Coming and Becoming

COMING AND BECOMING

Pluralism in New York State History

Compiled by Wendell Tripp

1991
New York State Historical Association
Cooperstown, New York

The New York State Historical Association
Cooperstown, New York 13326-0800

Library of Congress Catalog Card No. 91-65601
ISBN 0-917334-19-1
Printed in the United States of America

Cover: Charles F. Ulrich's painting, In the Land of Promise, *depicts immigrants waiting for clearance at the Castle Garden landing depot in Manhattan, 1884. In the collection of the Corcoran Gallery of Art, museum purchase.*

CONTENTS

T his anthology has a simple and practical purpose—to provide a convenient body of readings as a resource for undergraduate courses in New York State history. It is, at the same time, a collection that will stimulate and inform anyone who has an interest in United States history and in the history of this state. It deals with cultural diversity and especially with ethnic pluralism, a central aspect of that history, an aspect that has been the subject of highly charged discussion among educators in the recent past. The intensity of the exchange reflects the importance of ethnic pluralism in the American experience and especially in the experience of New York State, which, throughout its history has been a place of entry, funnel, and home for untold millions of people from all parts of the world.

It would be impossible to make a valid presentation of New York State history or national history without some emphasis on multiculturalism. This still permits differences of opinion on the manner in which the subject is approached. Thus, in 1989, a task force on minorities, appointed by New York Commissioner of Education Thomas Sobol, suggested that racial composition was the structural basis for understanding American history. The task force, on which historians were not represented, also condemned what it perceived as a bias toward European culture, which would, it believed, damage the psyches of young Americans whose ancestors were not Europeans. The New York State Board of Regents endorsed the report. Numbers of historians condemned it, professing their own belief in a pluralistic interpretation of American history but protesting the polemical character of the report and its perceived misunderstanding of history as an intellectual discipline.

This controversy informed a meeting, in February 1990, of the Advisory Committee on Teaching New York State History at the College and University Levels, attended by F. Daniel Larkin (chair) of State University of New York College at Oneonta; Bruce W. Dearstyne, of the New York State Archives and Records Administration; Kathleen S. Kutolowski of SUNY College at Brockport; Natalie A. Naylor of Hofstra University; John F. Roche of Fordham University; Mark Van Sluyters of Hoosic Valley Central School; Judith Wellman of SUNY College at Oswego; Daniel R. Porter III, director of the New York State Historical Association. Among a number of pertinent statements in behalf of the importance of New York state and local history in the curriculum, the committee declared that "New York local history is the best national case study of U.S. multicultural history." Among several additional recommendations, it urged the New York State Historical Association to recruit its director of publications, Wendell Tripp, to compile a selection of secondary readings on the theme of "pluralism." This anthology, *Coming and Becoming,* is the result.

As the title suggests, the emphasis of the volume is upon people in groups who have come to New York State from other nations and other continents, or, like Native Americans and New Englanders, were already here but displayed the characteristics of a distinct national group. An appropriate subtitle might have been "Ethnic Pluralism in New York State," but a broader term, "multiculturalism," also seems appropriate. Though the essays do not deal explicitly with all groups and topics that compose a multi-faceted culture, they do offer implicit insights and specific examples relating to religion, gender, education, the family, children, rites of passage, work and play, and other strands of culture. The essays also address, usually implicitly, certain persistent themes in the history of New York: Regionalism has been a factor in our history from the colonial period to the present. The ancient upstate-downstate dichotomy is related to the state's distinct cultural milieus—one urban, one rural—which themselves vary from region to region, and to which we should add a third cultural entity, suburbia. Long Island encompasses all three and at the same time has a pronounced sense of self as a distinct and separate region. On the other geographic and cultural extreme, the North Country is predominantly rural but equally aware of itself. Several other vaguely delineated regions, possessing a greater or lesser degree of self-consciousness, divide the state.

These factors have influenced the selection of essays, but ethnicity, broadly defined, is both rubric and central theme, though physical limitations prevent the inclusion of essays on each group included in New York's demographic spectrum. All major immigrant groups are included, however, and selected essays on smaller groups—the Welsh or Lebanese, for example—represent, if imperfectly, the experience of other relatively small groups who settled in specific communities or regions.

These several considerations aside, no easily definable point of view influenced the selection. Individual readers, teachers and students, will utilize the essays in accordance with their own interests and needs. The essays, taken altogether, do reveal our unceasing demographic ferment, from colonial times to the present. Each group that came to New York interacted with existing cultures and existing circumstances and, in time, was changed. And, in time, each group contributed to the common culture, sometimes broadly, sometimes in a limited theater. Ferment often included conflict—between new immigrant groups and older established groups, among racial groups, among various ethnic groups, and even within ethnic groups. But conflict and antagonism, individuality and separation, should not be overemphasized. The essays also suggest a broadening consensus to which the various groups contribute in the course of time. It is not a perfect or complete consensus, far from it, but neither are we out of time.

A majority of the essays are reprinted from *New York History,* the quarterly journal of the New York State Historical Association. The remainder are reprinted, with permission, from *Afro-Americans in New York Life and History; Long Island Historical Journal;* the *International Migration Review,* with permission of the Center for Migration Studies; Louis M. Vanaria, ed., *From Many Roots: Immigrants and Ethnic Groups in the History of Cortland County, New York* (Cortland, N.Y., 1986), with permission of Cortland County Historical Society; Nancy Foner, ed., *New Immigrants in New York* (New York, 1987), with permission of Columbia University Press; Salvatore J. LaGumina, ed., *Ethnicity in Suburbia: The Long Island Experience* (1980), with permission of Salvatore LaGumina.

A large number of generous individuals responded to my plea for advice and suggestions about the contents of a reader on pluralism in New York: Patricia U. Bonomi, Thomas E. Burke, Jr., Gould Colman, Bruce W. Dearstyne, David M. Ellis, Louis Filler, Charles Gehring, Laurence M. Hauptman, Graham Hodges, Carol Kammen, Cynthia A. Kierner, Milton M. Klein, Kathleen S. Kutolowski, F. Daniel Larkin, Natalie A. Naylor, John F. Roche, Donald M. Roper, Herbert A. Wisbey, Jr., Andrew P. Yox. I am especially indebted to Robert Kuhn McGregor and Keith Melder for specific suggestions and extensive commentary on the subject. Needless to say, neither this group of scholars, nor any one of them, is responsible for the shortcomings of this volume, though their suggestions have been essential to its value. Finally, I am indebted to Stefan Bielinski for his commentary, and to Jane Anne Russell for her assistance throughout the project.

Wendell Tripp
Cooperstown, New York

A View of FORT GEORGE *with the* CITY *of* NEW YORK *from the* S W.

In this view of New York, made about 1730 by John Carwitham, churches domi-nate the skyline: Trinity Church, Lutheran Church, New Dutch Church, the Presbyterian Church or the Quaker Meeting, the French Church, the Old Dutch Church, and the church in the fort. From Stokes, Iconography of Manhattan Island.

Shaping the American Tradition: The Microcosm of Colonial New York

By MILTON M. KLEIN

The determinative role of New York, as province and state, in the evolution of the American people has been misunderstood and neglected. Milton Klein is Professor of History at the University of Tennessee, Knoxville.

NEW YORKERS ARE a beleaguered lot these days. Everything seems to be going wrong in the Empire State. There is too much snow in Buffalo and not enough energy in New York City. The state's population and its electoral vote have both taken second place to California, and refugee New Yorkers are escaping to the Sunbelt far away instead of to their own suburbs and exurbs. Albany can't help its major cities bail themselves out of their always imminent bankruptcy because the state's own fiscal condition is precarious. The "Big Apple" has become the "Big Trouble," but none of the state's urban centers are free from the problems of crime, violence, and racial tensions that seem to plague Gotham more than ever. And the rest of the country appears to have little pity for the once proud Empire State and its great metropolis. Public opinion polls reveal that other Americans would prefer to live almost anywhere but New York, and New Yorkers are caricatured for their provincialism—most recently by a map showing that insofar as Gothamites are aware, the rest of the United States begins and ends not very far west of Hoboken.

Historians are neither psychiatrists nor physicians, and they cannot ease the pain by instant potions nor relieve the

This essay was originally presented on October 13, 1977 in a lecture series sponsored by the New York State Museum.

New York History   APRIL   1978

anxieties by any known forms of psychotherapy. But they can provide some comfort by means of the historical dimension. The history of humankind is a moving train that began some thousands of years ago and will continue on indefinitely until nature or man himself ends the journey by some physical trick by which everyone is destroyed. We board the train and remain on it for an instant present, born too late to have seen the beginning and dying too early to see the end. History remedies at least one of these defects: It permits us to extend our collective memory backward so that we can know better how and why it all began.

For New Yorkers in a defensive mood it may come as some comfort to learn that their state's present difficulties are not so unusual and that, indeed, New York is in the good company of many of its national neighbors. Even more, armed with knowledge of their own history, New Yorkers may be able not only to meet their sister states' verbal assaults but even to blunt the attacks. The fact is that the history of New York is not some deviant from the national norm of which Yorkers have to be ashamed but rather a mirror of the national past. Whether they admit it or not, Americans at large will have to concede that New York *is* the United States and that they can no more allow it to go down the drain today than they can escape inseparability from its past. The rest of the country and New York have for three hundred years or more marched to the tune of the same drummer; New York was or was always becoming what the rest of the nation turned out to be. As New York changed, so did the country; as New York turned out to be the gateway through which millions of the nation's future citizens entered the American republic, so did it prove to be the funnel through which were channeled the tides of change that transformed English colonists into American citizens.

If the people of America are "scared of New York City," as one writer in the *New York Times* commented several years ago, it may well be because they see in the metropolis the present or future problems they themselves must face.[1] Or they find its vastness, its variety, its dynamism just too much to comprehend. It may be too much to say, as Norman Cousins once did, that Gotham on the Hudson mirrors the whole

---

1. Richard Reeves, quoted in Neal R. Peirce, *The Megastates of America* (New York, 1972), p. 81.

Economic change is reflected in two views of Cooperstown, top view in the 1860s and the bottom in 1978, as farm land gives way to forest and to housing developments. New forest growth made it impossible to take the bottom photo from exactly the same site as the top photo. Top photograph from Special Collections, New York State Historical Association; bottom photo by Amy Barnum.

human race, but it surely is the world's capital, symbolized by the towering U.N. Secretariat on its East River shore.[2] For Americans, however, New York, city and state, offers a micro-cosm of the larger country: a blend of rich farmlands, rugged mountain scenery, and bustling cities; rural and urban; nature's beauty and man-made wonders; whites and blacks and Hispanics and Chinese; rich and poor and those in between; and a people who are the composite Americans: energetic, cosmopolitan, materialistic, and brash, but also convivial, humane, tolerant, and idealistic. That one state alone should be able to encompass in itself so many of the virtues and limitations of the American people is a measure of New York's unique role in the nation's history. New York is big enough to do so because, as Carl Carmer has remarked, "York State is a country."[3]

That most New Yorkers are not aware of their native state's distinction as the bellwether of the country is not surprising. Historians have tended to pass New York by in telling the story of the country's past. Consult the catalog of a public library for a scholarly account of the history of the state's and the nation's first city. The last ones were published before 1900.[4] Not until the bicentennial year did we have at least an introduction to the city's history from its Dutch beginnings to the present.[5] (The *New York Times* did not bother to review it.) For the history of the state, the researcher is even more limited: an excellent textbook published in 1967 and a superb collection of essays in ten volumes; but the latter appeared forty years ago.[6]

2. The Norman Cousins remark appeared in the *Saturday Review*, Nov. 15, 1975.

3. *Dark Trees to the Wind* (New York, 1949), p. 5; also *Listen for a Lonesome Drum* (New York, 1950), p. 3.

4. For example, David Valentine, *History of the City of New York* (New York, 1853); Martha J. Lamb, *History of the City of New York*, 2 vols. (New York and Chicago, 1877, 1880); Theodore Roosevelt, *New York* (New York, 1891); and James G. Wilson, ed., *Memorial History of the City of New York*, 6 vols. (New York, 1915-1928). Cleveland Rodgers and Rebecca B. Rankin, *New York: The World's Capital City* (New York, 1948) is useful and interesting, but it is not a scholarly history, rather a panorama of the city's contemporary problems viewed in historical perspective. I. N. P. Stokes, *New York, Past and Present, 1524-1939* (New York, 1939), is a brief chronology, heavily illustrated.

5. Milton M. Klein, ed., *New York: The Centennial Years, 1676-1976* (Port Washington, N.Y., 1976).

6. David M. Ellis and others, *A History of New York State* (Ithaca, 1967); Alexander C. Flick, ed., *History of the State of New York* (10 vols.; New York, 1933-1937).

The colonial history of New York has been neglected even more. To 1919, the best history of the province was written by a contemporary New Yorker and published in 1757![7] Over 150 years later, there appeared a volume summarizing both the Dutch and English experience in some 200 pages. The defect was not remedied until two years ago, when thanks to Michael Kammen, we have the best one-volume scholarly account of New York's history from its settlement to the Revolution.[8]

General histories of the American colonies do scant justice to New York. A few recent publications are illustrative. Daniel Boorstin has written a three-volume account of the American experience for which he won the Bancroft, Parkman, and Pulitzer Prizes. The first volume deals with the colonial period, and its integrating theme is how successful colonies shed their European dogmas and ideologies and adapted to the New World social environment.[9] The New England Puritans and the Virginia planters are cited as examples of such success, the Quakers of Pennsylvania and the secular utopians of Georgia as failures. New York, despite its supremely pragmatic and accommodative colonial experience, is omitted entirely from Boorstin's pages. In 1969, William Goetzmann published a small volume of documents and interpretive essays designed to illuminate the creation of an American culture. Interested more in "process" than "pageantry," Goetzmann was content to seek the beginnings of "American values, institutions, and modes of behavior" on the shores of Massachusetts and Virginia. Goetzmann found their experiences to be most "relevant" to his theme.[10] And just two years ago, a well-known colonial historian prepared an otherwise excellent brief interpretation of our colonial origins intended to demonstrate that "a new and different society, . . . akin to Europe but not European" emerged in British North

7. William Smith, Jr., *History of the Province of New-York* (London, 1757). It was republished with a continuation to 1762 as *The History of the Late Province of New-York* (2 vols.; New York, 1829). A revised version of the latter, with volume two taken from Smith's own manuscript of the original, was edited by Michael Kammen and published in 1972 by the Harvard University Press.

8. Maud W. Goodwin, *Dutch and English on the Hudson* (New Haven, 1919); Michael Kammen, *Colonial New York: A History* (New York, 1975).

9. *The Americans: The Colonial Experience* (New York, 1958).

10. The full title is *The Colonial Horizon: America in the Sixteenth and Seventeenth Centuries* (Reading, Mass., 1969).

America. Again, two colonies are used to illustrate the
historical process; again, they are Virginia and Massachusetts.[11]

What accounts for the perennial neglect of early New York
by the nation's historical guild? How could the writers who
streamed to New York City in such large numbers in the nineteenth and twentieth centuries to make it the country's literary
capital overlook the very region which gave them shelter
and cultural nourishment? It was perhaps precisely because the
city was the nation's capital that these authors bypassed it in
their writings. They saw themselves not as New York writers—
although they were—but American writers in New York.
Their myopia did not permit them to recognize in the variegated patterns of New York society the contours of the larger

11. William W. Abbot, *The Colonial Origins of the United States: 1607-1763*
(New York, 1975).

Wouter van Twiller as illustrated in Irving's
Knickerbocker's History of New York *(1894).*

America they sought to portray in their pages. Or perhaps they feared being typed as New Yorkers in a nation that caricatured Gotham as a den of sin and crass commercialism.

Columbia University nurtured generations of historians, but, again, seeking to enact a role as a national institution, it encouraged aspiring doctoral candidates to write their dissertations on almost every subject other than New York. This negative parochialism changed after World War II, but the damage to our historical literature was immense. Historians elsewhere were beguiled by the same ethnocentrism which viewed our past through the twin Anglo-Saxon prisms of Jamestown and Plymouth. It did not matter that the American people were already in 1776 a nation of nations and certainly more so by the nineteenth century. Historians persisted in portraying the country's history as a stage on which John Smith and Miles Standish, Pocahontas and Priscilla Alden were the leading characters. The Walloons, Dutch, Huguenots, Germans, and Jews who peopled New Netherland and later New York did not seem fit progenitors of the citizenry of the new American republic. Nor did it help that when New York emerged into literature, it was in the caricature of Washington Irving's Dutchmen: fat, simple, stupid, and bibulous.

It did not help, either, that while the millions of Europeans who now poured into the country were spread throughout the landscape, so many of them were concentrated and made glaringly visible on New York City's lower East Side. For the nation, while it was already becoming a land of urban dwellers, remained suspicious of large cities, preferring to regard the country's Arcadian past as the image of its industrial present. Politicians from Thomas Jefferson to William Jennings Bryan made capital of anti-urbanism in their pursuit of high office, and historians used their chronicles to express their own hostility—as Americans of Anglo-Saxon stock—toward the polyglot masses who were jostling them in college classrooms. As recently as 1963, the president of the American Historical Association expressed regrets that so many younger historians were of "lower middle class or foreign origins" and could hardly be expected to appreciate the "shared culture" which was the American past—as if that culture had been shaped out of Anglo-Saxon ingredients only.[12]

We should, I suppose, be more forgiving of earlier historians. Many of them were New Englanders, from Mercy
Otis Warren to George Bancroft and Henry Adams, and they
may be pardoned their filiopietistic affection for their ancestors—or their tendency to view all American history as the
unfolding of the Puritan design to create a godly commonwealth in the New World. After all, they saw Providential
intervention in the development that guided the Puritans to
the New World, made our Revolution, and put two Adamses
in the White House. And colonial New England seemed an
easy subject for this kind of simplistic interpretation of our
history. The voyage of the Pilgrims, the escape from European
intolerance to the free air of America, the Puritan mission
to establish a "city upon the hill" as a beacon for all who
sought perfection, the beginnings of constitutional democracy
in the Mayflower Compact, and the heroic efforts of the
minutemen at Lexington and Concord were all ready-made
vignettes for the larger drama of the nation's history. Southern
historians painted their American landscape from similar
prideful ingredients: the first planting of English civilization
in the New World, even the first white child born on American
soil, and also the first representative assembly, the best
cash crop, and later, the stirring oratory of Patrick Henry, the
eloquent language of Thomas Jefferson, and the indomitable
generalship of George Washington.

Of course, these historians could not—or did not—know
that the bulk of the passengers on the Mayflower were
adventurers rather than religious seekers, that Boston quickly
became a heterogeneous commercial center rather than a
peaceful English village even before John Winthrop's death,
that in other towns the Puritan ideal of a community of
saints was upset by conflicts between first settlers and newcomers, small farmers and large proprietors, ministers and
their congregations, orthodox Calvinists and dissident
Baptists. As New England historians forgot the intolerance
of their forebears toward witches, so did southerners mini-
mize the monstrous evil of slavery on which the South's freedom was built.

New York's colonial history is not a canvas of uninterrupted

---

12. Carl Bridenbaugh, "The Great Mutation," *American Historical Review*,
LXVIII (1963), 322–323.

progress or unblemished liberalism, but in many ways it was more typical of the later history of the United States than were its sister colonies. New Yorkers were among the last to recognize their typicality. It may come as a source of some embarrassment that it awaited a midwesterner and the great historian of the American frontier, Frederick Jackson Turner, and a southern political scientist, Woodrow Wilson, to call attention to the many ways in which New York and its neighbors of the middle region prefigured that later United States. What may have freed them from their provincialism was that Turner's parents were both New Yorkers, while Wilson was teaching in New Jersey when he wrote approvingly of the middle colonies.

Turner asserted that the Middle Atlantic colonies and states were "typical of the deep-seated tendencies of America in general"—geographically, politically, and socially. Without the "peculiarities" of either New England or the South, this middle region exhibited the traits which were to become characteristic of the nation as a whole: It was national in outlook, easy and tolerant in its social attitudes, composite in its demographic makeup, individualistic and competitive in its manners.[13] For Wilson, the Middle Atlantic colonies and states were "more distinctively American in constitution and character than either their northeastern or southern neighbors." Chiding historians for chronicling the nation's past as if it were merely the expansion of New England, Wilson cautioned that "the life of the nation cannot be reduced to these so simple terms." It was the middle region from which the rest of the country drew inspiration for the methods by which the continent was peopled:

> Here from the first were the mixture of population, variety of element, combination of type, as of the nation itself in small. . . . The life of these [Middle Atlantic] States as from the beginning the life of the country: they have always shown the national pattern.[14]

13. Turner's appraisal of the significance of the middle region may be found in a number of his writings. See especially "Problems in American History" (1892) and "The Significance of the Frontier in American History" (1893) in Everett W. Edwards, ed., *The Early Writings of Frederick Jackson Turner* (Madison, 1938), pp. 78–79, 217–218; *The Rise of the New West* (New York, 1906), pp. 29–30; "Some Sociological Aspects of American History" (1895), and "The Development of American Society" (1908), in Wilbur R. Jacobs, ed., *Frederick Jackson Turner's Legacy: Unpublished Writings in American History* (San Marino, Calif., 1965), pp. 163–164, 177; *The United States, 1830–1850* (New York, 1935), pp. 92, 94, 112, 138, 143.

Today's historians are only beginning to enumerate in detail the role of New York and its close neighbors to which Turner and Wilson alluded.

What strikes a researcher most is the frequency with which colonial observers noted how much New York seemed to be the capital of British North America. Even before the completion of the Erie Canal and the entrance of millions of immigrants through its harbor, New York was already regarded as the gateway to the Continent. And even before nineteenth-century southern travelers found it the mecca to which their northern odysseys directed them, both Americans and Europeans were drawn to New York as the focus and the climax of their explorations. The tendency to regard New York as the premier American city extends back almost to the beginning of England's acquisition of the colony. Richard Nicolls, the Duke of York's first governor, had hardly settled into his new duties before he reported to his patron that New York was "the best of all his Maj[es]ties Townes in America." Some thirty years later, another governor, the Earl of Bellomont, put the matter more acutely and with a prescience he could not be expected to possess. New York, by its situation,

being much in the center of the other colonies Challenges a preference to all the rest and ought to be looked upon as the capital Province or the Cittadel to all the others; for secure but this, and you secure all the English Colonies, not only against the French, but also against any insurrections or rebellions against the Crown of England. [15]

(Almost a hundred years later, it was on just such a presumption that the British occupied New York City and held it throughout the years of the American Revolution.)

The perception of New York's importance was not accurately grounded in fact: On the eve of the Revolution, the province's population was exceeded by four others, Philadelphia was larger than New York, and the volume of shipping clearing the city's docks was smaller than that of Philadelphia, Boston, or Charleston. But when an English

14. "The Proper Perspective of American History," *The Forum*, XIX (1895), 544–546. See also "Mr. Goldwin Smith's 'Views' on Our Political History," *ibid.*, XVI (1893–1894), 494–496, and "The Course of American History," *Collections* of the New Jersey Historical Society, VIII (1900), 186–189.

15. Edmund B. O'Callaghan, ed., *Documents Relative to the Colonial History of the State of New York* (15 vols.; Albany, 1853–1887), III, 106 (Nov. 1665), 505 (April 17, 1699).

mercantilist proposed, in 1698, a reorganization of the system of imperial administration by a union of the English mainland colonies, he suggested New York as the site of the intercolonial congress. William Penn was offering the same suggestion at about the same time.[16]

New Yorkers were not backward in reinforcing these impressions of their importance. When Lewis Morris, a wealthy New York land magnate, urged upon English authorities the establishment in America of a college for the training of Episcopal ministers, New York, as "the centre of English America," was suggested as its site.[17] European visitors often remarked on New York's singular position. Peter Kalm, a Swedish naturalist touring North America in 1750, observed Philadelphia's and Boston's harbors at first hand, but he was certain that New York carried on a more extensive commerce than any other city on the mainland. A visitor from Maryland was similarly puzzled. He knew that Philadelphia's trade was greater than New York's, but he confessed that he saw more ships in the harbor of Peter Stuyvesant's old town than he had in Penn's city of brotherly love. New Yorkers themselves bluntly declared their first city to be "the best Mart on the Continent." A French traveler in 1765 agreed: "The Situation of new york with regard to foreign markets Is to be prefered to any of the Colonies," he recorded in his diary. "It lies in the Center of the Continent." Lord Adam Gordon, a visiting British army officer, was surprised to find that New York did not come up to either Philadelphia or Boston in size or population, since at home it had "long been held . . . the first in America." And in far-off Scotland, an anonymous reporter of American affairs recorded his belief that New York's location marked it as the "Capital of Engl[ish] Govern-[men]t" in America.[18]

16. Charles Davenant, *Discourses on the Publick Revenues and on the Trade of England* (London, 1698). On this and Penn's plan, see Louis B. Wright, ed., *An Essay upon the Government of the English Plantations on the Continent of America* (San Marino, Calif., 1945), pp. xiv, 12.

17. Lewis Morris to the Society for the Propagation of the Gospel in Foreign Parts [1703?], quoted in Morgan Dix and others, *A History of the Parish of Trinity Church* (6 vols.; New York, 1898-1962), I, 145n.

18. *The America of 1750: Peter Kalm's Travels in North America*, ed. Adolph B. Benson (2 vols.; New York, 1937, 1964), I, 134; *Gentleman's Progress: The Itinerarium of Dr. Alexander Hamilton, 1744*, ed. Carl Bridenbaugh (Chapel Hill,

By the close of the eighteenth century, the impression was widespread that New York was the Liverpool of America, even a London in miniature. And it was already acquiring a reputation as a center of taste and fashion. A Maryland clergyman assured George Washington on the eve of the Revolution that New York City was a proper place for the education of an American gentleman. It was "the most fashionable and polite Place on the Continent." A residence there could well substitute for the grand tour of Europe and provide a young man with an opportunity "for receiving that Liberality of Manners, which is one of the best uses of Travel, mixing occasionally with truly well-bred people." [19] When, years later, southern planters exclaimed over New York as the most dazzling of all northern cities—"What an empire, or rather what a world is this New York City, and how insignificant do all other places appear when compared [sic] to this," one wrote—they were merely confirming an impression created at least a century earlier, when a still half-rural, partly Dutch town had already begun to cast a spell of fascination on those who heard of it and who visited it. [20]

What astonished visitors in the eighteenth century was the babble of strange tongues, the multiplicity of houses of worship, the large number of blacks, the "stirr and frequency upon the streets," the hum of activity at the waterfront, the gay and fashionable women, even the crowds of prostitutes who seemed even more visible in New York than anywhere else in English America. But what impressed British officials even more than these signs of New York's vitality was the strategic position of the entire province on the North American mainland. For almost a hundred years after the

---

1948), pp. 43–44; "A French Traveller in America, 1765," *American Historical Review*, XXVII (1921), 83; "Journal of an Officer's Travel in America and the West Indies, 1764–1765," in Newton Mereness, ed., *Travels in the American Colonies* (New York, 1916), 414; "Note on American Colonies, 18th Century," [1760?], Scottish Record Office, Edinburgh, GD 248/471; William Livingston and others, *The Independent Reflector*, ed. Milton M. Klein (Cambridge, Mass., 1963), p. 104.

19. Allan Nevins, ed., *American Social History as Recorded by British Travelers* (New York, 1931), p. 56; Wilson, ed., *Memorial History of the City of New York*, III, 150; Jonathan Boucher to George Washington, June 19, 1773, *Columbia University Quarterly*, XXIV (1932), 144–145.

20. The southern comment, made in 1851, is in John Hope Franklin, *A Southern Odyssey* (Baton Rouge, 1976), p. 21.

removal of the Stuarts from the English throne, New York figured as the centerpiece in the military planning of French, English, and American generals. The Hudson River-Champlain waterway was the most direct path to Canada, and during the Anglo-French wars that continued from 1689 to 1763, it was the Albany-Montreal corridor which both sides sought to control and through which they directed attacks at each other.

Great Britain recognized New York's military value by stationing in the colony the only sizable contingent of regular troops she maintained in America until after the French and Indian War.[21] Albany, still not more than a village, early became the site of conferences with the Indians; and here in 1754 was held the famous congress which not only renewed the "covenant chain" with the Iroquois but also attempted to create a defensive union of the English colonies. Father to that scheme was Benjamin Franklin, but its godfather was surely Archibald Kennedy, a New York official, who in 1751 proposed a colonial union, a superintendent of Indian affairs, and a fair and consistent policy towards the natives.[22] The Five Nations were regarded as important less for their role in the fur trade—it had already begun to decline—than for their value as an obstacle to French expansion.[23] New York officials assured the home government that Albany was the linchpin of empire, "the key and Centre of all their Ma[jes]tyes Territories on the Main of America," the frontier of all the colonies, and "the only bulwark and safe guard of all Their Majesty's plantations on the main of America."[24]

From 1763 to 1789, New York was the military center

21. On this, see Stanley Pargellis, "The Four Independent Companies of New York," in *Essays in Colonial History Presented to Charles McLean Andrews* (New Haven, 1931), pp. 96–123, and William A. Foote, "The American Independent Companies of the British Army, 1664–1764" (unpublished Ph.D. dissertation, UCLA, 1966).

22. On Kennedy, see Milton M. Klein, "Archibald Kennedy: Imperial Pamphleteer," in Lawrence H. Leder, ed., *The Colonial Legacy*, Vol. II (New York, 1971), pp. 75–105.

23. On the fur trade, see Allen W. Trelease, *Indian Affairs in Colonial New York: The Seventeenth Century* (Ithaca, 1960), and Thomas E. Norton, *The Fur Trade in Colonial New York, 1686–1776* (Madison, 1974).

24. On Albany's importance, see Arthur W. Buffinton, "New York's Place in Intercolonial Politics," New York State Historical Association *Proceedings*, XVI (1917), 51–62. See also *New York Colonial Documents*, III, 785.

of North America. Here was headquartered the permanent army created by the mother country to administer its enlarged empire. Here was felt the pulse of colonial discontent, as General Thomas Gage reported to his superiors the Stamp Act riots, the constitutional arguments that emanated from the congress convened in New York to protest the new tax, and the first official act of disobedience from the colonial legislatures—New York's refusal to comply with the new Quartering Act. The colony's crabbed lieutenant governor, Cadwallader Colden, wrote to the home government that "whatever happens in this place has the greatest influence on the other colonies. They have their Eyes perpetually upon it and they govern themselves accordingly."[25]

The Revolution only reaffirmed New York's strategic importance. It was New York City which the British military decided should be occupied as the "anvil on which to hammer the New England rebels." Here commenced the first large-scale operations of the war, during the summer of 1776, and here, even as the Howe brothers almost crushed Washington's army, Lord Richard Howe met with Franklin, John Adams, and Edward Rutledge in a conference to attempt a last-ditch reconciliation. When "Gentleman Johnny" Burgoyne failed in his expedition from Canada, using the familiar Lake Champlain-Hudson Valley campaign route, and surrendered his army at Saratoga, the British continued to retain possession of New York City. It was in their opinion the only vital city among all the provinces, since it commanded communications between New England and the Middle Colonies. The Hudson Highlands were important, too; British control of the up-river country could prevent easy movement northward by Washington from his headquarters in New Jersey. Hence, Britain's negotiations with Benedict Arnold for the seizure of West Point in the "blackest treason" of the war.[26] It was more than symbolic of New York's considerable role in the Revolution that the final dramatic moments of the war were played out on its soil: the departure of the British army from America and Washington's tearful

25. Colden to Secretary of State Henry Conway, Dec. 13, 1765, *Colden Letter Books*, 2 vols. (New York, 1877–1878), II, 66.

26. For the importance of New York in British strategy, see Piers Mackesy, *The War for America, 1775–1783* (Cambridge, Mass., 1963).

General Amherst's British-American army in the Mohawk Valley en route to Oswego and to Montreal, 1760. Drawing by Nelson Greene. Copy in New York State Historical Association.

'farewell to his officers at Fraunces Tavern. Of course, Washington could not know that within six years he would be returning to that same city to take the oath of office as president of the new republic in its first capital.

Eighteenth-century visitors could hardly be expected to measure New York's importance by its role in an as yet unforeseen civil war. When they commented on the fantasy that was New York, they had in mind rather its extraordinarily cosmopolitan character, the pageant of European nations enacted before their eyes on the city's streets, the richly variegated social composition of its population. Even under the Dutch, the colony had begun to develop a diversity that adumbrated its future complexity. The first settlers in New Netherland had been Walloons, and to them were soon added, besides Hollanders, Swedes, Norwegians, Germans, English, and Scots. Blacks came, too, enough to give New York the largest number of Africans of any colony

north of Maryland—between 12 and 15 percent.[27] Under
the Dutch, slaves were treated with considerable casualness,
even tolerance, but English rule brought the same kind
of racial conflict that characterized black-white relations
generally. New York had two slave riots, in 1712 and 1741,
which were put down with a brutality not witnessed elsewhere; but New York also nurtured the first black poet in
the colonies, Jupiter Hammon, a friend of the more celebrated Phillis Wheatley.[28]

Englishmen, accustomed to the homogeneity of their own
country, were irritated by New York's polyglot peoples.
"Our chiefest unhappyness is too great a mixture of nations,"
one complained in 1692. Seventy years later, another English-
man was baffled by what he saw in the province: "Being . . .
of different nations, different languages, and different
religions, it is almost impossible to give them [New Yorkers]
any precise or determinate character."[29] The visitors could
not appreciate that it was precisely this diversity which
would give New Yorkers their distinctive cast as a tolerant,
easy, practical, exciting, and unstable people—just as the
rest of the nation became. Neither the Dutch nor the English
set out to establish a haven for the dispossessed of Europe on
the shores of the Hudson. In matters of religion, the Dutch
expected to extend the Reformed Church of the fatherland.
And the English conquerors, although they granted religious
liberty to the Dutch, made vigorous efforts to Anglicize
the whole province after they became its possessors. However, both the Dutch and the English discovered that these
intentions clashed with conditions that came to exist in their
colonies. When Peter Stuyvesant urged the removal of
Lutherans, Jews, and Quakers as threats to religious uni-

27. On blacks in New York, see Edgar J. McManus, *A History of Negro Slavery
in New York* (Syracuse, 1966), and David Kobrin, *The Black Minority in Early
New York* (Albany, 1971).

28. For Jupiter Hammon's poetry, see Stanley A. Ransom, ed., *America's First
Negro Poet: The Complete Works of Jupiter Hammon* (Port Washington, N.Y.,
1970). For a brief account of Hammon and Phillis Wheatley, see Sidney Kaplan,
The Black Presence in the Era of the American Revolution (New York, 1973),
pp. 150–180.

29. Charles to Francis Lodwicke and Mr. Hooper, Sept. 5, 1692, New York
Historical Society *Collections*, 2 Ser., Part I (New York, 1848), p. 244; Andrew
Burnaby, *Travels through North America* [1759–1760], ed. Rufus R. Wilson (New
York, 1904), p. 117.

formity in New Netherland, the Dutch West India Company commanded him to shut his eyes to such eccentrics, "at least not force people's consciences, but allow everyone to have his own belief, as long as he behaves quietly and legally, gives no offence to his neighbors, and does not oppose the government." What Dutch officials were really suggesting was the policy that the good burghers of old Holland had long pursued. Officially, they stood for religious conformity, but as a practical matter they connived at all deviations from orthodoxy which were not disruptive of social order. It was this policy of practical toleration that had made Holland the wealthiest and most cosmopolitan of all European states; there was even more reason to follow it in their overseas plantation, where people were at a premium.[30]

The English attempted early in their administration to establish the Anglican Church by law, and the Assembly reluctantly complied in 1693 with an act permitting towns in the four lower counties to impose a church tax to support "a good and sufficient Protestant minister." But ardent Anglicans soon discovered that the law was a huge jest played on both the governor and the churchmen who had pressed for the measure. Since the Anglicans were a tiny minority in the colony and a majority in almost no single community, the new law, in effect, provided a public subsidy for non-Anglican churches. One Anglican layman learned that the Church of England would gain more friends by abandoning the law than trying to enforce it: "It is not an easy task to persuade men to change their Religion," he conceded, "and I think a great point is gained when they [i.e., dissenters] are prevailed upon to have as good an opinion of ours as their own."[31]

As the lesson was taken to heart, the English authorities came to wink at the unorthodox in their midst, and New York became the bane of churchmen and the pride of liberal

---

30. Dutch West India Company to Stuyvesant, April 16, 1663, in E. C. Corwin, ed., *Ecclesiastical Records of the State of New York* (7 vols.; Albany, 1901–1916), I, 530. Dutch connivance is discussed in George L. Smith, *Religion and Trade in New Netherland* (Ithaca, 1973), and his "Guilders and Godliness: The Dutch Colonial Contribution to American Religious Pluralism," *Journal of Presbyterian History*, XLVII (1969), 1–30.

31. Lewis Morris to the SPG, Jan. 1, 1712, SPG Letterbook, A, VII, 12, SPG Archives, London.

New Yorkers. A Dutch minister reported in 1741 that all
was confusion "because there is here perfect freedom of
conscience for all, except Papists. . . . Everybody may do
what seems right in his own eyes, as long as he does not
disturb the public peace." And a German clergyman complained that in New York the church was "like a vineyard
without a hedge, . . . a city without walls, . . . a house without
a door and a lock."[32] One New Yorker, preparing an almanac
in 1716, quipped about the bewildering variety of religions
in the colony in verse:

> In their Religion they are so Uneven,
> That each Man goes his own By-way to Heaven.
> So shy of one another they are grown,
> As if they strove to get to Heaven alone.

But other New Yorkers praised diversity as a positive good.
The variety of churches prevented any one of them from
striving for supremacy over the other. And even the Deists
served a useful purpose by reminding good Christians to
examine the strength of their own convictions.[33]
   As for church finance, instead of compulsory public
taxation, each denomination turned to its own communicants
for voluntary support. This was the path which America took
as a nation when it provided in the First Amendment to
the Constitution that "Congress shall make no law respecting
an establishment of religion." New York had preceded the
nation in its own constitutional proviso that "the free exercise
and enjoyment of religious profession and worship, without
discrimination or preference, shall for ever hereafter be
allowed," one of the most liberal expressions of the principle
of religious freedom in any of the new state constitutions.[34]
When the New York framers explained that their aim was
to prevent "that spiritual oppression and intolerance, where-
with . . . wicked priests and princes, have scourged mankind,"
they were recalling the dogmatic efforts of some Anglicans

---

32. *N.Y. Ecclesiastical Records*, IV, 2756; John B. Frantz, "The Awakening of
Religion among the German Settlers in the Middle Colonies," *William and Mary
Quarterly*, XXXIII (1976), 273.

33. *The American Almanack for the Year 1716* (New York, 1716), Unpaged;
Independent Reflector, ed. Klein, pp. 391, 396.

34. The constitution of 1777 is readily available in William A. Polf, *1777: The
Political Revolution and New York's First Constitution* (Albany, 1977).

to impose religious uniformity during the period of English rule. And by their grant of religious freedom they institutionalized the spirit of tolerance that had long before been so eloquently expressed by the residents of Flushing when they refused Peter Stuyvesant's order to bar Quakers from their homes. "We desire," they said, "not to judge least we be judged, neither condemn least we be condemned, but rather let every man stand and fall to his own Master."[35]

For historians as for contemporary observers of the New York scene from elsewhere, accustomed to the homogeneity of New England and Virginia, the mystery of colonial New York was why its heterogeneous society did not come apart at the seams. There was neither the sense of special mission of the New Englander nor the common racism of the Virginian to knit them together. But New Yorkers did have a bond of unity, perhaps only dimly perceived and certainly rarely articulated. It was their common interest in making money and a set of political values which caused them to immerse their energies and diffuse their hostilities in politics.

Colonial New Yorkers were widely regarded as a materialistic lot. Cadwallader Colden's criticism bespoke a broadly held sentiment: "The only principle of Life propagated among the young People is to get Money and Men are only esteemed according to what they are worth, that is, the money they are possessed of."[36] Englishmen attributed the mercenary qualities of New Yorkers to their Dutch ancestry. Of the merchants of old Amsterdam it was once said that if they thought they could make a profit by passing through Hell, they would risk burning the sails of their ships to try. The Dutch surely set the tone of New York's commercial character; they came to the New World, it was said, "to enjoy life, not to establish creeds; to secure a domestic fireside, not to make converts to political opinions." Under English rule, New Yorkers continued to follow the practice of old Holland, where, a visitor reported as early as 1662, "Next to the freedom to worship God, comes the freedom for all inhabitants to make one's living."[37]

---

35. *N.Y. Colonial Documents*, XIV, 402–403 (Dec. 27, 1657).

36. Colden to Hezekiah Watkins, Dec. 12, 1748, SPG MSS, B-20, 86–88, SPG Archives, London.

English New Yorkers found it difficult to resist the colony's material advantages: a rich hinterland linked by easy water passage to an excellent harbor. The colony's wheat and bread, considered the finest in America, brought a prosperity that was augmented by cattle raising and a range of industries producing linen, woolens, hats, glass, iron, rum, sugar, soap, candles, shoes, cordage, beer, and ships. With a smaller volume of commerce than three other colonial cities, New York nevertheless became the center of a complicated network of trade linking the northern and southern mainland colonies, the West Indies, and Europe. When British manufacturers had to dispose of surpluses by quick sales, it was to New York that the goods were sent, and when the French government had to buy quantitites of wheat and flour in 1770 to combat a famine crisis, it was New York to which they turned for the purchase.[38]

New York's prosperity was reflected in the stability of its paper currency, its numerous civic and social organizations, its ability to support its poor citizens and also to finance a variety of public improvements, and its hospitality to artists and craftsmen. There was little "high culture" in colonial New York and few prominent native authors, but then as now, creative talent flowed to its principal city. It was even then the "open market for ideas," the "glorious vehicle . . for the cross-fertilization of minds," that it has been ever since.[39]

Next to Philadelphia, New York was the busiest book mart in the colonies, housing some seventy-six printers between 1633 and 1800. The first American edition of Milton's *Paradise Lost* was published in New York, and the first American printing of Daniel Defoe's *Robinson*

---

37. Margaret Marshall, *Five Generations* (New York, 1930), p. 3, quoting an unidentified early historian; Henri and Barbara van der Zee, *A Sweet and Alien Land: The Story of Dutch New York* (New York, 1978), p. 21.

38. On New York's colonial commerce, see Curtis Nettels, "The Economic Relations of Boston, Philadelphia, and New York," *Journal of Economic and Business History*, III (1930–1931), 185–215; William Sachs, "Interurban Correspondents and the Development of a National Economy before the Revolution: New York as a Case Study," *New York History*, XXXVI (1936), 320–335; and Jacob M. Price, "Economic Function and the Growth of American Port Towns in the Eighteenth Century," *Perspectives in American History*, VIII (1974), 123–186.

39. The quotations are those of Jacob Javits and Robert Alden, in Peirce, *The Megastates of America*, pp. 80–81, 97.

Crusoe. Twenty newspapers and magazines came from New York's presses before 1783, and in them may be traced not only the lively political controversies of the times but also the progress of the arts and sciences. A variety of private schools offered instruction in practical subjects but also in dancing, music, and foreign languages. The evening school was a distinctive New York institution which spread to other colonial cities.[40]

New York was less a producer than a consumer of the arts, attracting painters like John Singleton Copley and Benjamin West; sculptors like Patience Wright, with her miniature waxworks; theatrical producers like David Douglass, who offered Sheridan's *She Stoops to Conquer* only months after its London premiere; a number of German and Italian musicians, several of whom offered the first nearly complete performance of the *Messiah* in 1770. The city was also affluent enough to support such varied cultural organizations as the Society Library, a Harmonic Society, a law debating club, and a chamber of commerce—the latter, the first of its kind in the colonies.[41]

If New Yorkers were more materialistic than aesthetic, they merely prefigured the character of later Americans. When the Reverend Samuel Miller surveyed the cultural scene in 1800, he conceded that the spirit of the American people was commercial: "*the love of gain* particularly characterizes the inhabitants of the United States."[42] But in New York, commerce was the handmaiden of a utilitarian culture that sheared off the rough edges of the wilderness from its inhabitants and introduced the embellishments of the arts to a broad spectrum of its people. The two combined to make New York a collection of individuals who were

40. John Tebbel, *A History of Book Publishing in the United States* (2 vols.; New York and London, 1972, 1975), I, 52–55, 83, 87, 93–94; Flick, ed., *History of the State of New York*, III, 84–86; Robert E. Seybolt, *The Evening School in Colonial America* (Urbana, Ill., 1925).

41. On New York's receptivity to artists, painters, dramatists, and musicians, see Kenneth Silverman, *A Cultural History of the American Revolution* (New York, 1976), and Rita S. Gottesman, comp., *The Arts and Crafts in New York, 1726–1776* (New York, 1938); for libraries, see Austin B. Keep, *The Library in Colonial New York* (New York, 1909); and on the city's many social, cultural, and philanthropic organizations, Jacquetta M. Haley, "Voluntary Organizations in Pre-Revolutionary New York City, 1750–1776" (unpublished Ph.D. dissertation, State University of New York at Binghamton, 1976).

42. *A Brief Retrospect of the Eighteenth Century*, 2 vols. (New York, 1803), II, 407.

New York election scenes. Above, discussion at the ticket booth; opposite: upsetting a ticket booth in the Twentieth Ward. From Frank Leslie's Illustrated Newspaper, *November 13, 1858.*

different but who had learned that both culture and commerce required hospitality to outsiders. The society that developed in colonial New York was no "melting pot" but rather a system of stable pluralism, individuals and ethnic groups contributing to the richness of the colony's material and cultural life while resisting the intrusion of the whole on their individual autonomies. A Marylander expressed his admiration in 1773 for New York's receptivity to strangers, and two hundred years later an Irishman paid his tribute to the city on the Hudson in the reminder that "the test of a city is the ease with which you can see and talk to people."[43] New Yorkers had passed that test in the crucible of three centuries of experience in learning to talk to each other!

And finally, then as now, it was politics that not only absorbed the attention of multitudes of New Yorkers but also taught them in still another sphere the virtues of compromise and accommodation. New York was not a democracy by modern standards, but its inhabitants early learned to

43. *Brendan Behan's New York* (New York, 1964), p. 12.

play the game of politics in a way that enlisted large numbers of the citizenry. The province had its patricians, as did the other colonies, but they did not exercise unchallenged authority. The Dutch—who continued to be a sizable part of New York's population well into the eighteenth century— proved to be a contentious sort—"stubborn for liberty," as one recent historian describes them. Under English rule, they were in the courts for the offense of "contempt of authority" more often than any other ethnic group, reflective of their highly individualistic temper and their traditional suspicion of the agencies of government.[44] Presbyterians, Lutherans, Quakers, Jews, German Calvinists, Dutch Calvinists, and French Calvinists all eyed each other with a proper wariness, and all of them were suspicious of the

44. Alice P. Kenney, *Stubborn for Liberty: The Dutch in New York* (Syracuse, 1975); Douglas Greenberg, *Crime and Law Enforcement in the Colony of New York, 1691– 1776* (Ithaca, 1976).

Anglicans. New Yorkers divided also on economic and sectional lines: wholesale fur traders and retailers; those who bought directly from the Indians and those who preferred to buy pelts in Montreal; city merchants desiring to monopolize the export of flour and up-river millers who fought such a monopoly; landowners who wanted taxes on trade and merchants who urged taxes on land; Long Islanders who wanted to carry on business directly with Connecticut and Massachusetts and New York City merchants who insisted that such commerce be funneled through its harbor.

What might have produced intense intergroup violence instead was converted into vigorous politicking. Men with similar interests organized into political factions, and factions became parties, employing much of the paraphernalia of modern politics: petitions to the legislature, appeals to the voters in newspapers and pamphlets, parades and mass meetings, electoral tickets and party platforms. New Yorkers were considered a "factious people," but their politicking was not meaningless or mindless. Elections were the battleground on which the province's pluralistic society competed for control of the legislative machinery. The extraordinary diversity of the colony's citizenry compelled its political leadership to build coalitions, court other interest groups, balance tickets, awaken political consciousness, and enlist the support of large numbers of voters. N ɑ even a nominally restrictive franchise prevented tenants on the great Hudson Valley estates or artisans in the cities of Albany and New York from joining in the great game. In 1820 a Rhode Island newspaper commented that "Electioneering in New-York is conducted with greater acrimony and zeal than we have ever known exhibited in any other state." But a visitor had discovered the same phenomenon in New York in 1775: "Men, women, children, all ranks and professions mad with Politics."[45]

45. The Rhode Island comment is from Michael D'Innocenzo, "The Popularization of Politics in Irving's New York," in Andrew B. Myers, ed., *The Knickerbocker Tradition: Washington Irving's New York* (Tarrytown, 1974), p. 12, the 1775 comment from Philip Padelford, ed., *Colonial Panorama: Dr. Robert Honeyman's Journal for March and April 1775* (San Marino, Calif., 1939), p. 31. On the general theme of New York's contentious politics, see Patricia U. Bonomi, *A Factious People: Politics and Society in Colonial New York* (New York, 1971), and her essay, "The Middle Colonies: Embryo of the New Political Order," in Alden T. Vaughan and George A. Billias, eds., *Perspectives in Early American History* (New York, 1973), pp. 63–92.

In an age which looked on political factionalism as disruptive of public order, New Yorkers accepted it as the legitimate vehicle for checking arbitrary power and preserving the liberties of the province's diverse population. "To infer," wrote one mid-eighteenth-century pamphleteer, "that the Liberties of the People are safe and unendanger'd, because there are no political Contests, is illogical and fallacious."[46] It is no coincidence that when the legitimacy of political opposition reached fruition in the party battles of the Jackson era, its fullest expression was in New York and with men like Martin Van Buren.[47] Colonial New York had already introduced the citizens of the Empire State to the special role which parties were to play in the life of the democratic republic: "They provided vehicles for political participation, . . . for offering effective choices to the electorate, and brought new order into the conduct of government."[48]

New York's arts and sciences may have languished during the colonial period, and its population and trade may have lagged behind those of some of its neighbors, but the tumultuous and pluralistic society that developed on the Hudson and on Long Island had taught the other English colonies a precious lession: That free, popular government could thrive on the foundations of social diversity, religious difference, and humane cosmopolitanism. It was a lesson from which the new American republic profited and from which it drew the inspiration for its future greatness.

46. *Independent Reflector*, ed. Klein, p. 148 (Feb. 22, 1753).

47. This theme is expounded in Richard Hofstadter, *The Idea of a Party System* (Berkeley and Los Angeles, 1969), chap. 6, and Michael Wallace, "Changing Concepts of Party in the United States: New York, 1815–1828," *American Historical Review*, LXXIV (1968), 453–491.

48. William N. Chambers, *Political Parties in a New Nation: The American Experience, 1776–1809* (New York, 1963), p. [vii].

A view of New Amsterdam and its waterfront, as depicted by Peter Schenk, about 1673. From Stokes, Iconography of Manhattan Island.

How Dutch Were the Dutch
of New Netherland?

By DAVID STEVEN COHEN

The settlers of New Netherland are traditionally pictured as sturdy Dutch burghers. A fresh look at the sources suggests that the colonists, though sturdy, were not burghers and half of them weren't Dutch. David Cohen is Coordinator of the Folklife Program at the New Jersey Historical Commission in Trenton.

EUROPEAN HISTORIANS HAVE stressed the urban, middle-class, and democratic character of the Netherlands. "The solidarity of the Dutch people," wrote Johan Huizinga, "springs from their bourgeois character. Whether we fly high or low, we Dutchmen are all bourgeois—lawyer and poet, baron and labourer alike."[1] According to Pieter Geyl, the "Holland regent class is not only the most important political factor, but also the most notable social phenomenon in the Netherlands throughout the seventeenth century and beyond."[2] The emphasis has been, not only on one class, but on one province: Holland. Again, Huizinga said it best:

Though we, who are attached by ties of memory, kinship and love to all parts of our country, cannot forget the beauty and goodness of incomparable Friesland, noble Guelders, the prosperous and pious medieval towns on the Ijsel, we must remember that, seen from Holland itself, the Republic looked like a flimsy embroidery round a strong and colorful central pattern.[3]

This myopia is reflected in the common misconception that

This article is a slightly revised version of a paper presented at the Conference on New York State History in Binghamton, New York, on April 25, 1980.

1. Johan Huizinga, "The Spirit of the Netherlands," in *Dutch Civilization in the Seventeenth Century*, trans. by Arnold J. Pomerans (New York, 1968), p. 112.

2. Pieter Geyl, *The Netherlands in the Seventeenth Century* (London and New York, 1961), I, 248.

3. Huizinga, "Dutch Civilization in the Seventeenth Century," in *Dutch Civilization*, p. 14.

The seal of New Netherland, given by Peter
Stuyvesant to the city in 1654. Courtesy of the
Museum of the City of New York.

the name "Holland" refers to the entire country, not just to
one province.

American scholars, writing about the Dutch in New
Netherland, have been influenced by this orientation. Alice
P. Kenney stresses the "Dutch patricians" of Albany, who,
she argues, emulated the traditions, values, and behavior
of the wealthy merchants of the Low Countries. She states that
"the colonists who settled in towns—particularly New York,
Albany, Schenectady, Kingston, Brooklyn, and New Brunswick—recreated the way of life of Dutch burghers."[4] But
Kenney focuses on the political and economic elite, without
paying sufficient attention to their social and geographical
origins in Europe.

Alan Gowans divides architecture in New Netherland
into two types: the urban houses of the merchants and the
rural houses of the farmers. The urban houses, he argues, "re-

4. Alice P. Kenney, "Dutch Patricians in Colonial Albany," *New York History* XLIX
(July 1968), 253. Quotation from Alice Kenney, *Stubborn for Liberty: The Dutch in
New York* (Syracuse, N.Y., 1975), p. 69.

produced those of the rich burghers of Amsterdam and Haarlem and Delft who first financed and governed the New Netherland settlement,"[5] but the rural houses were "not, like the urban type, an expression of Dutch (or Flemish, or any other) national traditions transplanted to the New World."[6] Gowans, however, presumes that only the upper classes are capable of producing lasting cultural contributions, despite evidence to the contrary.

Thomas J. Condon argues that the Dutch were more interested in the fur trade than in planting agricultural settlements. Since this commercial spirit was essentially the same as that in Virginia and New England, the history of New Netherland, he argues, "is not the story of the gradual development of a distinctively Dutch society in the New World but rather the story of why such a society did not take shape."[7] He concludes that "the end result in New Netherland was a combination of the forms that developed in Virginia and New England, which can be explained by historically conditioned factors rather than by exclusive ethnic or regional concepts."[8] Condon bases his conclusions solely on political and economic institutions, which, of course, ended with the English conquest of New Netherland.

Donna Merwick recently argued that "the strong town tradition of the Low Countries" led to a distinctive social history in New Netherland "that exalted town life over rural existence," as opposed to weaker town tradition of the English.[9] Merwick selectively cites evidence to further her thesis and fails to note that the Dutch settlers had to be ordered to settle in towns as a defensive measure in the 1640s.[10]

5. Alan Gowans, *Architecture in New Jersey* (Princeton, N.J., 1964), p. 19.

6. Alan Gowans, *Images of American Living: Four Centuries of Architecture and Furniture as Cultural Expression* (Philadelphia and New York, 1964), p. 60.

7. Thomas J. Condon, *New York Beginnings: The Commercial Origins of New Netherland* (New York and London, 1968), p. 120.

8. Ibid., p. 178. For a different interpretation see Van Cleaf Bachman, *Peltries or Plantations: The Economic Policies of the Dutch West India Company in New Netherland, 1623-1639* (Baltimore, Md., 1969).

9. Donna Merwick, "Dutch Townsmen and Land Use: A Spatial Perspective on Seventeenth-Century Albany, New York," *William and Mary Quarterly*, 3rd Ser., XXXVII (January 1980), 53–78.

10. Albert S. McKinley notes that "town life developed late and with difficulty among the Dutch [in New Netherland]." He cites instructions dated July 7, 1645, sent to the Director and Council at New Amsterdam that "(t)hey shall endeavor

Because they are wrong about the backgrounds from which the seventeenth-century settlers in New Netherland came, these historians miss the cultural processes that shaped a distinctive Dutch culture region. My own research tells a different story. I have determined the exact places of origin of more than 900 settlers who immigrated to New Netherland in the seventeenth century, as revealed by ship passenger lists, genealogies, collections of colonial documents, and ethnic and local histories.[11] The data include those people whose place of origin was listed in the population of New Amsterdam in 1660, the population of Rensselaerswyck from 1630 to 1657, passengers on ships arriving between 1654 and 1664, as well as many of the founders of Dutch families still living in New York and New Jersey. I carefully compared the sources in an effort to avoid duplicating individuals mentioned in more than one source.

These 900 settlers represent a large part of the total Dutch population of New Netherland. In 1647, Director General Stuyvesant estimated the population, excluding the three English villages on Long Island, as 250 to 300 men capable of bearing arms. In 1673, the Dutch population including women and children was estimated to be 6,000. The first census for New Jersey was not taken until 1726, but based on figures of people swearing oaths of loyalty to the English government, it is estimated that the total population of East

---

as much as possible, that the colonists settle themselves with a certain number of families in some of the most suitable places, in the manner of villages, towns, and hamlets, as the English are in the habit of doing, who thereby live more securely." McKinley, "English and Dutch Towns of New Netherland," *American Historical Review* VI (October 1900), 1–18.

11. Rosalie Fellows Bailey, *Pre-Revolutionary Dutch Houses and Families in Northern New Jersey and Southern New York* (New York, 1936; reprinted 1968); Bailey, "Emigrants to New Netherland, Account Book, 1654 to 1664," *New York Genealogical and Biographical Record* XCIV (October 1963), 193–200; Henry G. Bayer, *The Belgians: First Settlers in New York and in the Middle States* (New York, 1925); Van Brunt Bergen, "A List of Early Immigrants to New Netherland, 1654–1664," *New York Genealogical and Biographical Record* XIV (1883), 181–90; 15 (1883), 34–40, 72–77; Bergen, "Early Immigrants to New Netherland, 1657–1664," Holland Society of New York *Yearbook* (1896), pp. 141–58; John O. Evjen, *Scandinavian Immigrants in New York, 1630–1674* (Minneapolis, 1916); Cornelius Burnham Harvey, *Genealogical History of Hudson and Bergen Counties, New Jersey* (New York, 1900); "List of Passengers, 1654–1664," Holland Society of New York *Yearbook* (1902), pp. 5–37; I. N. P. Stokes, *The Iconography of Manhattan Island, 1498–1909* (6 vols.; New York, 1915–1928), II; Helen Wilkinson Reynolds, *Dutch Houses in the Hudson Valley Before 1776* (New York, 1929; reprinted 1965); A. J. F. Van Laer, ed., *Van Rensselaer-Bowier Manuscripts* (Albany, N.Y., 1908), pp. 805–46.

Jersey was 548 during 1665–1668 and 1,955 in 1673. Using the estimate of Capt. Mathias Nicolas, Secretary of the Province of New York, that the average family in East Jersey consited of five individuals, our data represent about one-half the families in New York and East Jersey.[12]

The names on the ship passenger lists constitute only a part of the overall data, but these lists provide the previous occupations of the immigrants in their country of origin, as opposed to the occupations they assumed in New Netherland, which in several cases were not the same. Occupations are listed for 177 individuals who immigrated between 1654 and 1664. Of that number, one-third were farmers, more than one-quarter were soldiers, and another quarter were craftsmen. The remainder were farm laborers, servants, fishermen, and laborers (see Table 1).[13] While several of these immigrants became the founders of wealthy merchant families in New York and New Jersey, their social origins in their country of origin were more humble. Certainly, they were not of the ruling, regents class.

The same phenomenon has been discovered in the social

12. Edmund B. O'Callaghan, ed., *Documents Relative to the Colonial History of the State of New York* (15 vols.; Albany, N.Y., 1853–1887), I, 44; Peter O. Wacker, *Land and People: A Cultural Geography of Preindustrial New Jersey* (New Brunswick, N.J., 1975), pp. 129–30.

13. Compiled from "List of Passengers, 1654–1664," pp. 5–57; Bailey, "Emigrants to New Netherland," pp. 193–200.

TABLE 1

OCCUPATIONAL BACKGROUNDS OF IMMIGRANTS TO
NEW NETHERLAND, 1654–1664

Farmers	59	33.3%
Soldiers	49	27.7%
Craftsmen	45	25.4%
Laborers	10	5.6%
Farm laborers	8	4.5%
Servants	4	2.3%
Fishermen	2	1.1%
Total	177	100.0%

SOURCES: "List of Passengers, 1654–1664," The Holland Society of New York *Yearbook* (1902), pp. 5–28; Rosalie Fellows Bailey, "Emigrants to New Netherland, Account Book, 1654 to 1664," *New York Genealogical and Biographical Record*, XCIV (October 1963), pp. 193–200.

origins of seventeenth-century emigrants from England to America. Mildred Campbell compiled data on 10,000 individuals who left from the port of Bristol for America between 1654 and 1685. She shows that 36 percent were yeomen and husbandmen, 22 percent were artisans and tradesmen, and fewer than 1 percent were gentlemen and professionals. "Thus the farmers outnumber the skilled workers almost two to one, and the combined farmers and skilled workers outnumber the laborers more than five to one."[14]

When one looks at the social origins of some of the wealthiest Dutch families in New York and New Jersey, the same phenomenon is observed. For example, Philip Pietersz Schuyler was the son of a baker. He emigrated from Amsterdam in 1650, and married Margareta van Slichtenhorst, the daughter of the director of Rensselaerswyck. Schuyler became one of the wealthiest men in the colony. Frederick Philipse, who became the landlord of Philipsburg Manor, was born in Bolswaert, a small town in the province of Friesland in the Netherlands. His father was a slater, and he became a carpenter. He immigrated to New Netherland in 1647, where he married Margaret Hardenbroeck, a wealthy widow, who was herself a businesswoman and trader. Oloff Stevensen Van Cortlandt, the founder of Van Cortlandt Manor, was probably of Scandinavian ancestry, although he was born in the town of Wijk near Utrecht in the Netherlands. He resided in the Duchy of Courland, opposite the Swedish Island of Gothland. He came to New Netherland in 1637 as a soldier, and later owned a brewery in New Amsterdam. Dirck Jansen Dey, the founder of one of the wealthy and influential Dutch families in New Jersey, was a soldier from Amsterdam employed by the Dutch West India Company. He was sent to New Netherland in 1641. His grandson, also named Dirck Dey, was a member of the New Jersey Assembly, and his great-grandson, Theunis Dey, was a colonel in the militia, a member of the New Jersey Assembly and the Provincial Council. He married into the Schuyler family.[15]

---

14. Mildred Campbell, "Social Origins of Some Early Americans," in James Morton Smith, ed., *Seventeenth-Century America: Essays in Colonial History* (Chapel Hill, N.C., 1959). pp. 71, 73.

15. Van Laer, *Van Rensselaer-Bowier Manuscripts,* pp. 841–42; *Philipsburg Manor* (Tarrytown, N.Y., 1969), pp. 8–9; Evjen, *Scandinavian Immigrants,* p. 145; Stokes, *Iconography,* II, 251–52; Bailey, *Pre-Revolutionary Dutch Houses,* p. 504.

A major exception to this pattern, however, was the Van Rensselaer family. Kiliaen Van Rensselaer, a director of the Dutch West India Company and landlord of the patroonship of Rensselaerswyck, sent his eldest son, Jan Baptist, to New Netherland in 1652 to be the director of his patroonship. When Jan Baptist returned to the Netherlands in 1658, his younger brother Jeremias replaced him as director in residence of the colony. [16] He founded the American branch of the Van Rensselaer family. While these examples are hardly typical of the average Dutch settler in New Netherland, the social origins of the founders of these wealthy Dutch families, notwithstanding the Van Rensselaers, suggests the fallacy of placing too much emphasis on the wealthy merchant tradition in the towns of Holland.

The present study of place of origin of settlers in New Netherland further refutes the past emphasis on the single province of Holland. Most previous studies of the origins of settlers in New Netherland have been either filio-pietistic genealogies of purely antiquarian interest, or exercises in ethnic chauvinism trying to prove which nationality came first or contributed more. [17] National boundaries have changed considerably since the seventeenth century (see map, p. 50). For example, territory that was then part of the Spanish Netherlands (Belgium) is today part of France. Furthermore, cultural boundaries tend to cut across political boundaries. There was then little difference either in language or house types between peasants in Friesland in the Netherlands and those in East Friesland in Germany. It is therefore more instructive to list places of origin by provinces, duchies, and principalities—using the political boundaries that existed in the seventeenth century, and utilizing gazetteers to determine the town, province, duchy, or principality in which each place of origin was located. [18]

Of the 904 persons listed in sources as immigrants to New

16. Robert G. Wheeler, "The House of Jeremias Van Rensselaer, 1658–1666," *New-York Historical Society Quarterly* XLV (January 1961), 79.

17. Bailey, *Pre-Revolutionary Dutch Houses;* Harvey, *Genealogical History;* Bayer, *The Belgians;* Evjen, *Scandinavian Immigrants.*

18. Angelo Heilprin and Louis Heilprin, eds., *Lippincott's New Gazetteer* (Philadelphia, 1906); Leon E. Speltzer, ed., *The Columbia Lippincott Gazetteer of the World* (New York, 1962).

Europe in the mid seventeenth century. Map by Adele L. Johnson.

Netherland during the seventeenth century almost half (445) actually came from places outside the Netherlands (see Table 2, p. 52). The largest group (about 37.5 percent [167] of the non-Dutch emigrants) came from Germany, mainly from places either adjacent to the Netherlands (Aachem, the Duchy of Cleves, East Friesland, Westphalia, Bremen, Hamburgh, and Oldenburgh, which became a possession of Denmark in 1667) or further up the Rhine River (Cologne, Bonn, Hesse, Baden, the Lower Palatinate).[19] For example, Wessel Wesselse Ten Broeck came from the town of Wessen near Munster in Westphalia. He emigrated to New Netherland in 1659, where he lived first in New Amsterdam and then in Kingston. Meyndert Barentszen came from Jever in Oldenburgh and emigrated to New Amsterdam, where he lived in 1659 and worked as a cooper. Pieter Claesen Wyckoff came from Norden, a town near Ems in East Friesland. He emigrated to New Netherland in 1637, and lived consecutively in Rensselaerswyck, New Amsterdam, and Flatlands (Amersfoort).[20]

The next two largest contributors of colonists from outside the Netherlands were France and the Spanish Netherlands, each with approximately 14 percent of the non-Dutch immigrants. Many of the emigrants from France were French Huguenots from the city of Calais, the provinces of Picardy and Normandy, which are adjacent to the Spanish Netherlands, or the city of La Rochelle, which was the site of a suppressed Huguenot rebellion in 1627. Some French Huguenots fled first to the Palatinate, and later came to New Netherland. For example, Abraham and Jean Hasbrouck were two brothers from Calais who came to New Netherland in 1678 by way of the Palatinate, Rotterdam, and England. They were two of the original patentees at New Paltz. David Demarest (Des Maree) was born in Beauchamp, near Amiens, in

---

19. The Palatinate was the domain of the electors Palatine, who were high princes of the Holy Roman Empire. It consisted of two geographically separate territories. The Lower Palatinate, situated on the Rhine, was divided among Baden, Hesse, and Nassau in the nineteenth century; the Upper Palatinate, situated to the southeast, became part of Bavaria in the eighteenth century. The town of New Paltz, New York, is named after the Palatinate (*Pfalz* or *Pfalts* in German).

20. Evjen, *Scandinavian Immigrants*, pp. 402, 434–35; Reynolds, *Dutch Houses*, p. 220; E. B. O'Callaghan, ed., *Documentary History of the State of New York* (4 vols.; Albany, N.Y., 1850), III, 36; Bailey, *Pre-Revolutionary Dutch Houses*, pp. 89–90; Morton Wagman, "The Rise of Pieter Claessen Wyckoff: Social Mobility on the Colonial Frontier," *New York History* LIII (January 1972), 5–24.

TABLE 2

PLACE OF ORIGIN OF 904 IMMIGRANTS TO NEW NETHERLAND
(NEW YORK AND NEW JERSEY) IN THE SEVENTEENTH CENTURY

The Netherlands (N = 459; % = 50.8)*

NORTH HOLLAND (N = 142; % = 16)	
Alckmaer (Alkmaar)	3
Amsterdam	90
Blarcom (Blaricum)	2
Edam	4
Haerlem (Haarlem)	6
Hilversum	3
Hoorn	11
Medemblick	2
Naerden	8
Other	13

GELDERLAND (N = 88; % = 10)	
Aernheim (Arhem)	6
Beest	8
Betawe	2
Buren	5
Doornyck (Doornik)	2
New-kerk (Niewkirk)	13
Newenhuys	2
Putten	2
Thillerwarden (Thillerwaerd)	4
Tiel (Teyl)	7
Tricht	2
Wagening	7
Other	26

UTRECHT (N = 68; % = 8)	
Amersfoort	15
Breuckelen	3
Bunnick	4
Hilversam	2
Houten	6
Leerdam	5
Loosdrecht	2
Maersen (Maarssen)	2
Soest	3
Westbroeck	2
Ysselstein	3
Other	21

SOUTH HOLLAND (N = 45; % = 5)	
Delft	2
Dort (Dordrecht)	3
Gorcum (Gorichem, Gorkem)	7
Ter Gouw (Gouda)	3
Leyden	13
Rotterdam	5
Schoenderwoert	6
Other	6

FRIESLAND (N = 25; % = 3)	
Harlingen	5
Workum	3
Other	17

DRENTHE (N = 22; % = 2)	
Meppel	5
Ruinen	2
Other	17

NORTH BRABANT (N = 16; % = 2)	
Breda	7
's Hertogenbosch	3
Other	8

OVERIJSSEL (N = 21; % = 2)	
Deventer	3
Hasselt	2
Kampen (Campen)	5
Oldenseel (Oldenzaal)	2
Steenwyck	5
Swoll (Zwolle)	3
Other	1

LIMBURG (N = 7; % = 1)	
Maestricht (Maastricht)	2
Other	5

ZEELAND (N = 18; % = 2)	
Middleburg (Middelburgh)	6
Veere	2
Vlissingen (Flushing)	3
Other	7

GRONINGEN (N = 7; % = 1)

Spanish Netherlands [Belgium]
(N = 63; % = 7)

WALLOON PROVINCES (N = 30; % = 3)	
Avesnes	2
Liège	3
Hainaut (Henegouw)	2
Tournai (in Hainaut)	3
Valenciennes	7
Artois	5
Richebourg (in Artois)	2
Other	6

FLEMISH PROVINCES (N = 31; % = 3)	
Antwerp	5
Leeuwen (Leuven, Louvain)	2
Bruggen (Bruges)	4
Iperen (Yprés)	2
Other	18

BRUSSELS (N = 2; % = .2)

Germany (N = 167; % = 18)

EAST FRIESLAND (N = 20; % = 2)	
Embden (Emden)	9

*N = number of settlers; % = percentage of the 904 immigrants.

Norden	4
Other	7

OLDENBURGH (N = 23; % = 3)

Oldenburgh	12
Jever	8
Other	3

WESTPHALIA (N = 18; % = 2)

Münster	5
Other	13

BRUNSWICK-LÜNEBURG (N = 6; % = 1)

Brunswick	3
Wolfenbüttel	2
Other	1

BREMEN (N = 18; % = 2)

HAMBURG (N = 7; % = 1)

HANOVER (N = 2; % = .2)

CALEMBURG (N = 2; % = .2)

OSNABRUCK (N = 2; % = .2)

COLOGNE (N = 3; % = .3)

CLEVES (N = 5; % = .6)

AACHEM (N = 2; % = .2)

BONN (N = 5; % = .6)

LIPPE (N = 2; % = .2)

HESSE (N = 12; % = 1)

Darmstadt	7
Other	5

BADEN (N = 3; % = .3)

Mannheim	2
Other	1

LOWER PALATINATE (N = 2; % = .2)

THURINGIA (N = 2; % = .2)

WURTEMBURG (N = 2; % = .2)

POMERANIA (N = 2; % = .2)

SAXONY (N = 4; % = .4)

BRANDENBURG-PRUSSIA (N = 7; % = 1)

Magdeburg	2
Other	5

BAVARIA (N = 5; % = .6)

Nürnberg	4
Other	1

OTHER (N = 13; % = 1)

France (N = 64; % = 7)

PICARDY (N = 10; % = 1)

Amiens	2
Calais	4
Other	4

NORMANDY (N = 9; % = 1)

Dieppe	2
Other	7

SAINTONGE (N = 4; % = .4)

La Rochelle	3
Other	1

PAYS DE VAUD (now in Switzerland) (N = 8; % = 1)

PARIS (N = 3; % = .3)

LANGUEDOC (N = 2; % = .2)

OTHER (N = 28; % = 3)

Schleswig-Holstein (N = 60; % = 7)

Barlt	2
Dithmarschen	11
Flensburg	4
Holstein	26
Husum	2
Lübeck	7
Nordstrand	2
Schleswig	3
Other	3

Denmark (N = 11; % = 1)

ZEALAND (SJAELLAND) (N = 4; % = .4)

Copenhagen	2
Other	2

JUTLAND (N = 5; % = .6)

OTHER (N = 2)

Sweden (N = 24; % = 3)

Götenborg	4
Stockholm	8
Vesterås	2
Varberg (in Scania)	2
Other	8

Norway (N = 47; % = 5)

Bergen	5
Fleckerö	3
Frederikstad	3
Sant	3
Sleewyck (Sleviken)	2
Other	31

Poland (N = 3; % = .3)

Other (N = 6; % = .7)

Total = 904

Picardy. He fled to Middleburg in Zeeland, then to Mannheim, and then came to America in 1663. He lived for a while on Staten Island, then moved to Harlem, and then to Bergen County. Other French Huguenots came by way of the Netherlands. For example, Jacques Cousseau was a merchant from La Rochelle. He immigrated to New Netherland by way of Holland in 1658 and subsequently lived in New Amsterdam and then in Harlem. Still others were Waldensians—members of the brotherhood known as the Pauvres of Lyon, founded by Peter Waldo in the twelfth century. During persecutions in 1655, they fled to Holland and then came to New Netherland to settle on Staten Island and Long Island. [21]

In the sample of emigrants from the Spanish Netherlands (Belgium), roughly half (30) came from the Walloon provinces (Hainault, Namur, Liege, Luxembourg, Artois, South Brabant) and half (31) from the Flemish provinces (West Flanders, East Flanders, Antwerp, Limbourg, North Brabant). The term "Walloon" comes from the Flemish and Dutch word *Waalsch*, which is the Germanic form of the French word *Gaulois*. The Walloons are the descendants of the Gallic Belgae, who were the Celtic inhabitants of Belgian Gaul. Their language is *Waalsch* (Walloon), a Romance language related to French. The Flemings (*Vlamings*) are a Teutonic people whose Germanic language is related to Dutch. In 1648, Spain ceded to the Dutch Republic the northern parts of Flanders, Limbourg, and Brabant. In 1659, Artois, part of Luxembourg, and the southern parts of Flanders and Hainault were ceded to France. And in 1678, additional cities in Hainault and Flanders were ceded. Thus, many emigrants thought to have been French Huguenots and Dutch were actually Walloons and Flemings (see map, p. 56).

After the founding of the Dutch Republic in 1579, Walloon and Flemish Protestants fled to the Netherlands—some by way of Germany—and later many of them came to New Netherland. According to the seventeenth-century Dutch historian Nicolaes Van Wassenaer, the first, permanent settlers to arrive in New Netherland in 1624 aboard the ship *Nieu Nederlandt*, commanded by Cornelis Jacobsz May from

---

21. Reynolds, *Dutch Houses,* pp. 203–04; Katherine Bevier, *The Bevier Family* (New York, 1916), p. 15; Bailey, *Pre-Revolutionary Dutch Houses,* pp. 284–85; Adrian C. Leiby, *The Huguenot Settlement of Schraalenburgh* (Bergenfield, N.J., 1964), pp. 6–8.; Stokes, *Iconography,* II, 273–74; Bayer, *The Belgians,* pp. 175-78.

Hoorn, consisted of "a company of thirty families, mostly Walloons."[22] One of these settlers was George Jansen de Rapelie (Rapelje), thought to have been from Valenciennes, who married Catelina Trico and, after immigrating to New Netherland, lived in succession at Fort Orange (Albany), Manhattan, and Long Island.[23] Descendants of the Rapelje family also settled on Staten Island. Louis du Bois, the leader of a group of Walloons who settled at Esopus in 1660, was born in Wieres near Lille, and, as a young man, he migrated to Mannheim in the Lower Palatinate, where he married in 1655 Catherine Blanchan, also a Walloon.[24] One of the first settlers at New Paltz was Louis Bevier, thought to have been born near Lille, who married Marie Le Blanc in 1673 in the Palatine bishopric of Speier and came to America two years later. In fact, several of the leaders of the colonial effort were originally from the Spanish Netherlands. Peter Minuit, director general of the colony from 1626 to 1632, was the son of Walloon refugees who settled in the town of Wesel in Westphalia, Germany. William Usselinx, one of the founders of the Dutch West India Company, was originally from Antwerp. Jan De Laet, director of the Amsterdam Chamber of the Dutch West India Company, was a Fleming born in Antwerp who migrated to Leyden. Cornelis Melyn, the patroon of Staten Island, who came to New Netherland in 1638, also was a Fleming originally from Antwerp.[25]

Approximately 14 percent (60) of the non-Dutch emigrants were from Schleswig-Holstein, at that time part of Denmark. Laurens Andriessen Van Boskerk, for example, emigrated from Holstein about 1654, settling first in New Amsterdam and then in Bergen County. Although he was a turner by trade, he became a justice of the peace and a member of the governor's council. Jan Pietersen Slot (Sloat) also was from Holstein. He immigrated to Amsterdam and then to New

22. J. Franklin Jameson, ed., *Narratives of New Netherland, 1609–1664* (New York, 1909), p. 75.

23. The place name "Wallabout Bay" near the Brooklyn Navy Yard comes from *Waal-Bocht*, which means in Dutch "Walloon Bay." It was so named because it was adjacent to the land bought by George de Rapelje on Long Island.

24. Bayer, *The Belgians*, pp. 167–70, 180–85. The name "Wallkill" comes from *Waal-Kill*, literally the "Walloon's Creek."

25. Bevier, *Bevier Family*, pp. 11–13; Bayer, *The Belgians*, pp. 70, 96, 163–65, 175, 178, 190, 194, 195, 221.

UNITED
NETHERLANDS

1 North Holland
2 Gelderland
3 Utrecht
4 South Holland
5 Friesland
6 Drenthe
7 North Brabant
8 Overijssel
9 Limburg
10 Zeeland
11 Groningen

•Norden

•Harlingen
5
11
•Workum
6
•Steenwyck
•Ruinen
Medemblick
Meppel
Alkmaar
1
•Hoorn
Campen
•Hasselt
8
•Edam
•Zwolle
Haarlem
•Doornik
Amsterdam
Blaricum
•Deventer
•Oldenzaal
Leyden
Naerden
•Putten
Breuckelen
•Kiewkirk
2
3
Amersfoort
Bunnick
Houten
•Arhem
4
Delft
Gouda
Wagening
Rotterdam
•Buren
Betawe
Gorkem
Beest
•Teyl
Hertogenbosch
Veere
10
Middelburgh
Breda
Flushing
7
•Bruges
•Antwerp
9
Flanders
Schelde
•Ypres
•Louvain
Maastricht
•Brussels
•Tournai
Artois
•Liège
•Valenciennes
•Aresnes
SPANISH
NETHERLANDS
Rhine

*The United Netherlands in the mid seventeenth century. Map by Adele L.
Johnson.*

Netherland, where he took up residence in Harlem. Another 2.5 percent (11) came from the rest of Denmark. Perhaps the most notable of them was Jonas Bronck, for whom The Bronx is named. He was the son of a Lutheran pastor from Thorshavn on the Faroe Islands. He came to New Netherland in 1639 and obtained a large tract of land in what is today known as Morrisania.[26]

Another 11 percent (47) of the non-Dutch immigrants came from Norway. According to John O. Evjen, "the Scandinavians, especially the Norwegians and Danes, had, for many years, been accustomed to see their sons and daughters go, for a longer or shorter time to Holland. The commerce between Norway and Holland was large. The vast forests of Norway furnished the Dutch with timber. And Norwegians and Danes joined the Dutch fleet in great numbers."[27] Two brothers, Arent Andriessen Bradt and Albert Andriesse Bradt, came from Fredrikstad, Norway, and settled in Rensselaerswyck. Albert Bradt built a mill a few miles south of Albany. Albert was known as *de Noorman* (the Norwegian), and the stream on which he built his mill was called *de Noorman's Kill*. (today known as Norman's Kill).[28]

Approximately 5 percent (24) of the non-Dutch immigrants came from Sweden. Together the Scandinavian countries contributed 32 percent (142) of the non-Dutch immigrants to New Netherland.

Of those colonists who came from the Netherlands, the largest number (90) came from the city of Amsterdam. But they represent only about one-fifth (19.6 percent) of the total Dutch immigrants. Even when those from Amsterdam are included, the number of individuals from North Holland was only 31 percent (142) of the total Dutch immigrants. Several of these came from Hoorn, a seaport on the Zuider Zee, and included David Petersen De Vries, onetime patroon of Staten Island and Vriesendael, and Jan Pieterse Haring, one of the original shareholders in the Tappan Patent. Approximately 10 percent (45) of the Dutch emigrants came from South Holland, including Pieter Gerritse Van Alen from Rotterdam,

---

26. Bailey, *Pre-Revolutionary Dutch Houses,* pp. 210, 265, 314; Evjen, *Scandinavian Immigrants,* pp. 167–81, 276.

27. Evjen, *Scandinavian Immigrants,* p. 12.

28. Ibid., pp. 19–36; Reynolds, *Dutch Houses,* p. 64.

Walloons landing in Albany. From Bayer, The Belgians.

who settled in the Saddle River Valley of Bergen County, and Peter Van Ecke, a planter from Leyden who immigrated in 1659. Rutger Jacobsen, the founder of the Rutgers family, came from Schoonderwoert, a village near Utrecht, in South Holland. He started out as a farmhand, became a foreman at Rensselaerswyck, and became a prominent man in Beverwyck (Albany), also owning a house in New Amsterdam.[29]

About 15 percent (68) of the Dutch colonists came from the province of Utrecht. A significant number (15) came from the town of Amersfoort. Wolfert Gerritsz van Couwenhoven came from Couwenhoven, an estate near Amersfoort in the province of Utrecht. He was hired by Kiliaen van Rensselaer to supervise the establishment of farms and the purchase of cattle in Rensselaerswyck. Cornelis Anthonisz van Schlick

29. Bayer, *The Belgians*, pp. 174–75; Bailey, *Pre-Revolutionary Dutch Houses*, pp. 293, 312; O'Callaghan, *Documentary History*, III, 35; Evjen, *Scandinavian Immigrants*, pp. 214–15; Van Laer, *Van Rensselaer-Bowier Manuscripts*, p. 812.

was a carpenter and mason from Breuckelen, in the province of Utrecht, who emigrated in 1634 and settled in Rensselaerswyck. The province of Zeeland, along the coast in the southwestern corner of the Netherlands, contributed about 4 percent (18) of the sample of Dutch immigrants. They came from places, such as Middelburgh and Vlissingen (Flushing). Claes Martenszen van Rosenvelt, the founder of the Roosevelt family in America, came from the town of Rosenvelt in the province of Zeeland.[30]

Almost 20 percent (88) of the Dutch colonists came from the province of Gelderland, through which the Rhine River flows on its way across the eastern part of the Netherlands. Newkirk (Nykerck, Niewkirk) contributed the largest number (13), but individuals also came from Aernheim, Beest, Buren, Thillerwarden, Teyl, and Wagening. For example, Arent van Curler, the commis of Rensselaerswyck from 1642 to 1644, came from Nykerck. And Gerrit Gerritse, the founder of the Van Wagoner family, emigrated from Wageningen in 1660 and settled in Communipaw (now part of Jersey City).[31]

Lesser numbers of Dutch colonists came from the provinces of Friesland, 5.4 percent (25); Drenthe, 4.8 percent (22); Overijssel, 4.6 percent (21); North Brabant, 3.5 percent (16); Limburg, 1.5 percent (7); and Groningen, 1.5 percent (7). But taken together, these provinces represent 21.3 percent (98) of the total Dutch immigrants—more than the number that came from the city of Amsterdam—and included some very important people in New Netherland. For example, Pieter Stuyvesant was born in the province of Friesland. Epke Jacobse Banta, founder of the Banta family of Bergen County, New Jersey, came from Harlingen in Friesland. Steven Coerte van Voorhees and Joris Dircksen Brinkerhof both came from the province of Drenthe; and Dirck Storm and David Ackerman both came from the Mayory of Bosch (s' Hertogenbosch) in North Brabant. Also from North Brabant was Adriaen van der Donck, the patroon of Colendonck (present-day Yonkers). He was originally from the town of Breda in that prov-

---

30. Van Laer, *Van Rensselaer-Bowier Manuscripts*, pp. 805, 809; Alvin Page Johnson, *Franklin D. Roosevelt's Colonial Ancestors* (Boston, 1933), pp. 16–18.

31. Van Laer, *Van Rensselaer-Bowier Manuscripts*, p. 817; Bailey, *Pre-Revolutionary Dutch Houses*, p. 523; O'Callaghan, *Documentary History*, III, 35.

ince. And finally, Gerrit Hendricksen, the founder of the Blauvelt family, was born in Deventer, Overijssel. He worked as a shoemaker in Nykerk, before going to New Netherland in 1637.[32]

What overall conclusions can be drawn from these data? First, the emphasis of both American and European historians on the middle class, burgher tradition in the Netherlands does not explain the Dutch experience in New Netherland. Most of the immigrants were farmers, soldiers, or craftsmen, even among the ancestors of the families that gained great wealth in New York and New Jersey. Second, the emphasis on the single province of Holland has masked the fact that the majority of the Dutch immigrants came from other provinces. And, third, almost half the immigrants to New Netherland were not from the Netherlands, but from places adjacent to the Netherlands. We tend to think in terms of political boundaries instead of in terms of ethnic and linguistic groups. Political boundaries changed frequently during the seventeenth century. Only when we look at the cultural boundaries and how they relate to the place of origin of Dutch settlers in New Netherland do we understand the cultural processes that shaped the Dutch culture in New York and New Jersey.

32. Adrian Leiby, *The Early Dutch and Swedish Settlers of New Jersey* (Princeton, N.J., 1964). pp. 41–42; Bailey, *Pre-Revolutionary Dutch Houses,* pp. 180–81, 270, 277, 281, 320; Reynolds, *Dutch Houses,* p. 376; O'Callaghan, *Documentary History,* III, 39; Van Laer, *Van Rensselaer-Bowier Manuscripts,* p. 824.

Cultural Adaptation in Colonial New York: The Palatine Germans of the Mohawk Valley

By ROBERT KUHN McGREGOR

Millions of immigrants have endured the experience of making a new life in a new world. One eighteenth-century group provides a model for study of immigrant adaptability to life in America. Robert McGregor is a member of the History Program at Sangamon State University, Springfield, Illinois.

IN THE EARLY YEARS of the eighteenth century, a group of German immigrant families completed an odyssey of fifteen years duration by accepting freeholds on the westernmost frontier of Provincial New York. These families had departed the Rhineland in 1709, for a host of political, economic, and climatic reasons. They carried with them their immediate personal belongings and a set of cultural values that may best be described as traditional and corporate. These Germans, coming to America as indentured servants of the English government, faced an almost completely different physical and social environment in the New World. To survive and maintain cultural identity, they began an adaptive process which resulted in the development of a social structure bearing characteristics of both a competitive "modern" society and the traditions of the Old World. The behavior of this immigrant community in the colony of New York, as presented in a broad array of scattered documents, reveals the nature of their adaptive process and, by projection,

I wish to thank Dr. Bernard Mason of the State University of New York at Binghamton for his gracious assistance, David Zipkin for his contributions, and the State University of New York at Binghamton Foundation for a research grant that helped underwrite the costs of archival research.

nourishes an assessment of the manner in which less visible groups accommodated themselves to the American experience.[1]

The group in question are the Palatine Germans who settled New York's Mohawk River Valley during the 1720s. Many of these Germans had entered the colony as early as 1710 and had been moved from place to place as the object of a number of economic experiments undertaken by the Provincial government with the blessing of the Crown. After fifteen years of setbacks and humiliations, they received patented lands in the Mohawk country, an outcome which left many of their number alienated from colonial authorities. All the Palatines were isolated from the rest of New York's settlements, both socially and politically. By the outbreak of the Revolution some fifty years later, however, these Germans felt an identity with the patriot cause which inspired them to make a major contribution to its success. To understand the nature of this transformation it is necessary to examine the composition of the corporate society of the immigrants and the subsequent effects of their life in the Mohawk Valley.[2]

The corporate society, virtually universal in the Europe of the seventeenth and early eighteenth centuries, is one of mutually shared responsibilities. The structure is relatively rigid, with the few wealthy and honored persons at the top controlling the political and economic regimen of the society. Beneath these few stand a number of middling groups of descending social importance, including yeoman and husbandmen, craftsmen, tradesmen and artisans. Under these come the general mass of the society, including laborers, tenants, and paupers. Women occupy a subservient position in all parts of such a social organization.

1. The discussion of social change in the New World reaches back at least to J. Franklin Jameson and Carl Becker. For an articulation of the controversy surrounding the emergence of individualist society, consult James Henretta, "Families and Farms: *Mentalité* in Pre-Industrial America," *William and Mary Quarterly* 35 (1978): 3-32.
2. The most comprehensive chronicle of the Palatine experience in America is Walter Allen Knittle, *Early Eighteenth Century Palatine Emigration* (Philadelphia: Dorrance and Company, 1937). See also Nelson Greene, ed. *History of the Mohawk Valley: Gateway to the West*, 4 vols. (Chicago: S.J. Clarke Publishing Company, 1925), especially volume one.

The smaller numbers at the apex of the social pyramid share a responsibility to the masses beneath them, a responsibility met through the exercise of the power of government, and also in more personal ways. Perhaps the best measure of one's social standing was the number of servants one possessed. These servants were drawn from among the minors of families whose positions left them unable to afford their maintenance. Service was a means by which the rich took direct responsibility for the welfare of the poor. In addition, they assumed obligation for poor relief, adjudication of disputes, and general protection of the population. In return, the masses below gave deference to their betters, referring to them by titles and offering virtually no opposition to their operation of societal affairs.

At the heart of the corporatist society was the belief that such organization was imperative, that a challenge to the hierachy or an attempt to seriously alter the social structure would lead only to catastrophe. The men at the top of the structure occupied such a position because they were the best elements, and must rule of necessity.[3]

Traditionally, the Christian church, itself hierarchically organized and constituted to imbue the virtues of servility and deference, had anchored and re-enforced the corporate nature of the society. In Germany, the role of religion had diminished during the seventeenth century, in large measure because of ecclesiastical conflicts and the insensitivity of church and political leaders. The middle classes still abided the authority of the churches at times of birth, marriage, and death, but religion had become less significant in the day-to-day lives of the people.[4]

A reaction to the rigid orthodoxies of the period took root in Germany in 1675 with the publication of *Pious Wishes* by Philipp Jacob Spener. His call for a practical, experimental faith ruled by the heart rather than the mind came to be

3. Peter Laslett, *The World We Have Lost* (London, 1965); Pierre Goubert, *Louis XIV and Twenty Million Frenchmen*, trans. A. Carter (New York, 1969).
4. Ernest F. Stoeffler, ed. *Continental Pietism and Early American Christianity* (Grand Rapids, Michigan: William B. Eerdmans Publishing Company, 1976), Introduction, esp. pp. 9-10; David Warren Sabean, *Power in the Blood* (Cambridge: Cambridge University Press, 1984).

known as Pietism. By 1700, the Reverend August Hermann Francke had centered the movement at Halle University, where he benefited from a proclamation of protection by the civil authorities of Brandenberg. This governmental support guaranteed that Pietism would exist as a reform movement within the Lutheran and German Reformed Churches, rather than becoming a separatist doctrine. By the time of the Palatine emigration in 1708-09, religious debate had become a part of life in the German states.[5]

Like all of Germany, the Palatinate had suffered the tragedies and terrors inspired by religious controversy during the Thirty Years' War. The Treaty of Westphalia (1648) left the states under the rule of Protestant Electors. Because of its location along the Rhine River near the borders of Louis XIV's France, the Palatine states quickly became a haven for French Huguenot refugees, as well as for victims of persecution from Switzerland and elsewhere. An unusual degree of toleration and cooperation developed as the Palatines strove to adjust to the confused religious situation. Reformed German (Calvinist), Lutheran, and Roman Catholic devotees not only occupied the same villages; they at times also shared church buildings. The problems posed by German religious orthodoxy could nonetheless be found in the region. At Gross Aspach, the parson ran a wine business in addition to his clerical duties, but the village schoolmaster was described as a man of piety.[6]

Life in the Palatine states became increasingly difficult as the seventeenth century drew to a close. The seemingly continuous series of continental wars inspired by the expansionist designs of Louis XIV resulted in repeated invasions of the region. The states were devastated in 1674, in 1688-89, and again in 1707. Each invasion brought an epidemic in its wake, killing still more people. To make matters worse, the most terrible winter in more than a century blighted the region in 1708-09, killing trees and destroying vineyards. The combina-

5. Harry Julius Kreider, "Lutheranism in Colonial New York," Ph.D. Dissertation, Political Science Department, Columbia University, 1942.
6. Mack Walker, *The German Homes Towns: Community, State and General Estate* (Ithaca: Cornell University Press, 1971); Heinriche Rembe, "Emigration Materials From Lambsheim in the Palatinate," trans. Donald Yoder, *Pennsylvania Folklife* 22 (Winter, 1973-74): 40-42; Paul A. Wallace, *Conrad Weiser: Friend of Colonist and Mohawk* (Philadelphia: University of Pennsylvania Press, 1945), 4.

tion of military and climatic disasters inspired a number of Palatine residents to emigrate. Although the Pastor of Weltrod referred to them as "more or less lazy and indolent fellows," most were of the middling classes.[7]

German clerical leaders had petitioned the English government for relief, and had found a sympathetic receptor in Queen Anne, a devout Protestant who had inherited William and Mary's opposition to French Catholic designs. American colonial land agents, who apparently circulated a gold-framed book bearing the Queen's picture and a description of the American colonies, may also have played a role in inspiring the removal. Several English clerics supported and assisted the emigration, including most importantly Anton Wilhelm Boehme, an alumnus of Halle University and court advisor to Queen Anne. Boehme, a Pietist, provided a critical link between the German Protestant churches and the English government.[8]

The Palatines arrived in London from Holland in the autumn of 1709 and were temporarily sheltered in refugee communities outside London while the government decided their ultimate fate. By the end of the year, approximately 13,000 had journeyed to England. The vast majority were husbandmen and vinedressers, but twenty-nine other crafts and occupations were represented, including weavers, carpenters, smiths, tailors, masons, and shoemakers. English writer and journalist Daniel DeFoe found the Palatine immigrants both industrious and religious in outlook. Although defined as members of the middle classes by virtue of their former occupations, the emigrants had carried little with them, and were by all accounts destitute.[9]

The English quickly returned the Catholics among the immigrants to Germany and divided the remainder into small groups consigned to colonies in Ireland, the Virgin Islands,

7. Knittle, *Early Palatine Emigration*, 3-21; Wallace, *Conrad Weiser*, 5; Lucy Forney Bittenger, *The Germans in Colonial Times* (New York: Russell and Rusell, 1968), 15-60; Henry Z. Jones, *The Palatine Families of New York*, 2 vols. (Universal City, Cal., 1985), 1:vii.

8. Knittle, *Early Palatine Emigration*, 3-21; Wallace, *Conrad Weiser*, 4-9; Henry Eyster Jacobs, *The German Emigration to America, 1709-1740* (Lancaster: The Pennsylvania German Society, 1898), 16.

9. Daniel DeFoe, *A Brief History of the Poor Palatine Refugees* [1709] (Los Angeles: The Augustan Reprint Society, University of California, 1964).

New Jersey, Virginia, and the Carolinas. In early 1710, the balance of the population—roughly 3,000—were sent to the Province of New York, where they were to be settled into economic communities devoted to the manufacture of naval stores for Her Majesty's government. Royal officials also discussed the possibility of awarding the Palatines land grants in one of New York's interior river valleys, although knowledge of the colony's geography was vague.[10]

A smaller advance group of Palatines from the Village of Landau had set out for New York the previous year, and had established an encampment at Newburgh in the Hudson River Valley. Of the forty-seven immigrants, nineteen changed their religion to become Pietists upon arrival in the colony. The Provincial Governor, Lord Cornbury, was called out to arbitrate the ensuing religious dispute, and was relieved to determine that all the Germans remained Christian. The incident provides the first record of Pietist influence in America.[11]

Of the second New York contingent, 470 Palatines died en route to the province. Children orphaned in consequence were separated from the group and apprenticed to New York City tradesmen. The rest were assigned to temporary camps along the Hudson River, while New York's Governor Hunter attempted to find means to carry out the British government's intentions. Two years of confusion and repeated failure followed. The Germans relocated at least twice, were given no accurate instructions in the manufacture of naval stores, and continually petitioned Hunter and others for the freeholds they felt they had been promised. The experiment fell completely apart in 1712.[12]

10. Knittle, *Early Palatine Emigration*, 22-134; Hugh Hastings, ed., "The Conditions, Grievances and Oppressions of the Germans in His Majesty's Province of New York in America," *Ecclesiastical Records of the State of New York*, 8 vols. (Albany: J.B. Lyon Company, 1902), 3:2158-73. (*Ecclesiastical Records hereafter referred to as ERNY.*)

11. *ERNY*, 3:1742-43; Bittenger, *Germans in Colonial Times*, 59-60; Theodore G. Tappert, "The Influence of Pietism in Colonial American Lutheranism," in Stoeffler, *Continental Pietism*, 13-33.

12. Knittle, *Early Palatine Emigration*, 135-87; Edmond B. O'Callaghan and Berthold Fernow, eds., *Documents Relative to the Colonial History of the State of New York*, 15 vols. (Albany: Weed, Parsons and Company, 1853-1887), 5:113-95, 450-79. (*New York Colonial Documents* hereafter referred to as *NYCD.*)

One hundred-sixty Palatine families then moved to a portion of the Schoharie Valley of their own accord, claiming the lands in fulfillment of English promises. Two years later, they were informed that they had squatted on property owned by a group of Albany merchants, entitled the "Seven Partners Patent." Years of acrimonious controversy ensued. At one point, the women of the community attacked and repulsed the Sheriff of Albany County, who had come to force their evacuation. The Germans in the meantime petitioned London, to no avail. In the end, several families admitted defeat and paid the owners for deeds to the properties they farmed. Others refused to capitulate, insisting that the government by right owed them freeholds without cost—if not in the Schoharie Valley, then elsewhere.[13]

A solution was reached in 1723, when twenty-six Palatine families were awarded land in the Mohawk Valley, at the behest of the new royal governor, William Burnet. The governor was frank in declaring his purpose in granting the patent. His conditions stated that "it not be nearer than a fall in the Mohocks River which is 40 miles above Fort Hunter & four score from Albany by which the frontier will be so much extended . . . ." The Germans were placed in the valley to serve as a buffer against the Iroquois Indians and the French in Canada.[14]

The Palatines moved no further after taking up residence in the upper Mohawk Valley. Isolated from the rest of the colony, close to potentially hostile French and Indian neighbors, and surrounded by largely unbroken wilderness, the group faced a physical and social environment very unlike that of Germany. The large expanse of open, unclaimed land in the region posed a vast potential whose exploitation was limited initially only by the settlers' lack of resources and small numbers. In the Mohawk Valley, the Germans found themselves free to develop a new social and economic identity.

The settlers received 12,700 acres of land in this first grant,

13. Knittle, *Early Palatine Emigration*, 188-204; Jeptha R. Simms, *The Frontiersmen of New York* (Albany: George C. Riggs, 1882), 146, 152, 182.
14. Burnet to the Board of Trade, *NYCD*, 5:634.

located mostly on a plateau overlooking the valley, removed from the river itself. Portions had been cleared by the Iroquois, giving the Palatines some small compensation for the loss of the improvements they had made in the Schoharie. For reasons which remain obscure, the settlers called the grant Stone Arabia. They divided enough of the patent to allow each family fifty acres of farmland. The group held the remainder in common and set aside the entirety for division by later generations. A small glebe lot was also set aside and divided in half for the construction of two churches, one Lutheran, the other German Reformed. Devotees of the two faiths were roughly equal in number.[15]

More Palatine Germans moved into the valley over the next eight years. Several families bought lots in the Harison Patent, granted to Lewis Morris and others in 1722, and in the Alexander Patent, given to a group of New York City merchants and lawyers in 1725. Also in 1725, Governor Burnet awarded a patent of 9,400 acres to a group of thirty-seven families (ninety-four persons in all; one hundred acres per person). Originally called Burnetsfield, this patent became generally known as German Flats. The settlers derived from two groups, some from the Schoharie, the remainder from a newly-arrived immigration from Europe. Apparently, all were members of the German Reformed Church.[16]

Two more small grants were made to the Palatines during this period. The Province awarded the 1,637-acre Waganaer Patent to three families in 1725, and 2,000 acres were granted to Harmtman Wendecker in 1731. By 1725, the German population in the valley stood at approximately 110 households, composed of 440 people.[17]

The patterns of land distribution among the Palatine popu-

15. Land Papers, Colonial and State, 1642-1683, 63 vols., Manuscript Division, New York State Library, 6:138 (hereafter referred to as Land Papers); Greene, *History of the Mohawk Valley*, 401-07.

16. Lou D. MacWethy, *The Book of Names, Especially Relating to the Early Palatines* (Baltimore: Genealogical Publishing Company, 1969), 180, 189-91; Land Papers, 9:22, 48, 174; Nathaniel S. Benton, *A History of Herkimer County* (Albany: J. Munsell, 1856), 50-64.

17. Specific information regarding the dates, acreages, and identities of patentees is derived from Original Letters Patent, Engrossed in Books of Letters Patent, 1664-1786, 17 vols., Manuscript Division, New York State Library (hereafter refer-

lation suggest a few salient facts concerning their social organization. In all of the patents save Burnetsfield, the lands were appointed to individual families. At Stone Arabia, where an entire community of Germans possessed direct control over the allotments, fifty acres were given to each family by lot, and the remaining 8,000 acres were held in common by the group for distribution to future generations. Each family settled on its own tract; there was no common village. Individual ownership of property was an established fact at Stone

red to as Original Letters Patent). Essential to the use of these documents is Charles Hooper's unpublished Card Index of Letters Patent, Manuscripts Division, New York State Library. The estimate of population is based on the lists of patentees, the lands distributed to each family, and evidence of actual occupation from church records, militia rolls, or land deeds. See n. 31, below.

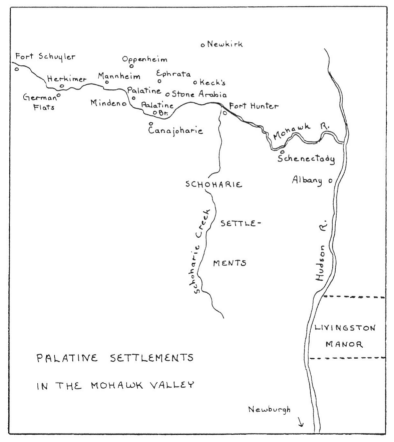

Location of Palatine settlements in the Mohawk Valley. Utica, the site of Fort Schuyler, is included for the sake of orientation. Map by Adele L. Johnson.

Arabia, and in the Harison and Alexander Patents, where separate lots were purchased from the original owners by solitary families. The Waganaer Patent was divided between two family units; a single household owned the Wendecker Tract.[18]

At Burnetsfield, the organization was vastly different. The Provincial government granted 100 acres to each person in the group at German Flats, but the acreage was not allotted in a single 100-acre parcel. Most commonly, a person received thirty acres in the flats by the Mohawk River, and another seventy acres in the uplands. A family's combined holdings might include several small parcels scattered along both sides of the river.

Unlike Stone Arabia, a central village was established at German Flats, where most of the members of the community resided. All in all, the German Flats population organized their community in a manner reminiscent of the Old World, with each family owning several small tracts surrounding a common village. It is difficult to establish the reason for this departure from the behavior of the other German settlers, but it is suggestive that among the Burnetsfield population were several persons newly emigrated from Germany. Since the German immigrants of the period tended to emigrate as members of a cohesive group, often emanating from the same villages, it seems probable that these new arrivals influenced the establishment of an "Old World" system of settlement. The other Palatines, already long-time dwellers on the American landscape, opted for a system of individual parcels contained within a single boundary.[19]

Table 1 illustrates the amounts of land acquired by the Palatines in the years 1723-1731, and in addition breaks down those holdings into amounts available for various potential economic uses. Almost three-fourths of the German holdings

18. "Ancient Stone Arabia: Schedule of Titles Produced 1723 to 1792," a map and accompanying documentation produced by the St. Johnsville, N.Y. *Enterprise and News*, 1931, from documents then on file at the Margaret Rainey Memorial Library, St. Johnsville. Information on spatial relationships in other patents is based on the study of patent maps on file at the New York State Library, Manuscripts Division, Maps Collections.

19. A copy of the original map of land distribution at German Flats may be found in MacWethy, *Book of Names*, 190. The original is in the Maps Collections of the New York State Library, Manuscripts Division. See also Benton, *Herkimer County*, 41-51.

possessed less than 11 percent slope, suiting them admirably for crop agriculture. The Palatines could at least utilize most of the remainder for grazing, and a mere 3,443 acres were too steep for any agricultural purpose. Even these lands were largely forested, from which some economic profit could be derived. After several years of ill-use by the Provincial government, the Palatines were at last provided with lands which were not merely adequate, but of enormous agricultural potential.

The patents received by the Germans were only one part of the overall distribution of lands in the Mohawk Valley. In all, the Province of New York granted 147,849 acres in the region between 1705 and 1731. There was no orderly distribution of the territory. The royal governors most often granted patents as political favors, usually with little regard for the necessities of settling and defending the frontier. Since the Mohawk was under the hegemony of the Iroquois confederacy, authorities in London directed that the valley be patented and settled in

TABLE 1

QUALITY OF PALATINE LANDS, IN ACRES, 1722-1731

Patent	Year	Suited for planting	Suited to grazing	Unsuited to farming	Total acreage
Harison	1722	8,640	2,520	840	12,000
Stone Arabia	1723	10,160	1,905	635	12,700
Burnetsfield	1725	7,144	1,974	282	9,400
Alexander	1725	4,400	2,160	1,440	8,000
Waganaer	1725	1,391	0	246	1,637
Wendecker	1731	2,000	0	0	2,000
Total		33,735	8,559	3,443	45,737

Source: Original Letters Patent. Data concerning the potential of the land in each patent was derived in the following fashion: Land suited to planting is defined as ground with a slope of less than 11 percent. Land with a slope of greater than 11 but less than 17 percent is considered suitable for pasturage only. Land with a slope of more than 17 percent will not support agricultural endeavor. (Source: New York State Department of Soil Conservation, Personal Communication, 1985.) To determine the slope percentages for each of the pertinent patents, eighteenth-cenutry maps of the Mohawk Valley were compared with modern United States Geographical Survey Maps (1:24,000 scale) to discover changes in landform, stream beds, etc. After making allowances for such changes as had occurred (there were not many in these particular patents), the amount of land falling into each slope category was ascertained geometrically.

an orderly fashion. Provincial governors largely ignored these orders, granting lands to favorites who had no intention of settling, or to powerful landlords who could attract only a few tenants. The result was a patchwork of land grants of various shapes and sizes that left the isolated German settlements surrounded by thousands of acres technically owned but most often unoccupied. Such a haphazard frontier was difficult to defend, but it did have certain advantages. The Palatines were relatively undisturbed for a long time.[20]

Certainly it was not the intention of the colonial authorities to give the German immigrants the advantages of possessing some of the best lands in the Mohawk Valley. The Stone Arabia, Waganaer, and Wendecker patents were set well away from the river, in an era when water transportation was considered essential to economic success. With the exception of Burnetsfield, the government did not distribute the on-river grants directly to the Palatines, but gave them to various colonial grandees, who sold them to the Germans at a profit. Yet, as the statistics on land forms demonstrate, the Palatines in fact received some very good agricultural properties.[21]

Not only were the land forms within the patents conducive to agriculture; the soil was unsurpassingly favorable as well. In 1738, New York's surveyor general, Cadwallader Colden, informed the Board of Trade in London that "the soil of the Mohawks Country is in general much richer & stronger than that of the Southern parts of the Province & exceeds any soil that I ever saw in any part of America . . . . This soil, I am pursuaded will produce any thing, that can be produced in a Climate where the Winters are very cold."[22] Within a few

20. The total number of patents and their locations were derived from Claude Joseph Sauthier, "A Chorographical Map of the Province of New York" (London: William Fadden, 1779). Years in which the patents were granted, as well as their areas, were found in Original Letters Patent. Homes, occupations, and related information concerning the patentees was assembled from an entire bibliography of primary and secondary sources in the history of colonial New York. For a general discussion of Provincial New York land policy, see Patricia U. Bonomi, *A Factious People: Politics and Society in Colonial New York* (New York: Columbia University Press, 1971); and Ruth L. Higgins, *Expansion in New York* (Columbus: Ohio State University Press, 1931).

21. David Maldwyn Ellis, *Landlords and Farmers in the Hudson-Mohawk Region, 1790-1850* (New York: Octagon Books, 1967), 50-51.

22. Cadwallader Colden to the Board of Trade, 1738, in Edmund B. O'Callaghan,

years of their initial settlement in the Mohawk region, the Palatine Germans were putting this soil to profitable use.

Contemporary accounts of the Palatines from the time of their entry into New York through their years in the Schoharie Valley indicate that the people were desperately poor. They had carried very little with them from Germany, and English promises of cash allotments to each individual had not been fulfilled. As late as 1730, an Anglican minister officiating among the Palatines remaining in Schoharie advised his superiors that "the people are very poor and have not been able to contribute quite 30 pounds a year of that country money for his support . . . ."[23] Yet, within a few years of their establishment in the Mohawk region, the Palatines provide ample evidence of successful participation in New York's cash economy.

There is evidence that the Palatines pursued wheat production in the Schoharie Valley before moving on to the Mohawk, a practice they continued in the new location. Within twenty-five years of their initial settlements in the region, several observers had noted their success. Swedish naturalist Peter Kalm, writing in 1749, reported the Germans were reaping twenty bushels of wheat for every bushel sown (about four times the average produced in Europe). "The Germans . . . sow great quantities of wheat which is brought to Albany," he stated, "and from whence they send many yachts laden with flour to New York. The wheat flour from Albany is reckoned the best in all North America . . . ." Eight years later the acerbic but reliable William Smith related in his *History of the Late Province of New York* that "Our settlements on the north side extend to Burnet's field, a flat inhabited by Germans, which produces wheat and peas in surprising plenty." Richard Smith, a New Jersey official and land speculator who visited the Mohawk in 1769, observed that "The People of the German Flats bring their loads of Wheat in Sleighs down to Schenectady . . . ." Other estimates of wheat production among the Germans ranged from

ed., *Documentary History of the State of New York*, 4 vols. (Albany, 1849-1851), 4:113. (Hereafter referred to as O'Callaghan, *Documentary History.)*
    23. Reverend Mr. Ehlig to the Lord Bishop of London, March 19, 1731, *ERNY*, 4: 2535.

twenty to thirty bushels, compared to a general average of twelve bushels per acre found in most of the Mid-Atlantic region.[24]

Witnesses generally attributed the success of the German farmers to their enterprise. Sir William Johnson, Crown official, member of the Provincial Council, and largest single landowner in the region acknowledged that the Germans were "the most Industrious people" in the valley, although he generally found their behavior unorthodox. The Palatines seem to have employed agricultural methods somewhat at odds with those in use throughout the rest of the colony. They did rotate crops (which is essential to wheat production), using cultivation of peas to replenish the soil. Yet, they made little effective use of manures, instead piling the refuse on the frozen river in winter, allowing it to wash away with the spring floods. In addition, the Germans used horses rather than oxen for plowing, despite the greater expense.[25]

In the City of Albany, the Palatines employed the profits from their wheat sales to purchase a variety of necessities and a few luxuries as well. The account ledgers of Albany merchant Robert Sanders record transactions with several German farmers from both Stone Arabia and German Flats during the 1750s. Among the items they obtained in trade were kitchen utensils, farm tools, gunpowder, rolls of cloth, fur hats, and tea. Nor was the prodigious growth of wheat a temporary phenomenon. As late as 1802, the Reverend John Taylor noted during a visit to Stone Arabia that "the fields of wheat are numerous, and the crop in general is excellent." The boom seems to have lasted until roughly 1825, when a combination of invasion by grain moths and competition

24. Peter Kalm, *Travels into North America*, trans. John Reinhold Foster (Barre, Mass.: The Imprint Society, 1972), 325; Fernand Braudel, *The Structures of Everyday Life*, trans. Sian Reynolds (New York: Harper and Row, 1979), 120-124; William Smith, *The History of the Late Province of New York*, 2 vols. (New York: New York Historical Society, 1829), 1:265; Richard Smith, *A Tour of Four Great Rivers . . . in 1769*, ed. Francis W. Halsey (Port Washington, N.Y.: Ira J. Friedman, Inc., 1964), 27; Percy Wells Bidwell and John I. Falconer, *History of Agriculture in the Northern States, 1620-1860* (Washington: Carnegie Institution, 1925), 101.

25. Sir William Johnson to the Society for the Promotion of the Arts, February 27, 1765 *DHNY*, 3:348-50; Kalm, *Travels*, 325; *Transactions of the New York State Agricultural Society* (Albany: 1841-1870), 1841:136, 1851:516; Ellis, *Landlords and Farmers*, 93-97.

from western farmers forced the Mohawk residents to shift to dairy products.[26]

The wheat was a source of enormous profit for the Palatine farmers in the valley during the eighteenth century. Perhaps one of the finest indications of the degree of wealth quickly obtained among the German population can be derived from the report of a disaster. In November of 1757, the settlement at German Flats fell victim to one of the early attacks of the French and Indian War. The Germans, who had not suffered in previous colonial wars, were caught unprepared. As many as forty were killed, and another 150 captured and taken to Canada. The commander of the French and Indian raiders considerably inflated the amount of booty captured or destroyed in the assault, but even reduced by half or two-thirds, the numbers remain impressive. The list included vast quantities of grain, 3,000 horned cattle, 3,000 sheep, 1,500 horses, and numerous hogs. The village was patently wealthy and agriculturally successful. Even New York's lieutenant governor, James DeLancey, reported to the Board of Trade that "the loss is estimated at twenty thousand pounds this money, it is as fertile a piece of ground as any perhaps in the world the settlers were generally rich, and had good buildings on their lands . . . ."[27]

With the exception of the attack at German Flats in 1757, the Palatine settlers suffered few of the vicissitudes that so often characterized life in colonial America. By the 1750s, the vast majority of the group could be classified as yeoman farmers or husbandmen, members of the middling portions of society.[28]

By all accounts, the Palatine population in the Mohawk rose steadily between 1723 and 1775. The valley throughout most of the colonial period was included in the vastness of New York's Albany County, so no accurate census tallies exist. The following estimates are derived from the comments of contemporary observers, the militia muster rolls of the

26. Robert Sanders Ledgers, various years 1750-1763, New-York Historical Society; John Taylor, "Journal of the Rev. John Taylor On a Mission Through the Mohawk and Black River County in the Year 1802," O'Callaghan, *Documentary History*, 3:686; Bidwell and Falconer, *History of Agriculture*, 326-27.

27. O'Callaghan, *Documentary History*, 1:333-34; Benton, *History of Herkimer County*, 51-53.

28. Laslett, *World We Have Lost*, 45-46.

period, and the useful but incomplete church records of the various Palatine churches. The results (as shown in Table 2) are generally a bit lower than those of various nineteenth and twentieth century antiquarians, but reflect more probable demographic behavior.

Even given these relatively conservative population estimates, it is obvious that the numbers of people would have placed pressure on the original Palatine land holdings by the 1750s. The six original patents contained a total of 33,735 acres conducive to crop agriculture. Dividing this figure by the calculated number of households in 1755 provides an average of 93.7 acres per family—a little less than the size of the average farm at German Flats. Unless the Palatines obtained more land to support their growing population, the per capita wealth of the community would necessarily have declined. Either the Palatines would have had to reduce farm size, or many of their children would have to turn to other, probably more menial, occupations.[29]

29. The figure of 93.7 acres per family is based on my population estimates. If Halsey's or Greene's were to be employed, the resultant acreage would be even less.

TABLE 2

PALATINE GERMAN POPULATION IN THE MOHAWK VALLEY

Year	Number of Households	Total Population
1725	110	400
1755	360	2,100
1775	680	4,000
1790	950	5,800

Note: The population estimate for 1725 is based on the numbers of persons who claimed land in the original patents, and for whom there exists independent evidence of *actual occupation*. At German Flats, every person was granted a share; at Stone Arabia, every family. Records for the remaining original patents vary, necessitating an estimate rather than an exact number. (Source: Land Papers and Original Letters Patent.) Estimates for 1755 and 1775 are derived from militia muster rolls of those years (as listed in MacWethy, *Book of Names*), complemented where possible by the birth and marriage records of the Lutheran and Dutch Reformed Churches of Stone Arabia, and the Dutch Reformed Church of German Flats (typed copies on file in the Montgomery County Archives, Fonda, New York). Population aggregates are considerably lower than those of Nelson Greene, *History of the Mohawk Valley*, or Francis W. Halsey, *Tour of the Four Great Rivers*, introduction.

The Germans had obtained their original grants largely through the largess of the English and Provincial governments. There could be little hope of further gifts. Acquiring further tracts of land through the Provincial patenting process was expensive. At each stage, the patentees paid fees to the officials involved, including the surveyor-general, the clerk of the council, and the provincial governor. For a patent of two thousand acres, the total cost of fees alone amounted to thirty pounds or more, exclusive of the cost of purchasing rights to the land from the Indians.[30]

TABLE 3

Quality Of Palatine Lands, in Acres, 1752-1765

Patent	Year	Suited to planting	Suited to grazing	Unsuited to farming	Total acreage
Herkimer	1752	1,929	116	279	2,324
Gunterman	1753	905	0	0	905
Klock	1754	6,240	6,080	3,680	16,000
Staley	1755	26,860	1,360	5,780	34,000
Timmerman	1755	2,520	900	180	3,600
Franck	1765	2,550	1,500	950	5,000
Total		41,404	9,956	10,869	61,829

Note: The source is Original Letters Patent, with lists of landholders in original grants compared with names of patentees in newer holdings.

Between 1752 and 1756, descendants of the original Palatine settlers obtained patents for an additional 61,829 acres (see Table 3). In addition, fragmentary evidence from the Albany County Deed Books of the period shows that several Germans were actively purchasing land in some neighboring tracts, such as Glen's Purchase and the Canajoharie Patent, which were owned by speculators. The degree of land acquisition activity alone demonstrates the wealth of German population, and their determination to maintain that wealth and economic independence in future generations. As late as 1825 —the first year for which there are any meaningful census

30. *NYCD*, 5:952-53; New York, *The Colonial Laws of New York from the Year 1664 to the Revolution*, 5 vols. (Albany: James B. Lyon, 1894), 1:638-53.

statistics—over four-fifths of the adult males in the predominantly German townships of the valley operated individual farms.[31]

The purchasers in the Klock Patent included six families from Stone Arabia, four from German Flats, and one each from the Harison and Wendecker tracts. In Staley's Patent, allotments were claimed by eleven families from German Flats, and two from the Harison Patent. One or two Palatine families residing in the various original holdings in the valley took up each of the smaller patents. In sum, virtually all of the Palatine families living in the Mohawk during the 1750s participated in the effort to secure additional property. By obtaining these six additional grants, the Germans were guaranteed possession of enough land to last for at least another generation, even though these newer holdings were not as conducive to agricultural pursuits as the original grants. A full 17.5 percent of the new holdings were too steep for any form of agricultural activity.[32]

Historians of America's colonial period will tend to the view that the aggressive nature of Palatine land acquisition is one evidence of a population imbued with the more "modern" values associated with market competition. There is considerable corroborative evidence to support such an interpretation. In the crucial realms of religious behavior and deference toward social betters, the Palatines acted in manners seemingly at odds with Old World corporate traditions.[33]

German behavior in religious matters was often rancorous. Contemporary observers cite several instances of discord, jealousy, and disaffection, while evidence of spiritual piety is decidedly lacking. The German Reformed Churches in the valley seem to have been especially troubled. In 1736, the Classis of Amsterdam wrote to the Minister of the German

31. Albany County, *Index to Deed Books, 1664-1775* (Fonda, NY: Montgomery County Archives); New York State, *Census for the Year 1825: Montgomery County* (Albany: 1827).

32. Original Letters Patent. Lists of landholders in the original Palatine grants were compared with the names of the patentees in the newer holdings.

33. See, for example, James T. Lemon's introduction to *The Best Poor Man's Country: A Geographical Study of Southeastern Pennsylvania* (Baltimore: Johns Hopkins Press, 1972), a study which also deals in large measure with a German population. The controversy between Lemon and James Henretta is, of course, well known. This paper attempts to address some of the issues they have raised.

Flats Church that "It grieves [us] to the heart, to learn from your writing and other reports that have come in, that it goes so badly with the affairs of the church in Albany (county) and vicinity. Concerning this field, we had high expectations, but instead of seeing it established and in a generally prosperous condition, it appears to have run to waste. It is brought into utmost confusion by internal divisions and strivings for the mastery."[34]

The Classis was also concerned by reports from Stone Arabia. The church there had suffered enormous difficulties in obtaining any minister at all. In July of 1751, thirty-two members of the church signed a statement expressing their satisfaction with the pastor they had recently hired. Such a statement was necessary because, as matters turned out, the man was neither properly trained nor qualified to be a minister at all. For the next fourteen months, letters crossed the Atlantic between church authorities in Holland and the Coetus in New York City. Their ultimate decision was to dismiss the unqualified pastor, despite the continued support of his congregation at Stone Arabia.[35]

Matters grew worse. The Coetus found another candidate for the position, one in whom they had confidence despite his lack of completed church training. The Classis disallowed this second minister as well. The result was anarchy. By 1757, the Coetus advised authorities in Amsterdam that Stone Arabia had dropped "the German Church Order altogether. She has now become a prey to confusion and to German tramps."[36]

The fault did not lie entirely with the church authorities in New York or Amsterdam. The first of the dismissed pastors, John Aemilius Wernig, wrote to a friend in September, 1752, describing the unfortunate aspects of his situation. After depicting the divisions and disruptions among his flock, he lamented the abuse he himself received from opponents within the congregation. There was, he stated, "a continual dislike and envy." The reason, to his mind, was not difficult to discover:

34. Classis of Amsterdam to Rev. George M. Weiss, *ERNY*, 4:2676.
35. *ERNY*, 5:3162, 3201, 3254-55, 3264-65, 3285-87, 3610-11, 3553, 3658-59, 3687.

> On the whole, this German people is one that cannot well bear the
> noble English freedom. They are like fat horses and oxen, which
> have gone to rich pasture for a long time and then refuse to take the
> bit or bear the yoke. It takes strong legs to bear propserity. The liber-
> ty, peace, wealth, and abundance which they enjoy cause them to be
> uncivil, wanton, proud, and violent.[37]

Wernig was undoubtedly overstating the case, but his observations on the effects of abundance ring true. The position of
the Germans, their resources, and most importantly, the
assurance that the bounty of the new land would allow none
of them to starve, may well have fostered a greater degree of
independence in their behavior than would generally have
been the case in Germany, in England, or in other parts of
America.[38]

The German Reformed was not the only church to experience difficulties in the Mohawk Valley. In 1768, the
Lutheran Church at Stone Arabia discovered that the deed to
their half of the glebe lot was missing. The German Reformed
members of the community then questioned the Lutherans'
right to possess a church on the site, a maneuver reminiscent
of the persecutions the Calvinists had visited upon the
Lutherans in Europe. The congregation was forced to appeal
to New York Council member Sir William Johnson, who was
able to provide them a new deed, guaranteeing their right to
half the glebe.[39]

The Lutherans apparently explored several avenues in their
search for religious satisfaction. Although Lutheran pastors
working in the Mohawk Valley had trained in Europe, no
continental supervision of their American activities existed.
During the 1750s, the pastors of all three Lutheran parishes in
the valley associated with the Pennsylvania synod of the
Reverend Heinrich M. Muhlenberg, a Pietist and supporter
of the Anglican Society for the Propagation of the Gospel in
Foreign Parts. In 1771, William Johnson wrote to the
Reverend Charles Inglis of the SPG to advise him of the
Lutherans' interest in converting. "I should tell you," he

36. Coetus to the Classis of Amsterdam, *ERNY*, 5:3708.
37. Rev. John Aemilius Wernig to his Patron, *ERNY*, 5:3285.
38. Laslett, *World We Have Lost*, 113-121.
39. Rev. Andrew Luther Dillenbeck, *Lutheran Trinity Church of Stone Arabia*
(St. Johnsville, NY: Enterprise and News, 1931). 11-14. This booklet is an anniver-
sary collection of original church documents by the then-current pastor. See also
Bittinger, *Germans in Colonial Times*.

wrote, "that the German Lutheran Minister at Stoneraby . . . has Expressed a desire to me of taking orders in our Church, & what is more extraordinary his Whole Congregation desire to become members of the same . . . ." The rumored conversion never took place, but it does suggest that the Lutheran devotees among the Palatines suffered from instability in their church as well. Religious disquiet was prevalent in the valley.[40]

While a confused religious situation was in part a tradition inherited from Europe, the extreme instability of such institutions among the Palatines in the Mohawk Valley is indicative of a subtle yet important shift in values. In Europe, the Pietist movement grew up to fill a void created by the insensitive orthodoxies of Lutheran and Reformed orthodoxies. The movement was an attempt to restore meaningful religious experience to the common people. In the Mohawk, although evidence of Pietist leanings was abundant, attempted control of church facilities in the face of European authorities resulted in virtual anarchy. The Palatines, aggressive middle class farmers, themselves provided the fuel for many of the controversies, for reasons ascribed to prosperity and pride. In a welter of conflicting interests, the influence of religion in the lives of the people diminished.

Evidence concerning the nature of deferential practices in the Mohawk is far more obscure, but there are several described incidents which, when taken together, seem to indicate a decline in the traditional manners. There appears to have been some rather obscure antagonisms between members of the Palatine population and the leading family in the valley, the Johnsons.

William Johnson had emigrated from Ireland in 1738 to manage his uncle's properties in the Mohawk, and over the next thirty-five years had forged an unassailable social position for himself and his relations. In 1746, he became sole Indian agent for the Province of New York, after which he

40. Kreider, "Lutheranism in Colonial New York," 144; Hermann Wellenreuther, "Image and Counterimage, Tradition and Expectation: The German Immigrants in English Colonial Society in Pennsylvania, 1700-1765," *America and the Germans: An Assessment of a Three Hundred-Year History* ed. Frank Trommler and Joseph McVeigh (Philadelphia: University of Pennsylvania Press, 1985), 85-105, esp. 90-93; Johnson to Inglis, O'Callaghan, *Documentary History*, 4:276-78.

became a leading military officer, land proprietor, and member of the governor's council. His political influence was tremendous, reaching as far as Albany, where he was able to successfully manage elections to the Assembly. Johnson was granted a baronetcy by the Crown in 1755. The family prestige in the valley was shared by a nephew and a son, the latter of whom became a baronet in 1765. Together, the Johnsons controlled over 80,000 acres in the Mohawk. Much of this land was unoccupied, although the family rented a significant portion to Ulster Irish and Scottish tenants. Much of the animosity which eventually surfaced between the Palatines and the Johnson family may be traced to the cultural antipathy between the German freeholders and the Ulster-Irish tenants.[41]

By traditional custom and right, the Johnson family should have expected something approaching absolute control of affairs in the Mohawk Valley. Such a condition did not exist. The Palatines, in the years between 1750 and 1775, manifested their antipathy to the Johnsons in a number of subtle ways. Some of these were in the nature of ongoing controversies. Leading Palatine merchants such as Jacob Klock and Jellis Fonda vented strong opposition to Sir William's Indian trade policies, which were designed to prevent fraud, but which also served to guarantee the baronet's absolute control. There may have been resentment to Johnson's control of Mohawk land transactions as well. When Staley's Patent was divided among patentees in 1765, William Johnson was granted a share, although he had paid none of the costs of ownership. The share was a payment for his influence in obtaining the patent.[42]

Minor incidents punctuated the relationship between the Johnsons and the Palatine residents. In 1757, the Palatines at German Flats ignored William Johnson's warning of an impending attack by the French, despite his position as Colonel of the District Militia. The result was a disaster.[43]

41. James T. Flexner, *Mohawk Baronet: Sir William Johnson of New York* (New York: Harper and Brothers, 1959).

42. Peter Marshall, "Sir William Johnson and the Treaty of Fort Stanwix, 1768," *Journal of American Studies* 1 (1967): 149-79; "Survey of the Franck and Staley Patents, 1765," New York State Archives, Albany.

Six years later, Peter Hasenclever, a German iron manu-facturer, wrote to Johnson to thank him for his rescue from the hands of an unhelpful and somewhat malicious Palatine guide. Hasenclever had sought to locate a colony of new Ger-man immigrants in the valley to manufacture potash, a proj-ect Johnson encouraged. Apparently the local Palatines were unsympathetic, and led poor Hasenclever a merry chase until Johnson himself intervened and obtained a tract for the proj-ect.[44]

Such incidents would seem trivial, save that they portended subsequent turmoil of a more serious nature. Yet, in the early 1770s, the Johnsons possessed seemingly absolute control over local politics. The Province established Tryon County out of Albany County at the behest of Sir William in 1772, an event which brought about a brief period of political tran-quility. Johnson family tenants won most of the new county offices, and elections were held without opposition candi-dates.[45]

The tranquility ended in August, 1774, when the Palatine District Committee of Safety organized. The committee was one of the first in the Province of New York, and its composi-tion was overwhelmingly German. Although the members held their initial meetings in secret, the very existence of such a committee threatened the hegemony of the younger John-sons (Sir William died in June, 1774). The committee passed a series of resolves condemning the Intolerable Acts, and con-tinued to meet sporadically over the next year. By June, 1775, all of Tryon County had organized under a Committee of Safety, over the opposition of the Johnsons and their ten-ants. One of the first actions of the full committee was to ad-dress a letter to Guy Johnson, now head of Indian Affairs, requesting him to use his influence among the Iroquois to maintain the peace. The situation was a truly volatile one, as the Indians, thoroughly loyal to the Johnson family, posed a

43. George Croghan, "A Summary Narrative, November 1757," O'Callaghan, *Documentary History*, 1:336-37.
44. Peter Hasenclever to William Johnson, May, 1757, *The Papers of Sir William Johnson*, 14 vols., ed. James Sullivan and Alexander C. Flick (Albany: New York State Division of Archives and History, 1921-1965), 5: 704-705.
45. John C. Guzzardo, "Democracy Along the Mohawk: An Election Return, 1773," *New York History* 57 (January, 1976): 30-52.

very real threat to any independent activity on the part of the committee. The Johnson tenants remained unaffected by the imperial crisis as well, meaning the Johnsons had a combined army of over a thousand in their support. The committee was undaunted, observing that "We cannot think that, as you and your family are possessing very large estates in this country, you are unfavorable to American freedom; although you may differ from us in the mode of obtaining a redress of grievances."[46]

The depth of Palatine resentment of the Johnson hegemony in their valley is revealed in a letter written to the Albany Committee of Safety in May, 1775. The members of the Palatine committee emphasize their efforts in the vanguard of opposition to England and the defense of liberty, and detail their actions in securing county support for the Association. They placed their difficulties in the latter regard at the feet of the Johnsons. "This Country," they observed, "Has for a series of Years been Ruled by one family, the different Branches of which are still strenious in dissuading people from coming into Congressional measures . . . . "[47]

Matters in fact had already reached the stage of violence. Sir John Johnson had broken up a mass meeting in support of the Association the previous week, confronting the gathering with 150 of his armed tenants. By July, the tide had turned. The Tryon County sheriff, a Johnson loyalist, arrested one of the county's more vociferous supporters of the Association, John Fonda, after a confrontation in the latter's wheat field. A mob quickly gathered at the Johnson-owned county jail and secured Fonda's release. The sheriff fled to the protection of the fortified Johnson Hall, but was subsequently ousted from office and forced to flee. A truce was then negotiated between the Tryon County committee and the Johnson family, but hostilities were quickly renewed. By January, 1776, the Johnsons, their tenants and retainers, and several Indians had removed to Canada, some in considerable

46. Maryly B. Penrose, *The Mohawk Valley in the Revolution* (Franklin Park, N.J.: Liberty Bell Associates, 1978), 1-7; Letter to the Johnsons, written by the Seventh Meeting of the Tryon County Committee of Safety, June 2, 1775, quoted in Simms, *Frontiersmen of New York*, 499.

47. Palatine Committee of Safety to Albany Committee of Safety, May 19th, 1775. Penrose, *The Mohawk Valley*, 4.

hardship. For the next seven years, civil war ensued, as the Johnsons led raid after raid into the valley.[48]

While most of New York dithered over the question of independence, the Palatines of the Mohawk Valley had declared theirs. All of the county's royal officials were deposed, most of those loyal to the Crown had been forced out. The committee of safety possessed sole control of county government long before the State of New York formulated an independent constitution.

The behavior of the Palatines in these several respects tends to support the interpretation that the Mohawk settlers were prototypes of the competitive individualist society that developed within the American nation following the Revolution. Combining the evidence of their aggressive market behavior with regard to wheat sales and land purchases, their lack of proper piety in religious matters, and their indifferent record of deference toward the Johnson family, the influences that shaped autonomous, individualist behavior seem easy to trace. Given the experience of the Palatines during the preceding half-century, their position at the forefront of the independence movement is readily comprehended. Yet, to portray the Germans of the Mohawk in this light is to tell only half the story. There exists another body of evidence to indicate that these were genuinely people of the Old World culture.

Many of the evidences for the retention of Old World corporate characteristics revolve around the nature of the Palatine household and their agricultural practices. Outside observers were responsible for the reports of these characteristics, observers who compared the Germans with their knowledge of other American cultural groups. Most of these reporters were post-Revolutionary, and express shock that the Palatines were so backward and out-of-step with American behavioral norms. They were, by and large, unfriendly sources.

The Reverend Samuel Kirkland, a missionary influential with the Oneida Indians, recorded his observations of a Pala-

48. Simms, *Frontiersmen of New York*, 528-29; Edward Countryman, *A People in Revolution: The American Revolution and Political Society in New York, 1760-1790* (Baltimore: Johns Hopkins University Press, 1981), 146-47, 150; Simms, *Frontiersmen of New York*, 512-96.

tine Christmas in 1769. "They allow no work or servile labour on ye day and ye follow'g—their servants are free," he stated, "but drink'g fight'g and frolic'g are not only allowed, but seem to be essential to ye joy of ye day." This is the only extant indication that the Germans commonly kept servants, but several others noted the custom of heavy drinking, including the Reverends Timothy Dwight, President of Yale University, and John Taylor. Taylor perceived "as yet, but one great defect in the morals of the people—they are too much addicted to drink."[49]

Taylor also noted what he labelled "singular customs" with regard to German burials. "When a person dies," he said, "nothing will influence ye connections, nor any other person, unless essentially necessary, to touch the body. When the funeral is appointed, none attend but such as are invited." Such practices may have been unusual in late eighteenth-century America, but they were not at all uncommon in seventeenth- and early eighteenth-century Germany, where memories of the danger of epidemic and plague were very recent and very real. The Palatines had emigrated in part to escape an epidemic of "Hot Fever," which accompanied Louis XIV's invasion of 1708-09.[50]

Timothy Dwight, who travelled through the Mohawk region in 1799, wrote of several German circumstances he considered strange. One such was the German houses he saw, "ordinary houses built in the German manner, with few windows, many doors, dark sheds over the principal doors, *leantos* behind, and awkward additions at the ends. They are of one story, and in a few instances of a story and a half, and frequently look like a collection of kitchens." They were, in short, houses of the Old World. The style was in sharp contrast to the barns prevalent in the region, which were very im-

49. "Reverend S. Kirkland's Journal, 1769," O'Callaghan, *Documentary History*, 4: 639; Rev. Timothy Dwight, *Travels in New England and New York*, ed. Barbara Miller Solomon, 4 vols. (Cambridge, Mass.: Belknap Press, 1969), 3:118-19; Taylor, "Missionary Tour," O'Callaghan, *Documentary History*, 3:686. Dwight added gambling and horse racing to his list of immoral habits practiced among the Palatines. As all of the witnesses to the vice of alcohol were ministers, it is difficult to determine if this was a genuine problem, or even a culture-specific trait.

50. Taylor, "Missionary Tour," O'Callaghan, *Documentary History*, 3:685; Braudel, Structures of Everyday Life, 81-88; William McNeil, *Plagues and Peoples* (New York: Vantage Press, 1976); Wallace, *Conrad Weiser*, 5.

posing and generally covered an area fifty feet by thirty. The size and design of a German's barn was seen as an indicator of social status, unlike the New Englanders who entered the region after 1783. The newcomers emphasized house construction.[51]

Even more novel to Dwight was the sight of German women working in the fields. "Women in New England are employed only in and about the house," he advised, "and in the proper business of the sex. I do not know that I was ever more struck with the strangeness of any sight than with the business and appearance of these German females." Michael Guillaume Jean de Crevecoueur, writing some thirty years earlier, noted the same custom, though he was not so surprised. To the French diarist, the women were assuming an active and legitimate interest in an essentially family enterprise. "German women," he stated, "vie with their husbands and often share with them the most severe toils of the field . . . . "[52]

In addition to this collection of characteristics, so out of step with American cultural norms and highly reminiscent of European traits, there were the previously mentioned German agricultural practices. These included a single-minded devotion to production of wheat (despite William Johnson's dire prediction that the crop would soon be "a drug" on the market), a neglect of even simple methods of prolonging field productivity, and a devotion to horses. Taken together, such characteristics indicate a culture transplanted to America in which the customs of the Old World withered very slowly, if at all.[53]

To successfully comprehend the nature of Palatine society in the Mohawk River Valley, historians must abandon the dichotomy between Old and New World social organizations; forsake the notion that individualist traits necessarily denote a breakdown of corporatism. The Palatines were in fact an *adaptive* society, attempting to adjust their manner of living

51. Dwight, *Travels*, 122; Braudel, *Structures of Everyday Life*, 274-75.
52. Dwight, *Travels*, 142; J. Hector St. John de Crevecoeur, *Letters From an American Farmer* (New York: New American Library, 1963), 79.
53. Sir William Johnson to the Society for the Promotion of the Arts, February 27, 1765, O'Callaghan, *Documentary History*, 3:348.

to new and vastly different circumstances while retaining as much as possible of their familiar traditional patterns. Adaptation is essentially a cautious process, in which the adaptive group alters only enough of their behavior to conform to the needs of survival in the differing environment.

Adaptation is a word much used by historians, to a degree in fact that it is in danger of losing any real meaning. Often, adaptation is employed as a mere synonym for "transitional." In this study, I am employing the concept in a narrow sense to mean the process by which a species alters only those characteristics necessary to meet the challenge of a changed physical and social environment. The concept derives more closely from evolutionary biology than any of the social sciences, although I must emphasize that the altered characteristics are *cultural*, and not biological.[54]

As an immigrant group, the Palatines underwent considerable cultural turmoil between 1709—the year they left Germany—and 1723. Uprooted, herded into refugee camps in both England and America, shunted from one economic experiment to another, and finally cast adrift, these Germans lived for a considerable period in an unkind and confusing world. To survive, they retained as much as they could of the familiar ways of the Old World, a life well-ordered and habitual. Ultimately, they found themselves settled on the Mohawk, where, without interference, they were able to resurrect their former customs. The Palatines then constructed houses and barns such as they had known in Germany; they employed traditional agricultural methods. Women took their accustomed places beside the men in the fields. They constructed German Reformed and Lutheran churches, side by side. The immigrants of 1725, who had experienced the fewest opportunities to observe or adopt American practices, established nucleated farming villages. And even in death, in a new and healthful country, the Palatines guarded against the scourge of Europe: the plague.

But New York was not the Rhineland. Their abilities to retain the customs of the Palatinate were challenged by essen-

54. See Stephen Jay Gould, *Ever Since Darwin: Reflections in Natural History* (New York: W. W. Norton and Company, 1977), esp. 91-96.

tial differences in geography and circumstance. Land was plentiful in America, and people were not. Virtually the entire population now belonged to the middling echelons of society, possessed of freeholds that produced immeasurably greater yields than the European norm. The combination of unaccustomed wealth and the availability of open land not only allowed the original immigrants to live in comparative plenty, it also provided them the means to pass on this unaccustomed standard of living to their children and grandchildren. More than anything else, the wealth of the New World offered opportunity, and the Palatines took advantage. They adapted. They did not change, become unrecognizable to their German counterparts still in Europe, they simply altered their approach to life enough to profit from the differing circumstances.

The adaptation did not occur without cost. To become aggressive in the marketplace, the Palatines suffered the price of societal contentiousness, which became most visible in their religious practices and their relations with social superiors. Both the Lutheran and the German Reformed churches in the Mohawk were wrought with internal divisions, while German interactions with the Johnson family were often antagonistic. The effects can be viewed in either a negative or a positive light. While the Palatines lost some of the security of the old customs, their new independence of attitude did make it possible for them to be among the initial leaders of the Revolution, which began in New York in 1774.

The significance of the Palatine experience in the Mohawk lies in the fact that the adaptive process is so visible. Unlike many immigrant groups, the Palatines were not located in close proximity to other culture groups, either immigrant or long-term Americans. The alterations that occurred in their social make-up took place at their own pace, and were not dictated by the presence of neighbors. The Germans were purposely isolated, placed forty miles to the west of the nearest colonial settlements. They remained unaffected by the presence of other settlers for a very long time. Prior to the Revolution, virtually their only competitors for space and activity were the Johnsons and their tenants, who tended to remain separate from the German communities. William Johnson's overweaning control of the Indian trade and relations with the Provincial government may have been nettlesome, but the evidence clearly indicates the Palatines maintained a forceful independence with regard to their internal affairs. Free from interference, they were able to adapt to the valley's clear opportunities for economic gain without undermining their accustomed ways of living.

The Palatines of the Mohawk enjoyed a circumstance which many immigrant groups did not. Most often, immigrant groups were thrown into proximity with others, meaning that their own adaptive processes were neither so obvious nor so clear cut. Their response to the American environment was muted and conditioned by the influence of close neighbors. Still, certain parallels may be seen among isolated cultural groups in other colonies, including perhaps the Scots Highlanders in Georgia, the Ulster Irish in North Carolina, or the Swiss Mennonites in Pennsylvania.[55]

The importance of the Palatines to the modern historian is their role as a model to assess the alterations that took place in American society during the eighteenth century. To say that the Palatines, like all of American society, were in transition is meaningless, for all societies are "in transition." Historians must view them as adaptive, altering their social mannerisms enough to meet peculiar American circumstances. Once the modifications began, continuation was the logical tendency.

55. For examples of potential leads, see Fussell M. Chalker, "Highland Scots in the Georgia Lowlands," *Georgia Historical Quarterly* 60 (1976); Grady McWhiney and Forrest McDonald, "Celtic Origins of Southern Herding Practices," *Journal of Southern History* 51 (May, 1985); John L. Ruth, "A Christian Settlement 'In Antiquam Silvam': The Emigration from Krefeld to Pennsylvania in 1683 and the Mennonite Community of Germantown," *Mennonite Quarterly Review* 62 (October, 1983).

New York's Long Black Line: A Note on the Growing Slave Population, 1676-1790

By THOMAS J. DAVIS

B lack people go back a long way in New York history. They go back, in fact, to the beginning to European settlement of the land here. For even before the place was called New York, blacks slaved on its lands. Starting on Manhattan Island at the Dutch trading post called New Amsterdam, they arrived first in 1626 as a "parcel" of eleven males.[1] Their number made them about one-tenth of the population here then—excluding Indians. Three black women arrived in 1628 and were joined shortly by an unspecified number of other Africans described as "Angola slaves, thievish, lazy, useless trash."[2] More arrived intermittently to keep their number larger than that in any other community north of Maryland. By 1790 when the new national government took its first census, New York's slave population numbered 21,329 and ranked fifth in size among the United States.[3]

What follows here proposes simply to relate the growth, composition and distribution of the slave population in New York from its beginnings to the federal census of 1790. To suggest the reasons, consequences and implications of the demographic patterns that

Reprinted from *Afro-Americans in New York Life and History* 2 (January 1978), 41-59.

Thomas J. Davis is Associate Professor of History at Howard University.

1. Bernard Fernow, ed., *Records of New Amsterdam, 1653-1674* (7 vols.; New York, 1897), 1:27; Arthur Peterson and George Edwards, *New York as an Eighteenth Century Municipality* (1917: reissue, Port Washington, New York, 1967), 4. Arrival of the first enslaved blacks often was placed during 1625 or 1626 on the basis of Director-General William Kief's notation in 1644 that the slaves had then served the West Indian Company for "18 to 19 years"; see E. B. O'Callaghan, ed., *Laws and Ordinances of New Netherland, 1638-1674* (Albany, 1868), 36. A36. Also see E. B. O'Callaghan, ed., *Voyages of the Slavers "St. John" and "Arms of Amsterdam"* (Albany, 1867), 13, 202.

2. Edwin Vernon Morgan, "Slavery in New York with Special Reference to New York City," in *Half Moon Series: Papers on Historic New York,* ed., Maud Wilder Goodwin, et al., 2nd ser., 2 (1898), 3.

3. U. S. Bureau of the Census, *Negro Population 1790-1915* (Washington, D.C., 1918), 57.

follow could form an extensive history, and that is clearly beyond the scope here. This treatment aims only to introduce the data and their development. It notes some interrelations. Also, it illustrates some directly observable features that characterized the population. The intention is, however, only to contribute an accessible common and clear base for future discussions that interpret the data in their relations to aspects of their setting in New York's history.

That setting started sparsely during the years when the Dutch were masters here. For although they were great slave traders, the Dutch did not immediately bring in large numbers of blacks. Even when the English and others neighboring New Netherland repeatedly petitioned to be supplied with slaves, and when patroonships such as Rensselaerwyck requested "any suitable black available," the Dutch West India Company was slow to ship in slaves.[4] Part of their reason was the better prices that they got by selling their black cargoes elsewhere.

Nevertheless, in time the company listened to Peter Stuyvesant, their colony's director-general, who recommended that it import blacks "to promote and advance the population and agriculture."[5] But the company still delivered only one large black cargo to New Netherland. It contained about three hundred Africans. And, perhaps signaling developments to come, they arrived in August 1664, only days before the Dutch surrendered to the English.[6]

Then Stuyvesant cursed the blacks' arrival. It was not that he did not want them, he had practically begged for them earlier. But they arrived at a bad time. At a time when he was marshaling his resources to fight attacking Englishmen nearly on his doorstep, he did not want to guard three hundred new slaves. Moreover, besides diverting his manpower, the black cargo also cut into his already thin food supply, for he reported that they seemed to be "half-starved."[7] Consequently, he credited them, with speeding his surrender. Historians seldom note that black contribution to the English take-over in 1664.

4. A. J. F. VanLaer, ed., "The Van Rensselaer Bowier Manuscripts," New York State Library, *History Bulletin,* No. 4 (1908), 642.

5. O'Callaghan, *Voyages of the Slavers,* 202. For background of the Company's position, see: Van Cleaf Bachman, *Peltries or Plantations: The Economic Policies of the Dutch West India Company in New Netherland, 1623-1639* (Baltimore, 1969), esp. chaps. 1 & 2.

6. E. B. O'Callaghan and Berthold Fernow, eds., *Documents Relative to the Colonial History of the State of New York* (15 vols.; Albany, 1856-1887), 2:504—referred to hereafter as *N.Y. Col. Docs.* Also see, David T. Valentine, "Slaves and the Slave Trade in New Netherland," in *Manual of the Corporation of the City of New York* (New York, 1863), 582, 594.

New York began, then, with a population that included between 700 and 850 slaves. There was no precise count, however, until a generation after 1664. Even then the records showed only sketchy figures. Yet, eleven fairly complete censuses conducted at irregular intervals between 1698 and 1790 provided valuable information about how the slave population grew in New York. The years of these censuses were 1698, 1703, 1723, 1731, 1737, 1746, 1749, 1756, 1771, 1786 and, of course, the first federal census of 1790.[8]

The counts were far from perfect, and debates about their reliability have long raged. For the purposes of this essay, the most salient imperfection was a failure before 1786 to distinguish between slaves and free Negroes. They simply used the terms "slaves" or "blacks" or "Negroes" as interchangeable. But that did not distort the magnitude of the slave population. For it was only in the 1780s that the number of free blacks grew appreciably. By 1790, for example, free Negroes formed only 1.4 percent of the state's total population, and 18.4 percent of its total black population. Its proportion before then was never so large. Thus, the lack of distinction in the censuses did not severely affect calculations.

Another problem with the censuses arose in the age used to distinguish between adults and adolescents, for the census of 1737 used age ten years and the others used sixteen years as the cut off. That point was not crucial, but it did affect calculations of the rate and degree of change among the age groupings. However, because only one census used a different age, only the calculations between it and the immediately preceding and succeeding censuses (1731 and 1746) were affected.

Three other deficiencies in the censuses seemed worthy to note. First, in 1698 the returns from Dutchess and Ulster counties were entered as a single total, so no separate figures from each county were available. Worse, in 1703 the returns from Dutchess were omitted altogether from the census list. Another omission occurred in 1746 when the population of Albany County was "not numbered

---

7. Ibid.

8. The sources for the census are as follows: 1698, Governor Bellomont to Board of Trade, in *Calendar of State Papers, Colonial Series: America and West Indies, 1697-1698,* 532, No. 978; 1703, Governor Robert Hunter to Board of Trade, in *Calendar of State Papers, 1711-12,* 301-302. No. 454, and in *Documentary History of New York,* E. B. O'Callaghan, ed., (Albany: Weed, Parsons & Co., 1850), 1:691; 1723, *Documentary History of New York,* 1:693; 1731, ibid., 1:694; 1737, ibid.; 1746, ibid., 1:695; 1756, ibid., 1:713; 1771, ibid., 1:697; 1786, in Franklin B. Hough, *Statistics of Population of the City and County of New York* (New York: New York Printing Company, 1866), viii. The figures from these sources are used with corrections found in Evarts B. Green and Virginia D. Harrington, *American Population before the Federal Census of 1790* (New York: Columbia University, 1932), 88-105.

because of the enemy." While the deficiencies made calculations rougher, they were not serious faults.

Two counts other than the censuses taken in the eleven years added to the data. One count taken in 1755 listed slaves aged fourteen years or more and it named their holders. That information helped to answer questions about the distribution of slaves in holdings, questions such as who held slaves, what was the range of slaveholding and what was the size of the average holding? Unfortunately, answers could be only partial, for the list lacked returns from three counties—Suffolk, New York and Albany. And the last two were the largest slaveholding counties then. The returns there, like those missing in 1746, were omitted probably as a security measure that reflected the fact that many white New Yorkers feared slaves and felt insecure about their large number. Especially during times of turmoil, whites suspected that slaves were really not loyal to them. In time of war they reasoned that attackers might well find slaves a ready fifth column. So, they tried to make the number of slaves in their midst, at vulnerable places, a secret. Thus, at the time of the French and Indian War (1754-1763), they did not publish the returns from Albany on the exposed northern frontier nor for New York County and Suffolk on the coastal southern and eastern frontier worried by threats of invasion. The feared attack never came, nor were the census returns ever published.[9] In 1776, however, Suffolk did count its residents, and that formed the second set of additional data here. Valuable for suggesting certain trends at the dawn of the Revolution, the data showed that in Suffolk, slaves were growing in number.[10]

In fact, the number of slaves in New York at large grew almost tenfold during the ninety-two years between 1698 and 1790. At the beginning of the period, 2,170 slaves lived in all New York, by the latter date the number was listed at 21,329. On the average, during these years 1 in every 8 (12.4 percent) New Yorkers was black. That declined for a time, however, and in 1790 it was at a low of about one in thirteen (6.3 percent). The percentage varied in each county; slaves in Kings County, for instance, formed 21.9 percent of its population in 1749—the largest ever for any county. The smallest percentage was 1.6 recorded in Albany during 1698 (See Table 1).

9. See New York *Post-Boy,* 18, 25, June and 2 July 1744; and, Howard R. Pecham, *The Colonial Wars 1689-1762* (Chicago: University of Chicago, 1964).

10. New York, *Census of Slaves 1755* (Albany: Weed, Parsons & Co., 1850); *New York Calendar of Historical Manuscripts Relating to the War of the Revolution in the Office of the Secretary of State* (Albany: Weed, Parsons & Co., 1868), 1:378-417.

Exactly how much the slave population increased by natural reproduction or by importation was not clear for the whole period. The collector reported in 1726 that since 1701 the port of New York had received 2,395 blacks. His year-by-year figures when matched with the census counts from 1703 and 1723 suggested that the imports then accounted for slightly more than six of every ten (63.2 percent) new blacks in New York during those two decades.

TABLE 1

Slave Population in New York, by Age, Sex and Percentage of
Total Population, 1698-1790

POPULATION

| YEAR | ADULT | | CHILD | | TOTAL | | % |
	M	F	M	F	SLAVE	COLONY	SLAVE
1698	--	--	--	--	2170	18067	12.0
1703	707	702	467	382	2258	20665	10.9
1723	2186	1810	1178	997	6171	40564	15.2
1731	2932	1853	1402	1044	7231	50286	14.4
1737	3551	2714	1397	1279	8941	60437	14.8
1746	2893	2034	1964	2216	9107	61589	14.8
1749	3317	2656	2379	2240	10592	73348	14.4
1756	4290	3198	3280	2780	13548	96790	14.0
1771	6220	5197	4416	4050	19883	175364	11.3
1781	9521	9368	--	--	18889	238897	7.9
1790	--	--	--	--	21329	340211	6.3

Source: cf. n 8. Note the absence of breakdown by age or sex in 1698 and 1790 data. Also, note the absence of breakdown by age in 1786 data.

The peak year of their importation was 1718 when 447 arrived from the West Indies and 70 directly from Africa. Over the whole quarter-century, 1,573 of the blacks came from the West Indies and 822 directly from Africa.[11]

Historians have generally used that count to suggest that New Yorkers demanded blacks from the West Indies as they wanted to buy slaves already seasoned.[12] They reasoned simply that blacks would know more of their role and work as slaves after time in the islands than they would know if brought immediately from freedom in their African homelands. But although a preference for blacks from the West Indies was clearly expressed by New York slave buyers such as John Watts, it was not an overwhelming demand as historians have previously suggested.[13] Historians failed to take full account of the trade factors that created a natural New York-West Indian connection nor of those factors that connected African and the West Indies more directly than Africa and New York in buying and selling slaves. Simply, prices for fresh Africans were higher in the islands than up north. So slave traders direct from Africa were more likely to deal first with the West Indies; then they visited the southern colonies, and if they had a surplus in their cargoes they might find their way to New York. A direct connection between Africa and New York, therefore, was minor in the slave trade. New Yorkers had more direct trade with the West Indies. As they supplied the islands with foodstuffs, they developed an easy exchange of their products for blacks that West Indian planters wanted to sell. Thus, New Yorkers bought slaves from the Caribbean more because of convenience than because of any absolute demand: it was the natural pattern of trade relations, then, that established the old and long black West Indian connection with New York.

Patterns in the slave population differed, of course, from county-to-county. Between 1698 and 1771, New York's censuses listed ten counties, and in 1790 the federal census listed fifteen. The ten original counties were Albany, Dutchess, Kings, New York, Orange, Queens, Richmond, Suffolk, Ulster and Westchester. Although their names have remained the same, their shape and size have not all remained the same. Westchester, for example, then included the Bronx, and Suffolk included Nassau. Also, Albany spread almost

---

11. *Documentary History of New York,* 1:707; *NY Col. Docs.,* 5:768, 814.

12. See Edgar J. McManus, *A History of Slavery in New York* (Syracuse: Syracuse University, 1966), esp. 28-31.

13. John Watts, *Letter Book of John Watts Merchant and Councillor of New York, January 1, 1762-December 22, 1765* (New York: New-York Historical Society, 1928), 31-32, 150-151.

boundlessly during most of the colonial period, and many of the present northern counties came from lands once associated with it. For instance, the five new counties that showed up in the 1790 census came from lands ceded by Albany. The first two of those counties were formed in 1772 under the names Tryon and Charlotte, but in 1784 they were renamed Montgomery and Washington to honor two heroes of the American Revolution; the other three counties were formed between 1786 and 1789 with the names Columbia, Clinton and Ontario.[14]

Albany County

By 1790 Albany was a large and populous county. Almost perennially it ranked among the leaders in population. But the uncertainties of life on an unexposed frontier dampened its development until late in the eighteenth century. For the French and Indians frightened away more than a few settlers. During the colonial wars Albany appeared, in fact, to lose population. The difference between its population in 1737 and 1749 was a loss of 47, for example, during that dozen years which included the War of Jenkins' Ear (1739) and King George's War (1744-1748). That suggested that threats did not necessarily drive people away wholesale, but neither did it suggest that people flocked in eagerly to settle. After 1763, however, settlement in Albany took off as its population increased rapidly. Apparently reflecting the beginning of the new era that Lawrence Henry Gipson said followed after the French withdrew from Canada, Albany "waxed rich and strong."[15] Its population doubled between 1756 and 1771, and it nearly doubled again between 1771 and 1790. Also, after 1756 it had the largest black population of any county, and that population also doubled by 1771 (See Table 2).

New York County

While blacks were increasing in Albany, they were decreasing in New York County which until 1756 had the biggest concentration

---

14. Charles W. Bardeen, *A Brief Descriptive Geography of the Empire State* (Syracuse: C. W. Bardeen, 1895), 62; Robert J. Rayback, *Richard's Atlas of New York State* (Phoenix, N.Y.: Frank E. Richards, 1965), 19, Thomas C. Cochran, *New York in the Confederation: An Economic Study* (Philadelphia: University of Pennsylvania, 1932), 3-4.

15. Lawrence Henry Gipson, *The Coming of the American Revolution 1763-1775* (New York: Harper & Row, 1962), chaps. 1, 2; Douglass E. Leach, *The Northern Colonial Frontier 1607-1763* (New York: Holt, Rinehart and Winston, 1966), 37-43.

of slaves. In 1790 the number of slaves on Manhattan Island was only one more than it had been in 1749. But even though New York County lost its leadership, blacks continued to be a large part of its total population. At its high point (1746) blacks constituted 20.8 percent of the population in New York County. Albany County had a high of 15.3 percent in 1737. Beyond their numbers, however, the blacks in Albany County lived in a different regime than they did in New York County. Up on the northern frontier, holders worked their slaves at the rough clearing of land and other back-breaking tasks they needed to begin profitable farming. They demanded strong men for their initial work, and the censuses showed that: adult black males were the single largest group in Albany's slave population. Until 1749, for instance, black males outnumbered black females almost two-to-one. After that the ratio evened, and by 1786 Albany had only twenty more black males than females. In contrast, holders in New York County seemed to use their slaves for personal and household service and for somewhat skilled assistance in trades. They never built any overwhelming holding of black males. In fact, adult black females were usually the largest group among New York County's black population, and that suggested a trend of domestic service. Moreover, the number of adult black males in Manhattan decreased precipitously after the slave plot there in 1741 which dramatically impressed upon whites an idea that black males were really dangerous.[16] But it was not only the slave uprising that affected New York County's population, its troubled economy also had an effect (See Table 3).

Dutchess County

Not only did Manhattan fall behind Albany in its pace of development, it also fell behind Dutchess where settlement and slavery picked up rapidly, particularly after 1750. Its whole population, for example, rose between 1723 and 1790 by 44,193 persons, but 37,364 (84.5 percent) of them came after 1750. That was nearly twice Manhattan's increase of 24,883 over the sixty-seven years. The numbers of blacks followed much the same pattern, for the slaves in Dutchess grew from 43 in 1723 to 1,856 in 1790. Further, more than half (939) of that growth occurred between 1749 and 1771. Reflecting the farming economy in Dutchess, black males there consistently

16. New York *Weekly Journal,* 27 April, 27 July, 1741; *Letters and Papers of Cadwallader Colden, 1711-1775* (New-York Historical Society: *Collections,* Vols. 66, 67-68, 1917-1923, 1934-1935), 2:225-227, 8:282-289; Herbert Aptheker, *American Negro Slave Revolts* (New York: International Publishers, 1943, 192-195; Thomas J. Davis, ed., *The New York Conspiracy* (Boston, 1971), esp. vii-xxv and 5-12.

TABLE 2

Slave Population in Albany County, by Age, Sex and Percentage of
Total Population, 1698-1790

POPULATION

| YEAR | ADULT | | CHILD | | TOTAL | | % |
	M	F	M	F	SLAVE	COUNTY	SLAVE
1698	--	--	--	--	23	1476	1.6
1703	83	53	36	28	200	2273	8.8
1723	307	200	146	155	808	6501	12.4
1731	568	185	346	174	1273	8573	14.8
1737	714	496	223	197	1630	10681	15.3
1746	--	--	--	--	--	--	
1749	472	365	309	334	1480	10634	13.9
1756	862	603	658	496	2619	17424	15.0
1771	1350	980	876	671	3877	42706	9.1
1786	2335	2355	--	--	4690	72360	6.5
1790	--	--	--	--	3929	75921	5.2

Source: cf. n 8. Note the absence of breakdown by age or sex in 1698
and 1790 data. Also, note the absence of breakdown by age in 1786 data.

TABLE 3

Slave Population in New York County, by Age, Sex and Percentage of
Total Population, 1698-1790

POPULATION

| YEAR | ADULT | | CHILD | | TOTAL | | % |
	M	F	M	F	SLAVE	COUNTY	SLAVE
1698	--	--	--	--	700	4937	14.2
1703	102	288	131	109	630	4375	14.4
1723	408	476	220	258	1362	7248	18.8
1731	599	607	186	185	1577	8622	18.3
1737	674	609	299	207	1719	10664	16.1
1746	712	569	419	735	2444	11717	20.8
1749	651	701	460	556	2368	13294	17.8
1756	672	695	468	443	2278	13046	17.5
1771	932	1085	568	552	3137	21863	14.3
1786	896	1207	--	--	2103	23614	8.9
1790	--	--	--	--	2369	33131	7.2

Source: cf. n 8. Note the absence of breakdown by age or sex in 1698
and 1790 data. Also, note the absence of breakdown by age in 1786 data.

outnumbered black females. Yet the farms there were worked primarily by yeomen not slaves. Slaves never were more than one-fourteenth (7.6 percent) of the county's total population (See Table 4).

Ulster County

Even Ulster, which ranked fourth among the counties in total population in 1790, enjoyed more increase than New York County. Its increase—like that in Dutchess—was overwhelmingly in its white population and occurred after 1750. But its black population also grew greatly, increasing between 1723 and 1790 by 2,340. Moreover, its largest increase in slaves appeared after the American revolution, for between 1771 and 1786 it added to its rolls 738 slaves. As in Dutchess, male slaves consistently outnumbered female slaves in Ulster. The farmers there heavily relied on blacks, too, judging from the large portion that they formed in the total population. In

TABLE 4

Slave Population in Dutchess County, by Age, Sex and Percentage of Total Population, 1698-1790

	POPULATION						
YEAR	ADULT		CHILD		TOTAL		%
	M	F	M	F	SLAVE	COUNTY	SLAVE
1698*	--	--	--	--	156	1384	11.3
1703*	63	36	31	15	145	1649	8.8
1723	22	14	2	5	43	1083	4.0
1731	59	32	13	8	112	1724	6.5
1737	161	42	37	22	262	3418	7.7
1746	186	100	106	108	500	8806	5.7
1749	176	79	103	63	421	7912	5.3
1756	323	162	211	163	859	14157	6.1
1771	451	328	299	282	1360	22404	6.1
1786	830	815	--	--	1645	32636	5.0
1790	--	--	--	--	1856	45266	4.1

Source: cf. n 8. Note the absence of breakdown by age or sex in 1698 and 1790 data. Also, note the absence of breakdown by age in 1786 data. *The 1698 and 1703 data represent total combined with Ulster County.

1746, for example, more than one of every five (21.1 percent) of Ulster's inhabitants was black (See Table 5).

Westchester County

In Westchester County, too, adult male blacks were usually the most numerous group among the slaves. Its farming economy needed their labor and used them in large numbers, particularly between 1723 and 1771 when the number of slaves there increased by 2,983 blacks. More than three-fourths (76.2 percent) of that increase came after 1750 to send slaves in Westchester to their height in proportion to the county's population; that was a little more than one in seven (15.7 percent). The war brought dramatic change, however, as detailed later (See Table 6).

Orange and Suffolk Counties

Blacks grew greatly in Orange County, also, after 1750. Although only 996 slaves were in the county in 1790, that was 636 more than there had been in 1749. Again, black adult males were the largest group in the slave population (See Table 7). They also dominated in Suffolk's slave population which in 1698 had been more than one-fifth (20.8 percent) of the county's total. They were never again

TABLE 5

Slave Population in Ulster County, by Age, Sex and Percentage of Total Population, 1698-1790

| YEAR | ADULT | | CHILD | | TOTAL | | % |
	M	F	M	F	SLAVE	COUNTY	SLAVE
1698*	--	--	--	--	156	1384	11.3
1703*	63	36	31	15	145	1649	8.8
1723	227	126	119	94	566	2923	19.4
1731	321	196	124	91	732	3728	19.6
1737	378	260	124	110	872	4870	17.9
1746	374	264	244	229	1111	5265	21.1
1749	351	240	217	198	1006	4810	20.9
1756	486	360	328	326	1500	8105	18.5
1771	573	441	518	422	1954	13950	14.0
1786	1353	1309	--	--	2662	22143	12.0
1790	--	--	--	--	2906	29397	9.9

Source: cf. n 8. Note the absence of breakdown by age or sex in 1698 and 1790 data. Also, note the absence of breakdown by age in 1786 data.
*The 1698 and 1703 data represent total combined with Dutchess County.

TABLE 6

Slave Population in Westchester County, by Age, Sex and Percentage of
Total Population, 1698-1790

POPULATION

| YEAR | ADULT | | CHILD | | TOTAL | | % |
	M	F	M	F	SLAVE	COUNTY	SLAVE
1698	--	--	--	--	146	1063	13.7
1703	74	45	50	29	198	1946	10.2
1723	155	118	92	83	448	4409	10.2
1731	269	96	176	151	692	6033	11.5
1737	304	254	153	140	851	6745	12.6
1746	207	140	187	138	672	9235	7.3
1749	336	279	303	238	1156	10703	10.8
1756	495	280	296	267	1338	13257	10.1
1771	984	887	793	766	3430	21745	15.8
1786	649	601	--	--	1250	20554	6.1
1790	--	--	--	--	1419	23941	5.9

Source: cf. n 8. Note the absence of breakdown by age or sex in 1698
and 1790 data. Also, note the absence of breakdown by age in 1786 data.
*The 1698 and 1703 data represent total combined with Dutchess County.

TABLE 7

Slave Population in Orange County, by Age, Sex and Percentage of
Total Population, 1698-1790

POPULATION

| YEAR | ADULT | | CHILD | | TOTAL | | % |
	M	F	M	F	SLAVE	COUNTY	SLAVE
1698	--	--	--	--	19	219	8.7
1703	13	7	7	6	33	268	12.3
1723	45	29	42	31	147	1244	11.8
1731	85	47	19	33	184	1969	9.3
1737	125	95	38	35	293	2840	10.3
1746	133	44	82	51	310	3268	9.5
1749	111	103	62	84	360	4234	8.5
1756	140	94	103	93	430	4886	8.8
1771	206	174	162	120	662	10092	6.6
1786	442	416	--	--	858	14062	6.1
1790	--	--	--	--	966	18478	5.2

Source: cf. n 8. Note the absence of breakdown by age or sex in 1698
and 1790 data. Also, note the absence of breakdown by age in 1786 data.

so large a proportion. Indeed, the blacks in Suffolk followed a curiously erratic pattern of rising and falling numbers. There were 558 of them in 1698, but in 1703 only 188 remained as hard times befell the area and people moved on. By 1723, however, blacks had come back to number 975. Again that build up dissipated, and throughout the remainder of the century periods of lean years alternated with periods of fat years for the number of blacks in Suffolk (See Table 8).

Queens County

Blacks in Queens County did not follow an erratic growth pattern such as in Suffolk, but the whole county did suffer population losses. Particularly at mid-century when other counties began to spring ahead, Queens dropped back. Losing 1,700 inhabitants between 1746 and 1749, for example, the county plummeted from the second most populous county in 1723 to be eighth in 1790. And it lost blacks as well as whites. Between 1749 and 1756, for example, blacks in Queens County decreased by 846. Still, in 1771 one of every five persons (20.3 percent) was black. There, also, males outnumbered females among black people (See Table 9).

Kings County

In neighboring Kings County the black population grew slowly but steadily. It increased threefold between 1723 and 1790. Its larg-

TABLE 8

Slave Population in Suffolk County, by Age, Sex and Percentage of Total Population, 1698-1790

			POPULATION				
YEAR	ADULT		CHILD		TOTAL		%
	M	F	M	F	SLAVE	COUNTY	SLAVE
1698	--	--	--	--	558	2679	20.8
1703	60	52	38	38	188	3346	5.6
1723	357	367	197	54	975	6241	15.6
1731	239	83	196	83	601	7675	7.8
1737	393	307	203	187	1090	7923	13.8
1746	445	310	329	315	1399	9254	15.1
1749	396	293	305	292	1286	9384	13.7
1756	337	236	278	194	1045	10290	10.2
1771	448	334	350	320	1452	13128	11.1
1786	567	501	--	--	1068	13793	7.7
1790	--	--	--	--	1098	16440	6.7

Source: cf. n 8. Note the absence of breakdown by age or sex in 1698 and 1790 data. Also, note the absence of breakdown by age in 1786 data.

est proportion of the whole population was approximately one-third (34.3 percent) in 1698. Like Manhattan, Kings had a predominance of adult black males among its slaves until 1759 when the sex ratio began to even out (See Table 10).

Richmond County

Richmond, the last of the ten original counties, steadily increased its proportion of blacks in its total population during the eighteenth century. In 1698 one of every ten (10 percent) of its residents was black, and by 1786 that had grown to more than one-in-five (21.9 percent). And males consistently outnumbered females among the black population (See Table 11).

The economic bases and differences among the counties needs to be developed for a fuller understanding of what the slaves were doing in New York. Here it might be noted, however, that if slavery began purely as an economic system in New York, it was soon woven into the entire fabric of life. It became an aspect of social distinction—among other things. The lines of such distinction showed in patterns of slaveholding.[17]

17. See Jackson Turner Main, *The Social Structure of Revolutionary America* (Princeton: Princeton University, 1965), 197-220.

TABLE 9

Slave Population in Queens County, by Age, Sex and Percentage of Total Population, 1698-1790

POPULATION

| YEAR | ADULT | | CHILD | | TOTAL | | % |
	M	F	M	F	SLAVE	COUNTY	SLAVE
1698	--	--	--	--	199	3565	5.6
1703	117	114	98	95	424	4392	9.7
1723	393	294	228	208	1123	7191	15.6
1731	476	363	226	199	1264	7995	15.8
1737	460	370	254	227	1311	9059	14.5
1746	527	361	365	391	1644	9640	17.1
1749	429	349	300	245	1323	7940	16.7
1756	618	470	581	500	2169	10786	20.1
1771	782	534	374	546	2236	10980	20.4
1786	1160	1023	--	--	2183	13084	16.7
1790	--	--	--	--	2309	16014	14.4

Source: cf. n 8. Note the absence of breakdown by age or sex in 1698 and 1790 data. Also, note the absence of breakdown by age in 1786 data.

TABLE 10

Slave Population in Kings County, by Age, Sex and Percentage of
Total Population, 1698-1790

POPULATION

| YEAR | ADULT | | CHILD | | TOTAL | | % |
	M	F	M	F	SLAVE	COUNTY	SLAVE
1698	--	--	--	--	296	2017	14.7
1703	135	75	72	61	343	1912	17.9
1723	171	123	83	67	444	2218	20.0
1731	205	146	65	76	492	2150	22.9
1737	210	169	84	101	564	2348	24.0
1746	199	152	140	154	645	2331	27.7
1749	265	149	232	137	783	2283	34.3
1756	235	197	212	201	845	2707	31.2
1771	309	295	297	261	1162	3623	32.1
1786	695	622	--	--	1317	3986	33.0
1790	--	--	--	--	1432	4495	31.9

Source: cf. n 8. Note the absence of breakdown by age or sex in 1698
and 1790 data. Also, note the absence of breakdown by age in 1786 data.

TABLE 11

Slave Population in Richmond County, by Age, Sex and Percentage of
Total Population, 1698-1790

POPULATION

| YEAR | ADULT | | CHILD | | TOTAL | | % |
	M	F	M	F	SLAVE	COUNTY	SLAVE
1698	--	--	--	--	73	727	10.0
1703	60	32	4	1	97	504	19.2
1723	101	63	49	42	255	1506	16.9
1731	111	98	51	44	304	1817	16.7
1737	132	112	52	53	349	1889	18.5
1746	102	94	92	95	383	2073	18.5
1749	130	98	88	93	409	2154	19.0
1756	122	101	145	97	465	2132	21.8
1771	174	137	177	106	594	2847	20.9
1786	369	324	--	--	693	3152	22.0
1790	--	--	--	--	759	3835	19.8

Source: cf. n 8. Note the absence of breakdown by age or sex in 1698
and 1790 data. Also, note the absence of breakdown by age in 1786 data.

Slaveholding, of course, indicated a level of wealth. Slaves were property, and property reflected prestige on its holder. Even a glance at the slave holders listed in the census of 1755 indicated that the persons atop the list of slaveholders in New York were distinguished in society. Lewis Morris, for example, had the largest holding at his estate, Morrisania (now a section of the south Bronx). He was chief justice of New York, speaker of the assembly, member of the Common Council and first separate governor of New Jersey.[18] A pattern of slaveholding prevailed among federal officeholders in New York between 1789 and 1805. Eight of these men held more than five slaves in 1790 and 1800. Overall, in both 1790 and 1800, forty-five of the seventy-five men (60 percent) held slaves.[19]

The distribution of slaves among holders as indicated in the 1755 census showed the prevalence of the institution then. The census listed 2,435 slaves fourteen years or older. There were 1,371 males and 1,064 females, and they were held by 1,113 individuals. The holders were predominantly men, but slave holding was not an exclusive male prerogative. Sixty-three females showed up in the census as holders. Together they had 115 slaves—73 males and 62 females. Twenty-nine of the women slaveholders were recorded as widows which suggested that their holdings may have been bequeathed by their husbands. The woman with the largest holding was Ann Garting of Marbletown; she had 7 slaves—4 males and 3 females. They put her relatively high among all holders. For five or more slaves was a significant holding.

As might be expected, the general pattern of holding resembled a pyramid. At the base, 1,032 persons held fewer than five slaves. Seventy-two persons held between five to nine slaves. Six men— Thomas Dongan of Staten Island, Martinus Hoffman of Dutchess County, David Jones of Oyster Bay, Litgert Van Brunt of New Utrecht and Isaac Willet of Westchester—held ten slaves. Peter DeLacey of Westchester held twelve. At the apex, of course, was Lewis Morris with his twenty-nine slaves.

The list showed the average holding to be about two adult slaves. Also, it showed widespread holding. Neither individuals nor families concentrated holdings. Indeed, the list of New York slaveholders showed only 138 patronymic groups—persons with the same

18. [Lewis Morris] The Papers of Lewis Morris, Governor of the Province of New Jersey, New Jersey Historical Society *Collections,* IV (1852), 41, 67.

19. New York, *Census of Slaves 1755;* Arthur J. Alexander, "Federal Officeholders in New York State as Slaveholders, 1789-1805," *Journal of Negro History* 28 (1943), 326-349.

last name residing in the same census district. Together they held 935 adult slaves, a little more than one-third (38.4 percent) of the total. So, in distribution, slaveholding was spread more widely in New York society than it was in Virginia, for example, where a relatively small number of individuals and families held the majority of slaves.

The pattern of slaveholding in New York changed little between the middle and the end of the eighteenth century. The second federal census (1800), for instance, listed 20,663 slaves and 8,439 holders in New York. That averaged 2.4 slaves per holder. As in 1755, the holdings in 1800 pyramided. At the base, 3,858 persons held one slave; 1,758 held two, and 1,005 held three; 633 held four and 434 held five. Then the number of holders narrowed more: 267 persons held 6 slaves; 164 held seven; 99 held eight, and 62 held nine. At the apex were 112 holders each with ten slaves. That spread clearly indicated that slaveholding had broad roots in New York.[20]

And those roots were not killed by the American Revolution, contrary to what historians have often suggested. Clearly, the war disrupted slavery in New York as it disrupted almost everything else. Yet after the war the growth in the number of slaves continued, as it had done in most of New York's counties during the war. It took a concerted movement to end slavery in the state and, then, that required a generation of gradual emancipation.[21]

New York's slave population did decline by five percent between 1771 and 1786. That certainly resulted directly from the American Revolution. But that decline was not uniform throughout New York. Indeed, only four counties—New York, Westchester, Suffolk and Queens—lost slaves during the fifteen year period. The other counties actually increased their holdings. Moreover, the decrease in the four counties was 3,696 slaves: Westchester lost 2,225 blacks; New York County lost 1,034; Suffolk lost 384; and Queens lost 53. The other counties together added to their lists 2,652 slaves. So the net difference reflected by the five percent drop was only 994 slaves. Thus, the decline was not what it first seemed: it did not represent the fact that New Yorkers were giving up their slaves. Instead, the loss was remarkably small considering the actual losses in the four counties and the opportunities for losses opened by the war.[22]

20. U. S. Census Office, *Second Census* (Washington, D.C.: William Duane, 1801), population, II.

21. See Arthur Zilversmit, *The First Emancipation: The Abolition of Slavery in the North* (Chicago: University of Chicago, 1967), esp. 146-151.

22. On conditions, see Thomas J. Wertenbaker, *Father Knickerbocker Rebels: New York City during the Revolution* (New York: Charles Scribner's Sons, 1948); and Wilbur C. Abbott, *New York in the American Revolution* (Port Washington, N.Y.: Ira Friedman, 1962; reprint of 1929 ed.).

Hundreds of slaves gained their freedom in New York through the Revolution, particularly in three ways worthy of note. First, all slaves who formally shouldered arms for the patriot cause in New York were emancipated by the state legislature. Second, the legislature freed those slaves held in estates that tories forfeited. The third and largest loss resulted, however, from circumstances which New Yorkers protested loudly. And it was those circumstances that largely accounted for the decline in the number of slaves in Westchester, Manhattan, Queens and Suffolk.[23]

The British occupied all or parts of those counties during the war. Indeed, they did not surrender control of New York City until late in 1783. And when they left, they offered free passage to almost any slave who wanted to leave with them. Fugitive slaves, abandoned slaves and slaves who had served His Majesty under arms all were evacuated.[24]

Sir Guy Carleton, British Commander in New York City during the evacuation steadfastly refused to deny transportation to any black, whether slave or free. He tried simply to register the slaves who left, noting who had held them and the amount of compensation that might be due holders for loss of slaves. That, of course, proved a needless task, for no compensation was ever forthcoming. Yet his directions produced a revealing document.[25]

The British commissioners under Carleton in New York listed an even 3,000 blacks—1,336 men, 914 women and 750 children—whom they evacuated on specified ships under His Majesty's command. But other blacks left unregistered on private vessels. Consequently, no one knows the precise number of blacks who left New York with the British before November 30, 1783, the date of final evacuation.[26]

23. See *Laws of New York,* 4th sess., chap. XXXII (1781); *Laws of New York,* 8th sess., chap. LVII (1785); Harry B. Yoshpe, *The Disposition of Loyalist Estates in the Southern District of the State of New York* (New York: Columbia University, 1939); Harry B. Yoshpe, "A Record of Manumissions in New York during the Colonial and Early National Periods," *Journal of Negro History,* 27 (1941), 78-107.

24. Carleton Papers, Colonial Williamsburg, doc. 766, cited in Wertenbaker, *Father Knickerbocker Rebels,* 262.

25. See Carleton Photostats, book of Negroes Registered & certified after having been Inspected by the commissioners appointed by His Excellency Sir Guy Carleton, K. B. General & Commander in Chief, on board Sundry Vessels in which they were embarked previous to the time of sailing from the Port of New York between the 23 Apr. and 13st July, 1783, both days included; Benjamin Quarles, *The Negro in the American Revolution* (Chapel Hill: University of North Carolina, 1961), ch. 9, "Evacuation with the British."

26. Ibid., 172.

Whatever the total number was, it provoked vociferous complaints from patriots. Elias Boudinot, President of the Confederation Congress, led the complainers. In a letter to Benjamin Franklin, Boudinot accused the British of purposely despoiling the property of New Yorkers by sending off their slaves.[27]

Thus, New York's drop of five percent in its slave population actually covered over both a more substantial loss of slaves and a determination by slaveholders in New York to add more blacks to those held in bondage. The drop did not reflect the press of anti-slavery ideology nor any powerful impact of liberal policies from the patriots. Nor did it indicate that the desire of New Yorkers to hold slaves had diminished. Quite to the contrary, to reduce the net loss to only five percent, as indicated, New Yorkers outside Westchester, Manhattan, Queens and Suffolk had added significantly to their holdings between 1771 and 1786. Moreover, between 1786 and 1790 the total number of slaves in New York increased more than an eighth (12.9 percent), rising from 18,998 to 21,329. So slavery was hardly over for black people in New York after the American Revolution.

New York's slaves had to wait for the lingering effects of the state's gradual emancipation acts of 1799 and 1817. Even then, after July 4, 1827, when the acts were supposed to have freed the mass of slaves in New York, some blacks remained legal bondsmen in the state. For more than two centuries they had found themselves in that position.

Thus, blacks came here with the earliest European settlers, and their number grew as New York grew. They labored to develop the land and life here, and their continued presence has formed a long black line that runs deep to New York's roots.

27. Boudinot to Franklin, 13 June 1783; Jane J. Boudinot, *The Life, Public Service, Addresses and Letters of Elias Boudinot, Lld., President of the Continental Congress* (New York: Houghton Mifflin & Co., 1896).

These workers in the International Cheese Plant in Cooperstown, New York, lived below the level of historical scrutiny, except for this 1912 photograph by Arthur J. Telfer. From the Smith & Telfer Photographic Collection, New York State Historical Association.

On Doing Local History in New York State

By CAROL KAMMEN

THE SEARCH FOR DIVERSITY

Local history has long been the preserve of old families, first settlers, famous sons, men of local power and those with some degree of national importance, politicians, men of the military. By and large in the nineteenth century, local history was written by men with some education and leisure who themselves came from or established prominent families. This pattern, with a few modifications—such as the emergence of women as custodians of local history—continued well into the twentieth century.

During the last ten years, however, local history has undergone a change. In the early 1970s the director of a historical society in an upstate city of 35,000 people was not interested in competing for a grant to study ethnicity in his city because "we have no ethnics." Ten years later, the same society—with a different director—has embarked on a search for people of every imaginable ethnic variation and has uncovered a rich past. Ethnicity has definitely found its way into local historical societies despite the origins of those organizations as the keepers of a particular past—generally a native-born Protestant past.

Not only ethnicity, but also the search for the historic role of blacks and of women has enlivened our study of the past. Diversity has become the catchword of the 1980s. Our older local histories were decidedly male in orientation—white male, to be precise. Women barely existed in them. Because the hearth was not regarded as important in the public realm, women were identified by their relationships to their husbands and fathers. "In March," notes one mid-nineteenth-century history, "following the September when they came in, the wife of John Dumond, presented to the world, the first white child born within the present limits of this county—who is still living and resides in Danby, the wife of Mr.

Benjamin Skeels." The mother of the child goes nameless through time; the baby, in case you are interested and want to give the good lady a bit of her own identity, was Sally. Throughout the nineteenth century our earliest settlers were carefully named in our histories so that each man would be known to those who followed. The women who came with them were usually ignored.

So too, our earliest local histories ignored the existence of blacks. If they were mentioned at all it was usually because they were fugitives from southern slavery seeking better conditions north of the Mason-Dixon line. Yet many of our towns have a black presence that dates back to settlement days. The Town of LaPeer, in Cortland County, received its first settler in 1799, a "colored man" by the name of Primus Grant, a native of Guinea. H.C. Goodwin's *Pioneer History of Cortland County* (1859)—copied almost word for word by H.P. Smith in his 1885 history—states simply that Grant "lived a number of years on his lot, and when he died was buried on one of the high bluffs that overlook the stream known as the Big Brook." In many other counties of the state, though census figures reveal free blacks and slaves, even less is known about them.

In contrast, local historians and historical societies today have broadened their focus to include people and conditions or events once thought to have little to do with the stuff of local history. This is partially due to recent academic interest in local history and is partially the result of national acceptance and celebration of our heterogeneity. This probably dates from the election of John F. Kennedy to the White House, from the emphasis in recent decades upon the heritage of minority people, and to such things as the Foxfire books, *Roots,* and the celebration of the Bicentennial.

The discovery of diversity in our past is obviously a good thing because it provides a more complete and therefore a more truthful portrait of that past. A minority group at one time, moreover, can become a majority group or an assimilated group at a later date. In one New York community, those who were on the edges of the mainstream might have been Welsh—and their treatment cordial— while in another place, the outsiders could be Irish Roman Catholics and their reception altogether different. Some years later, the Irish might be well established—if not yet politically powerful or socially elite, but at least a defined part of the fabric of a particular place—while Italians, or Hungarians, Jews, Syrians or Poles might be standing where the Irish once stood. The history of our minority past is also the history of their reception by those already on the scene, and it is the history of one ethnic group's reaction to another.

This type of history broadens our idea of "who was us" in the past. Most local historical societies, however, did not collect the archival flotsom and the material culture of these people. Searching for such people today becomes a process of identification through census data, church records, and other public documents, then finding artifacts that have survived. It means seeking clues to group identity through oral traditions.

The history of black New Yorkers offers a particular example. Black residency in New York goes back a long way, and blacks represent something of a special case in a discussion of our ethnic pluralism. In many communities, relatively little is known about black local history. Their story was not recorded, their artifacts not considered collectable, their oral traditions ignored. Even today, when ethnic programs at historical societies are put in place, blacks are often excluded.

So how do we find blacks in our local past? We turn to the census and to public records for a start. Rosemary Silbey describes such a project in her essay, "Nineteenth-Century Black Community History in Tompkins County," in *History for the Public* (1984), edited by G. David Brumberg, Margaret John, and William Zeisel, available from the New York Historical Resources Center at Cornell University or from the Institute for Research in History, New York City. Silbey searched through the manuscript census records and "recovered" all blacks listed. She noted on cards the family name, the number of persons in the family unit, their relationships, their address, and place of birth. The cards were helpful in locating individuals and in finding neighborhood and employment patterns, information about mobility, literacy, and family size.

The re-creation of a black past requires, in addition, a search for physical remains such as pictures, family Bibles, houses, and churches. Sometimes the material culture and oral tradition will reinforce each other. Sometimes cemetery records will solidify a family legend. Sometimes the legend proves false.

Not long ago a woman telephoned me in order to talk about her family. Her grandfather, she said, came to our part of the state during the Civil War. Family legends about him told of his birth in Maryland to a black woman. His father was the plantation owner, who had several other children living in the slave quarters. The boy carried his father's name and because of their relationship, which was acknowledged, escaped from the hard labor of the fields.

Charles Washington, however, was not ignorant of what the rest of the slave population suffered. He was present one day when a defiant slave broke the cradle scythe he was using and he heard the overseer threaten death if the worker was careless again. Family legend asserts that the slave broke the piece a second time and was shot dead on the spot.

Shaken by what he had seen, Charles Washington and his brother Webster decided to flee and that autumn they made their way north. Something of the terror of that trip could be heard as my friend intoned words she had obviously learned from her father, who had repeated the story to her. She said that the two boys moved only at night, hiding their shadows among the corn stalks stacked in pyramids in the fields through which they passed. By day they slept fitfully inside the piled corn, eating whatever came to hand. Webster settled permanently in Canada, while Charles married a Mohawk woman, and changed his name, becoming Charles Reed. He and his young wife made their way to central New York where they procured a farm and raised a family of thirteen children. My friend alone remains in the area to testify to their presence.

Another legend about Charles Reed concerns his eldest daughter, Mary, who became ill and frail and finally unable to talk. Yet, in the last minutes of her life, this dying girl began singing in a thin clear voice. The family gathered around and heard her plead with her father to join the church. This story we can confirm from church records which list Charles as a probationer and later as a member. The church records also tell of the babies that this couple laid to rest in the nearby graveyard. The federal census lists Charles Reed, locating him in central New York twenty years earlier than his family believed, yet they echo the family legends: that he was born in Maryland, that he was illiterate (it was illegal to teach slaves to read and write), that he married Mary, and that they had thirteen living children. After telling me about her ancestor, his granddaughter pointed to a portrait on the wall and said to me, "there he is, you know." So legend, public documents, and a portrait solidified the existence of a man largely forgotten.

Blacks belong in our expanded version of our forebears. They are a minority to search for. But we should not confine our efforts to studies of particular groups. To create a truly varied and accurate picture of society in the past we have to move beyond the usual and accepted story of progress and success in our communities to include all experiences that make the story complete. There is, after all, a history of the farmer or shopkeeper who did well and there is the history of those who failed, those who barely hung on, those whose luck changed for the worst. We are already conscious of those whose luck proved good, for our local histories are full of such tales. We need to know about the ill, the criminal, the insane. We need to ferret out the alternative histories and the multi-layered histories that have yet to be told. No community has a singular historical past. Every community has versions of the past that reflect varying opinions, various actions, many perceptions of what happened and why.

Local history often emphasizes commercial success, the oft-related tale of a young man who founds a business and the usefulness or beauty of his product. A multi-layered history of that business, however, includes more than an examination of the source of supply or the raw materials and sales figures. It should also include the history of those who worked in the factory, the conditions of their employment, their salaries, benefits, housing and compensation, if any. Such a multi-layered history would also look at attempts at organization on the part of the workers, their strikes, their demands. These are not the usual questions asked and answered in our local histories but they hold the possibility of our understanding a great deal more about ourselves than the simple fact that a particular town was known for the production of clocks or chairs or sewing machines.

Once, when talking with a woman who was writing the history of a local cheese factory, I asked who the workers were. She did not know and was not really interested. She knew the process used to make the cheese, the source of the baskets in which cheese was shipped about the state, and the range of the market. But who made the cheese in the factory? "Oh," she answered, "just some local women who came in on an hourly basis when they were needed." Just some local women. Here we have an example of wage-earning women about whom we knew nothing and about which the census will be mum.

These are not, however, the usual questions asked and answered in our local histories; posing them broadens the challenge of recapturing a complete past. Too often as we write local history or as we read through those that have come down to us, the story told is static and interchangeable, one community with another. A progressive history shows a community moving slowly but gracefully from a state of nature to a state of some degree of civilization which is defined by the number of improvements in the town and of the businesses established therein.

By opening up local history to a host of new people and new experiences we escape from a single-minded view of the past and reveal the diversity of our origins. Our people were, after all, of both sexes, of many national origins, and of varying abilities. Upon some the sun smiled, upon others it rained.

There is one caution in all this, however, and that is our search for diversity is not so important that we can overlook the part played in our local past by old established families. In our rush to embrace women and Irish and blacks and Italians, we cannot ignore the white Protestant native-born male who was, after all, central to much of the history we are interested in telling. To eliminate his role would be to write as biased and limited a history as that which has been passed along to us up to this time. To eliminate male history or white male history, would be to create a past inaccurate to its own time. So we search for minorities and the neglected not to supplant or deny the legitimate role played by those traditionally treated in historical studies, but rather, as a chord is built, we add other notes to those already in place in order to build a more complex sound—a richer, fuller view of the local past.

THE YANKEE INVASION OF NEW YORK, 1783-1850

DAVID MALDWYN ELLIS

NEW YORK by 1820 was becoming a "colony from New England"—to use the phrase of President Timothy Dwight of Yale.[1] The "Puritan Pope," as he was sometimes called, estimated that 60 to 67 percent of the people of New York had originated in the "land of steady habits."

The few thousand Puritans who had established a new Zion around Boston in the 1630's were a remarkably energetic, prolific, and self-assertive people. The thin soils on the hilly lands, the harsh winters, and the stern theology of John Calvin created a distinct community spirit and shaped a unique character. The township was the unit of economic, social, political, and religious life. An economy of small self-sustaining farms with cooperative features such as common pastures, mowing lots, and forests made emigration almost imperative as each generation grew to manhood. Not toleration but conformity was the basic tenet of religion. Sometimes formal action by town or church (often indistinguishable) but more usually critical comments by neighbors with over-size consciences kept individualists from straying too

The author was appointed Dixon Ryan Fox Fellow by the New York State Historical Association in 1948 and commissioned to help write a one-volume history of the State. The following article is adapted from a proposed chapter in this study. Dr. Ellis is Assistant Professor of history at Hamilton College.

[1] *Travels in New-England and New-York* (New Haven, 1821-1822), III, 266-267.

far from the Mosiac code. Not democracy but an obligarchy of God's elect at the beginning ruled each town. New England remained in 1800 a remarkably homogeneous community proud of its civilization so appropriately described as a "state of mind."

The isolation of the frontier, the ideas of the enlightenment, and the secular and cosmopolitan spirit of the seaports had gradually loosened the iron grip of the clergy, especially in the eighteenth century. But the Puritan virtues and vices still marked the citizens of New England and their transplanted compatriots in New York. Their thrift at times verged on stinginess; their self-esteem seemed arrogance to many; their soul-searching sometimes led to morbidity; their "conscience" tended to outrageous meddling in the lives of their neighbors. Their stamp on the character and institutions of New Yorkers has been unmistakable. Farm and factory, school and church all show the Yankee imprint. Who else but a Yankee such as John Brown of Providence would have designated several townships in the Adirondacks with such titles as Frugality, Industry, Enterprise, and Sobriety?

Prior to 1775 the great majority of restless Yankees were filling up the back country of southern New England, spreading up along the Maine coast, and following the Connecticut River northward into Vermont. Daughter towns, however, were springing up in New Jersey (New Ark), in Pennsylvania (Wyoming Valley), and especially in New York. As early as 1640 Yankees were beginning to invade Long Island and the eastern two-thirds soon became completely Yankee in population. Only a trickle during the seventeenth century, this population movement became an important stream during the first three quarters of the eighteenth century. By 1775 many Connecticut men had filtered into the eastern townships of Westchester and Dutchess Counties and across the Hudson into Orange County. After 1783 the influx became a torrent pouring into the Hudson Valley towns, sweeping up the Mohawk Valley, and spreading out across the rich lands of central and western New York. Within a generation the sons of New England could be found in every town and city of New York State.

The New England migration to New York is a thrilling chapter in one of the great folk migrations of all time. The Yankee came by land and by sea, in winter and in summer, in groups and as individuals. Sloops sailed up the Hudson laden with the household gear of families while sleighs and ox carts came overland through the steep hills fringing the border. The citizens of Albany watched a continual parade of restless people. During one three day period in February 1795 about 1200 sleighs freighted with men, women, children, and furniture passed through that city on the way to the Genesee country. During the summer settlers going up the Mohawk Valley got aboard the bateaux and Durham boats which profane rivermen poled upstream to the portage near Rome whence they could reach Oneida Lake and its connections with Lake Ontario and the Finger Lakes. Others preferred to take the turnpike westward. Rude wagons carried only the absolute necessities—pots, pans, beds, farm tools. The young, the old, and the sick rode; the able-bodied walked with the men leading the oxen; the young men drove the two or three milch cows and scraggly sheep. The mania for "turnpiking" which reached its peak between 1800 and 1807 opened up new highways to the west. New Englanders could drive their wagons westward over the New England network until they met roads leading eastward from Greenbush (opposite Albany), Hudson, and Pough-keepsie. At almost every river landing small boats were ready to carry them across the river. From Albany settlers could strike out for the west over the Cherry Valley turnpike or to Schenectady and thence up the Mohawk Valley. Other settlers used the turnpikes leading westward from Newburgh and Catskill.

Most Yankees were looking for farms although thousands headed for the counting houses of New York and the shops of artisans. The migration to the countryside was not an orderly procession which filled up eastern counties one by one. Rather the wave of newcomers seems to have swept into almost every valley except the recesses of the Adirondacks in the first decade following the close of the Revolution. Of course, the Hudson Valley counties were the first to feel the onrush, but Yankees were planting corn on the fertile intervales along the Genesee Valley long before the hill towns in the Catskill region had filled up. Almost every county save Dutchess and Westchester contained thousands of acres of unimproved lands after 1800. In fact, New York farmers were still clearing forest lands after 1850.

Land-hunger was the compelling drive behind the migration, although other factors swelled the bands of the discontented. In Massachusetts high taxes coming at a time of falling prices ruined thousands of farmers, whose attempt in 1786 to prevent mortgage foreclosures by following the rebellious Daniel Shays failed miserably. Settlers, braving the wild country near Lake George, declared to a traveler that the capitation tax in Rhode Island had driven them to New York. Others wished to escape the keepers of the New England conscience who enforced conformity with little charity and less humor.

Glowing reports of rich lands in New York picqued the curiosity of Yankees picking stones from their steep hillsides. Missionaries to the Iroquois sent back accounts of a new Eden. Many Yankee soldiers had carefully noted the fertile intervales as they followed General Sullivan in 1779 into the Finger Lakes region. They realized that the destruction of the Senecas and their allies would enable the white man to take over the corn fields of the red man within a decade. The first pioneers wrote stirring letters urging their relatives to join them. Hugh White, who claimed to be the first white inhabitant west of the German settlers on the upper Mohawk, sent back to his friends in Middletown, Connecticut, his tallest stalks of Indian corn, his largest potatoes and onions.[2] Agents distributed handbills offering new farms at

2 Pomroy Jones, *Annals and Recollections of Oneida County* (Rome, 1851), 790.

tempting prices and on long term credit. Small wonder then that Yankees hurried westward to the promised land. One authority estimates that between 1790 and 1820 the three states of southern New England lost approximately 800,000 people through emigration.[3] Most of these settled in or passed through New York.

A quick survey of various regions will bring out the extent and magnitude of the Yankee invasion.

The valley of the Hudson and especially the counties on the west side of the river attracted thousands, who almost submerged the small Dutch communities. For example, Stephen Van Rensselaer along with other landholders sent out broadsides advertising his vacant lands. As a result hundreds of Yankees leased farms in the hill towns back of the Helderberg escarpment. Other immigrants filled up the lands stretching northward from Albany to Lake Champlain.

The Mohawk and Schoharie valleys had only a handful of inhabitants in 1783. To the Yankees the rich alluvial soils looked as attractive as Canaan had appeared to the children of Israel. They bought unoccupied lands along the river bottoms and struck out into the hill country north and south of the Mohawk. The rugged Adirondacks formed a natural barrier some thirty miles north of the Mohawk. Some sanguine and unwary Yankees such as John Brown, the Providence merchant, tried to establish settlements in the mountains but with little success. Except for the inroads of lumberman and a few miners supplying the forges on the shore of Lake Champlain, the Adirondacks remained a wilderness until well after the Civil War. Thousands of Yankees found homes in the hill towns south of the Mohawk. Otsego county where William Cooper was land agent was the mecca for thousands. Throughout the Mohawk Country the sound of the ax was heard on every side. The experience of Herkimer County is typical. Within fifteen years some 10,000 immigrants from New England and the eastern counties had taken residence in that county.

The North Country, that is the region lying between Lake Champlain and Lake Ontario and southward from the St.

---

[3] Percy W. Bidwell, "Rural Economy in New England at the Beginning of the Nineteenth Century," *Transactions of the Connecticut Academy of Arts and Sciences*, XX (April, 1916), 352.

Lawrence River to the Adirondack fastnesses, became another colony of New England. Perhaps the title New Vermont (found on early maps) would be more precise because so many Green Mountain residents crossed Lake Champlain to this region in search of land, timber, and mill sites. About 1795 a stream of Vermonters began to leave that state and after the Embargo Act of 1807 it became a flood.[4] By 1850 about 52,000 Vermonters (one fifth the population of Vermont itself) were living in the Empire State. Town names in western New York such as Lyndon and Royalton betray the Vermont influence.

The region drained by the Delaware and the Susquehanna rivers likewise was overrun by New Englanders. To be sure, speculators from Pennsylvania and New Jersey often owned the land along the upper reaches of these rivers. A trickle of Pennsylvanians, Jersey men, and even Marylanders worked their way up these river systems. Legend has it, for example, that the town of Penn Yan on Keuka Lake was so named as a compromise between settlers from the two areas. The bulk of the settlers, however, were New Englanders who found the steep hillsides of the Southern Tier of counties reminiscent of their old home.

Central New York by 1800 had become almost as Yankee in population as Connecticut itself. Whitestown in Oneida County, which at first included all the state west of Utica, was typical. Elkanah Watson, himself a son of Berkshire, marveled at the influx in 1788 only four years after Hugh White of Middletown, Connecticut had cut a clearing and erected a log house. Watson wrote:

> Settlers are continually pouring in from the Connect-
> icut hive, which throws off its annual swarms of intel-
> ligent, industrious and enterprising settlers, the best
> qualified of any men in the world, to subdue and civil-
> ize the wilderness . . . . They already estimate three
> hundred brother Yankees on their muster list.[5]

Timothy Dwight, who traveled over New York during the first two decades of the nineteenth century, was delighted

[4] Lewis Stillwell, "Migration from Vermont (1776-1860)," *Proceedings of the Vermont Historical Society*, V (1927), 120.

[5] *History of the Rise, Progress, and Existing Condition of the Western Canals in the State of New York* (Albany, 1820), 13.

to find towns such as New Hartford and Clinton in Oneida County which reproduced in the wilderness the church, the school, and the "sprightliness, thrift, and beauty" of New England.[6]

The story of western New York is much the same. There was scarcely a town which did not have settlers from New England. The census figures tell a story of rapid settlement. The districts west of the Line of Property of 1768, exclusive of Oneida and Oswego counties, received about 60,000 inhabitants between 1790 and 1800. A decade later the poplation of this region neared 200,000. By 1820 it had passed 500,000. Ten years later it was over 700,000 and by mid-century over 1,000,000. The great bulk of these people were of New England stock.

The Yankee impact on New York's economy, politics, professional and social life was tremendous. Yankee axes cleared most of the forests. Ledgers kept by Yankee clerks for Yankee business men recorded most of the expanding trade nourishing New York and the upstate cities. Even industry, which had hardly bgun prior to 1825, felt their stimulus. Some of the leaders of the textile factories in Oneida County, for example, were former residents of Rhode Island. A high proportion of the men who preached the Gospel, pleaded before the bar, bled the patient, and used the birch rod to chastise the unruly student were also trained in the academies and colleges of New England. Moreover, many ingenious craftsmen migrated westward where their talents were in great demand to construct grist mills, forges, homes, and mercantile buildings.

Yankee brains stirred the old river ports to feverish activity. The port of New York won top place among the nation's ports largely under their direction.[7] Since the days of Peter Stuyvesant a few sons of New England had drifted to the wharves of Manhattan despite ministerial fulminations that the city was a re-creation of Sodom and Gomorrah. After 1800 their numbers swelled greatly until by 1820

6 Dwight, *op. cit.*, III, 179.
7 A good description of the Yankee impact on New York City is found in Robert Greenhalgh Albion's *The Rise of New York Port* (New York, 1939).

Yankees had become the largest but certainly not the most
digestible ingredient in the metropolitan melting pot. Before
long the quarter decks, ship yards, and counting houses
were virtual colonies of New England. Farm boys from the
towns along the Sound paced the procession. These lads
were indeed the prototypes for the heroes of Horatio Alger's
stories. By working hard, by seizing every opportunity, by
cutting corners and driving sharp bargains, and by avoiding
the pitfalls of wine, women, and song, a goodly number of
Yankee farm boys climbed to the pinnacles of New York life.
Other immigrants had an easier time of it. Several New
England families of substance moved their businesses to the
city. Boston firms often sent younger sons to set up branch
offices on Manhattan.

A new mercantile group gradually emerged overshadowing
the older aristocracy of New York. The Griswolds hailing
from Old Lyme, Connecticut, and the Lows from Salem
enticed most of the China trade from Boston. The Grinnells
formerly of New Bedford owned scores of trim ships. Edward
K. Collins originally of Cape Cod won fame with his Black
Ball packets. Edwin Morgan from Berkshire grew fat on the
import trade, directed the Hudson River Railroad in the
early 1850's and ended his career as Governor and Senator.
The Fish family of Rhode Island and the Macy family from
Nantucket also carved niches in the political and commercial life of New York. Yankees manned the helm on most
of the ships operating out of New York. They owned most
of the shipyards and directed most of the shipping lines.
Indeed they invaded every cranny of economic activity.
Later in the century Jim Fisk from Vermont titillated the
country with his prodigal amours and his unscrupulous deals.
J. P. Morgan from Hartford is another son of Connecticut
who towered over Wall Street around the turn of the century.

The old mercantile and landed families naturally resented
this invasion by the "locusts of the west." To the De Lanceys
the Griswolds were upstarts who had no manners, sang
psalms, and chased dollars avidly—and too successfully. The

old families tardily organized the St. Nickolas and the Knickerbocker Societies as a counterpart to the New England Society established as early as 1805. The newcomers were outspoken men quick to ridicule the proverbial lethargy of the native New Yorkers and tireless in extolling the virtues of the "land of steady habits." Their successful business careers seemed to confirm their claims to superior virtue. How the descendants of the old mercantile families must have writhed when they saw Yankees occupying the presidential chair of the New York Chamber of Commerce continually, except for one short period of eight months, between 1845 and 1875.[8]

The landed aristocracy smarting from the beating which the Green Mountain boys had already given them in regard to their land claims in the region of Vermont had additional cause to dislike the land speculators and settlers from New England. Yankees such as Oliver Phelps and Nathaniel Gorham got control of the choicest lands of western New York when Massachusetts sold off its claims in 1786. Millions of acres were dumped on the market during the 1790's cutting down the value of the older tracts in eastern New York. Furthermore, Yankee settlers brought with them a desire to hold land in fee simple, an idea which threatened the large estates developed under the leasehold. James Fenimore Cooper held the Yankee farmer as largely responsible for the anti-rent troubles of the 1840's. He wrote three novels attempting to justify the role of the landed aristocracy and to expose the nefarious designs of the antirenters, who were invariably depicted as knaves and scoundrels from New England.

Albany likewise felt the invigorating effect of Yankee enterprise. The inrush of thousands of immigrants into the upland regions both south and north of the Mohawk river was roughly matched by the increase in the population of Albany which tripled its numbers between 1790 and 1810. By 1803 the Yankees outnumbered the original inhabitants. Indeed they had become so powerful that they succeeded in

[8] The most thorough analysis of the transit of New England institutions to New York and the resulting cultural clash is found in the delightful essays *Yankees and Yorkers* by Dixon Ryan Fox.

pushing through an ordinance requiring the enraged Dutch burghers to cut off the long rainspouts which the Dutch had erected on their houses.[9] Six miles to the north of Albany, New England adventurers laid out the new town of Troy in 1787. Its citizens soon acquired a reputation for bold enterprise and civic pride which became the taunt and the despair of Albany merchants for the next century. The centennial bard of Troy no doubt exaggerated Albany's distress at the news of Troy's founding.

> At Albany it awakened
> The Dutchmen from their sleep
> And with prophetic terror
> Their flesh began to creep [10]

Nantucket whalers in 1783 banded together in an association to found the city of Hudson. The city became a port of entry and her schooners sailed directly to foreign countries. Across the river, Catskill showed a similar growth. In fact there grew up a cluster of houses and stores at the foot of "every considerable road" leading to the Hudson River. Canny Yankees thus invigorated the business life of the Hudson Valley.

Utica, Syracuse, Rochester, Buffalo likewise owe much of their early growth to the New England migration. To be sure, some of the founders such as Colonel Rochester came from Maryland and other states, but most of the early settlers came in from the east. The city of Rochester was soon noted not only as America's first boom town but also for its stern Puritan piety. Ambitious farm lads from New England dominated the commercial life of these upstate urban areas in the same way that their compatriots swept to the top in New York City.

Those Puritans and their children who settled in New York displayed more skill and leadership in national politics than those who stayed at home. Hardly had they cleared the forests before they were organizing town governments. Soon they were unraveling the twisted skein of state politics

---

[9] Joel Munsell, *The Annals of Albany* (Albany, 1850-1859), X, 196.
[10] Arthur James Weise, *Troy's One Hundred Years, 1789-1889* (Troy, 1891), 286.

which had been the private preserve of the influential colonial families for so many decades. The first generation of New Englanders tended to join the fight for democracy. The sturdy Yankee yeomen could not help but look askance at the semi-feudal land system of the aristocracy. Contrariwise the landed gentry looked with mingled distrust and disdain at the hustling Yankee merchant and with some alarm at rising industrial towns with a propertyless working class. A majority of the members of the Constitutional Convention of 1821, which established manhood suffrage, were of New England stock. Of course, the career of Martin Van Buren and still earlier that of George Clinton indicate that democratic impulses were stirring in the older pre-Revolutionary population. Nevertheless, by the 1830's practically all the most prominent political leaders stemmed from New England forbears. The Albany Regency boasted such Democratic worthies as Silas Wright, William L. Marcy, Azariah C. Flagg, John A. Dix, and Martin Van Buren. Only Van Buren could trace his roots deeply into New York background. Moreover, the outstanding leaders in the Whig and later the Republican party—William H. Seward, Thurlow Weed, Hamilton Fish, and Horace Greeley—were of New England origin.

The transit of Yankee culture showed some interesting sea changes. The new enviroment modified such typical institutions as the town, the church, and the school. The New York frontier was settled by individuals and almost never by organized groups. The salient characteristics of the New England town with its proprietors and its jointly-owned and used pasture, mowing, and forest lands seldom appeared except on Long Island. To be sure, the pioneers often laid out a village green on which the church and homes fronted. But most farmers lived in isolated homesteads not in nucleated villages. Furthermore, the town was much less important as a unit of local government in New York where the county performed many important functions.

White church steeples soon dotted the New York countryside. Oddly enough, many of them belonged to the Presbyterian rather than the traditional Congregational faith. This is one of the accidents of history, which some will insist illustrates how the canny Scots outsmarted their fellow Calvinists. During the 1790's the Presbyterian Church of the United States with its center in Pennsylvania and the Congregational Associations of the various New England states were cooperating closely especially in sending missions to frontier areas. It seemed foolish for denominations so similar in theology to compete for members in the sparsely-settled communities of the Susquehanna region. Jonathan Edwards, Jr., President of Union College, suggested a Plan of Union which was adopted in 1802 by representatives of both denominations. It permitted communicants of either faith in a new community to form a single congregation which might call a minister of either denomination. A majority of the congregation could elect to conduct their church polity and discipline according to the rules of either the Presbyterian or Congregational church. Most congregations, despite the Congregational background of their members, selected the Presbyterian discipline. The presbyterial organization seemed better suited to the needs of a frontier church.

But Presbyterians of Yankee background did not submit readily to the rigid rules and orthodox Calvinism imposed by their Scotch-Irish brethren. Each congregation followed its own wishes as before. The former Congregationalists tended to read the sermons of New England preachers who were beginning to question such doctrines as original sin. Unitarian ideas rising to the forefront even in such citadels of Puritanism as Harvard during the first decade of the nineteenth century were part of the intellectual baggage which Yankee divines carried with them to upstate New York. Denominational ties were so lightly regarded by these "Presbygationals" that they eagerly joined such interdenominational agencies as the American Bible Society. Their leaders shocked old-Guard Calvinists by damning slavery more vigorously than warning the people of eternal damnation. The Old School Presbyterians denounced these tendencies as heretical. In 1837 they got control of the General

Assembly and ousted four synods, including those of Utica, Geneva, and Genesee. The New School Presbyterians promptly organized a separate church. Gradually other synods and presbyteries joined their ranks as the slavery issue grew hotter. Eventually the New School group included nearly all the Presbyterians of the north. In 1869 the Old School rejoined their brethern.

The New England tradition continued to influence New York churches. Most of the preachers serving the Presby· terian, Congregational, Baptist, and Unitarian churches were reared in that region and educated in Harvard, Yale, Amherst, and similar colleges. For example, Charles Finney, who sparked the great revival of 1825 and following years, was a native of Connecticut brought up in Utica. New England even provided the leaders of several strange cults which grew up in the fertile soil of the "burnt-over district" of central-western New York. Joseph Smith, founder of the Mormon Church, and John Humphrey Noyes, founder of Oneida Community, hailed from Vermont. William Miller, who convinced thousands that Christ would return in 1843, was also a Yankee. Boston was to remain for decades the religious and intellectual capital of Yankees in Diaspora.

The little red school house, the elm-shaded academy, and the hill-top college were usually founded and directed by New Englanders. Ichabod Crane is only one of several fictional and many flesh-and-blood school masters who parsed sentences in a nasal tone. The New York system, or perhaps more accurately, lack of system of state-supported schools displeased Yankees accustomed to tax-supported schools open to all children. Significant it is that a New Englander, Gideon Hawley, was called upon to direct the first successful system of state-aided neighborhood schools. Private academies flourished throughout the state whenever New England influence was strong.

Columbia College was the only institution of college level in the state that was not stamped with the Yankee imprint. Even Union College, which attracted the support of the Dutch Reformed and Episcopalians, soon had such one hundred per cent Yankees at the helm as Jonathan Edwards, Jr. and Eliphalet Nott. No institution was more New England in character than Hamilton College. Samuel Kirkland of Connecticut had established in 1793 the Hamilton-Oneida Academy. Prior to the Civil War all save one of the presidents of the College founded in 1812 were Puritan divines and usually sons of old Eli. As Dixon Ryan Fox has ably shown in his admirable book of essays, *Yankees and Yorkers,* Colgate, Rochester, Hobart, and St. Lawrence displayed the Yankee stamp. These colleges drew most of their faculty from the east and modelled their curricula after Harvard and Yale.

Science and fine arts owed much less to immigrants from the eastern states. The singing society, however, was an import from New England. More literate—certainly more articulate—than the average New Yorker, the Yankee wrote most of the editorials and set most of the type. One need only mention Thurlow Weed and Horace Greeley to understand our state's indebtedness to New England for the development of the press before 1850.

These cocksure invaders naturally antagonized the early inhabitants of New York. They did not conceal the contempt which they felt toward the "churlish, ignorant, and unenterprising" Germans and Dutch. The natives struck back as best they could by circulating stories about "dirty Yankee tricks." The upper classes read with approval James Fenimore Cooper's novels which invariably described the Yankees as a particularly disagreeable race. Cooper pilloried their avarice, their arrogance, their cant. The whole catalogue of sins was theirs, from poor cooking to a "strong and unpleasant" dialect. In *Miles Wallingford* he writes: "near neighbors they did not love each other. The Yankees said the Dutch were fools, and the Dutch said the Yankees were knaves."

Gradually the passage of time softened these asperities into a feeling of mutual good will. The transplanted Yankee became more mellow and less angular. Many another besides Ichabod Crane found the Dutch lasses captivating. Moreover, the Dutch and Germans gradually lost their dialects, especially after the public school system was extended. The new aristocracy based on trade and manufacturing began to copy some of the manners and customs of the landed aristocracy. Marriage alliances and a common distrust of LocoFocos and radicals drew them together.

Perhaps the most decisive factor was the Irish invasion of the 1840's and 1850's. The older population forgot their minor differences in their common distrust of these newer immigrants who were fervently Catholic and disturbingly clannish. By the 1840's the transplanted Yankees, themselves the despised newcomers only one short generation earlier, were beginning to scorn this new wave of invaders. This inevitable but short-lived xenophobia was to greet each immigrant group in the future: the Poles, Italians, and the Jews after 1900; the Negroes in the 1920's; the Puerto Ricans in the 1940's. Fortunately the desire for "Americanization" has always been strong among immigrants. Even more fortunately the spirit of good will among New Yorkers has usually overcome bigotry and prejudice. No group of newcomers however, left a more permanent imprint upon the racial, cultural, economic, and political life of New York than the resolute and enterprising sons of New England.

Church and Market Streets, Albany, 1805. By James Eights. The New York State Historical Association.

The Irish Aristocracy of Albany, 1798–1878

By WILLIAM E. ROWLEY

*Albany's ancient aristocracy was "democratic" enough to wel-
come as equals those Irish newcomers with sufficient ability to
gain economic and political strength in the community. In describing the rise of this group, Dr. Rowley—a member of the
English department at the State University of New York at Albany—also examines the origin and growth of Albany's Irish
population.*

THE STEREOTYPE of the Irish immigrant to American cities
in the mid-nineteenth century is a gawky peasant, sweat-
ing through his native "woolens and flannels of stoutest tex-
ture," shuffling off a crowded ship into a hostile community
of strangers.[1] If he survived the rigors of canal digging or railroad building, and the temptation of rum, he might live to see
his son master a trade and perhaps to see a grandson enter a
profession. The way up, as the legend has it, was the hard
individualistic way—a way offered by a society that was said
to have been radically equalized by the reforms of Jacksonian
democracy, when the old aristocracy of the Colonial and Fed-
eralist periods was disappearing and before the new "manufacturing aristocracy" had been established to take its place.[2]
His story, when it had a happy ending, was the rise of a free
common man.

The legendary image fits the experience of some Irish immigrants, but for many others it is only half-true. Witness the
story of the Irish in Albany, in a society that was not equalized but one in which aristocracy persisted through the "age

---

[1] *Albany Morning Express,* July 22, 1854.
[2] Alexis de Tocqueville, *Democracy in America,* 2 vols. (New York:
Random House, Vintage Books, 1945), II, 168-171.

New York History July 1971

of the common man." The Irishman who came there in the 1820s to dig canals, or in the 1840s and 1850s to lay rails, was greeted not only by hostile strangers but by some quite friendly Dutchmen and Yankees and some well-established fellow countrymen, and he soon saw that the social structure in which he might climb was not an egalitarian democracy but a hierarchy, some of whose prominent places were occupied by Caggers, Traceys, and Cassidys. For Albany in the first half of the nineteenth century was not basically different from the aristocratic Albany of the eighteenth century or even of the seventeenth century, when some less impoverished Irishmen had found their places. Jacksonian democracy had not levelled it. The last Patroon, Stephen Van Rensselaer, and his family, continued to exercise feudal power in Albany politics until the anti-rent wars of the 1840s. The Albany Regency, which ran the Jacksonian Democratic Party, was allied with large landed proprietors and with business and banking interests, and resisted social reform in New York State. In fact, the supporters of The Workingmen's Party, which did advocate reform, called the Regency a "monied aristocracy."[3]

In the present essay "aristocracy" will be used as the "workies" used it, to mean not just the "best" (in merit, family, land) as James Fenimore Cooper wanted it to mean, but the "rich" who had status and power. Throughout the first half of the nineteenth century, two overlapping groups dominated Albany society. One was the merchant patriciate whose power had paralleled that of the landed Patroons in Albany since the seventeenth century. In her study of *The Gansevoorts of Albany,* Alice P. Kenney describes the Dutch merchant patriciate in a way that illuminates the traditionally hierarchical structure of Albany society and the conservative temper of its dominant families. She found the form for the Albany patriciate in the medieval Dutch town, where to the leading merchants "neither the individual nor the mass, but the local community, was the significant entity, and its purpose in acting [in politics] was neither to preserve liberty nor to seize power, but to protect and extend its particular privileges."[4] A Dutchman might rise from plebian to patrician, but he never

[3] *Albany Microscope,* Sept. 18, 1830. See Lee Benson, *The Concept of Jacksonian Democracy* (New York, 1964), chap. 2, and William E. Rowley, "Albany: A Tale of Two Cities, 1820-1880," unpublished Ph.D. thesis, Harvard University, 1968, on which this article is largely based.
[4] *The Gansevoorts of Albany* (Syracuse, 1969), p. xiv.

St. Mary's, the first Catholic church in Albany. From Bi-Centennial History of Albany (1886).

thought of erasing the class line. So it was for the New Englanders who invaded Albany after the Revolution and made it a Yankee city. Elkanah Watson as a young entrepreneur, Benjamin Knower as a hatter's apprentice, and Ezra Ames as a portrait painter, all emigrated as plebians from Massachusetts and rose to become bank presidents in Albany.[5]

The second aristocratic group, actually an outgrowth of the first, comprised those businessmen for whom the word "merchant" became too small to describe and who came to be called "manufacturers." Erastus Corning is the archetype. Emigrating from Connecticut early in the nineteenth century, as a plebian, he made his way up as a hardware merchant, and then as an iron manufacturer, president of the New York Central Railroad, and financier, to become Albany's wealthiest man, holding as lofty a patrician status, and as conservative an ideology, for his time as had Stephen Van Rensselaer for his.[6] Corning was a transitional figure: first a merchant patrician, then a member of the "manufacturing aristocracy." What Albany history shows is what Douglas Miller has found to be true in New York State, in his study of *Jacksonian Aris-*

[5] Hugh Meredith Flick, "Elkanah Watson: Gentleman-Promoter, 1758-1842" unpublished Ph.D. thesis, Columbia University, 1958, p. 107; Jabez D. Hammond, *History of Political Parties in the State of New York,* 3 vols. (Albany, 1842), I, 562, and Joel Munsell, *Annals of Albany,* 10 vols. (Albany, 1850-1869), X, 295; Irwin F. Cortelyou, *Ezra Ames of Albany* (New York, 1955), pp. 3, 120.
[6] Irene D. Neu, *Erastus Corning: Merchant and Financier, 1794-1872* (Ithaca, New York, 1960).

tocracy: that there was no hiatus between the old and the new aristocracies.[7] There was just a burst of democratic reform in the 1820s and 1830s that the perennial aristocrats were able to absorb. There was no hiatus between the merchant patriciate into which the Cassidys rose in the beginning of the nineteenth century and the manufacturing aristocracy in which Michael Nolan, the brewer who became Albany's first Irish mayor in 1878, and Anthony Brady, the utilities baron at the end of the century, found their places.

The story of the Irish immigration into Albany and of the establishment of Irish power there not only helps to explain how this city became as Irish as any in America. It also helps to explain how Albany has preserved its hierarchic social structure, and its conservatism, even into the twentieth century, as what a reformist Protestant clergyman recently called a "medieval fortress" against change.[8] The Irish not only adapted to that social structure with its conservative climate of opinion, they also reinforced it.

The story began back in the seventeenth century when Irishmen began trickling into the city. The first Irish settler of record was a farmer and collector of liquor excises with the "Hollandized" name of "Jan Andriessen de Iersman Van Dublingh." After him, other Irishmen migrated up the Hudson, some serving as soldiers in the British army and staying on to marry English and Dutch wives, some fighting against the British in the Revolution. Many of them disappeared, as Irishmen, from the historical record, as their names changed from Sullivan to Swillivaun, O'Connell to Coneel, Reilly to Reyley, and many lost their identity as Irishmen as they forgot their Catholic religion to become part of the Protestant Dutch culture. After the Revolution, a new group of immigrants, their Irish religion still fresh in their memories, established the first cohesive Irish Catholic community in the city.[9]

They were hospitably received, for Albany has a long tradition of tolerant pluralism dating back to 1643 when the first Protestant pastor, the Dutch Domine Megapolensis, had given haven to the Jesuit missionary, Father Isaac Jogues, in his

---

[7] *Jacksonian Aristocracy: Class and Democracy in New York, 1830-1860* (New York, 1967), pp. 80, 124, and *passim*.

[8] Sermon quoted in *Albany Knickerbocker News*, June 3, 1966.

[9] Franklin M. Danaher, " 'De Iersman Van Dublingh,' " pamphlet (Albany, 1907); Jacob I. Hotchkiss, "The Irish," in "Diverse Backgrounds of Old Albany," research manuscript (Albany Institute of History and Art, 1964), p. 3.

flight from the Mohawk Indians. They fraternized ecumenically with the Protestants. Thomas Cassidy, for example, who immigrated in 1790, joined the Mount Vernon Lodge of Masons, probably indifferent to rather than ignorant of the papal antagonism to Masonry. But they remained loyally Catholic, and in the late 1790s they gathered for Mass in the Cassidy home, in the Pine and Chapel Streets neighborhood, or at the James Duffy home in Court Street. And in 1798, with the blessing of Bishop Carroll in Baltimore, they laid the cornerstone of St. Mary's, the first Roman Catholic church upstate, at Pine and Chapel Streets. Priests were scarce in those days, so the president of the board of trustees, Thomas Barry, who had a tobacco store in State Street, conducted the ceremony, and some of the ritual, it is said, was Masonic. Albany Protestants gave money to help build the church, and the city donated the land.[10]

The small, square brick church served several hundred Irish Catholics of Albany into the 1820s, for the community grew only slowly in these years. In 1820, the identifiable Irish numbered some two percent of the 12,629 population of the city—a small community, perhaps, but a well-established one. In the second decade of the nineteenth century, the annual dinners of the St. Patrick's Society at Ladd's or Bements's coffee houses were social events that attracted the most respectable leaders of the Protestant establishment. In 1817, when Thomas Cassidy's son, John, was president of the society, as well as master of the Mount Vernon Lodge, he welcomed to the dinner Governor DeWitt Clinton and William James, that Presbyterian Irish financier who was to become the grandfather of Henry and William James.[11]

[10] George R. Howell and Jonathan Tenney, *Bi-Centennial History of Albany* (New York, 1886), pp. 750-752; Mount Vernon Lodge, No. 3, F.&A.M., *Charter, By-Laws, Condensed History, Officers,* (Albany, n.d.) p. 76; Martha J. F. Murray, "Memoir of Stephen Louis Le Couteulx de Caumont," *Publications of the Buffalo Historical Society,* IX (1906), 433-483; "'Masonic Emblems' Engraved on Cornerstone of St. Mary's Church, Albany, New York, and Laid with Masonic Ceremonies," *American Catholic Historical Researches,* XXIII (July, 1907), 255-258; Munsell, *Annals,* III, 179, and IV, 306.

[11] 1820 estimate based on count of 202 distinctively Irish names in federal MS census, and on *Souvenir of Centennial Celebration and Historical Sketch of St. Mary's Parish* (Albany, 1897), p. 12, report the congregation "numbered little more than 300" that year; *Albany Argus,* March 21, 1817. Seventy-six Albany Catholics, including Cassidys, Caggers, Goughs, and Mahers, were prosperous enough to sponsor publication of an American edition of *A Plain and Rational Account of the Catholic Faith* (Albany, 1814).

In the 1820s, the Erie Canal boom doubled Albany's entire polyglot population, drawing immigrants from England and Scotland and, especially, from New England. The old Dutch town became a predominantly Yankee city.[12] But the new immigration also included several hundred Irish, so that by 1830, the Irish had come to number somewhere between 1,000 and 2,000, or between five and ten percent of the city's total population of 24,211.[13] Many of the Irish newcomers were poor, for this was the time of the "real beginnings of poor emigration" from Ireland.[14] Some came up from New York City, more down from Canada, to work on the canals, and, in the slack winter months, to drift back into Albany. "The

[12] By 1820 only some five percent of the names in the federal MS census were distinctively Dutch, while most were Yankee or English or Scottish; Yankee predominance in the 1820s is described in Rowley, "Albany," chap. 1; by 1829, there were six Presbyterian churches, only two Dutch Reformed (Munsell, *Annals*, IX, 195-196); see also Timothy Dwight, *Travels in New-England and New York,* 3 vols., (New Haven, 1821), III, 529 and 534. By "Yankee" I mean a person of New England origin or descent.

[13] Estimate based on count of 588 distinctively Irish names in 1830 federal MS census and a probably scare guess by the anti-Catholic *Religious Monitor* ("Increase of Popery," VI, November, 1829, 286) that Catholics in the city "number 2,000."

[14] William Forbes Adams, *Ireland and Irish Emigration to the New World from 1815 to the Famine* (New Haven, 1932), p. 111.

Albany County Alms House, completed in 1826. From Reynolds, Albany Chronicles.

poor Irish have greatly increased in the streets," observed a
traveler revisiting the city; they came to number 40 of the 214
paupers in the Alms House; they lived in tenements and boarding houses along the canal basin waterfront, or in shanties in
the outskirts.[15] Driven from their homeland by the 1822 famine, they suffered the worst poverty Albany had ever seen and
in the winter of 1830 their plight moved the city fathers to
set up a soup kitchen in the basement of city hall.[16]

But the poor formed only the lower strata of the expanding
Irish community. Many settled Irishmen were rising in the
social order. Though census data for 1830 list sixty-three of
the Irish workingmen as "laborers," sixty were employed in
skilled building trades and manufacturing jobs or working as
cartmen and teamsters; twenty-nine other Irishmen had struck
out for themselves as grocers and merchants; and their community could boast two physicians, an attorney, a steamboat
captain, a brewer, a hotel keeper, and several teachers.[17] At
the top were those families—the Cassidys, Caggers, Goughs,
and Mahers—who had been running St. Mary's Church for
two generations and who now took the lead in erecting a new,
larger and handsomer structure. The business, social, and
political careers of two of these second-generation Irish-Americans illustrate the growing power of their community and of
what was coming to be its aristocracy.

One was James Maher. He was born in Ireland and spent
the first thirteen years of his life there until in 1797 his parents, who had emigrated to Albany when he was three, were
able to send for him. After apprenticing as a clerk in Thomas
Barry's tobacco shop, he ventured in 1810 into his own wholesale and retail grocery business, which came to handle
$150,000 a year in trade. When war came in 1812, he orga-
nized a group of Irish men into the Republican Green Rifle
Company and, as their captain, led them in the capture of
Little York on the Canadian border. He returned to Albany,
as a hero, to a prototypal career in Irish-American politics,
serving as the stalwart leader in the riverfront Fourth Ward
for Martin Van Buren's Albany Regency. As reward, the

[15] Mrs. Anne Royall, *The Black Book, or a Continuation of Travels in
the United States,* 2 vols. (Washington, 1828), II, 34; Munsell, *Annals,* IX,
198.
[16] MS minutes of the Albany Common Council, 1830-1831, p. 121.
[17] Based on count of distinctively Irish names in federal MS census and
city directory.

Regency made him clerk of the market, which must have helped his grocery business, and state librarian, a patronage post, and saw to it that he was elected alderman. In the fall of 1829, as the Irish population in the city increased and as some anxiously conservative Protestants grumbled about the "increase of Popery," the Regency decided to take the bull by the horns and run Maher for the countywide office of sheriff. The election campaign, in its focus on the religious issue, resembled the Al Smith presidential campaign one hundred years later. It is difficult to tell which party played the issue harder. The opposition, denying any bigotry, nevertheless noted Maher as a "native of *'the Emerald Isle,' and a devotee of the Church of Rome"* who could "command" the growing Irish vote; the Regency's *Argus* made all it could of his Irishness and called him as patriotic as John Carroll, the signer of the Declaration of Independence. Maher lost the election, but strengthened his party's hold on the Irish vote, and gained power in party councils. From the Yankee aristocrats who ran both the Democratic and Whig parties, Captain James Maher commanded respect; in his ward, he was boss; in the Irish community, at St. Mary's Church, where he was secretary, he was a patriarch.[18]

The career of John Cassidy was more significant, for it established a family tradition in the Irish community that compares with that of the Cornings in the Yankee community. He was born in Ireland, and emigrated to Albany with his father and mother in 1790. Starting as an apprentice butcher, he made his fortune as a meat and cattle dealer, and in 1812 he went to war as lieutenant in Captain Maher's Republican Greens. He emerged as the first political figure of his Irish community when in 1819 the Republicans (pre-Democrats) ran him for assistant alderman in the South End Second Ward. Not only did he win, but he helped carry the entire Republican ticket in this increasingly Irish ward. Politics buttressed the career of John Cassidy, as they did that of James Maher. The next year, both men were elected assistants, and in 1821 Cas-

[18] *Albany Argus,* Oct. 31, 1829; *Military Minutes of the Council of Appointment of the State of New York, 1783-1821,* ed. Hugh Hastings, 4 vols. (Albany, 1901), II, 1274; *Albany Advertiser,* Oct. 30, 1829; *Albany Argus,* Oct. 31, 1829; Thurlow Weed, *Autobiography* (Boston, 1884), pp. 448-449 (Weed, the Whig boss, wrote of his "warm personal friendship" for this "popular, adroit, and clear-headed Democratic leader."); *Albany Argus,* Oct. 16, 1829.

sidy was elected alderman, a position he continued to fill through the rest of the decade. He enjoyed the friendship not only of the Yankee leaders of the Van Buren Regency but of Governor DeWitt Clinton, whose opposition party occasionally supported him. In 1829, he and James Maher and Michael Cagger organized an Association of Friends of Ireland to make a citywide appeal for the Irish emancipation movement. And in the same year, Cassidy, as president of the board of trustees of St. Mary's Church, laid the cornerstone for the new church building, and angered the pastor by using the words of the Masonic ritual. Funds for the building came not only from the Irish parishioners, but from Protestant friends—Stephen Van Rensselaer, the Patroon, gave $100; Martin Van Buren, $50. The Protestant trustees of the Lancaster School loaned their building for masses during the construction period. The new church was designed by Philip Hooker, Albany's finest architect, who built the city's classically graceful Protestant churches and public buildings of this period. Cassidy's address, printed in the Albany papers as well as in the Catholic *Truth-Teller* in New York City, extolled the "principles of religious and political freedom and equality"—the pluralism—that had made the event possible. He, more than any other Irishman in Albany, had been accepted into the city's establishment. He sent two sons to its exclusive Albany Academy to prepare them, along with young aristocrats of the Dutch and Yankee communities, for prestigious careers. A year after the cornerstone laying, John Cassidy died, and *The Argus* said his funeral was the largest in the city since that of Governor Clinton. Coming to pay tribute were Governor Enos Throop, the city officers, and a "vast concourse of citizens" that included 300 Masons as well as members of the St. Patrick's Society.[19]

In obituary editorials, John Cassidy was, like most men of property, praised for being a "friend of the poor." And there is no doubt that he, and his Irish friends, and their political party and their church, did, as benevolent aristocrats, help

[19] *Memorial of William Cassidy* (Albany, 1874); *Military Minutes*, II, 1274; Munsell, *Annals*, VII, 140; *Albany Argus*, Sept. 29, 1820; Cuyler Reynolds, *Albany Chronicles* (Albany, 1906), p. 434; *New York Statesman and Advertiser*, Feb. 4, 1822; *Albany Argus*, Feb. 6, 1829; *Albany Daily Advertiser*, Oct. 15, 1829; Howell and Tenney, *Bi-Centennial History*, p. 752; *Souvenir of Celebration . . . of St. Mary's Parish*, p. 16; Munsell, *Annals*, IX, 216-217; Edward W. Root, *Philip Hooker* (New York, 1929), pp. 173-176; *New York Truth Teller*, Oct. 24, 1829; *Albany Argus*, April 26, 1830.

poor Irish newcomers in their struggle to survive. Before Cassidy died, St. Mary's, with the help first of a Protestant woman, then of three Sisters of Charity, had started the first parochial school in the city and an orphanage. In 1833, James Maher and his friends formed a Hibernian Provident Society to help the poor fund sickness insurance. Thomas Gough, who was vice-president of the St. Mary's trustees, was a bank agent and broker in emigrant tickets and remittances—those savings of Irish immigrants sent to their families abroad to help them come over. A door into Albany society had been opened, by 1830, for those thousands of poor Irish who would come over in the next twenty-five years.[20]

Between 1830 and 1855, the number of Irish in the city grew from some 2,000 to more than 23,000, to comprise 40 percent of the total city population.[21] This tremendous change was accomplished as peacefully as it was, and the struggle of the thousands of newcomers to survive was facilitated, in large part because of the existence of the aristocratically led Irish establishment.

The mid-nineteenth century newcomers were poorer to begin with than the early Irish settlers, and few of them would achieve the status of the Cassidys. They came into an Albany, and an America, where the industrial revolution was already hardening class lines; the Cassidys and Mahers had made their way up in the post-Revolutionary and Jacksonian eras, especially in the dynamically democratic 1820s.[22] Throughout the second quarter of the nineteenth century, the poor Irish crowded into the city. They came in a constant stream that became a torrent after the potato famines in the late 1840s, until in 1855 there were 14,165 Irish-born in the city.[23] They came from New York by steamboat and later by train, under arrangements made by Erastus Corning's New York Central with the immigrant agents; more came south from Canada,

[20] *Albany Argus*, April 24, 1830; Sister Mary Ancilla Leary, *History of Catholic Education in the Diocese of Albany* (Washington, 1957), pp. 1-3; Munsell, *Annals*, I, 242; *Albany Argus*, Aug. 26, 1852; Richard J. Purcell, "Irish Residents in Albany, 1783-1865," *The Recorder* (Bulletin of the American Irish Historical Society), XII (February, 1950), 12.

[21] The 1855 state MS census shows Irish-born and their children comprised 38.87 per cent of the total city population; with others of distinctively Irish names added, the percentage is 40.87.

[22] Miller, *Jacksonian Aristocracy*, p. 80 and chap. 4.

[23] In 1830, 3,199 of the city's population was foreign-born, mostly Irish (Sheet 352, 1830 federal MS census for Albany); in 1845, the figure was 5,759 (Munsell, *Annals*, X, 375); 1855 figure revealed by count in state MS census, which gives places of birth.

down through Lake Champlain and the canal, by boat, or on foot through Vermont; a few came over from Boston.[24] Some walked all the way. In the terrible cholera summers of 1832, 1849, and 1854, the Irish suffered not only the disease but the scorn of natives who blamed them for bringing it. In the summer of 1832, when 400 died in Albany, some immigrants died in the boats bringing them down from Canada; some were driven back by armed posses; 700 were quarantined on Green Island near Troy, and those who reached Albany were shunted into a hastily constructed quarantine shanty town.[25] The poor Irish begging in the streets had disturbed the respectable Yankees in the late 1820s; in the next thirty years the growing numbers of poor stirred greater uneasiness, as the city newspapers gave the impression that the Irish were a poor, ignorant, hard-drinking, and violent people.

They made a pathetic picture on their arrival on the docks and at the depot, where confusion sometimes led to riots provoked by hustling runners, often Irishmen themselves, who fought each others for the privilege of selling them over-priced or worthless tickets to the west, or boarding house reservations in Albany.[26] The newcomers slept overnight in freight cars or on the docks, or went to a boarding house, or the Alms House, to revive themselves for the search for work.

Their first homes in Albany were likely to be tenements, crowded with as many as a dozen families, in the South End or in "Gander Bay" (Canal Street in Sheridan Hollow), which was the worst slum in the city, or shanties on the outskirts. Through the window of a "rude" shack in Gander Bay, a newspaper reporter saw an Irishman and his wife and two children sitting around their table with a loaf of bread, a small piece of butter, and a broken pitcher of tea. In the bad winters of 1854 and 1855, police picked up and took to the Alms House such poor Irish folk as two young girls caught stealing wood for a fire from a neighbor's yard; a young mother found lying "insensible" with her infant child in the snow-covered street; a seventeen-year-old girl, well along in pregnancy,

[24] Harry H. Pierce, *Railroads of New York* (Cambridge, 1953), p. 65; the predominance of the Canadian route is suggested by the birthplaces of Irish children in the 1855 state MS census—of the children born on the migration to Albany, 113 were born in Canada, 99 in New York City, and 29 in Massachusetts.
[25] *The Cholera Record* (Albany, 1832); *Niles Register,* June 23 and Aug. 25, 1832; Charles E. Rosenberg, *The Cholera Years* (Chicago, 1962), p. 94.
[26] Friedrich Kapp, *Immigration and the Commissioners of Emigration of the State of New York* (New York, 1870), pp. 66 and 78-79.

found sleeping in a woodlot; a sixteen-year-old boy in rags and "nearly famished," wandering aimlessly in the streets; a boy and four infants found "literally wallowing in filth" in a condemned shack, in the care of two "abandoned females" who were "beastly drunk."[27]

The bottle had a role in the last story, headlined "Squalid Depravity," as it did in the report of a physician attending cholera victims in a Gander Bay flat in 1854. As he entered one bare room, he found two corpses on the floor; a girl appeared, her eyes glazed, a pitcher in one hand, a glass in another. She poured herself a drink and a moment later "fell to the floor, a corpse." The physician reported "rot-gut" rum killed as many victims as the cholera in Canal Street, but he added with understanding: "Many drank to drown grief and keep fear at bay."[28] These were the despairing newcomers who had lost the fight.

Not all the drinking was desperate. The Irish drank exuberantly, too, supporting the nearly 800 Albany grog shops that dismayed the temperance leaders, and enlivening the more staid Dutch and Yankee culture of the city with their zest at dances and raffles, their fellowship at wakes, their lusty gaming in a tavern backroom turned into a cockfighting pit or in a countryside grove where boxers outdid the city ban and fought for prizes. Frequent newspaper stories of gang fights gave the Irish a reputation for violence. There were occasional fights between Irishmen and Orangemen, Germans, Negroes, and the police, but mostly the Irish fought among themselves: the "Fardoonians" against the "Corkonians" over railroad jobs; "the Hills" against "the Creeks" and the "Canal boys" against the "market boys" in neighborhood feuds. Poverty, oppression, despair, drink—the slum experience of immigrants from many countries in their first adjustment to America—help explain why the Irish dominated the police news and made up the largest ethnic group in the penitentiary.[29]

[27] *Albany Register,* Aug. 1, 1854; *Albany Argus,* Feb. 14, 1855; *Albany Evening Journal,* Jan. 12, 1854; *Albany Argus,* May 14, 1855; *Albany Argus,* March 6, 1855; *Albany Argus,* July 23, 1855.
[28] *Albany Express,* Aug. 1, 1854.
[29] *Albany Statesman,* Feb. 19, 1857; *Albany Examiner,* March 20, 1841; *Albany Microscope,* March 5, 1842 and Sept. 17, 1846 and July 9, 1842; *Albany Citizen,* July 10, 1843; *Albany Evening Journal,* June 9, April 18 and Aug. 12, 1856; *Albany Citizen,* Aug. 24, 1843; Munsell, *Annals,* III, 333; *Albany Microscope,* July 17, 1841; Munsell, *Annals,* II, 301, and III, 244; *Albany Times,* Sept. 29, 1856; *Albany Citizen,* July 6, 1843; *Albany Argus,* Feb. 14, 1855 and David Dyer, *History of the Albany Penitentiary* (Albany, 1867) pp. 135-138.

"The Emigration Agent's Office—the passage money paid." From Frank Leslie's Illustrated Newspaper, *January 12, 1856.*

The wonder is that so many Irishmen landed on their feet rather than in jail. Most Irishmen stayed out of trouble, doing the lion's share of the work that was making Albany prosper, and most of them were rising economically, socially, culturally, and in political power. The census of 1855, the first to reflect the results of the big famine immigration, showed that of the 5,300 Irishmen with listed occupations less than half—2,194 —were unskilled laborers, while 2,731 held skilled jobs in foundries and factories, on the railroads, in the building trades, and as cartmen and clerks. Another 369 were in businesses, some on the bottom rung as peddlers, some running their own small shops or groceries, some well established as merchants or manufacturers. Forty-two were in the professions.[30]

Which is not to say that Irish working men did not have to struggle through hard times. In 1855 when there was heavy unemployment in the city, Irishmen's wives and daughters were sometimes able to keep working when they were not. Besides the 1,629 Irish women, mostly unmarried girls, who worked out as domestics, others worked in various jobs, ranging from washerwomen up to school teachers. Sometimes, when the men were laid off, their sons, as young as twelve, were able to work as apprentices in the iron foundries. Mechanics resented the "Berkshire system" that made this possi-

[30] Compiled from 1855 state MS census.

ble, not only because it shared their work with boys, at boys' pay, but because it required them to take time training apprentices from the time they could spend on their own work, for which they were paid at piece-rates. Against this system, as against the system of contract prison labor that took hundreds of jobs out of Albany to be done at cheap pay at Sing Sing, the Albany labor unions fought.

But even if hardening class lines limited their opportunities, the Irish were assured of a place in Albany society. The census picture of the residential distribution of the Irish in 1855 suggests both how well they had been accepted and how stratified their community was becoming. They were not ghettoized but were spread throughout the city; in none of the ten city wards was the population less than twenty percent Irish.[31] The poorest, in that bad unemployment year, were in the Alms House (166, or sixty percent of the total number of inmates were Irish), in the penitentiary (117 Irishmen of the total 209), and in downtown slum tenements and riverfront shanties. The 600 families which received coal and food relief that winter probably included many of those Irish who clustered together in the working class sections of the South and North Ends and in Gander Bay.[32] Single Irishmen, some transient workers and some settlers who would later bring a bride from the old country or take one in Albany, boarded in the central downtown section. Sixteen hundred girls and women worked, and often lived, as domestics in the "quality sections." But some successful Irishmen and their families had moved into homes of their own in these sections. Of the 4,000 Irish families in the city, 809 owned property. Up on Capitol Hill in the respectable Chestnut Street neighborhood lived the families of Michael Masterson, a street paver and secretary of the Laborers Mutual Benefit Society, and his brothers—Philip, also a paver; Patrick, a machine tender; and Francis, a laborer. They had all come over to Albany as young men in the 1830s. A rung higher on the social ladder and farther out in the residential tenth ward lived such prospering Irishmen as James Savage, merchant; James Brown, contractor; and Dennis B. Gaffney, lawyer and politician. At the top of the ladder, in some of the finest homes in the city, lived the Tracey, Cagger, and Cassidy families. Most of the families who had moved out, and up, were the settled Irish, who had been in Albany twenty

---

[31] Data in this paragraph compiled from 1855 state MS census.
[32] *Albany Argus*, Feb. 10, 1855.

years or longer. Some of them took in newcomers as boarders or servants.

One of the factors in the acceptance and consolidation of the Irish in Albany was the demand for labor through much of the 1830–1855 period. In these years, Albany was a boom town, its population growing along with the railroads, the stockyards built alongside Corning's New York Central Railroad shops in West Albany, the tremendous lumber market along the canal basin, and the iron stove foundries downtown.[33] When the railroads and foundries were being built, the city fathers, headed by the Dutch patriarch Stephen Van Rensselaer and the Yankee Erastus Corning, advertised a welcome to "industrious mechanics," and contractors persuaded the pastor of St. Mary's Church to write a plea in the Catholic *Freeman's Journal* in New York for 300 men to lay rails.[34] The demand for their brawn gave the Irish economic power.

And their political power had increased steadily since the days when James Maher and John Cassidy had first been elected to office. The Irish constituted a large percentage of the voting population. They also helped provide the muscle on which both major political parties relied in the rough and rowdy vote-buying and bullying politics of this era. These were the years, 1835 to 1855, when the Whigs challenged the Democratic Regency, won most of the local elections, and gave Albany a taste of two-party government.[35] Bidding for the Irish vote downtown, Thurlow Weed, the Whig boss, organized his own gang under his Irish lieutenant, George W. Daly, to resist the Democratic gang of Captain James Maher.[36] But most of the Irish stuck with the Democratic Party. They moved into city patronage jobs and increased their influence in the firefighting and police forces.[37] While most of the aldermen in the 1840s and 1850s were Yankee and Dutch, Irishmen were frequently elected in the heavily Irish first, second, seventh, and eighth wards, and in 1858 ten of the twenty-two members of the City Democratic Committee were Irishmen.[38]

[33] Albany's population increased sharply each decade until the 1880s when it rose only 4.6 percent and then dropped in the 1890s. (*Eighteenth Census of the United States*, Vol. 1, Pt. 34, p. 9.) These Albany industries declined gradually after the Civil War.

[34] Munsell, *Annals*, X, 384-390; Purcell, "Irish Residents," p. 15.

[35] Munsell, *Annals*, X, 242, 267, 274, 279, 292, and Reynolds, *Albany Chronicles*, pp. 534, 546, 552, 566, 572.

[36] Weed, *Autobiography*, pp. 448-449.

[37] Thomas G. Ford, ed., *History of the Albany Fire Department* (Albany, 1924), p. 126 and *passim;* 1855 state MS census shows eleven Irish policemen.

Three more prestigious Irishmen—Dennis Gaffney who won
a local judgeship in the 1830s, the young lawyer Peter Cagger, and the young editor William Cassidy—became influential
in the Barnburner wing of the party in the county.[39]

If economic and political power helped the Irish become
established in Albany, so did their church, which grew in the
second quarter of the century to become the city's strongest
institution. The Catholic population very soon outgrew the
second St. Mary's Church, built in 1829. As the number of
its communicants multiplied, a second parish, St. John's in the
South End, was formed in 1837, and a third, St. Joseph's in
Arbor Hill, in 1843. By 1847, Catholics in Albany and in upstate New York had grown so numerous that the church established a new Diocese of Albany, and Bishop John Hughes of
New York sent up the tall, slender John McCloskey, a Brook-
lyn-born Irishman, to be its first bishop. For a few years he sat
at St. Mary's, putting his authoritative foot down on the independent lay trustees, and then between 1848 and 1852 he
built a $250,000 brownstone Gothic cathedral that seated
2,500 persons and towered up over the South End as a symbol

---

[38] Munsell, *Annals,* X, 340, 349, 361-362, 370, 378; *Albany Express,*
Sept. 11, 1858.
    [39] *Albany Mercury and Independent Examiner,* July 8, 1835; *Albany At-
las,* March 19, 1846; *Albany Argus,* April 10 and 14, 1846; *Albany Evening
Journal,* April 2, 1846.

Second St. Mary's Church, A▪
From Dillon, The Historic
of St. Mary's.

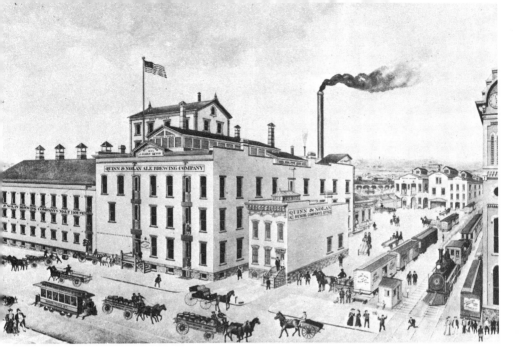

Quinn and Nolan Ale Brewing Company, watercolor, 1902, by James MacGregor. Collection Albany Institute of History and Art.

of Irish Catholic power. At the same time, the new diocese built a fifth church, Holy Cross, for its German members. By 1855, Roman Catholicism, with 13,000 communicants, had become the largest single denomination in Albany.[40]

Bishop McCloskey came to Albany not only as an authority to coordinate Irish Catholic power in the city, building churches and shoring up the Catholic faith, but also as a shepherd to the newcomers at the time of their greatest need. He helped to arrange their arrival and settlement, mediated between them and travel agents and city authorities, sought lost sons and daughters for their parents in the old country, raised funds for his people as they were "flying from starvation at home" to poverty in a strange city.[41] He and his church developed a system of charities to match that of the Protestants. They built two asylums to care for 150 orphans and organized a St. Vin-

[40] Howell and Tenney, *Bi-Centennial History,* pp. 753-754; Christine Sevier, *History of the Albany Cathedral of the Immaculate Conception, 1852-1927* (Albany, 1927), *passim.;* F. B. Hough, ed., *Census of the State of New York for 1855* (Albany, 1857), p. 444, reporting "usual number attending" church as 13,000 Roman Catholics and 13,835 Protestants. St. Joseph's, which became the parish of the Cassidys and several other aristocratic families, built a magnificent Gothic gray stone church in the late 1850s.

[41] Letters in John Cardinal McCloskey Papers at St. Joseph's Seminary, Dunwoodie, Yonkers, N. Y.: Bishop Fitzpatrick of Boston to McCloskey, May 8, 1850 (Box A-22); John Martin of Donegal, Ireland to McCloskey, Feb. 13, 1851 (Box A-25); McCloskey to Society for the Propagation of the Faith, 1850 (Box A-38).

Cathedral of the Immaculate Conception. From Weise, History of the City of Albany.

cent de Paul Society to distribute food, clothing, and fuel to poor families. They encouraged the rich Irish to help the workingmen build up the insurance fund of the Hibernian Provident Society. Irish Catholic charities were crucial in a city which spent less than ten percent of its public funds for the poor.[12]

Albany was also miserly in its expenditures for public education—providing schools for less than half of its school-age children—and it was to meet the need for education, as well as for Catholic teaching, that the church built its own parochial schools. By 1855, schools at St. Mary's, St. John's, and St. Joseph's had an enrollment of 600. That was a small fraction of the 6,000 in the public schools, but the church was beginning to build up a school system of its own that in the twentieth century would provide for nearly half the city's chil-

[12] "Report of Select Committee appointed to visit Charitable Institutions supported by the State, and all city and county poor and work houses and jails," *New York Senate Documents,* 80th Session, I, 97; *Albany Atlas and Argus,* March 3 and 8, 1856; *Albany Evening Journal,* April 1, 1845; "Chamberlain's Report of Receipts and Expenditures from November 1, 1877 to November 1, 1878," *Proceedings of the Common Council,* 1879, pp. 3-24 (even by this year the city was allotting only four percent of its expenditures to aid the poor).

dren—a greater proportion than in any other large city in the state.[43]

As Irish Catholic churches and schools grew, so did Irish Catholic culture. The Irish musician at the cathedral, Richard J. Carmody, was called by "Staccato," who reviewed church music for the Albany *Times,* the best organist with the best choir in town. Aspiring young Catholic intellectuals formed a Library Association, then a Catholic Literary Society, then a Catholic Lyceum, which brought to town such lecturers as Orestes Brownson and James A. McMaster. Some young Irish aristocrats in the predominantly Yankee lyceum, the Young Men's Association for Mutual Improvement, were influential enough to have its lecturers include Thomas D'Arcy McGee and Thomas Francis Meagher as well as Emerson and Oliver Wendell Holmes. The older Irish intelligentsia gathered at the Maiden Lane home of the widow Margaret Cassidy or in Bishop McCloskey's parlor to listen to music or to talk with their friends, Dr. Edmund Bailey O'Callaghan, the physician and former Irish nationalist reformer turned historian, and James Hall, the Yankee paleontologist and Catholic convert. Other guests would be such patrons of Irish culture and the church as Peter Cagger, the lawyer, and John Tracey, who with O'Callaghan, had fled Canada after the abortive Patriots' Revolution of 1837 to become, as a spirits distiller, the sixth richest man in Albany and the owner of the General Philip Schuyler mansion.[44]

The social and political growth of the Irish community by the 1850s was dramatically demonstrated by the careers of two of the sons of John Cassidy. William Cassidy, one of Albany's most distinguished and powerful newspaper editors, grew up in the family home in Maiden Lane, was classically

[43] "Public Education in Albany," *The New York Teacher,* I (April, 1853), 212, and *Annual Report of the Board of Education to the Common Council,* 1858, p. 3; Leary, *History of Catholic Education,* pp. 5-11; Records of Bureau of Statistical Services, New York State Education Department for 1967.

[44] *Albany Times,* Nov. 22, 1856; *Albany Evening Journal,* Jan. 11, 1854 and Nov. 28, 1855; lecture record books in Young Men's Association collection, Harmanus Bleecker Library, Albany; Mrs. Annie Blount Storrs, "Recollection of Bishop McCloskey," MS memoir in McCloskey Papers (Box A-37); *Albany Argus,* July 13, 1875; Amasa J. Parker, ed., *Landmarks of Albany County* (Syracuse, 1897), II, 5; list of Albany citizens paying taxes on income over $20,000 in 1863 in Joel Munsell, *Collections on the History of Albany,* 4 vols. (Albany, 1865-1871), II, 180; C. R. Roseberry, "South End Was Albany's Real Cradle," *Albany Times-Union,* Sept. 2, 1951.

educated at Albany Academy and Union College, and began to study law in John Van Buren's office. In the early 1840s, his interest turned to journalism as he began writing for Van Buren's Barnburner and Free Soil wing of the Democratic Party, and in 1843 he became editor of the wing's *Atlas*. For thirteen years he fought the more conservative *Argus* and the Hunker wing of the party, partly on grounds of principle, partly in protest against the *Argus'* state printing "monopoly" and the Hunkers' corner on patronage. In those years, he and his lawyer friend and brother-in-law, Peter Cagger, challenged Erastus Corning, the Hunker patriarch of what the *Atlas* called the "Bank Regency" of the party. It was not until 1856 that Governor Horatio Seymour was able to negotiate harmony in the party, to resolve the Barnburner-Hunker feud, to combine the two papers under Cassidy's editorship, and to unite these two young Irish aristocrats with Corning and the traditionally conservative Albany Democrats. Then for seventeen years, until his death in 1873, William Cassidy was the voice of that conservative Democracy, as well as of his own Irish Catholic people. They could count on him, as they could on Thurlow Weed of the Republican *Journal,* to preach tolerant pluralism and attack nativism; they didn't need an Irish nationalist paper of their own. Cassidy shunned the hurly-burly of the public politics, but he and Cagger became members of the state Democratic committee and with Dean Richmond, the chairman, ran the party. A tall, bespectacled man who "walked with his head inclined forward," he liked to translate French and Italian poetry in the study of the sumptuous house he built at 19 South Hawk Street, near the cathedral. At fifty, at the golden summit of his career, he made the American aristocrat's grand tour through Europe.[45]

The career of Cassidy's younger brother, DeWitt Clinton Cassidy, while less spectacular is nevertheless interesting as a symbol of the victory of the Irish over nativist reaction in Albany. He studied at Mount Saint Mary's College, became a lawyer, and was elected city attorney. Even more significant was his election in 1857 as the first Irish Catholic president of the Young Men's Association for Mutual Improvement. The

[45] Howell and Tenney, *Bi-Centennial History,* p. 358, and *Memorial of William Cassidy; Albany Atlas,* April 11, 1846; Herbert D. A. Donovan, *The Barnburners* (New York, 1925), p. 88; Stewart Mitchell, *Horatio Seymour of New York* (Cambridge, 1938), pp. 85-86, 149, 209; *Memorial of William Cassidy,* p. 100 and *passim; Albany Express,* Oct. 13, 1866.

William Cassidy. From Memorial of William Cassidy.

YMA, a pioneer in the national lyceum movement, was the cultural center of the city, bringing to it an impressive array of lecturers and channeling the drive of young men to "improve" themselves in its debates and in its reading rooms. While it had been dominated by the Yankees and the Dutch from its beginning in 1833, it had always included a handful of educated Irish members, and one of its founders had been the young lawyer Peter Cagger. Its capacity for tolerance was tested by the "Know-Nothingism" of 1855. That year Albany came as close as it ever did to "going nativist," when the American Party won 3,000 votes in the city, and when a nativist editor ran for president of the YMA. He was defeated by the more tolerant young men, Yankees as well as "Romanists," who then proceeded to take up the anti-nativist cause by choosing DeWitt Clinton Cassidy as their orator in the city's Fourth of July celebration. Speaking in the Third Presbyterian Church, Cassidy preached pluralism, extolling New York State's "cosmopolitan character" and "large heart" and its "widest freedom" and hospitality to "difference of language, of birth, of religion, all blending into a common allegiance." Two years later, when the "Know-Nothing" virus had abated, Cassidy ran for YMA president and won by a vote of 413 to 406. At least eleven new Irish members were taken into the YMA just before the election and their votes, and those of other Irish members, undoubtedly helped him. It was a victory for Irish political power as well as for Albany's pluralist tradition.[46]

In the quarter century following Cassidy's victory, the Irish population in Albany grew from 23,443 to 31,377, and continued to form the largest ethnic group in the city.[47] The Irish obviously had political power, which they demonstrated at the polls and in the patronage they held. Undoubtedly the Irish vote contributed to the dominance of the Democrats who won most of the mayoralty elections from 1856 to the end of the century.[48] In reward for faithful service, the Irish increased their share of city patronage; in 1875, for instance, Irishmen held the top four jobs at the Alms House, and there were 58 Irish policemen including Chief John Moloy and 28 Irish firemen including Chief James McQuade.[49]

And Irish economic power continued to grow. More Irish families owned property and more lived in better homes dispersed more widely throughout the city. While the number of Irishmen classified as laborers barely increased, from 2,169 to 2,317, the number of skilled workers nearly doubled, from 2,806 to 4,698, as did the number in business and the professions.[50] Fewer Irish women worked as domestics, more as factory hands, clerks, and teachers. Although the Yankees still controlled the great wealth and heavy industries of Albany, Irishmen like John Tracey and John McKnight came to dominate the liquor and beer manufacture industry. The real base of Irish economic power was in the labor movement, which

[46] *Albany Argus*, June 27, 1863; newspaper clippings and minutes books of YMA in Young Men's Association collection; Wallace K. Schoenberg, "The Young Men's Association, 1833-1876: The History of a Social-Cultural Organization," unpublished Ph.D. dissertation, New York University, 1962, *passim*; John J. Hill, *Reminiscences of Albany* (New York, 1884), p. 5; on American Party in Albany elections, see *Albany Express*, Nov. 6 and 7, 1855, and *Albany Evening Journal*, April 7 and 10 and June 13, 1856 and Rowley, "Albany," chap. 7, in which nativism in Albany is discussed; *New York Freeman's Journal*, July 21, 1855; YMA minutes of Feb. 2, 1857; *Albany Statesman*, Feb. 5 and 6, 1857; *Albany Times*, Feb. 4, 1857.

[47] Based on count of Irish-born, their children and others with distinctively Irish names in the 1875 state MS census. This indicates the Irish comprised 36 percent of the city population, compared with 40 percent in 1855. But Irish women who married either non-Irish or Irish without distinctively Irish names and their children were lost to the count. It is probable the Irish held their proportionate strength, if they did not actually increase it.

[48] Reynolds, *Albany Chronicles*, pp. 608, 640, 656, 662, 670, 680, 697, 702, 713, 720, 730, 738, 748.

[49] 1875 state MS census.

[50] 1875 state MS census.

John Tracey. From Cooney, St. Agnes' Cemetery.

emerged tougher from some bloody strikes against Yankee industry in the 1860s. Irishmen became the movement's leaders, dominating, by the mid-1880s, the painters, gas and steamfitters, brewery workers, and stove mounters' assemblies of the Knights of Labor.[51]

The Irish church grew, from five parishes in 1855 to ten in 1875, and its schools and charities expanded. While in 1855 only 600 Catholic children went to church schools, in 1875 more than 2,000 went to twelve parochial schools and two private high schools—the Christian Brothers Academy for boys and the Academy of the Sacred Heart for girls, which were the counterparts of the aristocratic Albany Academy and the Female Academy of the Yankee-Dutch community. Increasingly the church administered to the Irish poor and sick, through the work of the St. Vincent de Paul Society, the two orphan asylums, a home for the aged, and the Catholics' own hospital, St. Peter's, which was built in 1869 largely with money from the estate of Peter Cagger. Catholic charity was paltry compared with the hundreds of thousands spent to build churches, but it was impressive when compared with the city's expenditures for the poor. The Irish were cared for, in short,

[51] A. Bleecker Banks, compiler, *1686-1886. Albany Bi-Centennial. Historical Memoirs* (Albany, 1888), pp. 228-229.

by a church system of institutions that marked them off as a distinct community, if not a separate city. After 1867, they could even count on being buried in a separate St. Agnes Cemetery, next to the Protestant Albany Rural Cemetery. And there was no doubt that the system was Irish-dominated. After Bishop McCloskey went to New York to become archbishop, other Irish bishops succeeded him, and in 1875, the year that McCloskey became the first Amercian cardinal, twelve of the nineteen priests in Albany were Irish.[52]

There was a gap between the Irish Catholic and the Yankee-Dutch communities. That they could be coolly separate is suggested by the story of an Irishwoman on a horse-car who overheard two Yankee women talking about her people and her North Albany neighborhood. As the Irishwoman got up to leave the car, she tossed her head at them and said, "Let ye both move to hell. Ye'll find no Irish there." The same hatred and separation was expressed in a battle of tracts waged in

[52] *Sadlier's Catholic Directory, Almanac, and Ordo for the Year of Our Lord 1875* (New York, 1875), pp. 109-118; Leary, *History of Catholic Education, passim* (Sacred Heart had many Protestant pupils, pp. 186-187); Howell and Tenney, *Bi-Centennial History*, pp. 728-729; Munsell, *Collections*, III, 352 and 357; John Cardinal Farley, *Life of John Cardinal Mc-Closkey* (New York, 1918), pp. 216-217 and chap. 8.

Peter Cagger. From Cooney, St. Agnes' Cemetery.

the 1870s by the minister of the First Dutch Reformed Church and an Irish physician over whether the Protestant Bible should be used in public schools and whether public funds should support Catholic schools. The cold scorn of the minister's tone and the ranting anger of the physician's bespoke the limits of communication between the two communities.[53]

But the Irish, especially the aristocrats, found remarkable and subtle ways of bridging the gap, of making the necessary connections for the accommodation of power between the two communities. Working class and bourgeois Irishmen served mostly in their own militia companies, the Emmet and Worth Guards, but some aristocrats like Peter Cagger became life members of the city's elite Burgesses Corps. Young Catholic men and women went to their own Catholic Lyceum, but by 1880 nearly a hundred rising Irishmen had made it into the Young Men's Association. Gradually rich Irishmen were being elected directors of corporations. Erastus Corning's powerful Albany City Bank, for instance, took onto its board Peter Cagger in 1857, William Cassidy in 1869, Anthony N. Brady, the utilities and traction company financier, in 1888, and Charles Tracey in 1890. Irish power and patronage grew in the Democratic Party, and in 1864, when the elite of the party organized a City Democratic Association to discuss "principles" (and recruit young intellectuals), thirteen of the Irish elite were on the board of directors.[54] The keystone in the arch of accommodation was that most aristocratic institution in Albany, the Fort Orange Club, formed in 1880, to consist of

gentlemen who represented that which was best in Albany, the men of distinction, of culture, of good manners, of high character, of attainments, of social quality, the men who were born at the top, as well as those who possessed the qualities which make good men and had risen to the top.[55]

[53] Story told by C. R. Roseberry, "Old Albany: Lumber Brought Wealth," *Albany Times-Union*, Nov. 11, 1951; Rev. Rufus W. Clark, *The Question of the Hour: The Bible and the School Fund* (Boston, 1870) and Dr. James C. Hannan, *The Question Solved* (Albany, 1870).

[54] *Banquet of the Albany Burgesses Corps in Commemoration of its Semi-Centennial* (Albany, 1883); 1881 membership list (in scrapbook in Young Men's Association collection) shows 93 of the 1,204 members had distinctively Irish names; Herbert F. Prescott, *The National Commercial Bank of Albany. Three Quarters of a Century. Its Officers and Directors.* (Albany, 1901), p. 36—in 1971 an Irish aristocrat, Frank Welles McCabe, is chairman of the bank while Mayor Erastus Corning II, great-grandson

William D. Morange. From Cooney, St. Agnes' Cemetery.

Erastus Corning, Jr. was, naturally, the first president, but Michael N. Nolan, president of the Beverwyck Brewing Company, and John H. Farrell, publisher of *The Times-Union,* were founding members; later the sons of William Cassidy and John Tracey were taken in, and in 1898 Charles Tracey became the first Irish president of the club.[56]

Two priests, both intellectual aristocrats, also helped bridge the gap. One was the learned and sophisticated Father Edward Terry of St. Ann's parish in the South End, where he worked with a rabbi and a Lutheran minister to smooth Irish-German relations in the neighborhood. He had studied at the Universities of Louvain and Chicago, and in Albany, he fraternized with the elite at the Albany Institute of History and Art, where he was a member, and at the Fort Orange Club, where he became a non-resident member.[57] The other was the Yankee Protestant-born Clarence A. Walworth, son of State Chancellor Reuben Walworth, who went over to Rome in the Oxford Movement to become a pioneering Paulist missionary and

of Corning the First, sits on the board; *Constitution and By-Laws of the Albany City Democratic Association* (Albany, 1864), pp. 17-18.

[55] Grange Sard, *Historical Sketch of the Fort Orange Club of Albany, N.Y.* (Albany, 1902), p. 5.

[56] *Constitution, By-Laws, Officers and Members of the Fort Orange Club of Albany* (Albany, published annually), for these years.

[57] *History of St. Ann's Parish, 1866-1966* (Albany, 1966); Thomas F. O'Donnell and Hoyt C. Franchere, *Harold Frederic* (New York, 1961), pp. 42-44, pointing out Father Terry suggested to Frederic the character of Father Forbes in his novel, *The Damnation of Theron Ware.*

then served as priest at St. Mary's Church from 1866 to 1900. He had connections with the Protestant aristocracy—with the Pruyns, Townsends, and Van Rensselaers with whom he had gone to "the Academy"—and with the politicians who ran City Hall. An intellectual who wrote frequently for the *Catholic World,* he made his rectory a "rendezvous for cultured Catholics of Albany," such as the Caggers, Traceys, James Hall, Dr. O'Callaghan, and William Morange, a later president of the Young Men's Association. While his interest in science places him among the "liberals" in the Catholic Church in America, he was a conservative priest in conservative Albany. He ruled his parish with a firm discipline, preaching temperance and the rights of property and the "rights of labor" to work during strikes. Albany Yankee businessmen appreciated his "Rights of Labor" sermon, as they did the authoritative control the Catholic Church exerted over so many of their restive employees. In his old age, Father Walworth cut a Patroon-like figure as he walked through Albany streets in his cassock, his tall, broad frame "bowed with the weight and silvered with the honor of his eighty years," his arm thrown for support over the shoulder of Lem, his faithful black servant.[58]

The conservative climate of opinion of Albany had turned others back from their adventuring—Dr. O'Callaghan, who gave up revolutionary politics for the study of history, and William Cassidy, who moved from Free Soilism and Barnburnerism to the "harder" brand of Democracy preached by Corning and Seymour. As settled, affluent men, they felt no aching eagerness to change the structure of their society, to increase the working class' share in Albany's wealth, to share human rights with black people, to question such basic Albany values as prudence.[59] It was natural that Michael N. Nolan, the first Irishman to be elected mayor of Albany, was a conservative and prudent man.

Nolan's election as mayor in 1878 was the climactic victory

[58] Ellen H. Walworth, *Life Sketches of Father Walworth, With Notes and Letters* (Albany, 1907), p. 219 and *passim;* Robert D. Cross, *Emergence of Liberal Catholicism in America* (Cambridge, 1858), pp. 152-153 and 272; "Rights of Labor" sermon in *Life Sketches,* pp. 227-234; description of aged Walworth quoted in *Life Sketches,* p. 353.

[59] An editorial in Cassidy's *Albany Atlas and Argus* opposed suffrage for Negroes because they "are a separate race, which can never amalgamate with the white race and must always continue a distinct and peculiar people." (Nov. 7, 1860).

for Irish power in Albany in the nineteenth century. And it was a conservative Democratic, not a radically democratic, victory. Nolan, a portly, bearded man, had been born in Ireland, and after coming to Albany had made his way up in Horatio Alger style—bookkeeping at John McKnight's brewery, reading law in Peter Cagger's office, working as a ticket agent for the New York Central, and during the war, as an assistant superintendent for a railway in California. He married the daughter of an Albany brewer and after the war he and his brother-in-law, Terence Quinn, made the business the largest ale and beer manufactory in town. Nolan took over as president in 1876 when Quinn became the first Albany Irishman elected to Congress, and in 1878 he took over City Hall. He was elected mayor partly because Irish power had by then come of age and partly because he was a safe, conservative man. Some workers, disillusioned with the Democratic Party, nominated their own Independent Labor Democratic candidate to fight the competition of contract prison labor, and a

Michael Nolan. From Reynolds, Albany Chronicles.

group of businessmen, mostly Yankees, put up their conservative candidate for the Republicans. The regular Democratic
organization moved Nolan into the breach, touting him as
both a self-made businessman and as a "friend of labor," because he was a large employer, and also because he promised
to fight the prison contracts. He wooed enough of the dissident workers back into the Democratic fold to win 8,916
votes, compared to 5,358 for the independent labor man and
4,500 for the Republican. The loyal Democrats marched out
to his upper Broadway home to serenade him as the "first
Mayor of Irish birth," while he celebrated his inauguration day
by sending out brightly decorated wagons to distribute a new
Beverwyck lager beer to all the saloons in the city. Nolan was
a new kind of authority figure, holding his people in line
against the temptations of a labor reform movement. In his
first year in office, he won praise even from the Republican
Express for his "prudence and economy" in paring the budget
and keeping the tax rate down.[60]

The story of the Irish aristocracy's role in establishing the
power of the Irish community as co-equal with that of the
Dutch-Yankee community can end with Nolan's election. The
basic power structure of Albany had now been formed: It was
a *dyarchy,* the kind of structure that results when "two hier-
archies share a domain of power, and are equal in power
status."[61] Beginning with Nolan came a new generation of
Gilded Age Irish aristocrats to increase the power of their
community as well as their own fortunes.[62]

The influence of the pre-Civil War Irish aristocracy faded.
Charles Tracey kept his father John's name alive—with his

[60] *Albany Times-Union,* June 1, 1905; *Albany Argus,* June 19, 1878;
Reynolds, *Albany Chronicles,* p. 674; *Albany Argus,* April 10 and May 9,
1878; *Albany Express,* Dec. 20, 1878.
[61] Harold D. Lasswell and Abraham Kaplan, *Power and Society* (New
Haven, 1950), p. 204.
[62] After Nolan's re-election in 1880, his administration aroused a reform
movement to attack its mounting expenditures and patronage appointments
and its dealings with contractors and the electric street lighting company.
(See *Annual Report of The Council of Thirteen of the Citizens' Association
of Albany for the Year 1881-2* [Albany, 1882]) When Nolan's re-election
in 1882 was challenged in court on charges of vote frauds, he yielded
to his Yankee reformist opponent, Dr. John Swinburne, and to the "pressure
of his business interests" and went back to his brewery and fine racing
horses. (*Albany Argus,* June 23, 1883; Reynolds, *Albany Chronicles,* p.
717.) Other Irish aristocrats of the Gilded Age included Edward Maher,
manager of the street lighting company and mayor in 1888, and Anthony
N. Brady, utilities and traction company tycoon. (Reynolds, *Albany Chronicles,* p. 712, and *Dictionary of American Biography,* II, 582.)

service in the Holy Land and Rome with the Pontifical Zou-
aves, his glittering marriage to a French-Canadian girl in the
cathedral in Montreal, his liquor business, his three terms in
Congress, and his election to the presidency of the Fort Orange
Club in 1898.[63] The Cassidy family retired from public life,
one of William's sons becoming a gentleman artist. After Peter
Cagger was killed in a carriage accident in New York, where
he was on State Democratic Committee business, his family
was remembered chiefly for its gifts to St. Peter's Hospital.
But while the Cassidy-Cagger-Maher elite gave way to that
of the Nolans, Bradys, and Farrells, the dyarchic power structure of Albany society, which they and the always conservative
Albany Catholic Diocese had helped build, persisted. Their
Democratic Party kept the labor movement in loyal line, safe
from such temptations as the Greenback Labor movement,
because, as an Irish orator put it in 1886, his people had "too
much gratitude to the land of their adoption" to flirt with
socialism or "to permit them to destroy or aid in destroying
the institutions and laws they have sworn to obey."[64] The Irish
aristocrats accommodated the power they had, with the loyal
support of their lower class countrymen, to the power of the
Dutch-Yankee aristocracy, to form a stable dyarchic social
order, resistant to change. It would persist for years to come,
even as aristocrats of other newcomer groups—German, Jewish, Italian, and even to a small extent some black bourgeoisie
leaders—were let into the ruling circle and Albany became,
technically, an oligarchy. The Dutch Patroons and merchant
patricians had started it, the Yankees learned the way, and the
Irish reinforced it. There was something in the character of
the Irish community that meshed with what a perceptive Albany journalist said about his city in 1842: ". . . in no other
place in the Union is this aristocratical feeling carried to such
an extent . . . We have aristocrats here without number."[65]

[63] Parker, *Landmarks*, II, pp. 5-6; *Albany Argus*, June 15, 1883.
[64] Hugh Reilly, quoted in Banks, *Albany Bi-Centennial*, pp. 282-283.
After the failure of the Independent Labor movement against Nolan in the
spring of 1878, the National Greenback Labor Party was able that fall to
muster less than 3,400 votes in the city. (*Albany Express*, Nov. 6, 1878.)
[65] *Albany Microscope*, Feb. 26, 1842.

Making It in America: Social Mobility in Mid-Nineteenth Century Poughkeepsie

By CLYDE GRIFFEN

Comparing Poughkeepsie with Boston, as revealed in Stephan Thernstrom's recent study, Clyde Griffen of Vassar College offers a method of examining the relationship between ethnic origin and social mobility in America. This essay was originally presented at the Organization of American Historians meeting in Los Angeles in April 1970.

Many cities in the northeastern United States provided a major test in the mid-nineteenth century for the national faith in equal opportunity, the belief that men could make it in America on their merits alone, regardless of race, religion, or previous condition. The national experiment with Reconstruction in the South aroused hopes and expectations in the small black populations of these cities at the very time when mass immigration from northwestern Europe, especially Ireland and Germany, brought large numbers of alien newcomers to them.

We know quite a bit about prejudices and overt discrimination against both groups, but much less about the opportunities for particular ethnic groups except in a few large cities, and very little about how the experience of these minority groups compares with that of native whites in different types of urban communities.[1] At the extremes, we do not know

---

[1] Terminology: In the text of this essay, "native whites" will refer to all third or more generation Americans. In the tables "NBNP" will refer to these native-born of native parentage. In comparing my results for Poughkeepsie with those of Stephan Thernstrom for Boston, the reader should

New York History October 1970

151

whether immigrants, blacks, and their children fared better or
worse in a metropolis with many large factories and a complex commercial and financial life or in a small city with diversified manufactures and commerce conducted largely in
small shops. The present essay hopes to provoke more interest
in this kind of comparative study by relating a close examination of the experience of various ethnic groups in one small
city—Poughkeepsie, New York—to Stephen Thernstrom's
pioneering investigation of social mobility in Boston.[2] (Table
1).

Beyond the obvious contrast in scale and complexity of
economic life, the two cities differed in ethnic composition
and in the response of manufacturing interests to a greatly increased supply of cheap labor. In Boston the huge influx of
Irish in the late 40s created a higher proportion of foreign-
born by the 1850 census. Thereafter the proportion in Boston
declined; in Poughkeepsie, it increased. By 1880 first and second generation Americans constituted nearly one-half of the
population of this small city.

More important, although the Irish predominated among
immigrants in both cities, they constituted the vast majority
only in the metropolis. Whereas the German population in
Boston, always small, grew slowly, being less than 2% of
all inhabitants by 1865, the German-born in Poughkeepsie

remember that he has used the label "WASP" for third or more gener-
ation Americans in his "Immigrants and WASPS: Ethnic Differences in
Occupational Mobility in Boston, 1890-1940," Thernstrom and Richard
Sennett, eds., *Nineteenth Century Cities: Essays in the New Urban History*
(New Haven, 1969). All references for comparison to tables published in
Thernstrom's or my previous essay on Poughkeepsie in that book appear
in parentheses at the end of citations, as do references to tables in Oscar
Handlin's *Boston's Immigrants*. References to my tables in this essay ap-
pear in the text itself; subsequent references in footnotes appear without
parentheses.

I have preferred the contrasting terms "white collar" and "blue collar"
to "manual" and "non-manual," but I have used "low manual" to refer
to unskilled and semi-skilled workers combined and occasionally used
"manual" to refer to all blue collar workers. All foremen, supervisors, and
boss craftsmen are classified "white collar" in my study.

[2] The comparison in this paper with Thernstrom's investigation is based
on his essay cited above. Since that investigation starts with workers first
listed in the 1880 census whereas mine covers workers listed in all federal
censuses in Poughkeepsie, 1850-1880, the comparison is inexact. My Table
1 does differentiate ethnic mobility for workers by year of their first listing
in Poughkeepsie (less than 30 years of age at that listing) so the reader
can contrast Thernstrom's 1850-1859 birth cohort with this 1840-1855
cohort. Almost all of my second generation Americans in every table fall
in the latter cohort.

TABLE 1

CAREER MOBILITY BETWEEN FIRST AND LAST JOBS FOR
PARTICULAR ETHNIC GROUPS IN POUGHKEEPSIE

	Starting White Collar		Ending White Collar		Blue Collar Starters Climbing		White Collar Starters Skidding		Number of Cases
(BC: 1820-35) 1850 Entry									
Blacks	5%	(21)	10%	(21)	5%	(20)	0%		21
Irish	5%		17%		14%		40%	(5)	103
British	5%	(22)	32%	(22)	29%	(21)	0%		22
German	11%	(27)	37%	(27)	33%	(24)	33%	(3)	27
NBNP	34%		49%		27%		9%		326
(BC: 1830-45) 1860 Entry									
Blacks	0%		21%	(14)	21%	(14)	0%		14
Irish	2%		9%		9%		50%	(2)	107
British	18%	(28)	43%	(28)	35%	(23)	20%	(5)	28
German	11%		41%		35%		13%	(8)	76
2nd gen:									
Irish	7%	(15)	13%	(15)	14%	(14)	100%	(1)	15
British	27%	(22)	50%	(22)	31%	(16)	0%		22
German	0%		33%	(6)	33%	(6)	0%		6
NBNP	32%		42%		19%		10%		313
(BC: 1840-55) 1870 Entry									
Blacks	3%		7%		7%	(29)	100%	(1)	30
Irish	4%		9%		5%		0%		92
British	18%	(17)	35%	(17)	29%	(14)	33%	(3)	17
German	10%		32%		28%		33%	(6)	60
2nd gen:									
Irish	16%		34%		29%		43%	(14)	86
British	14%	(28)	18%	(28)	13%	(24)	50%	(4)	28
German	20%		39%		27%		10%	(10)	51
NBNP	38%		45%		18%		11%		304

Note: BC = Birth Cohort; NBNP = Native-born of native parentage.
See footnote 1.
Unless otherwise specified, all tables include all males first listed in the
1850, 1860, and 1870 federal censuses who were less than 30 years old
at first listing and 30 or more years at last listing. Wherever the divisor
is less than 30 cases, the number of cases has been put in parentheses
after the percentage.

comprised 8% of the male labor force even in 1850. By
1880 the percentage for first and second generation combined
had doubled. In that year, both generations of the Irish
formed only a slightly higher proportion of the male labor
force than had the foreign-born alone in 1850, 25% com-

Market Street, Poughkeepsie, in 1865. From Platt, The Eagle's History of Poughkeepsie.

pared to 21%.[3]

The proportion of black Americans was slightly higher in Poughkeepsie than in Boston, but much smaller absolute numbers meant less opportunities for blacks to rise through shops or professions serving their race. In both cities, the number doubled during Reconstruction, but most of the increase in Poughkeepsie came from within New York State, less than one-tenth of the newcomers having been born in the South. A large majority of blacks and first generation Irish in both metropolis and small city were unskilled or semi-skilled; the blacks, however, far more often were listed at specific occupations rather than as day laborers.[4]

Diversified manufacturing in small shops characterized

[3] Oscar Handlin, *Boston's Immigrants* (New York, 1968), pp. 52, 243 (Table VI), and 246 (Table IX): *Statistics of the Population of the United States at the Tenth Census* (1880), Vol. II, p. 864; *Nineteenth-Century Cities,* p. 56 (Table 2).

[4] Handlin, *op. cit.,* pp. 52-53.

both cities in 1850, but only in the larger city was surplus labor sufficiently numerous to stimulate rapid development of large factories.[5] In Poughkeepsie before 1870 only six firms employed more than 100 men. In the decade immediately after 1850 only one booming trade—coopering—provided many jobs for alien newcomers. Boston very quickly took advantage of its surplus labor; Poughkeepsie did not.[6]

Most of the large factories in Poughkeepsie did not appear until two decades after the first great influx of immigrants. Moreover, more than half of the employees of the new factories were women and children. In 1880 less than one-tenth of the city's male labor force worked for firms with more than 100 employees. The implication is obvious. Since Pough-

[5] Handlin, *op. cit.,* pp. 74-83; Tenth Census, II, p. 864; *Nineteenth-Century Cities,* p. 55.

[6] The consequences were severe for the least skilled of the newcomers, especially for the Irish who came to the area as construction workers on the Hudson River Railroad but found themselves without jobs when the railroad was completed in 1851. Three quarters of all day laborers listed in the 1850 census had left the city by 1860; the proportion among the Irish was larger. *Nineteenth-Century Cities,* pp. 62 (Table VI) and 68 (Table VIII).

Main Street, Poughkeepsie, in 1860. From Platt, The Eagle's History of Pough-keepsie.

keepsie remained predominantly a craft-oriented and small shop economy, alien newcomers had to find trades in which they could excel or at least compete by accepting lower wages if many of them were to escape menial labor.

Recognizing that Boston and Poughkeepsie differed both in ethnic composition and in economic development, it remains to be seen whether there was a comparable difference in opportunities for social mobility. Perhaps the most striking difference is in the smaller proportion of all workers in Poughkeepsie, regardless of national origin, who begin their occupational careers in non-manual employment. (Table 2). As

TABLE 2

CAREER MOBILITY BETWEEN FIRST AND LAST JOBS BY ETHNIC GENERATION

	Start White Collar in %	End White Collar in %	Blue Collar Starters Climbing %	White Collar Starters Skidding %	Number of Cases
Blacks (All NB)	3	11	10	50 (2)	65
1st gen. (FB)	7	24	19	25	528
2nd gen. (NBFP)	17	34	26	27	213
NBNP	35	45	22	10	944

in Boston, native whites had an immense advantage over blacks and the foreign-born, but even this most privileged group found fewer opportunities for white-collar work in a small city with a less specialized economy. Clerks of every description account for 11% of Boston's labor force in 1880 whereas they account for only 8% in Poughkeepsie.[7]

A higher proportion of white-collar workers in the smaller city were proprietors rather than clerical or sales workers employed by others. This fact favored the immigrant if he came with a skill or with any talent for small retail and service ventures. The alien who had neither the proficiency in English nor the formal education needed for clerical work had far more likelihood of achieving petty proprietorship, either by excellence in workmanship in a craft-related shop or by superior service in retail ventures catering at first to his country-

[7] *Nineteenth-Century Cities,* p. 134 (Table 2); see my Table 2, "Start White Collar."

men. If achievement of white-collar status is any criterion, many immigrants in Poughkeepsie benefited from its simpler economy. The proportion of the foreign-born who rose from skilled status at first census listing to white-collar at last is consistently higher than for native white, and the frequency of this achievement by Germans is extraordinary.[8] (Table 3).

TABLE 3

CAREER MOBILITY BY YEAR OF FIRST JOB LISTING

	NBNP		1st and 2nd generation		Black	
	Number	End White Collar	Number	End White Collar	Number	End White Collar
Starting Low Manual (Unskilled and Semi-skilled)						
1850	83	20%	93	9%	19	0%
1860	66	17%	105	14%	14	21%
1870	75	19%	144	16%	26	4%
Starting High Manual (Skilled)						
1850	134	31%	50	40%	1	100% (1)
1860	146	20%	127	30%	0	0%
1870	113	18%	149	24%	3	33%
Starting Non-Manual						
		End Blue Collar in %		End Blue Collar in %		End Blue Collar in %
1850	110	9%	9	33%	1	0%
1860	101	10%	22	18%	0	0%
1870	116	11%	41	29%	1	100%

The German record does suggest, however, that ethnic origin, regardless of the nature of the economy, may be critical in explaining differences in social mobility. This suggestion is supported by examination of the frequency with which sons of blue-collar fathers achieve white-collar status by the time of their last listing in the community. (Table 4). No significant difference appears between native whites and all second generation Americans, seemingly emphasizing the importance of class origin. But once again, the Germans prove distinctive, the second generation rising more frequently than native whites. The importance of ethnic origin is supported also by consideration of black Americans who fall well be-

[8] The percentages for Germans who start as skilled workers and climb to white collar status are 54% (1850 group), 44% (1860), and 31% (1870).

TABLE 4

CAREER MOBILITY BETWEEN FIRST AND LAST JOBS
OF SONS BY NATIONAL ORIGIN

	Start White Collar		End White Collar		Blue Collar Starters Climbing	White Collar Starters Skidding		Number of Cases
	Sons of Blue-Collar Fathers							
Blacks	5%	(20)	5%	(20)	5% (19)	100%	(1)	20
2nd gen:								
Irish	10%		22%		19%	58%	(12)	116
British	7%		19%		15%	33%	(3)	43
German	14%		25%		14%	11%	(9)	65
NBNP	14%		21%		14%	37%		300
	Sons of White-Collar Fathers							
Blacks	0%		17%	(6)	17% (6)	0%		6
2nd gen:								
Irish	31%	(26)	65%	(26)	50% (18)	0%		26
British	27%		68%		48% (21)	6%	(16)	37
German	35%		70%		57% (28)	7%	(15)	43
NBNP	67%		78%		42%	5%		277

hind the second generation Irish in frequency of upward mobility.

In the less specialized small city, men who began at white-collar work—regardless of national origin—more often ended their careers in blue-collar jobs. As in Boston, this downward mobility within career is much higher among sons of blue-collar fathers, emphasizing the handicap of working class origin and its presumed corollaries, lesser formal education and fewer cultural opportunities. In the small city, however, no difference appears between second generation Americans and native whites whereas in the metropolis the latter sustain white-collar status twice as often. The Germans make the difference; the sons of the Irish fall back as frequently as in Boston.[9]

The remarkable success of the Germans in achieving and sustaining white-collar status requires explanation. In this thirty-year period, the Germans far outdistanced the Irish in Poughkeepsie. The key to that difference lies in the record of

[9] Compare *Nineteenth-Century Cities,* p. 143 (Table 4); and my Table 4, "White Collar Starters Skidding." The significance of this ethnic difference in the second generation is questionable. Few sons of working class fathers in Poughkeepsie began at white-collar work; few subsequently attained that status, and among the latter, there is no appreciable difference in frequency of rise between ethnic groups.

the first generation. A much higher proportion of the German-born began as skilled workers and more of these craftsmen, in turn, ended their careers as employers or shop-owners.[10] Among second generation Americans, therefore, the Germans began with a distinct advantage; two-fifths of their fathers had achieved white-collar status compared to one-fifth of the fathers of the second generation Irish.

Men born in Germany rarely appear as clerical or professional workers; their success came almost entirely through proprietorships. Examining the occupations through which they achieved upward mobility helps to explain why German craftsmen rose more frequently than any national origin group, including the first and second generation English and Scotch and native whites. (Table 5). Crafts varied widely in

TABLE 5

CAREER MOBILITY BY INDUSTRY (SKILLED AT FIRST JOB)
AND NATIONAL ORIGIN

			1st and 2nd generation			
	NBNP		Irish		German	
		End White		End White		End White
	Number	Collar	Number	Collar	Number	Collar
Metal Trades	82	23%	26	12%	17	35%
Wood Trades	78	10%	12	17%	19	37%
Building Trades	101	20%	37	22%	14	21%
Food and Apparel Trades	42	45%	18	33%	75	41%

average size of shops and capital required with corresponding differences in the ratio of employers to total work force. Remarkably, Germans concentrated most often in trades where opportunities for proprietorship remained highest and the capital needed for proprietorship least; the native-born, by contrast, cluster disproportionately in crafts where the size of shops increased and the ratio of employers to total work force decreased markedly in this period.[11] (Table 6).

Within the rapidly expanding metal trades, the number but

[10] Percentages starting skilled are 68% for the Germans and 27% for the Irish; percentages of those starting skilled who end white collar are 45% for the Germans and 16% for the Irish, for all years of entry combined.

[11] Note that there are more Germans in the food and apparel trades than in the metal, wood, and building trades combined.

TABLE 6

CAREER MOBILITY BY INDUSTRY AND YEAR OF FIRST JOB LISTING

	1850 Census		1860 Census		1870 Census	
	Number	End White Collar	Number	End White Collar	Number	End White Collar
Metal Trades	34	32%	47	19%	56	20%
Wood Trades	29	17%	56	25%	40	13%
Building Trades	31	32%	61	16%	70	16%
Food and Apparel Trades	46	48%	55	44%	45	38%

not the size of foundries, machine shops, and furnaces remained relatively constant. Native whites and the English and Scotch accounted for more than four-fifths of the machinists and engineers; the Irish predominated among moulders by the end of the period. By contrast, the number of blacksmith, tin, and jewelry shops, most of them employing one or two workers and rarely as many as ten, increased by half. Germans appear frequently as owners of tin and jewelry shops.[12]

But the Germans fared best of all in the food and apparel trades, the very trades in which opportunities for self-employment remained highest throughout the period and trades which the Germans entered far more frequently than workers of any other ethnic group. Nearly one-half of the young men first listed in these trades in 1860 subsequently achieved white-collar status compared to less than one-fifth in the metal and building trades.[13] In several of these crafts, notably tailoring and butchering, first and second generation Germans account for a majority of all workers and employers by 1880; in

[12] In the woodworking trades, cooperages, sash and blind, and carriage factories tended to employ between twenty and thirty workers. Native-born workers and employers predominated. By contrast, cabinet making, upholstering, and piano making shops were smaller and here German proprietors were common. The number of male workers for all shops producing goods valued at $500 or more annually is given in the manuscript schedules of the federal manufacturing census. The total number of shops has been derived from the business directory appended to the annual city directory. For the proportion of the first and second generation in various skilled trades, see *Nineteenth-Century Cities*, pp. 75-76, (especially Table II).

[13] I have used 1860 for comparison rather than 1870 to ensure the possibility of at least two subsequent census listings in the period. The careers of all first and second generation Americans have been traced in the city directories to 1900—and the results do not change appreciably—but since this tracing has not been completed for native whites the comparison here is limited to mobility, 1860-1880, in the census.

The J. O. Whitehouse Boot and Shoe Factory, Poughkeepsie, in 1882. The factory was built in 1870, burned and rebuilt in 1879. From Smith, History of Dutchess County.

the others. Germans constituted a large minority. Shops rarely had as many as ten workers although at the end of the period cheaper factory or sweatshop-made shoes and garments increasingly favored larger and largely retail shops in these lines with some decline correspondingly in total number of shops.

This selectivity in the occupations through which Germans advanced does raise a serious question about the significance of that advance. Were the social status and economic reward of first and second generation owners of small meat markets, bakeries, and tailoring shops greater than those of native white employees in highly skilled, well-paid trades like machinist and engineer? This question seems even more important when one discovers that first and second generation Americans also account for a majority of proprietors in those retail and service ventures most likely to be petty in character, such as groceries, saloons, cigar shops, and variety stores.

The notorious frequency of failures in these small businesses, many of them conducted at home at least initially, suggests that they may not have represented any significant advance over well-paid employment by others. The suggestion is reinforced by other analyses. First, the sons of many petty proprietors did not maintain their fathers' white-collar status.

At the extreme, nearly three-fifths of the sons of saloonkeepers in Poughkeepsie appear as blue-collar workers at last
listing.[14]

Second, examination of the previous occupations of grocers
and saloonkeepers who achieved that status at a second or
later listing in the census shows that a majority of them came
from low manual or skill-diluted occupations.[15] By contrast
workers in the most highly skilled crafts rarely attempted such
ventures. Nor do they seem to have suffered in social status
by their lesser interest in self-employment. They resided in
prosperous middle class neighborhoods at least as frequently
as petty proprietors.

Analysis of the careers of small shop owners and their sons
by ethnic group does indicate, however, that questions about
the advance this status represents apply more forcefully to the
Irish than to the Germans. In addition to the slightly greater
frequency with which second generation Germans sustain their
fathers' advance, the amount of real estate reported by the
Germans together with the frequency with which their shops
appear in the heart of the central business district suggest a
more substantial and permanent improvement.[16] By contrast,
many of the Irish ventures in both first and second generation
were located in largely residential areas where their own
countrymen predominated.

Comparing the more limited advance of the Irish with that
of other immigrants from northwestern Europe inevitably
poses the question of how their religion influenced their mobility. Since some cities, and especially Boston, received comparatively few Catholic immigrants who were not of Irish descent, the temptation is strong to regard the poor showing of
the Irish as an index for the influence of Catholicism on social
mobility.[17] In Poughkeepsie, however, nearly one-third of the

[14] Only 3 out of 11 native white sons of saloonkeepers end white collar,
4 out of 13 second generation Irish, and 8 out of 12 second generation
Germans. More than half of the sons of hucksters and peddlers also fail
to sustain their fathers' status.
[15] Of 33 saloonkeepers with previous census listings at other jobs, 10
had been in skill-diluted trades—primarily shoemaking and woodworking—
and 8 had been day laborers. Of 38 grocers, 9 came from skill diluted
trades and 7 had been day laborers.
[16] See my Table 4, "End White Collar" for sons of white-collar fathers.
[17] In an unpublished paper, "Religion and Occupational Mobility in Boston, 1880-1963," Thernstrom finds that the difference between religious
groups does not disappear when ethnic group is controlled. My reservation about this finding is based primarily on the small number of Germans

numerous German population can be identified as members of Nativity Church, the German Catholic parish, permitting a comparison of the achievement of Catholics and Protestants within an ethnic group which did not begin with the obvious disadvantages of the overwhelmingly agrarian, unskilled, and propertyless Irish.[18]

The comparison does favor the Protestants, but only slightly. (Table 7). First and second generation Protestants

TABLE 7

RELIGION AND CAREER MOBILITY: THE GERMANS

	Start White Collar		End White Collar		Blue Collar Starters Climbing		White Collar Starters Skidding		Number of Cases
First Generation									
Protestant	17%		37%		27%		15%		238
Catholic	15%		35%		27%		18%	(17)	113
Jewish	55%	(29)	90%	(29)	77%	(13)	0%		29
Second Generation (White-Collar Father)									
Protestant	35%		63%		46%		5%	(20)	57
Catholic	41%	(22)	55%	(22)	31%	(13)	11%	(9)	22
Jewish	88%	(8)	100%	(8)	100%	(1)	0%		8
Second Generation (Blue-Collar Father)									
Protestant	14%		23%		10%		9%	(11)	80
Catholic	12%		25%		18%		20%	(5)	43
Jewish									0

begin a little more often than Catholics at white-collar jobs, the only exception being the sons of white-collar fathers where the number of Catholic cases are few and offset by a higher proportion of Protestant sons at that status at last listing. Among the sons of blue-collar fathers, by contrast, the proportion of Catholics rising after a manual start is higher. The achievement of the two groups in the first generation in

---

involved, but as I suggest subsequently there may be greater differences between German Catholics and Protestants after the first great period of migration.

[18] A substantial proportion of German Protestants in Poughkeepsie came from predominately Catholic areas like Bavaria and a fair number of Catholics came from predominately Protestant areas like Prussia. I have no exact controls for province yet, but do not think they will appreciably affect my analysis of the two religious groups. The Jewish achievement in Poughkeepsie as elsewhere is extraordinary, but included here only as a contrast.

rising from blue-collar status is identical. The one consistent difference for both generations appears in the greater tendency among Catholics beginning in white-collar work to fall downward to manual status, but the cases are few in number and the percentage difference not that large.

First generation Protestants do more frequently report amounts of real estate of $5,000 or more, with the difference between religious groups most pronounced for those with $10,000 or more. (Table 8). But at the other extreme, the

TABLE 8

OWNERSHIP OF PROPERTY: FIRST GENERATION GERMANS

	None	$1-999	$1,000-2,999	$3,000-4,999	$5,000-9,000	$10,000 or more	Number of Cases
Protestant	42%	16%	13%	8%	12%	8%	238
Catholic	38%	18%	12%	18%	10%	4%	113
Jewish	17%	14%	24%	14%	10%	21%	29

Protestants show a higher proportion with no property. Catholics concentrate in the middle range, 30% of them reporting real estate between $1,000 and $5,000 in value compared to 21% of the Protestants. Moreover, the significance of these differences lessens when one considers that a larger proportion of the Protestants resided in Poughkeepsie by the time of the 1850 census. The last property figures available come from the 1870 census, giving the earlier arrivals more likelihood of substantial acquisition by that time.

This comparison does not support Max Weber's thesis that Catholics show less tendency toward economic rationalism, insofar as that thesis stresses the importance of the so-called Protestant virtues—sobriety, industry, frugality, and ambition —for economic success. But a reformulation of the Weber thesis may be useful in exploring differences between Catholic and Protestant Germans beyond the period now under consideration, for there is evidence even in this period that German Catholics were more preoccupied with keeping their faith in what seemed a hostile environment and, therefore, more likely than German Protestants to limit their intercourse with the native Protestant majority.

Both groups of Germans emphasized preservation of their

native language and customs in a variety of voluntary associations, but the Catholics stressed the importance of this preservation for the future of Catholicism among their children. The *Golden Jubilee Book* of Nativity Church, published in 1897, admonished parishioners at length on the importance of their mother tongue. "Sad experience has taught that who abandons the Muttersprache, frequently abandons his religion. The both of them—language and religion—are intimately connected." The book insisted that English must be learned well. Indeed, it explicitly urged, "In English count and calculate your dollars," but added immediately, "In your family German should be spoken; do not tolerate your children's speaking English to you, otherwise the sweetest family ties will loosen, religion will be harmed, and the respectfulness due you from your children and your power over them will be destroyed."

How well parishioners heeded this advice escapes the historian, but it does seem significant that only the Catholics established a parochial school emphasizing instruction in German. Moreover, if tendency to reside near their church and fellow countrymen be any indication, then German Catholics in Poughkeepsie showed more tendency to insulate themselves from native Protestants. By 1880, 28% of the German Protestants resided in predominantly native-born neighborhoods to the east of the area where all the German churches and most of the German population concentrated; but only 17% of the Catholics did. More important, prosperous German Protestants in the second generation sometimes married middle class women of British ancestry whereas German Catholics, if they married outside their community, took women of Irish ancestry as brides. Using Milton Gordon's helpful distinction, the German Catholics might assimilate to American mores in their dealings in the marketplace, but they show a much stronger aversion than German Protestants to structural assimilation.[19]

The success of the Germans in Poughkeepsie, Catholic as well as Protestant, raises one other fundamental question about social mobility in mid-nineteenth century America, the question of whether immigration improved opportunities for most native whites. In small cities with fewer clerical and su-

[19] See Milton Gordon, *Assimilation in American Life* (New York, 1964).

pervisory jobs, native white advantages in competition with the newcomers may have been considerably less than in large cities, especially if the newcomers brought as much skill and ambition as the Germans did. In Poughkeepsie, native whites starting at blue-collar jobs seem to have had no appreciable advantage over the newcomers in comparable skill levels. Skilled first and second generation workers climbed more frequently throughout the period; unskilled and semi-skilled native whites first listed in 1850 did climb twice as often as the foreign-born, but by the end of the period their advantage over first and second generation combined had largely disappeared.[20] (Table 9). Regardless of ethnic origin, the oppor-

TABLE 9

Career Mobility of Workers Starting at Low Manual Jobs

	Remain at Low Manual	Climb to High Manual	Climb to Non-Manual	Number of Cases
Blacks	92%	2%	6%	64
1st gen:				
Irish	82%	10%	8%	208
British	40%	40%	20%	15
German	66%	20%	14%	44
2nd gen:				
Irish	55%	19%	26%	47
British	60%	20%	20%	15
German	50%	13%	37%	8
NBNP	58%	24%	18%	204

tunities for this lowest occupational group were depressing. No more than half achieved skilled or white-collar status subsequently; among the blacks a mere 8% did.

Had the unskilled and semi-skilled comprised a negligible and diminishing proportion of all native whites, these facts wou'd be less significant. But the proportion remained relatively stable and surprisingly high; one-fourth of all native whites in the 1880 census appear at low manual occupations. The percentage of day laborers alone was 12% in 1850 and still 9% in 1880. Furthermore, a comparison of the frequency with which workers first listed as skilled appear subsequently at unskilled or semi-skilled jobs indicates that

[20] For comparison of rise to white-collar status between skilled and low manual workers, see my Table 3.

native whites had no advantage over first and second generation Americans, regardless of ethnic group; on the contrary,
the only large group of skilled workers who show almost no
downward mobility are the German-born. (Table 10). If year

TABLE 10

DOWNWARD MOBILITY FROM SKILLED TO LOW MANUAL
(NUMBER OF CASES)

	Less than 31 Years	*31-44 Years*	*45 Years or Older*
NBNP	15	25	26
First Generation			
Irish	—	11	15
British	1	2	4
German	1	2	4
Second Generation			
Irish	4	2	—
British	1	—	—
German	5	—	—
TOTAL	27	42	49

of first listing in the census is considered, then the native
whites show a higher frequency of downward movement at
the end of the period. One-fifth of the young native whites
who first appeared at skilled work in 1870 and remained in
Poughkeepsie through the decade of depression were listed at
unskilled or semi-skilled work in 1880. Finally, native white
craftsmen had no greater security of employment in old age;
two-fifths of all downward mobility among skilled workers
occurred after age forty-four. The proportion varies little between ethnic groups, but the comparison does not favor native whites.

All these facts suggest that for many native white blue-
collar workers remaining in Poughkeepsie at least a decade,
the coming of the immigrants meant no great improvement in
status or opportunities. A possible exception might be those
native whites starting at low manual work who subsequently
list themselves at crafts with high average wage rates, usually
in the metal and building trades. But even this exception de-
pends upon the questionable assumption that latecomers to
these crafts were rewarded as well and found employment as
regularly as those who had apprenticed in them. It seems more

likely that many of these workers performed more specialized tasks requiring less general skill and correspondingly were less well-rewarded. Among machinists and engineers who began their careers in Poughkeepsie at other jobs, for example, one-third had been day laborers and in a few cases appear at last job again as laborers or at more specialized work like grinding or steel polishing.

Whether skilled designation, especially late in life, represents a major improvement in status and reward over low manual work is open to serious question. And while the question applies also to such advances by first and second generation Americans, it has special significance, at least in Poughkeepsie, for native whites. When native whites who began at low manual work in this small city rose at all, they tended more often than the newcomers to climb into skilled rather than into white-collar jobs.[21]

The more general implication of my questioning of the meaning of skilled designations in the census, like my questioning previously of petty proprietorships, is the suggestion that social mobility usually took the form of fairly small steps up or down a finely graded occupational ladder. This may

[21] See my Table 9, "Climbing to High Manual."

Immigrants arrive at Cork—a scene on the quay. From Illustrated London News, *1851.*

have been less true in a small city with little large-scale manufacturing, but even in comparatively small craft-oriented businesses in Poughkeepsie there seem to be significant gradations
in status and reward with corresponding differences in subsequent mobility for fathers and sons.

The importance of this stratification seems greatest for the
one group most obviously injured by the influx of immigrants
—those native white families where fathers and sons alike remained largely confined to low manual occupations. Contrary
to the expected pattern that the less successful tend to move
on in search of better opportunities elsewhere, this group in
Poughkeepsie, many bearing English or Dutch names common there for generations, remain with surprising frequency.
A variety of evidence suggests that the label "lumpenprole-
tariat" is appropriate. Alone among native whites this group
show frequent convictions for intoxication and theft and, perhaps more important, frequently reside on the few streets
where blacks concentrated, occasionally sharing houses.

For the blacks, this mingling with depressed whites, even
when they belonged to old Poughkeepsie families, must have
been slight consolation for their frustrations in this period.
The numerous conventions of "colored people" reported in
the city during the late 1860s and early 70s bespeak high aspirations, especially the frequency with which they resolve to
create academies for their children to escape inferior education in the city's segregated public schools. Yet in these very
years when some of Poughkeepsie's native white elite bestirred
themselves on behalf of freedmen in the South, local blacks
experienced no significant improvement in condition.

Unlike Boston, where a larger black population made retail
and craft-related shops catering to other blacks more feasible,
only a handful of blacks in Poughkeepsie achieved either
skilled or white-collar status.[22] (Table 11). In a black labor
force which ranged from 93 males in 1850 to 173 in 1870,
only two workers, a gardener and a steward, reported real estate of $5,000 or more by 1870. Of the few who achieved
white-collar status at any listing, only the steward, a clergyman, and three proprietors of jewelry, dyeing, and barber
shops, sustained that status for more than one listing. Of the

---

[22] Compare with the rates of persistence for blue collar occupations in
Nineteenth Century Cities, p. 62 (Table 6).

TABLE 11

NUMBER AND PERSISTENCE OF BLACKS IN POUGHKEEPSIE

	Unskilled		Semi-skilled		Skilled	White Collar	TOTAL	
Census	Number	Persist. in %	Number	Persist. in %	Number	Number	Number	Persist. in %
1850	50	38%	30	33%	11	2	93	39%
1860	50	28%	26	54%	6	6	88	40%
1870	102	30%	57	35%	5	9	173	33%
1880	71	—	63	—	5	11	150	—

Note: The numbers of skilled and white collar workers are too small for meaningful percentages on persistence. The rates are somewhat higher generally, but vary sharply from census to census.

few who listed themselves as skilled craftsmen, several appeared at low manual jobs subsequently.

As in Boston, about 90% of the blacks at every census were in low manual occupations, but more often in service and other specified occupations than the Irish-born. Blacks predominated among hotel waiters, hostlers, porters, and white washers and constituted a large minority of coachmen and barbers, but the Irish increasingly displaced blacks in the former occupation and Germans in the latter. Blacks in these specified occupations show about the same rate of persistence in Poughkeepsie as workers of other ethnic groups, even during the decade of depression, 1870-1880. But the similarity ends when the subsequent occupations of these survivors are compared. Only one of the blacks remaining in 1880 climbed beyond the low manual occupational universe and several changed jobs within it. By contrast, half of the second generation Americans in this category had achieved skilled or white-collar jobs.

This picture of the black community is not improved by discovery of the frequency of job changes within career of those who persist, the much lower frequency of acquisition of real estate than among first generation Irish who shared this occupational universe, nor by the frequency of men who list themselves without wives or families or with young children at one census listing who are not at home at the next.

Despite Boston's greater size and reputation for sympathy to blacks, their experience in Poughkeepsie is so similar as to suggest a universal condition. So does the obvious handicap in both cities of the least skilled immigrants, the Irish. Beyond these obvious extremes, the frequency of upward mobility is more difficult to interpret. A minority of low manual as well as skilled workers climb to white-collar status, very often to petty and perhaps marginal proprietorships in Poughkeepsie. Skilled status provided a much more frequent stepping stone only for the first generation Germans. But the ambiguity of skilled designation itself has been suggested, most obviously for those achieving it after low manual work.

The result is a picture even for the small city of a fairly finely graded occupational ladder with most social mobility consisting of short steps up or down. Native whites as a whole had the expected and decided advantage over immigrants and blacks, but there is evidence suggesting that a larger proportion of native whites than we usually assume received no boost upward from the presence of the newcomers. Indeed, as the German record shows, an immigrant group whose background prepared them to take advantage of a still largely craft-oriented economy could at least in the small city climb more often than native whites. Whether the differences suggested here between Boston and Poughkeepsie are due primarily to the different scale, economy, and ethnic composition of the two cities is, of course, speculation. Perhaps this comparison may provoke studies of similar cities which will suggest whether the speculation is well- or ill-founded.

"Paddy O'Dougherty, the Irish emigrant." [Illustrated News, *November 5, 1853*.]

Immigration and Social Stratification in Pre-Civil War New York

by

DOUGLAS T. MILLER

I T IS generally held by present-day historians that immigration did not adversely affect the American economy in regard to such factors as workers' wages and social mobility. The coming of the immigrants is viewed as a dynamic force, operating from below, helping to push persons from the earlier lower ranks to higher job levels. As one of the leading historians of immigration, Oscar Handlin, writes: "Immigration . . . endowed the social structure with fluidity. In the expanding culture it was difficult to preserve fixed forms, to establish rigid class distinctions that might limit opportunities. Diversity and mobility became characteristic features of life in the United States."[1]

Over an extended period the Handlin thesis may be true. However, if one considers only the effects of heavy immigration in the single generation preceding the Civil War a contrary picture emerges. A close examination of New York society in the pre-Civil War period indicates that heavy immigration widened the gulf between classes and increased class consciousness. During these years the fluid social and economic conditions of the Jacksonian era moved toward a state of social stratification.

Professor Miller is a member of the history department at Michigan State University.

[1] Handlin, *Immigration as a Factor in American History* (Englewood Cliffs, N.J., 1959), pp. 2-3; see also: Handlin, *Race and Nationality in American Life* (Boston, 1957), pp. 188-207; David M. Potter, *People of Plenty* (Chicago, 1954), pp. 94-5.

Immigrants landing at Castle Garden. [Frank Leslie's Illustrated Newspaper, *December 29, 1855.*

The prominence of New York City as a port of entry undoubtedly meant that the mass immigration of the 1840's and 1850's had a more significant impact on the Empire State than any other area in America.[2] Yet even if the New York experience were unique, which seems unlikely, it is important enough to warrant a re-examination of the commonly held generalizations about immigration. The present study will attempt to make some tentative suggestions, indicated by evidence drawn largely from the New York experience, regarding the effects of immigration on pre-Civil War America.[3]

[2] Over two-thirds of the more than five and a half million aliens who arrived in America between 1815 and 1860 entered this country through the port of New York. It is also significant that, relative to the total population, immigration during the two decades prior to the Civil War was the largest in American history. See: Alexander C. Flick, ed., *History of the State of New York* (10 vols., New York, 1933-37), VII, 42-3, 55-8; Marcus Lee Hansen, *The Atlantic Migration, 1607-1860* (New York, 1961), p. 280; Maldwyn Allen Jones, *American Immigration* (Chicago, 1960), pp. 92-4.

[3] The generalizations made in this and the following paragraphs stem mainly from the author's research for *Jacksonian Aristocracy: Class and Democracy in New York, 1830-1860* (New York, 1967).

A good illustration of the adverse economic effects of large scale immigration is the general reduction in workers' real wages between the 1830's and the Civil War. A frequent complaint during this period was that recent immigrants, working for a pittance, made it difficult for other workers to earn decent wages, or, in some cases, even to find work. A writer in 1850 fretted that Germans working for low wages had "caused a great reduction in the price of labour." He described a German who, speaking no English, arrived in Buffalo and took away from a native American a job chopping firewood. This sort of thing, the writer concluded, caused the Germans to be "utterly disliked by the labouring Yankees, and, indeed by all except those who employ them."[4]

Grumblings of this sort were well-founded. Wages for an unskilled laborer dropped from an average of a dollar a day in the early 1830's to less than seventy-five cents a day a decade later. Wages for skilled workers, though less affected, declined also. The pay of journeymen hatters fell from an average of twelve dollars a week in 1835 to about eight dollars a week

[4] [George Nettle], *A Practical Guide for Emigrants to North America* (London, 1850), pp. 28-9.

The hatter. [*From* Popular Technology *(1842) by Edward Hazen.*]

The tailor. [*From Hazen's* Popular Technology.]

in 1845. Similarly, New York cabinetmakers complained in 1846 that wages had fallen to less than eight dollars per week from a high of nearly fifteen dollars in 1836. Employers, they fretted, "are constantly on the watch for German emigrants who can work at Cabinet Making—going on board the ships before the emigrants have landed and engaging them for a *year* at $20 or $30 and their board. . . . This it is which has ruined the Cabinet Making business, and the complaints on the part of the journeymen are incessant." A lament of native-born tailors was that German immigrant competition had cut in half the price of coats from 1842 to 1847, making it nearly impossible for a tailor to sustain himself and his family. One group of skilled workers seeing the trend in wages asked in 1845: "How much can a mechanic lay up for sickness and old age—and what comforts the mechanic in New York can enjoy from his wages, in comparison with those engaged in some sort of business, are questions which we should like some of the brethren in New York to answer."[5]

[5] *Young America* [New York], February 14, 1846; *Champion of American Labor* [New York], April 3, 1847; John R. Commons and others, eds., *A Documentary History of American Industrial Society* (10 vols., Cleveland, 1910), VII, 47-8, 217-18. Though evidence is sketchy, it is possible that wages for New York's skilled workers increased slightly between 1830 and 1860; however, in most trades real wages declined due to rising living costs. For a sampling of information on wages see: John R. Commons and others, *History of Labour in the United States* (4 vols., New York, 1918-35), I, 487-8; Philip S. Foner, *History of the Labor Movement in the United States* (2 vols., New York, 1947), I, 168, 220; Foster Rhea Dulles, *Labor in America* (New York, 1960), pp. 77-8; Junius H. Browne, *The Great Metropolis* (Hartford, 1869), p. 548; Thomas Mooney, *Nine Years in America* (Dublin, 1850), pp. 22, 82; Samuel I. Prime, *Life in New York* (New York, 1847), p. 95; Charles Loring Brace, *The Dangerous Classes of New York and Twenty Years' Work Among Them* (New York, 1872), pp. 168-70; *New York Daily Tribune*, January 18, February 9, 1850.

The emigrant agent's office. [Frank Leslie's Illustrated Newspaper, *January 12, 1856.*]

That immigrants took only jobs that native Americans scorned was simply not true. In many instances Yankee workers, such as the Buffalo wood-chopper, were put out of jobs by foreigners willing to work for less, or else were forced to accept reduced pay. This was true not merely of unskilled jobs, but, as is indicated by the complaints of the cabinet-makers and tailors, even in the craft trades. One newspaper writer bemoaned in 1844:

> Our labouring men, native and naturalized, are met at every turn and every avenue of employment, with recently imported workmen from the low wages countries of the world. Our public improvements, railroads, and canals are thronged with foreigners. They fill our large cities, reduce the wages of labor, and increase the hardships of the old settlers.

Even small businessmen felt the pressure of immigrant competition. "Look at the Irish and Dutch grocers and rum-sellers," charged an 1844 nativist circular, "monopolizing the business which properly belongs to our native and true-born citizens."[6]

Much of the impetus underlying nativist reaction to foreign-born Americans in the 1840's and 1850's was economic

[6] *The Native American* [Philadelphia], November 29, 1844; *Daily Plebian* [New York], April 20, 1844.

Emigrants embarking. [Frank Leslie's Illustrated Newspaper, *January 12, 1856.*]

in nature. Many factors other than immigration, of course, contributed to the lowering of working-class living standards during the decades preceding the Civil War, and undoubtedly the immigrant often served as a convenient scapegoat for a variety of frustrations. However, nativism was not simply a matter of anti-Catholic, anti-foreign bigotry. Immigrants did, as one labor paper stated, "throw many of our mechanics out of employment." Some of the leading supporters of nativist organizations were skilled craftsmen who felt economically threatened by the immigrants. Often nativist meetings were called specifically to protest the economic consequences of immigration. For instance, an 1847 circular announcing a meeting of mechanics and workingmen invited to attend "all who feel the effects of the depression of labor in consequence of the number of laborers from Europe, thrown upon the city and country, and are disposed to adopt measures for self-preservation, by restricting immigration. . . ."[7]

[7] *Voice of Industry* [Boston], June 11, 1847; *Champion of American Labor,* April 3, 1847. Traditional accounts of pre-Civil War nativism such as Ray Allen Billington, *The Protestant Crusade, 1800-1860* (Gloucester, Mass., 1963) and Louis Dow Scisco, *Political Nativism in New York State* (New York, 1901) almost completely ignore the economic factors underlying nativism. An article which does emphasize the economic causes of nativism is, Robert Ernst, "Economic Nativism in New York City During the 1840's," *New York History,* XXIX (1948), 170-186. See also: John Higham, *Strangers in the Land: Patterns of American Nativism 1860-1925* (New York, 1963), pp. 45-6.

Heavy immigration also contributed to the boom-bust cycle of the American economy, which greatly hurt the laboring classes. During prosperous times such as the mid-'thirties or early 'fifties, increasing immigration helped prolong the boom by keeping labor available and wages low. But once a depression set in, as it did in 1837 and again in the late 1850's, its severity was much greater and longer lasting because of the numerous unemployed and destitute immigrants.[8]

Large-scale immigration also made unified action on the part of labor difficult. After the collapse of the New York labor movement in the wake of the 1837 depression, the increasing availability of low-priced Irish and German laborers greatly hindered the effective revival of unions. Similarly, this labor surplus tended to counteract the safety-valve effect of cheap land and the frontier in drawing off workers from New York and other eastern cities. After 1840 the magnitude of the emigration to America came close to creating a permanent semi-pauperized working class.[9]

Not only political nativists, but Americans as a whole, regarded recent immigrants as inferior beings, little better than the Negro. Immigrants, observed a contemporary, "are singled out and kept apart, from the mere circumstances of their birth, as a distinct and inferior caste—denounced in the degrading vocabulary of every native American, as unworthy of a more intimate fellowship with him, and in no wise fitted for the enjoyment of that rational freedom and independence, which at another time he claims as of man's inheritance—the inborn right of every human being."[10] Even an Irish emigrant agent felt compelled to warn his fellow countrymen not to be too proud and think that America was a land of freedom where one man was as good as another. "It is true," he wrote, "that at the legal tribunal and at the voting booth all are equal, but there the equality ends. . . . Every demand for a fellowship with respectable society, grounded upon the *law* of the land, will be rejected with contempt. . . ."[11] Another Irishman com-

[8] Harry Jerome, *Migration and Business Cycles* (New York, 1926), p. 252; William F. Adams, *Ireland and Irish Emigration to the New World From 1815 to the Famine* (New Haven, 1932), p. 359.

[9] Norman Ware, *The Industrial Worker, 1840-1860* (Boston, 1924), pp. 10, 12; Adams, *Ireland and Irish Emigration*, p. 355; Dulles, *Labor*, pp. 78-9; Miller, *Jacksonian Aristocracy*, pp. 87-99, 128-39.

[10] Francis Wyse, *America, Its Realities and Resources* (3 vols., London, 1846), I, 51.

[11] Mooney, *Nine Years in America*, pp. 87-8.

plained: "There is often a more intimate sympathy between the Alabama planter and his African *slave* than between a Yankee employer and his Irish help."[12] This class feeling, coupled with the fact that immigrants as a whole filled the most menial positions in society, made social stratifications more pronounced.

This is well illustrated by the changing status of domestic servants. Prior to the flood of foreign immigration in the 1840's and 1850's, native Americans were mainly employed as domestic servants; they were called and generally treated as "help," not as servants, and class lines were not tightly drawn. "The native men," wrote a Britisher in 1830:

> seem adverse to servitude, and are rarely to be found in this capacity. The women are somewhat more ready to *help* out; but servants entertain such notions of equality and independence as fit them poorly for this station of life, and tend greatly to abridge the comforts of their employers. . . .[13]

By the mid-'forties, however, the Irish came to form the most numerous and important group engaged in domestic employment. German women also entered this profession in growing numbers and by the early 'fifties were second only to the Irish. With the increased use of the foreign-born, class lines tightened, and fewer native Americans entered into service. The term "servant" was once more introduced and the wearing of livery—the hated badge of servitude—became common. These workers came to be a semi-permanent class of domestics, serving the needs of the wealthier classes.[14]

The growing number of servants in New York and other cities was perhaps the clearest index of the rise of an urban aristocracy. Advertisements such as the following from the *New York Tribune*, January 30, 1851, were frequent: "WANTED—Situations for about seventy excellent servants. . . ." Mrs. Anna Mowatt in her play *Fashion*, a delightful social satire of the mid-'forties, has Zeke, the Negro ser-

---

[12] D. W. Mitchell, *Ten Years in the United States* (London, 1862), pp. 148-9.
[13] John Fowler, *Journal of a Tour in the State of New York in the Year 1830* (London, 1831), p. 218.
[14] Lucy M. Salmon, *Domestic Service* (New York, 1897), pp. 62-5, 70-72; Carl R. Fish, *The Rise of the Common Man, 1830-1850* (New York, 1927), p. 113; Thomas L. Nichols, *Forty Years of American Life, 1821-1861* (New York, 1937), p. 255.

vant of the pretentious Mrs. Tiffany, say of his uniform: "Dere's a coat to take de eyes ob all Broadway! Ah! Missy, it am de fixins day make de natural born gemman. A libery for ever!"[15] Zeke had enough actual counterparts to give this satire a firm basis in reality.

Complaints of bad and insufficient servants continued to be heard, but not as frequently as in the Jacksonian period. Foreigners no longer found servants so inconveniently democratic. An English woman visiting America at mid-century said: "So far as the observations and enquires of sixteen months could elicit such facts, I have not discovered that the servants in the United States are of a worse description than the same class of persons in England."[16]

Few foreigners, unless they came to America with wealth or special skills, rose above menial, subordinate positions in the pre-Civil War period.[17] They generally ate and drank better than in Europe, but this was usually the extent of their advancement. As a British resident in America wrote: "but a very limited proportion indeed of the numbers—the many thousands who annually migrate to the United States, ever reach to mediocrity, much less to affluence or station. . . ."[18]

"Have we as a people," asked the Reverend Stephen Byrne, "paid sufficient attention to the proper establishing of ourselves in a state, not merely of prosperity, but of simple competency or independence in this great country? Let the crowded tenement-houses of the Eastern cities, where the very atmosphere is poisoned by the occupancy in one house of from twenty to forty families, and where morality itself is greatly endangered on account of associations that cannot be avoided, answer. Let the unnamed and unnumbered graves along the

---

[15] Mowatt, *Fashion; or Life in New York* (New York, 1849), p. 1.

[16] Quoted in Arthur W. Calhoun, *A Social History of the American Family* (2 vols., New York, 1960), II, 147-8, 233; see also: Robert Ernst, *Immigrant Life in New York City, 1825-1863* (New York, 1949), p. 67; Allan Nevins and M. H. Thomas, eds., *The Diary of George Templeton Strong, 1835-1875* (4 vols., New York, 1953), II, 22; Mrs. C. M. Kirkland, *The Evening Book* (New York, 1851), pp. 159-64, 166, 168.

[17] That this continued to be true after the War, at least in some areas, is indicated by a recent and important study: Stephan Thernstrom, *Poverty and Progress: Social Mobility in a Nineteenth Century City* (Cambridge, Mass., 1964).

[18] Wyse, *America*, III, 31; see also: Jesse Chickering, *Immigration into the United States* (Boston, 1848), p. 64; John A. Hawgood, *The Tragedy of German-America* (New York, 1940), p. 258.

canals and railroads of the United States, answer. Let the for-
lorn and forgotten creatures who, having neither homes or
friends, lie down and die in common hospitals of the country,
answer."[19]

Not finding the promised plenty that they had been led to
expect, many immigrants repented of ever having come to
America. A Welshman living in New York wrote of his fellow immigrants: "The chief want and disadvantage which I
saw among them was the scarcity of circulating money; they
were ready enough to worship the DOLLAR, could they have
seen one." "I have encountered many of my fellow-country-
men," he concluded, "who would go back to their native land
if they could, but Oh! without having the means. . . ."[20]

After seeing the poor prospects for immigrants, Francis
Wyse, a Britisher who spent several years in the United States
during the 1840's, wrote a three-volume work *America, Its
Realities and Resources,* which aimed at dissuading future
Europeans from emigrating. Wyse was critical of the two
standard economic motives for migrating to this country—
cheap land and high wages. There was abundant land, he admitted, but the expenses and difficulties involved in creating a
successful farm he found "almost insurmountable" for a poor
man. As for wages, although somewhat higher than in England, Wyse saw that much employment was seasonal and that
living expenses were higher. All too often the immigrant was
left "at the end of a laborious struggle, with scarcely any better prospects than when he first started; and certainly without
making any very rapid advance in that independence, and
increased wealth, which he was so confidently promised as a
corollary to his labours at the outset."[21]

The second generation, of course, had better prospects of
advancement than did their parents, but even here social and
economic improvement was the exception rather than the rule.
A study of the relative status of first- and second-generation
immigrants in New York's predominantly foreign Sixth and
Tenth Wards, based upon the New York State Census of
1855, reveals that out of 201 second-generation immigrants,
largely Irish and German, only 44, or less than 22 per cent,

[19] Byrne, *Irish Emigration to the United States* (New York, 1873), p. 12.
[20] Rowland T. Berthoff, ed., "Life in America: A Disillusioned Welshman in New York," *New York History,* XXVII (January 1956), 80-84.
[21] Wyse, *America,* I, 40-41.

An emigration vessel, between decks. [Frank Leslie's Illustrated Newspaper, *January 12, 1856.*]

attained a higher status than their parents.[22] This is not to say that pre-Civil War immigrants did not eventually rise; the Civil War helped the Irish and Germans both economically and socially. But generally it was not until the massive foreign influx from southern and eastern Europe in the late nineteenth century that the older immigrant groups made substantial improvements.[23]

New York's upper classes were not threatened by immigration. Rather it was the reverse; large-scale immigration helped bestow prosperity on them. From the mid-'forties on, the newcomers brought a seemingly endless supply of unskilled, cheap labor, making possible the full introduction of factory production to the profit of some, but to the detriment of both native and foreign laborers. Yearly more and more workers found themselves in the category of permanent wage earners, while social positions became more fixed and distinct. The great use of cheap immigrant labor made laboring less respectable than it had been. Mechanics employed in factories began to consider themselves as "wage slaves" in a very real sense.

The foregoing evidence, taken collectively, suggests that immigration rather than increasing social mobility presented a major challenge to America's egalitarian ideals, causing increased social stratification and class consciousness. It is quite

[22] Ernst, *Immigrant Life,* pp. 220-21.
[23] Brinley Thomas, *Migration and Economic Growth* (Cambridge, Eng., 1954), pp. 152-3.

possible that periods of heavy immigration, from colonial times until the restrictive laws of the 1920's, have always increased class divisions. Marked social stratifications are only possible where there exists an inferior group willing to perform the most menial tasks. The penniless Irish and Germans provided such a class in the 1840's and 1850's. If it could be shown that slaves, indentured servants, and redemptioners in the colonial period, and the "new" immigrants of the late nineteenth and early twentieth centuries served in a similar manner, then clearly the traditional generalizations concerning immigration are in need of revision.

Bonds of Community:
Buffalo's German Element, 1853–1871

By ANDREW P. YOX

In responding to the cultural and political forces of the new homeland, Buffalo's German community was influenced by cultural and political forces of European origin. Andrew Yox is a member of the Department of History at The Pennsylvania State University, Shenango Valley Campus, in Sharon, Pennsylvania.

THE GERMAN IMMIGRANTS who came to America in the mid-nineteenth century established a counterculture they called *Deutschtum*. In medium-sized cities like Buffalo, Cincinnati, and Milwaukee, the German quarter consisted of Gothic steeples, rows of small frame cottages, open-air markets, and the ubiquitous saloon. Unlike the sedate neighborhoods of the Anglo-Americans, the German district rustled with sounds. Beer gardens, brass bands, shops, dance halls, and "slumber-breaking" bells, installed in the steeples to rouse the artisans for work, teamed up to deprive the Yankees of their once-quiet weekends. The German community was younger, more tolerant with regard to beer and dancing, and more populated than the native American sectors. With respect to other immigrant enclaves, the German colony usually was larger and more developed. In the major cities, *Deutschtum* consisted not only of stores and saloons, but banks, hospitals, orchestra halls, and elite social clubs.[1]

Though it was a bewildering mixture of Protestants, Catholics, Prussians, Bavarians, workers, and merchants, the German community achieved a unity that seems surprising when one considers that Germany itself did not become a nation until 1871. Immigrants from the provincial countries of central Europe came together as a single nationality despite the lack of a national heritage, the lack of common class interests, the lack of religious unity, and without a

1. Joseph G. Kennedy, *Population of the United States in 1860* (Washington, 1864), 621; *Buffalo Commercial Advertiser,* 10 June 1857; Louis Scisco, *Political Nativism in New York State* (New York, 1901), 126–140.

New York History APRIL 1985

common view of politics. Historians have tended to explain this phenomenon in negative terms, treating the cohesiveness of the German-American settlement as a reaction against American culture. They describe the mid-nineteenth century *Deutschtum* as a "stockade," an "island," a "decompression chamber," and a "fortress."[2] They view the mass of German-Americans as peasants who wanted to protect their village traditions or as ethnics who forged a sense of unity in reaction to nativist threats.

This interpretation may have a certain appeal, but it indicates that German-American unity was a negative force, a reactionary movement. An examination of the German community of Buffalo, New York, reveals the positive appeal of *Deutschtum*, that German unity stemmed from revolutionary ideals in Europe. The immigrants who formed the German associations remained committed to a pan-German culture, *Kultur*, as a superior and enjoyable mode of life. These organizers were neither ethnics, in the present-day sense of the term, nor traditionalists, but idealists who desired an effective fusion of European ideals and American opportunities. Their *Deutschtum*, rather than a conservative bulwark, was a prophetic innovation and a smasher of provincial traditions.

About 1 percent of all German immigrants to the New World in the 1840s and 1850s settled in Buffalo, known as the Queen City of the Great Lakes.[3] The imperial pretensions of the city stemmed from its strategic location as the intermediary between the Erie Canal and the Great Lakes. From the elevation on the northern side of the city, visitors saw a motionless view of what the canal and lake had bred: tall windowed grain elevators, neat rows of five-story dwellings, westside mansions, and a congregation of small frame houses on the eastern half of Main Street. Some cities such as Chicago and New York had entered the American imagination through spectacular initiatives, and others like Cincinnati and Baltimore had capitalized on natural advantages. But the growth of the Queen City had stemmed from the decision of outsiders, in this case the state's canal commissioners. The favorable correlation of the city's water table to the elevation of the lake, rather than the

2. La Vern J. Rippley, *The German-Americans* (Boston, 1976), 73–84; John A. Hawgood, *The Tragedy of German-America* (New York, 1940), xiv; Kathleen N. Conzen, *Immigrant Milwaukee 1836–1860* (Cambridge, 1976), 3; Richard O'Connor, *The German-Americans* (Boston, 1968), 120.

3. By 1860, 18,000 of the 1,301,000 German-born who lived in the United States, resided in Buffalo. F. Burgdoerfer, "Migration Across the Frontiers of Germany," in Walter F. Wilcox, ed., *International Migrations* (New York, 1931), 2:353; Kennedy, *Population in 1860*, xxxi, 346. In comparison, the German-born population of New York City in 1860 was 119,977. See Robert Ernst, *Immigrant Life in New York City* (New York, 1949), 198.

arguments of boosters, brought the western terminus of the canal to Buffalo. The city subsequently thrived as a point of transshipment. Without the disruptive influence of a major industry or large mines, Buffalo's population grew at a steadier, less erratic pace than most other major American cities.[4]

The image of the city as a safe bet, a quieter, less aggressive version of the east coast cities, may have helped to draw an anomalously high number of immigrants from the small towns of central Europe. The local canal economy lagged behind the east coast centers in modernizing the technology of production, and there were many openings for the pre-industrial occupations, for artisans, small proprietors, and laborers.[5] The German fathers who came to the Queen City from underindustrialized areas in Bavaria, the Prussian Rhineland, Hessia, Baden, and Wuerttemberg, tended to take these blue-collar jobs, leaving the wife the responsibility of turning a barren cottage into a home. Reinforced by a large and conservative Catholic Bavarian influx, the Germans tended to own their homes and remain in the city as long as they could hold jobs. In 1855, 38 percent of the German households owned land. Ten years later, this figure had increased to 50 percent. The German element became progressively entrenched. By 1855, over 350 German-American families had resided in the city for at least twenty years compared to the New Englanders who could have counted only 200 such families, the English with 130, and the Irish with about 80. The Germans who had come with the immigration tide of the late 1840s and 1850s thus were newcomers like most of Buffalo's population of 74,000 in 1855, but they appeared more prepared to stay.[6]

The coming of the Europeans inspired Yankees to move farther west. With their stiff woolen jackets and harsh accents, "the Dutch," as the Germans were called, seemed conspicuous, clannish, and old-fashioned. Joseph Ellicott, the agent of the Holland Land Company monopoly, had begun to encourage German settlements in western New York in the early nineteenth century. Thousands of non-English-speaking farmers and artisans had congregated in the villages of Bergholtz, Hamburg, Lancaster, Ebenezer (West Seneca), and the "Fruit Belt" on Buffalo's eastside.

4. *Fourteenth Census of the United States 1920: Population* (Washington, 1921), 1:79.

5. Theodore Hershberg, *et al.*, "Occupation and Ethnicity in Five Nineteenth Century Cities," *Historical Methods Newsletter* 7 (1974), 192–196; Andrew Yox, "Decline of the German-American Community in Buffalo" (Ph.D. dissertation, University of Chicago, 1983), 22.

6. 1855 New York State manuscript census schedules.

Yankee land dealers had also profited from the village ideal, and by 1855, over 75 percent of the city's Germans resided in four eastside wards. Segregated from Anglo-American merchants on the west side and Irish tenants on the south, the city's eastside German element was larger than the combined population of Germans in the states of Maine, New Hampshire, Vermont, Connecticut, and Rhode Island. The rural background of many immigrants was manifested by the way they dug wells by their houses and retained small farm animals to raise and slaughter.[7]

The conservative character of religious groups on the eastside sharpened the impression of a parochial and traditional community. The Buffalo Synod Lutherans, emigrés from the forced system of ecumenicalism in Prussia, were considered the most hierarchical and orthodox of the many German synods of nineteenth-century America. Their leader, J. A. A. Grabau, had viewed his church's arrival in Buffalo as the dawn of salvation in America.[8] The German Catholics of Buffalo also gained a reputation for their uncompromising positions. German Jesuits held well-publicized missions beside huge wooden crosses imploring the crowds to reaffirm their commitment to Jesus Christ. The newspaper, *Die Aurora*, the third German Catholic paper published in the United States, decried the pernicious influences of modern civilization and called on "cold Catholics" to return to the one true Church. These goals were furthered in 1854 when the editor of the *Aurora* and other eastside Catholics became the first advocates of the Central *Verein*, the voice of German Catholicism in America.[9]

For the many sons of New England who had forged a living from the commercial opportunities of the Queen City, the eastside immigrants confirmed the crudest of stereotypes of the downtrodden European peasant. The *Buffalo Commercial Advertiser*, the oldest and most prestigious daily in the city, contributed several caustic reviews of the German enclave:

> The fourth, fifth, sixth and seventh wards are as little American as the duchy of Hesse Cassel; their population speaks a foreign language, reads foreign newspapers, . . . isolates itself from the American element.
>
> . . . the most worthless pauper in Europe . . . comes here, reeking with filth and ignorant as swine . . . [10]

7. *Commercial Advertiser*, 22 July 1876. In 1855, 4,503 of the 5,764 household heads of German birth in Buffalo resided in wards four, five, six, and seven. 1855 ms. census schedules; Kennedy, *Population in 1860*, 621.

8. P. Buerger, *Chronik der Ersten Ev. Lutherischen Dreifaltigkeits Gemeinde in Buffalo N.Y.* (Buffalo, 1889), 11.

9. *Aurora*, 5 November 1853, 13 July 1855; Emmet H. Rothan, *The German Catholic Immigrant in the United States* (Washington, 1946), 59; *Buffalo Express*, 3 August 1913.

One can read descriptions like these and assume that the German immigrants had been transplanted from the sixteenth century. Certainly such "peasants" could not have been imbued with a spirit of national identity. But a look at the German press and folklore of the 1850s presents quite a different picture. Even in Buffalo, with its disproportionately high representation of rural Bavarians, and its lack of a sizable German-American elite, advocates of German solidarity stepped forward to organize an associational life which was at once popular and based on the ideals of German nationalism.

Without the financial resources of the westside merchants, the leaders of the German societies marveled at the growth of their own literary, musical, and athletic organizations in the early 1850s. Later spokesmen viewed this period as the "good old times," the Garden of Eden stage in the history of Buffalo's *Deutschtum*. Both prestigious associations such as the *Saengerbund* singing society and the *Turnverein*, as well as a number of other influential organizations, received their charters. These initiatives were powered by the immigration stream of the late 1840s and early 1850s. Half of the male German population of Buffalo by 1855 had arrived in the last seven years and many of these journeymen desired the German

---

10. *Commercial Advertiser,* 7 December 1855, 12 June 1857.

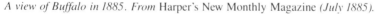
A view of Buffalo in 1885. From Harper's New Monthly Magazine *(July 1885).*

societies more than the young American women who walked together to church on Sundays. Fraternities came before families; the free-thinking element wanted to change their new situation before settling down in it. One group of newcomers, the Forty-Eighters, seemed especially single-minded in this effort. These ex-revolutionaries had served the liberal-nationalist cause in the German provinces during the 1848 upheaval which nearly toppled the monarchs of Prussia and Austria. Forty-Eighters in Buffalo such as August Thieme and Edward Storck were known as two of the most "active and spirited" German-American organizers in the city.[11]

To the American "rowdies" who ravaged the hall of the local *Turnverein,* and westside Yankees like the businessman, Elam Jewett, the cultural proclivities of the Germans seemed subversive and decadent. The activities of the German clubs, called *Vereine,* stirred up large crowds on the eastside who first attended the festivities, and then ended up in the saloons. The Turners sponsored outdoor athletic festivals which displayed the physical prowess of the young German men. The singing society featured a large ensemble of men who impressed an audience more by their resolve than by their virtuosity. The sober American could see how pathos blended into politics. The cultural character of the *Vereine* had proved useful in Germany where the provincial bureaucracies had suppressed nationalistic organizations. In the songs of the singing *Vereine* and in the fierce camaraderie of the Turners, members conveyed an enthusiasm for German unity and *Kultur.* For the hundreds of vocalists in the *Saengerbund, Liedertafel,* and other singing societies, crowd pleasers such as "The Watch on Rhine" and "Live Well My Fatherland" accented mystical ties to a politically fragmented German nation. One of the most prized possessions of the *Turnverein* was a bust of "Father Jahn," the European founder of the movement. Jahn, a vulgar nationalist who had preached against intermarriage with non-Germans and the adoption of "Latin" customs, had formed the gymnastic society as a front for military preparedness during the Napoleonic wars.[12]

Though Buffalo newspapers and directories indicate an absence of provincial Bavarian, Hessian, or Prussian *Vereine* which could have worked to preserve distinctive traditions, there were lodges and clubs on the eastside with a mythic appeal.[13] Alongside older

11. *Geschichte der Deutschen in Buffalo und Erie County* (Buffalo, 1898), 101, 149; Joseph Ehnes, *St. Anna Bote* (Buffalo, 1908), 97.

12. Frederick Hertz, *The German Public Mind in the the Nineteenth Century* (New York, 1975), 37–40; Carl Wittke, *Refugees of Revolution* (Philadelphia, 1952), v–vii.

lodges like Odin and Walhalla, three fraternities of the Harugari appeared in the mid-1850s. Harugari reportedly was a Teutonic priest who kept the "German spirit" alive during the days of the Romans. Like the priest they venerated, the Cherusker, Robert Blume, and Black Rock chapters joined together to "preserve and cultivate the German language, German customs, . . . German songs." In short, to help "Germanize" America. The spirit of the Harugari group also carried over to the German Freemasons, who of all the lodge groups had the strongest international connections. In the 1850s, the German lodge Modestia engaged in a recriminatory debate with the other American lodges over the necessity of keeping lodge notes in English.[14]

The center of the German-American community, the German Young Men's Society and German press, labored to promote a national consciousness among the Germans. The Alsatian, Swiss, and West German founders of the German Society in 1841 had dedicated the organization to the preservation of the "German language and spirit." One of the first presidents, F. A. Georger, wrote that for the Germans to achieve influence in America, the "preservation of the German language was not only necessary . . . but indispensable."[15] The Society showed its commitment to German nationalism in 1851 when it promoted the Buffalo visit of the Hungarian revolutionary, Louis Kossuth, and subsequently squandered hundreds of dollars in loans to liberal rebels in the German provinces. Despite these losses, the literary institution prospered as the office of community-wide picnics called "people's festivals," a library for the German speakers, and a forum for debates and speeches on German affairs. By 1855, the Society counted one member for every twenty-two German households in the city.[16] This effort to bring local Germans together through a discussion of European trends was paralleled in the press. The German-American newspapers dealt first with the central European situation or with United States news, secondly with events in the German provinces, and only incidentally with the activity of Germans in America.

Had the idea of common descent, or the need to recreate Old

13. *Buffalo Demokrat*, 1855; *Aurora*, 1855; *Directory of the City of Buffalo* (Buffalo, 1855).

14. *Buffalo Freie Presse*, 12 March 1886; H. Perry Smith, ed., *History of the City of Buffalo and Erie County*, 2 vols. (Syracuse, 1884), 2:380.

15. Die Deutsche Jungmaenner Gesellschaft, *Festschrift zur Feier ihres fuenfzigjahrigen Stiftungsfestes* (Buffalo, 1891), 12.

16. Yox, "German-American Community," 414.

World traditions proved fertile, one might expect to have found a Bavarian society, a Prussian enclave, or Saxon Lutheran churches. In fact, such provincial bodies probably did not exist. The records of many Evangelical churches and secular societies have perished, but when existing marriage records and membership lists are matched with the 1855 census, not one organization appears with a majority of members from any one German province (Table 1). The 1855 New York State manuscript census indicates further that the provincial groups scattered throughout the eastside. Certain factions like the Alsatians at St. Louis Church, or the Bavarians of the seventh ward, comprised strong pluralities, but even in these cases, village and descent ties probably were not very pervasive. The Alsatians at St. Louis, for instance, had immigrated from a variety of small towns. Parish nicknames such as "Ingweiler Schumacher," "Hagenau Andres," and "Wasseler Weber" identified the parishioner first by his hometown in Europe and second by his surname. Even the Buffalo Synod, known as the "Prussian Church," was not so clannish as its critics claimed. Grabau made a concerted effort to bring all conservative Lutherans into his synod. The church's 1842 hymnbook, the *Lutheranisches Kirchengesangbuch,* incorporated chorales from thirty-two different provinces in central Europe.[17]

The effort to organize by nationality may have alienated some immigrants. Perhaps over half of the Germans in Buffalo in the 1850s did not affiliate with a German church, lodge, or association.[18] The different German dialects of the provinces impeded communication among those immigrants who lacked a formal education and an exposure to "high" German. Many immigrants still looked further west and saw the Queen City and its social organizations as a trap. Other Germans admired the opportunities of the New World to such an extent that they dropped all ties to their countrymen. According to some accounts, these same pioneers often became the most vicious of nativists, calling the newly-arrived immigrants "dumb Dutchmen" to their faces.[19] But to the extent that formal organizations surfaced among the Germans,

17. *St. Louis Bazar Chronicle,* 25 October 1888; Johann A. A. Grabau, comp., *Evangelisch-Lutheranisches Kirchengesangbuch* (Buffalo, 1842).

18. The 1855 manuscript census indicates that only about 8,000 of the 31,000 German-born or German surnamed population of Buffalo affiliated with German churches. The combined membership of the *Vereine* probably did not exceed 2,000. See *Geschichte der Deutschen,* 108, 151, 159.

19. See Wilhelm Lautz's reminiscences: *Freie Presse,* 3 October 1904. The first German Republicans were often viewed as nativists. *Aurora,* 22 August 1856; *Demokrat,* 27 August 1857.

TABLE 1

Representation of Provincial Groups
in German Organizations and Wards: 1855

		Percent of Adults Born in:							
Group	N	Germany Unspec.[a]	Bavaria	Prussia	France[b]	Hessia	Baden-Wur.	Other	Total
Church Groups									
St. Boniface RC	25	24	20	12	12	4	12	16	100
St. Mary's RC	233	18	39	19	5	3	9	7	100
St. Michael's RC	24	36	30	8	22	4	0	0	100
St. Louis RC	119	14	20	8	46	5	6	1	100
First Trinity L.	21	35	15	15	10	5	5	15	100
St. John's Luth.	38	50	3	8	13	3	10	13	100
St. Paul's Evan.	20	40	5	5	20	5	10	15	100
Societies									
Ger. Young Men's	19	37	0	16	5	10	16	16	100
Liedertafel	27	26	22	0	7	0	15	30	100
Saengerbund	21	24	14	6	6	6	10	34	100
Turnverein	11	37	18	9	9	9	0	18	100
Eastside Wards									
Fourth	794	40	20	16	c	d	16	8	100
Sixth	1344	1	38	13	c	20	19	9	100
Seventh	1274	11	40	15	c	6	15	13	100

[a]Where the nativity was listed as "Germany."

[b]Most often refers to Alsace-Lorraine in the case of German organizations.

[c]Not coded.

[d]Enumerator failed to recognize Hessia as a province.

Source: Records of St. Boniface, St. Mary's, St. Michael's and St. Louis churches, Buffalo and Erie County Public Library.; Records at First Trinity Lutheran, St. John's Lutheran, and St. Paul and St. Mark's United Church of Christ. The samples of members in German societies were drawn from newspaper entries in the *Demokrat*, 1853–1856, and from *Geschichte der Deutschen in Buffalo and Erie County* (Buffalo, 1898), pp. 98–170. The names of members in the churches and societies were matched against an alphabetized printout of the 1855 census for Buffalo compiled by Lawrence Glasco of the University of Pittsburgh.

these associations thrived on the national tie. Bavarian patriotism or German-American nativism, though expressed, were positions of marginality and despair rather than popular sentiments, able to attract a following.

Due in part to provincial differences, the German community depended more on the abstract bond of *Kultur* than on a more concrete appeal to a special people. The non-ethnic, almost anti-ethnic character of this arrangement is striking. Ethnicity, when defined as a mutual feeling of common descent, or rather vaguely as a sense of "peoplehood" (thus making the term "ethnic group" redundant), generally refers to interrelated families, a historical community.[20] But the eastside had too many strangers, too many tradition-blind leaders and spokesmen to promote such a feeling. The lines of descent indeed failed to connect. Many of these immigrants did not have a strong family network in the city as the German-Americans did later. An alphabetical printout of the surnames in the 1855 census for Buffalo indicates that only one in eight of the German family names matched with at least one other in the city. By contrast, 25 percent of the Irish and 33 percent of the American-born households had matching surnames.[21] The idea of common descent thus had a much weaker mathematical foundation in the 1850s than later in the German-American experience when the yearly celebrations of "German Day" reminded the faithful about the achievements of their immigrant forebears. An ethnic feeling later brought German-born and American-born generations together, but in this community of immigrants in the 1850s the problem of a *Kultur*-less generation had not yet appeared.

Demographic factors sharpened the appeal of German culture as the one fundamental standard of the community. Unlike the German-American element in the twentieth century when over half of the household heads were American-born, over 95 percent of the fathers with German surnames in Buffalo in 1855 had experienced their most impressionable years in Europe. The German-Americans in the 1850s also tended to be younger on the average than in later years, more than half of the family heads being less than thirty-six years old in 1855. These relatively youthful guardians had viewed or heard of the 1848 revolution while in their twenties or late teens. Firsthand sentiments about the value of their *Kultur* also may have come from their parents who had experienced the deprivations caused by the Napoleonic invasions in the early nineteenth century. However difficult it was to preserve such Germanic

20. Milton Gordon has viewed ethnicity as a feeling of peoplehood in *Assimilation in American Life* (New York, 1964), 27. For other important definitions of ethnicity see: Max Weber, "On Ethnic Groups," in Talcott Parsons, ed., *Theories of Society* (New York, 1961), 306; William Petersen, "Concepts of Ethnicity," in Stephan Thernstrom, ed., *Harvard Encyclopedia of Ethnic Groups* (Cambridge, 1980), 234–235.

21. Lawrence Glasco, "Ethnicity and Social Structure: Irish, Germans, and Native Born of Buffalo, New York, 1850–1860" (Ph.D. dissertation, State University of New York at Buffalo, 1973), 156–157.

ideals in an English-speaking environment, the young German could point to the power of numbers. In 1855, Buffalo's Germans made up about 43 percent of the Queen City's population. By 1875, this figure had increased to 49 percent.[22]

The advance of German culture in Buffalo encouraged the nativist reaction of the 1850s. Though some historians have depicted the rise of German associations as a reaction to the political threat of nativism, in Buffalo the formation of the major German societies preceded the political successes of nativism.[23] By the summer of 1854, the major German organizations—the German Young Men's Society, *Liedertafel, Turnverein, Saengerbund,* and Harugari—were already in place. Political nativism merely encouraged this buildup further by attacking aspects of the German way of life head on. This assault came to life unexpectedly in the fall election of 1854 when a nativist candidate for governor, Daniel Ullman, captured the plurality of votes cast in Buffalo, and the temperance candidate, Myron Clark, won the election. Both forces threatened German culture: the nativists because of their insistence that the right of voting hinged on assimilation, and the temperance party for their attempt to outlaw beer, a German staple. The victory of the temperance faction seemed particularly anti-German, as the eastside immigrants monopolized the brewery industry and often thought of beer as one of life's most precious enjoyments. The new governor, an experienced back-country advocate of prohibition, successfully pushed through an "Act for the Prevention of Intemperance, Pauperism, and Crime" in 1855 which would have outlawed liquor in New York State. The prohibition bill, though later declared unconstitutional, drew a great deal of emotional crossfire from many German groups. The brazen resolve of German-American shooting societies and Turners not to accept the law helps to explain why it was never enforced in New York City and Buffalo.[24]

The new political situation emboldened the community spokesmen who had argued for a German front all along. The Buffalo *Demokrat* wrote that it was now "indispensable for the Germans to vote as a body." The German newspaper, the *Telegraph,* which had hitherto supported the Whig cause agreed with

22. 1855 ms. census schedules; A sample of 1,072 Buffalo households was drawn from the 1875 New York State ms. census schedules.
23. Hawgood, *German-America,* 235; Frank Nelson, "The German-American Immigrants' Struggle," *International Review* 10 (May, 1873), 39.
24. DeAlva S. Alexander, *A Political History of the State of The State of New York,* 2 vols. (New York, 1906), 2:210; *Demokrat,* 6–28 June 1855.

the viewpoint of the *Demokrat* and refused to follow the Anglo-American Temperance Whigs any further. The *Aurora*, though usually not only antagonistic to all Protestants but apolitical as well, reevaluated its position in tune with its secular rivals. The editor, Christian Wieckman, wrote that Catholics could support "honorable Lutherans and Calvinists." It was better to support a German Protestant who understood the needs of his countrymen than an Anglo-American who merely posed as a defender of the immigrants.[25]

The editorial support in the German press for a united front seems to have touched a majority of German voters. In the mayoral election of 1855, the four German wards drew 20 percent more voters than in 1854 and went solidly Democratic. The 1,259-vote majority gained by the Democratic candidate, Frederick Stevens, on the eastside generously offset the 400-vote majority given the Know Nothing or nativist candidate, William Bird, by the rest of the city. The subsequent elections clarified the meaning of this performance. In 1856, Buffalo's "most honorable" citizen, Millard Fillmore, ran for President as the candidate of the American party, the nativist organization. Though he obtained over 20 percent of the vote in Irish wards one and eight, this second generation New Englander won less than 10 percent of the sixth and seventh wards, the most concentrated German areas.[26] When the Know Nothing movement collapsed on the national level following the election, local nativists camouflaged their objectives behind the rhetoric of a reform party in 1857, designed to draw eastside votes. The *Telegraph*, a targeted ally, was not attracted to the bluff and wrote in rebuttal that the Germans would "not labor for a cause and for men who would degrade us to an inferior position." The Germans held out again as a bloc, and the Spearman correlation between the percentage ol German households in a ward and the percentage Democratic, indicates that Germans across the city tended to vote against the reform ticket (Figure 1). The persistence of this front stunned many westsiders. After the election of 1857, the *Commercial Advertiser* wrote that henceforth the "Irish" and "Germans" will "become our rulers."[27]

Ironically, nativism served to create what it had sought to de-

25. *Demokrat*, 19 September 1855; *Aurora*, 10 November 1854, 9 November 1855.
26. Fillmore received 9 percent of the 782 votes in the sixth ward and 6 percent of the 816 votes in the seventh. *Express*, 4 November 1856.
27. The *Telegraph* as quoted in: *Commercial Advertiser*, 13 June 1857; *Commercial Advertiser*, 10 June 1857.

FIGURE 1

German-American Voting Trends in Buffalo, 1853–1860

Spearman Correlation Coefficients

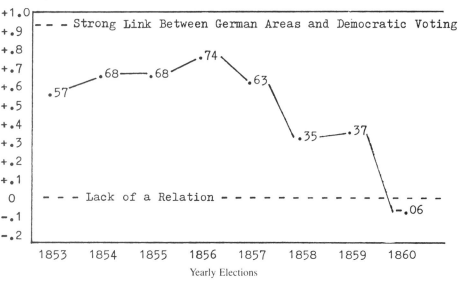

NOTE: Spearman rank correlations were used to determine the relation between two ordinal level variables: ward rank in percent German, and ward rank in percent Democrat. Data on yearly elections are from presidential, gubernatorial, congressional, and mayoral elections. SOURCE: *Commercial Advertiser,* 10 November 1853, 8 November 1854, 7 November 1855, 4 November 1856, 4 November 1857, 3 November 1858, 10 November 1859, 8 November 1860; 1855 New York State manuscript census schedules.

stroy, an alien political bloc. Sectional politics, by contrast, especially those pursued by the newly-formed Republican party, served to neutralize the foreign vote. The conflict over states' rights and the status of slavery in the west had simmered between North and South for forty years, but in the late 1850s the conflict suddenly had turned ugly and violent in Kansas. Northerners who wanted the new territory to ally with free states fought openly with partisans of the South who wanted another slave state. The sectional struggle, which threatened to plunge the nation into war and destroy the Union, also threatened the solidarity of German immigrants. Though an idealistic appeal to German unity could make sense on a local level, such an ideology had little applicability on a national scale. And it was now the specter of Civil War, not local issues, that dwarfed other concerns. The German-American community became paralyzed by the most pressing issue of the day. German immigrants resided in the South and in the North. Many Old Lutherans, Catholics, and southern Germans condoned slavery while Turners, free-thinkers, and Evangelicals condemned it in the strongest of terms.

German immigrants found it especially difficult to reach a consensus on national issues. Two sizable groups of Germans proved generally irreconcilable in local politics after 1857. The pioneers, represented in Buffalo by prosperous businessmen and professionals like Phillip Dorsheimer, Jacob Schoellkopf, and Edward Storck, criticized the Democratic party as an unimaginative and essentially corrupt coalition. These reformers favored the Republican party's strong stand on national unity and they generally opposed slavery. Their views brought them closer to the Anglo-Americans, and many agreed with Edward Storck who believed that the Germans needed Yankee know-how to succeed. The conservatives, by contrast, saw the Republican party as a new front for nativism. As workers, Catholics, and Democrats, these more segregated Germans were opposed to higher taxes and apprehensive about the government's meddling with temperance and parochial education.

Both sides retained their fascination for *Kultur*, but went along separate political routes. Schoellkopf and Dorsheimer invited imposing speakers like the Forty-Eighter Friedrich Hecker to win their countrymen to the Republican cause, but the conservatives proved able to counter these bids with rhetoric of their own. Hecker's fierce bombast in the name of Republicanism stirred the indignation of one of the city's most distinguished Germans, Francis Brunck, and a local backlash against the representative of Cincinnati's *Deutschtum* ensued. In New York State, the nativists had managed to claim the Republican name in the 1840s, and this association played havoc with the new party's determination to win the German vote. The *Demokrat* insisted that an alliance with the Republicans was not possible because these Americans "harbored great hostility toward the German-born...." The pioneers had fallen to the Republican temptation because they were offered offices "like bait" and a "false sense of honor." The charges and countercharges at times became cynical and malicious. The pioneers characterized the conservatives as "wife beaters" while the *Demokrat* compared the German progressives to "dogs" who groveled at the "feet of their nativist masters."[28]

The German society element known as the *Vereindeutsch* saw
their own power wane dramatically as spokesmen for the Germans
after 1857. *Verein* Germans in Buffalo tended to support the Republicans, but whichever way they turned, the cycle of protest,
unrest, and dissolution followed. The *Turnverein* broke up into two
rump organizations in 1857 when the majority voted to attend a
Republican rally. The economic contractions of that year added a
financial crisis to a morale problem and several lesser organizations such as the *Liederkranz, Harmonie,* and Thalia disbanded.
Even the German Young Men's Society appeared in danger of
failing. The membership of this cultural center declined from 275
in 1855 to 65 in 1860. When Karl Trieschman and H. F. Juengling
led the German Society in an attempt to reintroduce the People's
Festival in 1863, even the generally charitable *Demokrat* admitted
that the venture had failed. Perhaps the only bright spot for German
organization in Buffalo during the Civil War occurred with the
formation of a "German Women's Aid Society" to care for seriously wounded soldiers who had been returned to Buffalo. The
women explained that they saw their organization as a patriotic
duty and as a way to enhance the "honor of the German name"
in Buffalo.[29]

The outbreak of the Civil War made German unity seem trivial
and unnecessary. When Abraham Lincoln visited Buffalo before
his inauguration in 1861, the president-elect received a local delegation of Germans and told them that the country was as much
theirs as anyone else's. The newcomers therefore should "forget
that they were foreigners as soon as possible."[30] The Anglo-
Republicans were finally serious about power-sharing. Whole-
hearted German support for the war effort was the consolation
prize. Several Germans in Buffalo already had fired the musket-
loading cannons in Europe and one recently organized unit seemed
especially fight-worthy. The Buffalo *Express* commented that Buffalo had raised no finer collection of soldiers than the colorful,
well-trained Germans of Wiedrich's Battery. "When the adopted
citizens of a country respond like this to her call for aid, what hope
can there be for rebellion?"[31]

The German contribution to the war effort seemed generous
enough to console the nativists and boost the stature of the eastside

---

28. Scisco, *Political Nativism,* 40; *Demokrat,* 8 October 1856, 19 October 1860, 22, 27
August 1857; *Aurora,* 22 August 1856; *Freie Presse,* 10 May, 20 August 1870.
29. *Demokrat,* 17 February, 25 June 1863.
30. *Commercial Advertiser,* 18 February 1861.
31. *Express,* 24 April 1861.

community. About 16 percent of all German-American males aged nineteen to thirty-five by 1865 had served in the armed forces compared to 10 percent for the Anglo-Americans and 9 percent for the Irish. Though the perils of modern warfare seemed clear enough by the autumn of 1861, the Germans were less inhibited to volunteer than other groups. Wealthy Anglo-Americans when drafted could often afford to pay off a substitute. The future President of the United States, Grover Cleveland, living in Buffalo, avoided military service in this way. The Irish, on the other hand, often carried grudges against the Republican administration as they assumed that hordes of free Negroes might compete for their own jobs. In the summers of 1862 and 1863, angry Irish dockworkers looted and burned parts of the black neighborhood on Buffalo's lower eastside in search of scabs.[32]

Many Germans did not support the prolongation of the war effort. Both the Catholic *Aurora* and J. A. A. Grabau, spokesman for the Buffalo Synod, saw the fighting as a symbol of American decadence. By 1863, wards four and seven, which had gone Republican after 1857, moved back into the Democratic fold. But when the Union Army emerged victorious from the forests of Virginia, the war investment suddenly appeared to pay off with large political dividends. The anti-German bias in the city subsided. Later community historians noted that the Civil War ended the vogue of calling the Germans "Dutchmen" in Buffalo. When a German Civil War veteran on the city council, Richard Flach, made a motion to introduce German language instruction in the schools, the bid was accepted unanimously. After three failed ventures in 1839, 1851, and 1857, the Germans finally had incorporated their language into some of the city's primary schools. The School Superintendent, John Fosdick, wrote in 1866 that foreign language instruction did not come as a gift. The Germans had passed the test of citizenship and had earned it.[33]

Patriotic appeals rather than ethnic slurs came into fashion after

32. A 500-member sample of males, nineteen to thirty-five years of age, was drawn from the 1865 New York State manuscript census schedules. The 1865 enumeration listed whether a resident had served or was serving in the Union forces. The differences are significant at the .05 level of confidence. This score indicates that in less than 5 of 100 samples drawn randomly, the observed relationship would have occurred simply because of chance factors. For an account of the Irish uprising in Buffalo see: *Commercial Advertiser*, 7 July 1863.

33. *Commercial Advertiser*, 4 November 1863. Both George Baltz and Louis Buehl expressed the view in the 1870s that the Civil War had served to discourage the use of the term "Dutch" in place of "German." *Demokrat*, 19 May 1873, 1 March 1878. Fosdick's comments are recorded in the *Proceedings of the Common Council of the City of Buffalo* (Buffalo, 1866), 435, 440, 472.

the war. The identity of the immigrants began to change from "Dutch" to "German" to "German-American." The German-American celebrated a double sense of heritage and national pride. Simultaneously, he could reaffirm the advantages of German culture and the brilliance of American politics. *Kultur* and Constitution. He could profess, as the Buffalo *Freie Presse* did, that it was the "holy mission" of the Germans in America to accept the nation's democratic system and rise to the top of it in the arts, sciences, and politics.[34] Finally, the German-American was distinguished from his predecessor by the ability to speak English. It was much easer to insult the uncomprehending "Dutchman" than the German-American, as the latter could defend himself in English and swear on the bible of his Civil War record.

The acquisition of the English language paradoxically had a strong association with German-American idealism. The most fervent exponents of *Deutschtum* tended to learn English first, accepting the argument of Francis Brunck and others that German influence in the New World depended on a knowledge of two languages.[35] Bilinguists would become the power brokers of the new America as long as the *Deutschtum* maintained itself alongside the English-speaking American element. Many of the businessmen who frequented the *Verein* life followed this line, and by 1865 more than three in four were considered literate in English. More conservative church groups such as the Lutherans and Catholics showed more resistance to the new language even though they had persisted longer in the city. In a sample of fifty-seven *Verein* members drawn from newspapers and matched with the 1865 census, 86 percent were found listed as literate in English compared to 51 percent for the Lutherans, 37 percent for the Catholics, and 42 percent for other German Protestants. But over half of the Lutherans, many of whom had consecrated their homesteads after their arrival in 1839, were found in the 1855 census. Only 33 percent of the *Verein* Germans, by contrast, had resided in Buffalo for over ten years (Table 2).

The Lutherans, Catholics, and other conservative groups saw the members of the *Turnverein, Saengerbund,* and the German lodges as worldly and materialistic. This more self-consciously German element, the *Verein* Germans, seemed most apt to mix with the Americans. *Verein* members clustered in the fourth ward, rather than in the more segregated eastside wards: five, six and

34. *Freie Presse,* 29 March 1873.
35. *Buffalo Weltbuerger,* 11 December 1850; *Demokrat,* 5 September 1857.

TABLE 2

Literacy in English and Persistence for
German-American Groups in Buffalo in 1865

Group	N	Listed as Literate in English	Found in the 1855 Buffalo Census
Associational Groups		*Percent*	*Percent*
Catholics	88	37	37
Evangelicals	41	42	39
Lutherans	47	51	55
Verein Germans	57	86	33
Occupational Groups			
White Collar	131	73	26
Skilled Workers	371	53	26
Laborers	157	48	25
Unemployed	84	10	13
Neighborhood Groups			
Fourth Ward	89	83	33
Fifth Ward	224	22	19
Sixth Ward	192	37	24
Seventh Ward	172	59	23
All Germans	887	47	24

Note: Differences are significant at the .05 level of confidence.
Source: 1865 New York State manuscript census schedules.

seven (see Figure 2). Though the German population was to a great extent mixed together on the eastside, there was a decided preference for the *Verein* element to reside closest to the Anglo-American sector on the westside. This western quarter, the fourth ward, had the most conspicuous non-German population (40 percent) and the highest proportion of German adults who could speak English (84 percent) among the four eastside wards.

Even German immigrants who resided in Irish areas and other non-German neighborhoods tended to exhibit a lower inclination to learn English than the fourth ward Germans. Of the German heads of households in the southern wards—one, two, three, and thirteen—70 percent were literate in English at the time of the 1865 census. For northern wards eleven and twelve, only 46 percent of the German heads of households were considered able to employ

FIGURE 2

Residences of a Sample German-American Population
in Buffalo: 1865 (N 400)

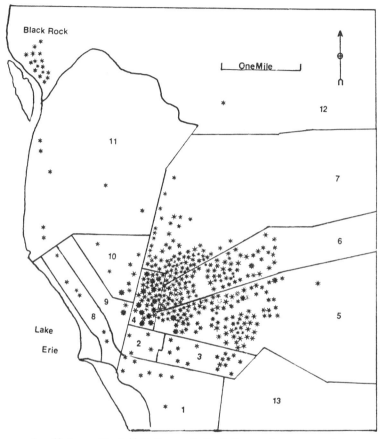

Key:✳=Evangelical,✲=Lutheran,✳=R. Catholic,✳=Unaffil.,✻=Verein Ger.

SOURCE: The relative sizes of the denomination and ward sub-populations were determined from the 1865 New York census schedules which indicate the size of districts and German churches. The relative size of the *Verein* element is an estimate based on membership information in *Geschichte der Deutschen in Buffalo und Erie County* (Buffalo, 1898), pp. 98-170. My estimate for 1865 is 500 adult males. The representation of church and *Verein* elements were apportioned on a ward by ward basis. A sub-sample of the *Verein* Germans was drawn from newspapers, directories, and biographical sketches. The sub-samples of denominational groups were drawn from marriage and baptismal records at the following churches: Trinity Old Lutheran, First Trinity Lutheran, St. John's Lutheran, St. John's United Church of Christ in Black Rock, St. Paul and St. Mark's Church of Christ, New Convenant United Church of Christ, St. Francis Xavier R.C., and St. Ann's R.C. Records for St. Boniface, St. Louis, St. Mary's, and St. Michael's R.C. Churches were drawn from the Buffalo and Erie County Public Library. Residences of members were found in *The Commercial Advertiser Directory for the City of Buffalo* (Buffalo, 1865).

the new language.[36] Many of these Germans who resided apart from their countrymen, as Figure 2 suggests, also tended to remain unaffiliated with the German associations. The heart of the community in ward four, rather than a segregated ethnic enclave, was one of the more cosmopolitan areas of the city with American, French, and English subpopulations living alongside a bilingual German majority.

By the early 1870s, this elite area around the fourth ward featured a German bank, a German insurance society, and many other German organizations such as the *Turnverein* and German Young Men's Society. Of particular interest were the new financial institutions which appeared after the Civil War. The bank and insurance society based their appeal solidly on the drawing power of nationality. Their agents could converse about money affairs in German and often generate a higher level of trust among immigrants than could many of the American institutions. But these organizations did not offer a cozy means to escape big city institutions. They were large money-making ventures which raised impressive edifices on Main Street and solicited an array of German groups to support them. The first board of directors for the German Insurance Society, for instance, included over eight members of the *Vereine*, at least two Lutherans, two Catholics, three German Evangelicals, Republicans, and Democrats.[37]

Though interest in the German-American community had subsided during the Civil War years, a revival of German national spirit was underway by the late 1860s even though the German-American population was more assimilated than before. New immigrants arriving now with greater frequency from Prussia and Mecklenburg undoubtedly infused a new sense of life into the *Deutschtum.* Yet the immigrants who left Germany after 1865 often were listless about the prospects of German unification, a political development which now seemed close at hand in central Europe. After wars with Austria (1866) and France (1870–71), Prussia was able to force a North German Confederation in 1867 and a German Union four years later. When the new "United States of Germany" was proclaimed, the city's Germans celebrated the event with more energy than the rallies held after Appomattox. Mapped out by the German Young Men's Society, the celebration included a three-

36. These figures concerning literacy in English are based on an 887-member sample of German-born household heads. The differences between groups is significant at the .05 level of confidence. 1865 ms. census schedules.

37. *Geschichte der Deutschen*, 258.

mile-long procession with three more divisions than the average Fourth of July parade in Buffalo. An estimated 5,000 marchers took part and tens of thousands more lined Main Street and Broadway to view the floats. Anglo-American newspapers such as the *Express*, *Commercial Advertiser*, and *Evening Post* admitted that the German festival either was, or might have been, the single largest municipal event witnessed in Buffalo.[38]

Such an event could have provided an opportunity to accent the ethnic dimension of the German-American experience, the history of the Germans in Buffalo, or the pride of the local *Deutschtum*. Instead, the speeches and floats focused almost exclusively on the political and moral significance of the new *Reich* in Europe. The myth of *Kultur* had come true; German unification and superiority over its enemies had ensued. Francis Brunck, a popular speechmaker in Buffalo circles, delivered a narration on German courage in the victory over France. George Baltz, a leading voice of the *Turnverein*, called for all Germans in America to follow Germany's bid for power and influence:

> Let this be henceforth our goal . . . to gain in this country that political and social position which is ours by right of numbers, intelligence and merit.[39]

Not only the *Verein* Germans, but also the evangelicals and pietistic Lutheran churches took part in the ceremony. An Evangelical pastor, Otto Burger, gave clear testimony to his belief in the implicit unity of all Germans:

> . . . one spirit animates the German race . . . and the Germany of old is risen again, more closely united than ever before. . . . . This makes every German heart beat more joyfully.
>
> Whatever has been achieved by Germany . . . constitutes our greatest and holiest glory.[40]

The ideal of a "German spirit," international and eternal, seemed to stir the fervor of the community spokesmen in 1871.

As the Peace Festival of 1871 afforded a glimpse of the community in its most dilated and vital form, a look at the celebration's symbols proves instructive. A viewer on the lower end of Main Street near the parade entrance might have first noticed the large *Reich* flag draped over the marchers. Horse-drawn wagons carried the exhibits of the *Vereine*, and these floats carried a few bizarre

38. *Express*, 29–30 May 1871; *Commercial Advertiser*, 29–30 May 1871; *Buffalo Evening Post*, 30 May 1871.
39. *Express, 29 May 1871.*
40. *Commercial Advertiser,* 29 May 1871.

sights for the American observer. The folklore of German nationalism appeared in the open. The German Young Men's Society
wagon carried a huge statue of Friedrich Barbarossa, the medieval
German monarch who had ruled over the last German *Reich*, 700
years before. The sign on the *Liedertafel* wagon poetically linked
the Rhine River to German unity and power. Another statue appeared: Arminus the Cherusker, the German warrior who had,
according to legend, defeated the Roman legions.[41]

Though the *Verein* Germans of the 1850s had made rapid strides
in learning the English language and participating in municipal
societies such as the Buffalo Club and the Science Museum, it was
this group rather than the post-Civil War immigrants who planned
and led the parade. Festival organizers, Edward Storck, Richard
Flach, Francis Brunck, Albert Ziegele, and Phillip Hauck, were all
long-term Buffalo residents and capable English speakers. Among
them, the mean number of years in America was 30.4. All five were
relatively wealthy, and whereas Brunck resided in a spacious
westside mansion, the others resided in the fourth ward.[42]

Though these middle-aged men proved to be spirited organizers
of a German holiday, they did help to soften the chauvinistic strain
of German nationalism. Edward Storck stressed to the city council
that the German celebration was a "Peace Festival," open to all
Buffalo residents, certainly not meant to insult the French-Amer-
icans. The American press in turn reviewed the festival graciously,
and frequently took the German-American point of view that the
new *Reich* was modeled after the United States Constitution. In
response to the often heard German notion of cultural superiority,
Anglo-American newspapers like the *Commercial Advertiser* and
Express interpreted this claim in a narrow sense. The American
press acknowledged the genius of Beethoven, Schiller, and Kant,
and admitted that the United States could use more *Kultur*. A sense
of conflict between Yankee virtures and the Germanic arts gave
way to a vision of overlap. Both America and its new counterpart,
Germany, would become a positive force of progress in the
world.[43]

It was easier to be magnanimous now that half of the eastside had
returned to the Republican fold and the nativist option had lost its
potential. The German community by 1871 was better organized
than in the 1850s. The membership of the German Young Men's

41. *Ibid.*, 30 May 1871.
42. See the "Biographischer Theil" in *Geschichte der Deutschen.*
43. *Commercial Advertiser,* 29–30 May 1871; *Express,* 29–30 May 1871.

Society again expanded, now to an all-time high of four hundred members. Eighty German associations appeared for the festival in 1871, more than many observers had thought existed. The circulation of German-American newspapers was also more extensive than ever before. For the first time in the history of the German-American press in Buffalo, there was an average of over one subscriber for every German household in the city.[44] Four dailies, the *Demokrat, Freie Presse, Taeglicher Telegraph,* and the *Volksfreund,* kept local readers informed about the course of the new Germany and the events of Buffalo's *Vereine.*

The revival of Buffalo's German-American community during the formation of the new *Reich* illustrated the electrifying potential of the national tie. The appeal of *Deutschtum* had extended originally to young immigrants with few family connections who relied on *Kultur* to maneuver socially on the eastside. By 1871, a mystical form of German nationalism continued to appeal to immigrants who were in many cases quite assimilated. The advocates of *Deutschtum* found the nationalist ideology useful not only to curb the influence of Anglo-Americans, but to promote their own political power and prosperity. Thus when the national front promised to raise the status of newly-arrived immigrants after 1850, or when the mythic promises of German nationalism appeared self-evident in 1871, the local *Deutschtum* waxed in popularity. But when German-American unity only complicated more fundamental concerns—such as the welfare of the country during the Civil War era—the community declined. Though a more dedicated sense of loyalty belonged to the nation that German-Americans had died for in the Civil War, the idea of *Deutschtum* was imported directly from Europe. The German-American community of the mid-nineteenth century already depended heavily on the promise of a foreign culture on American soil.

44. *Buffalo City Directory* (Buffalo, 1869), 48–56; *Demokrat,* 30 May 1871; Yox, "German-American Community," 413.

Captain Samuel George, about 1860. Painting by Sanford Thayer. The medallion is probably a peace medal. Courtesy of the Onondaga Historical Association.

Samuel George (1795–1873): A Study of Onondaga Indian Conservatism

By LAURENCE M. HAUPTMAN

History has neglected Samuel George, but Iroquois culture and independence survived its most difficult years because of leaders like him. Laurence Hauptman is Professor of History at the State University of New York College at New Paltz.

THE SIX NATIONS of the Iroquois Confederacy, whether they supported the colonial cause or remained loyal to the Crown, were all losers in the American Revolution. The loyalist groups were forced to give up their New York lands and remove to Canada; the remaining Iroquois, those who stayed in New York, very soon began to suffer incursions from the newly-independent Americans. They were almost completely at the mercy of white capitalists and politicians, and between 1784 and 1842, they lost 99 percent of their lands. In the subtler areas that made up an Iroquois way of life, they suffered the assaults of white missionaries and, inevitably, the endless impersonal bombardment of American civilization as it related to language, custom, consumer goods, communication. It is thus quite remarkable that throughout the nineteenth century there was a continuity in Iroquois society and that Iroquoian culture persisted in a variety of traditional forms. Many individuals contributed to this cultural tenacity, a number of whom have all but disappeared from the historical record. One of these was Samuel George of the Onondaga, a man whose career contributes to a fuller picture of Indian life in New York during a period when Iroquoian culture faced its greatest challenge.

New York History   JANUARY 1989

It should be noted.immediately that historical sources relating to George are not plentiful. His life spanned a period, 1795 to 1873, when the historical record was erratically maintained. Unlike later Iroquois leaders—Ely Parker and Clinton Rickard come immediately to mind—he did not live in a place or time that gave emphasis to the keeping of personal records, nor did he have a historical mentor to encourage him to do so. Samuel George was an Onondaga. Scholars writing on the history of the Iroquois in nineteenth-century New York have focused almost exclusively on the Seneca.[1] All these factors have combined to exclude George from his appropriate place in recorded history. F.D. Huntington, the Episcopal Bishop of Central New York, speaking in 1889, labelled him "the ablest pagan chief of this generation."[2] Despite a certain cultural myopia, Huntington's appraisal was accurate. George was among the most influential Onondaga of the century. He was also the consummate Onondaga conservative. Unlike other Onondaga leaders of the same period, such as Chief Albert Cusick who converted to Christianity, George held steadfast to his native beliefs.[3] He did not reject change outright and did permit western education among his people, but he was also a strong advocate of Indian sovereignty and treaty rights. Like Onondaga conservatives then and now, he urged a separate course for the Iroquois and opposed amalgamation into the American body politic.

Samuel George was born into the Wolf Clan of the Onondaga on the Buffalo Creek Reservation in 1795. This level and well-wooded tract of 83,555 fertile acres along Cayuga, Cazenovia and Buffalo creeks, which included much of the present-day City of Buffalo, was the central fire of Indian life in New York in the sixty years that followed the American

The author would like to thank Mr. George Hamell of the New York State Museum for his help in preparing this article.

1. For a more even-handed treatment of the several tribes, see Bruce G. Trigger, ed., *Handbook of North American Indians* (Washington, D.C., 1978), 15: 418–546.

2. New York State Assembly. *Report of the Special Committee to Investigate the Indian Problem of the State of New York . . .* (Albany, 1889), 390.

3. For the life of Albert Cusick, see William M. Beauchamp, Notebook: *Sketches of Onondagas of Note*, 219–21; William B. Beauchamp MSS., SC 17369, Box 3, New York State Library, Manuscript Division, Albany.

Revolution. It attracted a substantial number of Iroquois refugees from all member nations of the Six Nations. Although the Seneca were the most numerous and politically influential on the reservation, the Onondaga were well represented. In 1816, out of a total of 450 Onondaga in New York, 210 were residing at the Buffalo Creek Reservation. As late as 1837, there were 197 Onondaga on the reservation—approximately 40 percent of all Onondaga in New York State. They occupied a square mile tract on the southerly side of the reservation along Cazenovia Creek.[4]

The Seneca prophet, Handsome Lake, at times a resident of the Buffalo Creek Reservation, received his first vision in 1799, when George was still a small boy. The word of the prophet spread quickly. He spoke against the use of alcohol and against witchcraft and urged the Iroquois to return to traditional ceremonies. At the same time, he urged the Indians to learn to farm in the white manner, and he gave religious sanction to a male role in agriculture. He also preached the transformation of the Indian family structure—from the traditional extended family or clan to the parent-centered family structure of Europeans. And he urged his people not to give any more land to the white man and to take no part in the wars of the whites.[5] While clearly innovative in some respects, Handsome Lake's movement was basically conservative in that it called for the restoration of Iroquois beliefs and ceremonies that had fallen into disuse. He accepted the old gods and myths, the ancient dream rites, the old annual calendar.[6]

It is not surprising that Samuel George's nation, the Onondaga, was receptive to the prophet's conservative preaching.

4. Frederick Houghton, *The History of the Buffalo Creek Reservation*, Buffalo Historical Society, *Publications* (1920), 1-181; Beauchamp, Notebook, 172-73; Samuel George's Pension Application, New York State Division of Military and Naval Affairs, Adjutant General's Office, Claims, Applications and Awards for Service in the War of 1812, ca. 1857-1861, New York State Archives, Albany; Charles M. Snyder, ed., *Red and White on the New York Frontier: A Struggle for Survival: Insights from the Papers of Erastus Granger, Indian Agent, 1807-1819* (Harrison, N.Y., 1978), 30; Charles J. Kappler, comp., *Indian Affairs, Laws and Treaties* (Washington, D.C., 1904), 2:515-16.

5. Anthony F.C. Wallace, *The Death and Rebirth of the Seneca* (New York, 1970), 239-337.

6. Anthony F.C. Wallace, "Origins of the Longhouse Religion," *Handbook of North American Indians,* 15:447.

The Onondaga had clearly not prospered under white domination. The millions of acres that they had held in 1776 were gone. By the 1820s they were reduced to a reservation of 6,100 acres at Onondaga and to living with other members of the Six Nations at Buffalo Creek and along the Grand River near Brantford, Ontario. Divided by the events of the American Revolution, by the proselytizing of white missionaries, and by the power plays of their own leaders, they were impressed by Handsome Lake's call for solidarity and temperance. Many Onondaga converted to his ancient beliefs. The prophet died, in fact, while visiting the Onondaga Reservation in 1815 and was buried beneath the floor of the old Onondaga council house, a site marked today by a monument in the center of the reservation.[7]

Samuel George was twenty when the prophet died. The historical record, not surprisingly, gives no hint of contact between the two, and in one respect George, like many Iroquois, ignored Handsome Lake's message—proscription against Indian participation in the white man's wars. The Iroquois, including a sizeable detachment of Onondaga, served on the American side in the War of 1812. They viewed themselves as citizens of their separate nations and as allies of the United States under the direct command of their own chiefs, especially the Seneca leader Farmer's Brother. Onondaga, including Samuel George, followed the leadership of their chiefs, Captains Cold (Cole) and LaFort.[8] Ironically, the Onondaga came face-to-face with British-allied Iroquois, including Onondaga, from the Six Nations Reserve in Ontario. Once again, the Onondaga were split, participating as auxiliaries in the white man's "war of brothers," as they had done in the American Revolution.[9]

7. Harold Blau, Jack Campisi, and Elisabeth Tooker, "Onondaga," Handbook of North American Indians, 15:496. Interview of Ray Gonyea, Jan. 22, 1988, Albany. Mr. Gonyea, an Onondaga Indian, is the Specialist in Native American Culture, New York State Museum.

8. There is a need for a major study of the Iroquois role in the War of 1812. For good source material, see Snyder, Red and White on the New York Frontier. Arthur C. Parker's "The Senecas in the War of 1812," New York State Historical Association, Proceedings 15 (1916), 78–90. Other treatment of the Iroquois in this conflict is cursory and incomplete.

9. For the Iroquois on the British side, see Charles M. Johnston, ed., The Valley of the Six Nations: A Collection of Documents on the Indian Lands of the Grand

The Iroquois, including the Onondaga, derived little benefit from the war. They suffered casualties in battle and endured smallpox epidemics, while several of the fiercest en-
gagements of the war took place on their lands along the
Niagara River.[10] But for Samuel George, the war was a
theatre in which he displayed courage, endurance, and physical prowess, all of which play a role in the making of a leader
among the Iroquois. Serving along the Buffalo-to-Albany
corridor during the conflict, George was to excel as a runner.
A thin, sinewy man with strongly marked features, his physical appearance was frequently mentioned in the records. He
was viewed by one of these observers as "a noble specimen of
a man" for his athletic prowess and presence. George's greatest achievement during the War of 1812 was to run from
American headquarters at Buffalo to the arsenal at Canan-
daigua and back, a distance of 150 miles, in two days![11]

George's running abilities were legendary. Orlando Allen,
a man later involved in cheating Iroquois Indians out of their
lands, wrote that George was virtually unbeatable in foot
races. The only challenge to his string of victories came from
John Titus, a Seneca Indian from the Allegany Reservation.
According to Allen, Titus was able to defeat George only
once:

> On one occasion Titus achieved by strategy, what he could not by
> speed, and that was by keeping close up to George until within a few
> steps of the goal, and then just before crossing the line, putting forth
> all of his powers, slipped by leaving George no time to recover the

River (Toronto, 1964), 193-228; *The Journal of Major John Norton* (Toronto,
1970), 349-53; and G.F.G. Stanley, "The Significance of the Six Nations Participation in the War of 1812," *Ontario History,* 55 (1963), 215-63.

10. For the Iroquois role in the War of 1812, see William M. Beauchamp, Note-
book, 159-60; Jasper Parrish to Peter B. Porter, July 27, 1814, Asa Landforth to
Peter B. Porter, Sept. 7, 1814, Microfilm Reel 2, Peter B. Porter MSS., Buffalo and
Erie County Historical Society; E.A. Cruikshank, ed., *The Documentary History of
the Campaign Upon the Niagara Frontier, 1812-1814* (Welland, 1896-1908),
2:338-89, 406, 448; 3:145. For Indian casualties (at the Battle of Chippewa), see
John Brannan, comp., *Official Letters of the Military and Naval Officers of the
United States During the War with Great Britain . . .* (Washington, D.C., 1823),
368-73; "General Peter B. Porter's Description of the Battle of Chippawa [*sic*],
"*Public Papers of Daniel D. Tompkins: Governor of New York,* Hugh Hastings,
ed., (New York, 1898), 1:86-92; Snyder, *Red and White on the New York Frontier,*
80-81.

11. Beauchamp, Notebook, 173; "Clifton" Letter to Narragansett weekly quoted
in *Syracuse Standard*, July 26, 1858, newsclipping in Sanford Thayer file (relative to
portrait of Captain George), Onondaga Historical Association, Syracuse.

lost race, as he probably could have done in ten strides. George was exceedingly mortified at the result and was careful not to be thus out-witted again. I think he was on no other occasion beaten in these races.[12]

The importance of "runners" in Iroquois history should not be underestimated. They were not merely gifted athletes intent on "going for the gold." Iroquois runners summoned councils, conveyed intelligence from nation to nation and warned of impending danger. George's contemporary, Lewis Henry Morgan, in his classic *League of the Iroquois* (1851), observed: "Swiftness of foot was an acquirement, among the Iroquois, which brought the individual into high repute."[13] Consequently, George's rise to power and influence in the Iroquois councils was a direct result of his physical prowess. It is also important to note that the contemporary Onondaga of the 1980s still designate "runners," using the term to describe a person who serves the council as a conduit for the conduct of essential business, and who is accorded respect as a community leader worthy of other higher positions of authority and prestige in the nation. Significantly, runners still convey official messages and carry stringed wampum to symbolize their official role, diplomatic protocol and/or truth.[14]

George later received a pension of $120 for his participa-tion in the War of 1812. His pension request for three years of service in the defense of the Niagara Frontier is quite revealing. He asked to be compensated for the following: 1 hat ($5.00), ordinary (non-uniform) coat ($25.00), 1 vest ($3.50), 1 pair of "leggins" ($3.50), 2 blankets ($10.00), 1 knapsack ($3.00), 1 canteen ($.25), "use" of 1 rifle ($10.00),

12. Orlando Allen, *Personal Recollections of Captains Jones and Parrish*, Buffalo Historical Society, *Publications*, 6 (1903), 544.

13. Lewis Henry Morgan, *League of the Iroquois* (Rochester, 1851; reprint, New York, 1962), 441.

14. Interviews of Lee Lyons and Oren Lyons, Sept. 8, 1984, Syracuse. The late Lee Lyons, a Seneca Indian, served as a runner for the Grand Council of the Iro-quois Confederacy; his brother Oren Lyons is a Seneca Indian by birth and an Onondaga chief, who serves as an Iroquois faithkeeper. For the life of one modern day runner, see "Joyondawde Lee A. Lyons, Wolf Clan, Seneca Nation," *Akwesasne Notes*, 18 (Midwinter, 1986), 3. In July, 1984, I attended ceremonies at the Cattaraugus Indian Reservation at which time Iroquois runners were sent cross-country to the site of the Olympic Games in Los Angeles. For more on Iroquois run-ners, see Morgan, *League of the Iroquois*, 109–10; and Peter Nabokov, *Indian Run-ning: Native American History and Tradition* (Santa Fe, N.M., 1981), 18, 84, 178.

1 canoe ($6.00), 2 belts ($7.00), 2 pair of stockings ($1.00), 2 shirts ($4.00), 2 pair of moccasins ($2.00), 1 neckerchief ($1.50) and 1 "scalping knife" ($.50).[15] He also requested $2.00 compensation for his transportation expenses between Buffalo Creek and Fort Niagara (eighty miles round trip).

From the end of the War of 1812 until the mid-1840s, George virtually disappears from the historical record; it is nevertheless possible to reconstruct a part of this period of his life. George and his people came face-to-face with tribal destruction in the three decades after the War of 1812. Following the opening of the Erie Canal in 1825, population rapidly increased in central and western New York. The City of Buffalo was formally incorporated in 1831 and soon became a major Great Lakes port, creating further pressures for expansion; however, Buffalo Creek Reservation blocked the city's expansion to the southeast. Land speculators soon took advantage of the Iroquois, who were bitterly divided by a number of matters—land sales, methods of selecting chiefs, education, religion—that separated the Indians into different camps and made them susceptible to manipulation. Land speculators and corrupt federal officials took advantage of the situation, employed bribery and coercion, and induced some of the chiefs to sign the Treaty of Buffalo Creek in 1838, by which the Indians lost the Buffalo Creek Reservation.[16] Among the Iroquois signatories to the treaty were two Onondaga warriors, William John and Noah Silversmith, who acted without authority from the chiefs and received $2,000 for their "cooperation." The Onondaga were in fact the most resistant to change of all the New York Iroquois. One article of the treaty offered them cash compensation totalling $4,500 to move to the American West. Few of them did so, in sharp contrast to the substantial number of Cayuga and Oneida who left New York after the signing. The Onondaga and Tonawanda chiefs vociferously opposed the Seneca

15. New York State Adjutant General's Office, *Index of Awards: Soldiers of the War of 1812* (Baltimore, 1969), 571.

16. William N. Fenton, "The Iroquois in History," *North American Indians in Historical Perspective,* ed. by Eleanor Burke Leacock and Nancy Oestreich Lurie (New York, 1971), 161–62; Henry S. Manley, "Buying Buffalo from the Indians," *New York History,* 28 (July, 1947), 313–29. For the text of the Treaty of Buffalo Creek, see Kappler, *Indian Affairs, Laws and Treaties,* 2:502–516.

political revolution of 1848 which had overturned the old chieftain system of government and had established a republic, the Seneca Nation of Indians, an elected political system set apart from the Iroquois Confederacy. For more than two decades, they tried to restore the old chieftain system of government on the Allegany and Cattaraugus Reservations. Samuel George was one of the Onondaga leaders who gave support to Senecas attempting to restore the traditional government. Writing in 1850, he praised the Old Chiefs party at Cattaraugus and urged them "to defend the rights of the system of our old Indian government . . . so highly important to us all to maintain."[17]

Onondaga conservatism was also reflected in their resistance to missionaries. Jabez Hyde, a missionary at Buffalo Creek from 1811 to 1820, commented in his journal that the Onondaga were strongly opposed to conversion. Despite the frequent visits of Episcopal, Methodist, Presbyterian, and Quaker missionaries and the building of a Methodist and Episcopal church as well as an Episcopal school at Onondaga in the nineteenth century, a minority of Onondaga were converted. Although the Onondaga chiefs permitted these sects on the reservation, the missionaries' Christian message was not universally accepted. As late as 1890, there were only 68 Christians at Onondaga out of a population of 494 residents (including 86 Oneida).[18]

As a consequence of the loss of the Buffalo Creek Reservation in 1842 and after the death of Captain Cold (Ut-ha-wah), the Onondaga returned to their homeland in central New York. The Confederacy's council fire that had burned at Buffalo Creek was rekindled at the Onondaga Reservation and the sacred wampum was returned to the Onondaga longhouse in 1847. After a brief residence at the Cattaraugus Reservation in the mid-1840s, Samuel George moved his wife and five

17. Sam [sic] George and David Smith to the Chiefs at Cattaraugus, June 8, 1850, Marius B. Pierce MSS., Buffalo and Erie County Historical Society, Buffalo.

18. Jabez Backus Hyde, *A Teacher Among the Senecas: Historical and Personal Narrative of Jabez Backus Hyde,* Buffalo Historical Society, *Publication* 6 (1903), 247; United States Bureau of the Census, *The Six Nations of New York,* Extra Census Bulletin of the 11th Census of the United States, 1890 (Washington, D.C., 1892), 6–9. See also Laurence M. Hauptman, "Foreword" to Fred R. Wolcott, *Onondaga Portrait of a Native People* (Syracuse, 1986), 5–10.

children to Onondaga. It was there in 1850 that he became a chief, taking the name *Hononwirehdonh,* the "Great Wolf," the hereditary keeper of the wampum held by a member of the Wolf Clan of the Onondaga Nation.[19] The attainment of this League title, which he held until his death in 1873, was the culmination of four decades of apprenticeship for leadership. *Hononwirehdonh* was no ordinary title. As Annemarie Shimory states, "He is arbiter of disputes and the tie-breaker in voting. To him are left decisions of referral back to the individual phratries, and to him accrues the task of 'cooling down the fire' when arguments break out." He is also, she notes, "the wampum keeper of the League, and the only chief to constitute a phratry [a tribal social subdivision] all by himself."[20] Thus, at a time of bitter dissension caused by the Buffalo Creek Treaty of 1838 and its aftermath and continued talk by federal and state officials of Iroquois removal from New York, the *Hononwirehdonh,* with his responsibilities to help create consensus and pacify diverse elements, held a strategic position in the struggle for Iroquois survival.

George and the Onondaga Council of Chiefs were soon faced with repeated state policies of forced assimilation. This so-called Americanization process comprised a four-pronged formula: The christianizing activities of missionaries on reservations in order to stamp out "paganism"; the exposure of the Indian to white Americans' ways through New York State-supported schools established from the mid-1840s onward; the division of tribal lands among individual Indians to instill personal initiative, allegedly required by the free enterprise system; and finally, in return for accepting land-in-severalty, the "rewarding" of Indians with United States citi-

19. For Captain Cold, sometimes referred to as Captain Cole (Tayatoaque or Utha-wah), see Beauchamp, Notebook, 165–66; Elisabeth Tooker, "The League of the Iroquois: Its History, Politics and Ritual," *Handbook of North American Indians,* 5:436. In [Schoolcraft] Census of the State of New York, 1845, George is listed under "Senecas of Cattaraugus Reservation," entry No. 170, New York State Library, Manuscript Division; Beauchamp, Notebook, 172.

20. Annemarie Shimony, "Conflict and Continuity: An Analysis of an Iroquois Uprising," *Extending the Rafters,* 154. For the Great Wolf, see Morgan, *League of the Iroquois,* 65; William N. Fenton, "The Roll Call of the Iroquois Chiefs: A Study of a Mnemonic Cane from the Six Nations Reserve," *Smithsonian Miscellaneous Collections,* 111 (1950), 1–73; and Tooker, "The League of the Iroquois," 424–25.

zenship. The New York State Superintendent of Common Schools wrote in 1849: "Is it not obvious that the practical *communism* imposed by our laws upon the Indians, obstructs their advance in knowledge and civilization, and deprives them of the chief stimulus to industry and frugality." The Superintendent added: "If the Indian is to be civilized and educated, he must cease to be a savage. We must allow him to partition and cultivate his land, if we would not have all our efforts to educate and enlighten him prove illusive and futile."[21] Sixteen years later, this assimilationist message was even more elaborately presented by the Superintendent of the Onondaga Indian Schools. In his report in 1865, he advocated the state's abandonment of "the letter of old treaties" in order to save the Indians "from extinction." He urged that the course of citizenship and state jurisdiction work upon Indian lives in the same manner that it worked to fuse "the lower type of emigrants from foreign lands" into American society.[22]

Most Onondaga rejected this "Americanization" program; to preserve tribal identity they retained their separate existence, spoke their own languages, performed their ceremonies, continued to observe their native religion, not pushing for state or federal suffrage, and viewing themselves as citizens of sovereign enclave nation-states. Most importantly, they protested against every effort to undermine their tribal landbase. In the early 1850s, a bill to survey the Onondaga Reservation was introduced and passed in the New York State Assembly without the prior approval or knowledge of the Onondaga Council of Chiefs. When the chiefs learned of this bill, they protested, insisting that surveying was the first step in the division of the reservation into individual allotments and ultimate Indian land loss, "thereby destroying that bond of common interest which unites and holds Indian communities together."[23] The bill failed to pass the New York

21. New York State. Superintendent of Common Schools. *Annual Report, 1849* (Albany, 1849), 17.

22. New York State. Superintendent of Public Instruction. *Eleventh Annual Report, 1865* (Albany, 1865), 94–95.

23. Onondaga Chiefs to Nathan Bristol, April 3, 1853, Ely S. Parker MSS., American Philosophical Society, Philadelphia.

State Senate, but these efforts continued well into the late nineteenth and early twentieth centuries. It should be noted that the movement to survey and allot the reservation was supported by disgruntled Onondaga, some of whom were Christian converts, who objected to the power of the traditional Council of Chiefs. They accused the chiefs of personally profiting from their position by allowing whites to strip timber on the reservation. There is also evidence that some Onondaga did not welcome Indian refugees from the Buffalo Creek Reservation with open arms.[24]

During the Civil War, Samuel George was the leading spokesman of the Iroquois Confederacy in dealing with Washington. By 1863, he was given the honorary rank of Brevet General by federal officials and was acknowledged to be the "Principal Chief of the Six Nations." Well over 300 Iroquois Indians participated on the Union side during the American Civil War.[25] Although there appears to be Indian willingness to enlist in the conflict, the Iroquois reacted strongly to certain abuses in the recruitment process.

Much of the Iroquois criticism centered on the military conscription system. The Enrollment Act of 1863, which set categories of priority for conscription of all able-bodied male citizens, allowed a significant number of reasons for exemptions. The Act exempted anyone who could pay a $300 exemption fee or provide a substitute.[26] Though there seems to be little evidence that New York Indians were drafted during the Civil War, which is in sharp contrast to World War II and Vietnam, they were nevertheless affected by the Enrollment Act.[27] Because most of the Indians were poor, they found

24. Ibid.; David Hill to Ebenezer Meriam, Feb. 16, 1853, Nov. 17, 1854, Jan. 4, 1855 and Thomas LaFort to Meriam, May 31, 1853, Letters of Onondaga Indians, 1850-1855 MSS., American Philosophical Society, Philadelphia.

25. Laurence M. Hauptman, "The Tuscarora Company: An Iroquois Unit in the American Civil War," *Turtle Quarterly* 1 (Spring, 1987), 10-12; Laurence M. Hauptman, "Iroquois in Blue: From Reservation to Civil War Battlefield," *Northeast Indian Quarterly,* 5 (Fall, 1988), 35-39; William H. Armstrong, *Warrior in Two Camps: Ely S. Parker, Union General and Seneca Chief* (Syracuse, 1978), 71-121.

26. For the draft in New York State, see Eugene C. Murdock, *Patriotism Limited, 1862-1865: The Civil War Draft and the Bounty System* (Kent, Ohio, 1967), vii-41. For some modifications upon Murdock's work, see James W. Geary, "Civil War Conscription in the North: An Historiographical Review," *Civil War History* 32 (Sept., 1986), 208-28.

27. For Iroquois conscription in World War II and Vietnam, see Laurence M.

themselves subject to bounty inducements and many became substitutes. Non-Indian "bounty-brokers" actively recruited Indians as substitutes because of the attractiveness of the substitute fees to poor reservation residents. But the Indians were often the victims of unscrupulous brokers. By 1864, forty-three Iroquois, mostly Senecas, serving in the 24th New York Cavalry, 86th, 97th and 100th New York Volunteers and the 13th and 14th New York Heavy Artillery, asked to be released from service. They claimed they had never received their promised bounties or that they were underage recruits, some being only fifteen or sixteen years of age.

Iroquois leaders soon objected to the operation of the Act, and Samuel George led the protest. In November of 1863, he met with President Lincoln to discuss this matter. As a designated official of the Six Nations, George followed the traditional course established by earlier chiefs, who held that negotiations affecting the Iroquois must be made directly with the president of the United States on a nation-to-nation basis between equals.[28] In his talk with Lincoln, George undoubtedly reaffirmed the federal-Indian treaty relationship and questioned the right of Congress to pass legislation, such as the Enrollment Act, without the prior deliberation and approval of the League Council.

George convinced Lincoln to intervene on behalf of the Indian recruits. On November 20, 1863, Lincoln wrote Secretary of War Edwin Stanton: "Please see and hear the Sec. of Interior and Comm. of Indian Affairs with Genl. George, Indian Chief and discharge such of the men as the chief applies for and who have not received bounties." Seventeen days later, the Assistant Adjutant General's office issued Special Order No. 542 which allowed for the discharge of thirteen Iroquois Indians serving in the 13th New York Heavy Artillery and one in the 86th New York Volunteers.[29] On De-

---

Hauptman, *The Iroquois Struggle for Survival: World War II to Red Power* (Syracuse, 1986), 1–9.

28. "An Onondaga Chief at Washington," and "Affairs of the Six Nations," Nov. 25, 1863, newsclipping in Samuel George File, Onondaga Historical Association, Syracuse; Herman J. Viola, *Diplomats in Buckskin: A History of Indian Delegations in Washington City* (Washington, D.C., 1981), 95–96.

29. Roy Basler, ed., *Collected Works of Abraham Lincoln* (New Brunswick, N.J., 1953), 7:27; E.D. Townsend and C.S. Christinsen, Special Order No. 542, Dec. 7,

cember 23, thirteen of the fourteen Indians were released from their military service. Importantly, the order read: "Discharged by direction of the President at the request of the Chief of the Six Nations Indians."[30]

George was less successful in securing the discharge of the other Indians, though he and the Seneca frequently petitioned for their release. In June, 1864, Seneca leaders insisted that they had "authorized Samuel George head chief among the Onondagas and representative of the Six Nations to present our supplication." The Seneca reiterated George's arguments to Lincoln, maintaining that there was no law allowing for the drafting or enlistment of Indian minor children and objecting to conscription of Indians into military service without prior tribal consent, which went against historic precedents and treaties.[31] A month later, George wrote the Commissioner of Indian Affairs. Recalling his official visit to Washington and interviews with politicians nine months earlier, George repeated his stand about discharging the Indians: "We agreed [that] those who have not received Bounty [*sic*] from the Government shall be discharged from the service, notwithstanding many our young men taken away . . . I hope that you will discharge them without further delay."[32]

After substantial negotiations, the remaining Indians won the right to be discharged but only after they were required to pay back whatever bounty they had received. Unfortunately, most of these Indians had already spent the money, and though at least three repaid the bounty and were discharged, the majority stayed in military service to the end of the Civil War. At least two of these Indians, Privates Ira Pierce and

1863. Correspondence of the Office of Indian Affairs, Letters Received, 1824–1880, New York Agency, 1829–1880, Microfilm 590, Record Group 75, National Archives. (Hereafter cited as N.Y. Agency, Microfilm Reel 590, RG 75, NA.)

30. Quoted in Abstract, Muster Rolls: 13th New York Heavy Artillery—James Big Kettle (p. 242), Cornelius Fatty (p. 1058), James Halfwhite (p. 1381), Seth Jacob (p. 1669), Jesse Kenjockety (p. 1797), Wooster King (p. 1838), Young King (p. 1840), Murphy Longfinger (p. 1969), Stephen Ray (p. 2672), Martin Red Eye (p. 2678), Thomas Scrogg (p. 2879), Nathaniel Strong (p. 3165), and Dennis Titus (p. 3275); 86th New York Volunteers: John Thomas (p. 1939), Series 13775, Division of Military and Naval Affairs, New York State Archives, Albany.

31. Seneca Residing at Cattaraugus Petition to Abraham Lincoln, June 4, 1864, N.Y. Agency, Microfilm Reel 590, RG 75, NA.

32. Samuel George to William Dole, July 5, 1864, N.Y. Agency, Microfilm Reel 590, RG 75, NA.

Samuel George wearing an ostrich headdress adopted by the Iroquois after the American Revolution, with shell-embroidered sash and beaded Iroquois leggings of the period. From the William Beauchamp Collection, New York State Library. Courtesy of the New York State Museum.

John B. Williams, died in the conflict—Pierce at Petersburg and Williams as a prisoner-of-war at Andersonville Prison.[33]

33. 41. Ibid; E.R.S. Canby to J.P. Usher, Jan. 14, 1864; E. Townsend Special Order No. 126, March 24, 1864; N.T. Strong to General Sprague, April 12, 1864; J. Stonehouse to Edwin Stanton, April 1, 1864; John Sprague to William P. Doyle (sic), April 13, 1864; Samuel George to President of the United States, June 16, 1864, N.Y. Agency, Microfilm Reel 590, RG 75, NA; Abstract, Muster Rolls: 24th New York Cavalry: John Bennett (p. 122); 97th New York Volunteers: Titus Mohawk (p. 1616); and 14th New York Heavy Artillery: Oliver Silverheels (p. 374),

Despite his limited victory, George's efforts helped reinforce the Iroquois traditional belief in their own separate sovereignty. Reaffirming treaty rights, meeting with the Great Father in Washington City, and rejecting conscription without tribal consent are as strongly established in the convervative agenda of the Onondaga today as they were 125 years ago during the Civil War. Although success is important, symbolism, form, and style are equally important in the Iroquois traditional mind.[34]

Following the war, George continued to serve as Iroquois spokesman. In March of 1870, as "Head Chief," he wrote to

Series 13775, Division of Military and Naval Affairs, New York State Archives, Albany; Abstract, Muster Rolls: 24th New York Calvary: Ira Pierce (p. 1453); John B. Williams (p. 2046), Series 13775, Division of Military and Naval Affairs, New York State Archives, Albany. For Williams' death at Andersonville Prison, see Daniel G. Kelley, *What I Saw and Suffered in Rebel Prisons* (Buffalo, 1868), 30–43.

34. Laurence M. Hauptman, *The Iroquois and the New Deal* (Syracuse, 1981), 1–18; Laurence M. Hauptman, *Iroquois Struggle for Survival,* 205–43.

Colonel Samuel George, about 1860, wearing silver earrings. Courtesy of the Buffalo and Erie County Historical Society.

Governor John Hoffman of New York State to complain about timber stripping by whites on the Onondaga Reservation, to inquire about the status of an Indian agent, and to raise questions about leasing. In June of 1870, he asked Hoffman for information about moneys owed to the Indians by New York State.[35]

From 1869 to 1873, George was formally licensed to practice medicine and was appointed "government physician" to the Onondaga after a petition was signed by thirty-three leading Indians and non-Indians in the environs of Syracuse. His long involvement as a "traditional medicine man" is clear from the historic record. R.H. Gardner, the Indian agent at that time, formally endorsed George's appointment: "I believe Captain George can doctor the Indians as well as a white man. After considerable experience on the subject, I believe that the Indians live under his treatment and are as healthful as when treated by any other physician . . . ."[36]

During the last two decades of his life, George's gift of oratory was noted by observers of the Indian world. According to William Beauchamp, the Episcopal missionary and keenest observer of the Onondaga world of the nineteenth and early twentieth centuries, George "was both shrewd and eloquent" and "full of official dignity and seldom condescending to speak English." Although "thin and rather fun-looking," George was frequently a featured speaker at public events where his speeches were translated from Onondaga into English. His fame as a storyteller was widespread and undoubtedly added to his prestige and power among his own people and outsiders in the non-Indian environs of Syracuse. Beauchamp added: "I have heard him speak, and he was fond of story-telling, having a good stock to draw upon. He remembered when the Onondagas moved up the valley to their present reservation village, many building bark houses at that time."[37]

Oratory was the path to leadership among the Iroquois.

35. Samuel George to Governor John J. Hoffman, March 5, June 18, 1870, MS Item No. 17605 and 17606, New York State Library, Manuscript Division, Albany.
36. Beauchamp, Notebook, 174.
37. "Captain George's Speech at the Fourth of July dinner," *Syracuse Journal*, July 6, 1865, newsclipping found in Samuel George File, Onondaga Historical Association, Syracuse; Beauchamp, Notebook, 173-74.

Lewis Henry Morgan observed in 1851: "By the cultivation and exercise of this capacity [of oratory], was opened the pathway to distinction; and the chief or warrior gifted with its magical power could elevate himself as rapidly, as he who gained renown upon the warpath."[38] George's speaking abilities, in combination with his diplomatic and medical skills and his physical prowess, gave him a position of particular influence at the council fires of the Iroquois Confederacy. It is worth noting that oratorical skill is still valued in the Iroquois polity. One of the factors in the reemergence of Onondaga power within the Confederacy over the past two decades, apparently, is the substantial oratorical skills of two of the present Onondaga chiefs.[39]

Until his death on September 24, 1873, George lived in a small frame single-story house just northeast of the Onondaga Council House, about a quarter of a mile from the center of the reservation. He remained a "traditional" to the end, never converting to Christianity. Although a Christian sermon was presented by Bishop Huntington and other Episcopal leaders at his funeral, George was buried with Indian rites as prescribed by the Great Binding Law of his Iroquois people.[40]

Samuel George had witnessed striking changes in the status of the Iroquois during his lifetime. He was directly involved in two wars—in the War of 1812 as a combatant and in the Civil War as an Iroquois spokesman. He undoubtedly observed, as he was affected by, the Iroquois revitalization movement inspired by Handsome Lake's visions, which stimulated changes in the agriculture, the basic family patterns, and the religion of the Iroquois. He lived through a period of explosive growth in the white population of central and western New York—decades in which his people lost substantial amounts of land and suffered environmental deterioration and social circumscription. He endured a failed Indian leadership that was incapable of stemming the tide of

38. Morgan, *League of the Iroquois,* 107.
39. Laurance M. Hauptman, Iroquois Field Notes, 1971–1988.
40. "Funeral of an Indian Chief," newsclipping, Sept., 1873; and "Ho-no-we-ye-ach-te: Death of Capt. Samuel George, Head Chief of the Onondagas," *Syracuse Journal,* Sept. 25, 1873, Samuel George File, Onondaga Historical Association, Syracuse.

land specualtors and missionaries, as he endured the increased dependence of the Indian on the white man, caused by the
economic and political changes brought about by American
industrialization in combination with a shrinking Indian
landbase.

Despite these revolutionary changes, George remained an
Iroquois conservative to the end. His rise to influence among
his people had been along the traditional paths to authority.
His brand of conservatism allowed him to accept but modify
the teachings of Handsome Lake. Although he faithfully
ascribed to the ceremonials, kept his Iroquoian language
alive, and rejected alienation of Indian lands, he served the
American cause in two major wars. He also permitted missionaries and schools to be maintained on the Onondaga
Reservation and was a well-known and admired "personality" off the reservation. While dealing with the likes of Bishop
Huntington, Governor Hoffman or President Lincoln,
George attempted in a practical but mostly traditional way to
serve his people and to express Indian concerns despite the
often debilitating internal discord that was reflected in the
Iroquois polity and the incredible pressures from the non-
Indian world. Although today his reputation as "the runner"
remains in Indian oral tradition and overshadows his other
accomplishments,[41] George's steadfastness in maintaining
tradition, however flexible in approach, makes him worthy of
study and explains much about Iroquois survival well over a
century after his death.

41. Interview of John Fadden, Jan. 8, 1987, Albany. Mr. Fadden, a Mohawk-
Tuscarora Indian educator, co-directs the Six Nations Indian Museum in Onchiota,
N.Y.

"We Breathe The Same Air": Eastern Ontarian Migration to Watertown, New York In The Late Nineteenth Century

By RANDY WILLIAM WIDDIS

The small but bustling city in Jefferson County was a magnet for immigrants from eastern Ontario. It's history provides the material for a new view of the invisible Canadian. Dr. Widdis is a member of the Department of Geography at the University of Regina, Saskatchewan.

I N AN INTERVIEW conducted in his later years, James Pappa of Watertown, New York, observed, "I was ambitious and anxious to overcome my many deficiencies, hence I worked long hours and hard, making the most of my evenings by studying, thus endeavouring to compete with those of my own age." Recalling his early years in Watertown, he added, "If I were to place on paper the record of the first few years of my experience in this city in my effort to make good, it would take much valuable space."[1] James Pappa did make good. This Canadian immigrant from Newburgh, Ontario, established himself in the community and eventually became mayor of Watertown, one of New York's fastest growing urban centers at the end of the nineteenth century. He is also distinctive because, unlike so many of the thousands of nineteenth-century Canadian migrants settling in the United States, he did leave a record of the early years of his migration experience.

James Pappa was born in Newburgh on July 24, 1852, the son of a Canadian-born merchant tailor and an English-born mother. He was the youngest of four children, all maintained in "comfortable circumstances," although he was affected by health problems

---

Portions of this paper originally appeared in the March 9, 1985 edition of the Kingston *Whig-Standard*, Kingston, Ontario.

1. James Pappa's life story is compiled from an obituary appearing in the March 12, 1925 edition of the Watertown *Daily Times*. The obituary contains excerpts from an interview conducted with Mr. Pappa before his death.

which interfered with his formal education. Following in the footsteps of his older brother, a typesetter in the office of the Kingston, Ontario, *British Whig*, he became a printer. His first job was with the Newburgh *Beaver*, a six-column four-page weekly. He stayed there for a period of only seven months, disillusioned by the fact that he never received a cent of the $1.50 weekly wage promised to him. He took a moonlighting job as a fruit peddler at the Newburgh Fall Fair, and when Cephas Beeman, publisher of the *Beaver*, learned of this he planned to discharge Pappa, who forestalled Beeman by quitting. Apparently Pappa was not attracted by any of the few remaining opportunities available in Newburgh, including clerking in a store, driving a stagecoach, or working in a foundry or carriage plant. Like many others, he decided to move on to greener pastures.

The greener pastures, he concluded, were south of the border. His father was involved in a small business with his brother in Oswego and often spoke of the many opportunities in the United States. In September of 1871, the nineteen-year-old James left for Oswego. He took Finkler's stagecoach to Kingston and then boarded a ferry boat to Cape Vincent on the American side. His route to Oswego took him to Watertown where he stayed at the Globe Hotel. Exploring the town, James happened to pass by the Watertown *Daily Times* news room and he decided to make an application for work. At that point, James' good luck was about to begin:

> S. M. Washburn, the foreman, was the first and only person I ever asked for a job. Fortunately, as I learned later, Foreman Washburn was a former Canadian printer of Belleville, Ontario. This fact was doubtless in my favour and I was told I might report for work at 1 in the afternoon. I was there on time. This was my first introduction to the good people of Watertown and 12 years later I made it my permanent home and became an American citizen by naturalization.[2]

After his experience at the Newburgh *Beaver*, the salary he first received, $1 per day, must have seemed like a fortune to Pappa. After a period of time, he was promoted from compositor to the position of foreman in the book department of the job printing plant. A short time later, the *Daily Times* sold the building and the job plant to the Hungerford Printing Company, and Pappa was promoted to the business office. He subsequently worked as business manager of the *Times'* city circulation and then as a member of the editorial staff where he was assigned to reporting the city

2. Watertown *Daily Times*, March 12, 1925.

markets and compiling the "Looking Backward" column.

As Pappa became established in his career, his involvement in the city increased. A member of the Odd Fellows fraternity for over twenty years, he was also involved in city politics. In 1901, he was asked to run as the Republican candidate for the office of mayor. His campaign was successful and after a two-year term as mayor, Pappa served as supervisor of the second ward on two different occasions. Pappa's life in Watertown was a satisfying one. His was truly a success story.

In many ways, Pappa's story is representative of Canadian emigration to the United States in general. Many left home because of unfavorable circumstances and moved to nearby American cities and rural areas because of better prospects and the presence of friends and relatives. And it is also likely that many Canadians like James were hired by their fellow expatriates. Some undoubtedly achieved similar or even greater success than Pappa. Yet the experiences of English-speaking Canadians have not been the subject of comprehensive historical study because English-speaking Canadians have been perceived as "invisible" in the United States and because it is difficult to find sources which allow the researcher to break through this veil of invisibility.[3] For this reason, Watertown at the turn of the century is of particular interest. It was a major center of immigration from eastern Ontario; it had a flourishing daily newspaper, which included information on Canadians in residence. Of particular importance, in its notation of national origins, the United States manuscript census for 1900 lists individuals born in Quebec as being from French Canada and lists those from the Maritime Provinces in accordance with the province in which they were born. Those listed as originating in English Canada were therefore, for all intents and purposes, from Ontario, and the Canadians of Watertown are most suitably designated as Ontarians. The vast majority of this group came from both English and Celtic backgrounds and are best labelled as "Anglo-Celtics." In any case, the combination of economic adversity in Ontario and prosperity in Watertown influenced the movement of large numbers of English Canadians in the late nineteenth century and thus affords

3. See R. Berthoff, *British Immigrants in Industrial America* (Cambridge: Harvard University Press, 1953) and C. Erickson, *Invisible Immigrants* (Coral Gables: University of Miami Press, 1972). Both view British immigrants as being "invisible"; that is, they adapted readily to American life. But I would argue that English-speaking Canadians in general and Ontarians in particular were even less visible in the American scene. While the English, Scots, Irish and Welsh often formed cultural groups and associations, Ontarians rarely identified themselves as a distinct group.

an opportunity to examine a relatively neglected group.

In Ontario by 1855, almost one million people either owned or occupied land considered suitable for settlement. In less than fifty years, the agricultural frontier had ceased to exist and settlement and development had taken place in spite of the negative effects of land policies and of marked emigration.[4] The catalyst to development was immigration by which the sheer numbers of people coming into the province moved settlement along at a pace which surpassed government efforts and offset the significant numbers leaving. But the next four decades witnessed a series of crises which dramatically affected the agricultural sector and resulted in a mass emigration of people. During the period 1860–1900, the net loss of population was 661,000 as emigration (2,429,000) exceeded immigration (1,768,000).[5]

The decline of the wheat staple brought about by land shortages, soil depletion, western competition and the ending of the imperial preferences meant that Ontario farmers had to find markets for new exports. To offset this economic lethargy and stimulate industrial development, the National Policy was created by Sir John A. MacDonald and his Tory government in order to develop a domestic market in the West and the Maritimes for central Canadian industry. It was believed that such a strategy would result in benefits for both the industrial and agricultural sectors of the economy, but prosperity did not occur. The Americans responded to the protective tariff by restricting Canadian entry into United States markets. In 1890, the door was slammed with the McKinley Tariff. Prices dropped and demand decreased though costs remained constant.

Nowhere in Ontario were the effects of agricultural change felt as much as in the eastern part of the province. By 1880, much of eastern Ontario had passed its zenith and was in a gradual state of decline. Changing markets and the decline of the wheat staple combined with a limited agricultural base, population pressure on the land, and retarded industrial development to create an environment of exodus in eastern Ontario.[6]

4. For a discussion of the retarding effects of land policies, see G. Teeple, ed., *Capitalism and the National Question in Canada* (Toronto: University of Toronto Press, 1972).

5. M. Percy, *Migration Flows During the Decade of the Wheat Boom in Canada, 1900–1910: A Neo-Classical Analysis* (unpublished Ph.D. dissertation, Queen's University, 1977), 2–4.

6. For greater discussion of the decline of eastern Ontario, see B. S. Osborne, "Kingston in the Nineteenth Century: A Study in Urban Decline," in J. D. Wood, ed., *Perspectives on Landscape and Settlement in Nineteenth Century Ontario* (Toronto: McClelland and Stewart Ltd., 1975), Carleton Library Series, No. 91.

This stagnation affected both the economic and social structure of the area. Apart from localized population decline, this outflow also generated unbalanced sex ratios and unbalanced dependency ratios, with an increasingly aged population structure.[7] The noted Canadian historian, Arthur Lower, suggests that this outmigration deprived the region of its most productive elements:

> Every year, young people, except the fortunate few or the one or two children of the family who could find something to do, had to go away. In the days of the large Victorian family, this emigration of the young at their highest point of vitality, must have been like a constant bleeding. Some of the departing went to Toronto, others to Montreal. But Canada as a whole expanded slowly in the period 1861 to 1901, so the assumption can be made that most of them went 'across the line'. No doubt a town like Watertown, New York can find the origins of a majority of its people in our St. Lawrence river towns, Kingston, Brockville, Prescott, especially. It was a distinguished Kingstonian, Sir Richard Cartwright, who remarked of those bleak days that they 'began in Exodus and ended in Lamentations'. He was not far from wrong.[8]

An investigation of the United States manuscript census and other sources indicate that Lower's assumption is correct, that many eastern Ontarians moved to such northern New York centers as Watertown.[9] Watertown, in fact, is an ideal setting for a study of the English Canadian experience in the United States. In 1900, 779 or 15.3 percent of Watertown's 5,083 households were headed by English Canadians, many of whom originated in eastern Ontario. They were the dominant immigrant group in Watertown, composing 52 percent of the foreign-born population.[10]

Why did so many decide on Watertown? The visitor who looks at the city in the mid-1980s is struck by the juxtaposition of visible signs of past prosperity and present depression. The shells of once busy factories and mills which flank the Black River capture the viewer's attention. Large brick and stone mansions on tree-lined streets are impressive despite their dilapidated state in many cases. Many have been subdivided into small tenements and some stand

---

7. The social and economic consequences of this decline are discussed at length in J. MacDougall, *Rural Life in Canada* (Toronto: University of Toronto Press, 1973. Originally published in 1912).

8. A.R.M. Lower, "The Character of Kingston," in G. Tulchinsky, ed., *To Preserve and Defend: Essays on Kingston in the Nineteenth Century* (Montreal: McGill-Queen's Press, 1976), 25.

9. For a more complete description of sources, see Appendix 3 in R. W. Widdis, *With Scarcely A Ripple: The Eastern Ontarian Immigrant Experience in Northern New York At The Turn of the Century* (Ph.D. dissertation, Queen's University, 1984).

10. 1900 U.S. Manuscript Census.

empty with boards in place where elegant windows once sparkled in the sun.

It is, however, the large Public Square, the center of the city, that most dramatically underscores the contrast between the past and the present. One wonders why a small city in one of the most remote areas in New York possesses such an impressive central core. On the west side of the square sits the arcade, one of the first indoor shopping malls of its kind in the state. Just down the street is the Frank W. Woolworth building, the site of the first "5 and 10" cent store. But across the square, a "going out of business" sign is evident in a store window. Two vacant stores are present in the next block. And on the north side of the square, a large empty lot marks the site of the Woodruff House, for many years the largest hotel in the northern part of the state.

It is a curious city, a community that somehow seems lost in time. The inquisitive observer begins to wonder what Watertown

The Public Square in recent times. Photo courtesy of Randy Widdis.

was like during its "salad days." The indications of past prosperity still emanate through the pall of depression. It was this prosperity that prompted thousands of Canadians to settle in this city at the turn of the century.[11]

Watertown had originally been settled in 1800 by a group of New Englanders who recognized the site's potential for industrial and commercial activity, but the community was slow to make use of the resources of the Black River. During the first half of the century, the village grew slowly as it established its position as an agricultural and milling center. The first significant increase in population occurred when the Irish entered the area after the building of the Erie Canal in 1825. They came in even greater numbers in the late 1840s, "pushed" out of Ireland by the potato famine and "pulled" into the Watertown area with the extension of the railway into Jefferson County. German migration was also greatest at mid-century, while Italians and other eastern Europeans came largely during the 1890s and the first decade of the twentieth century.[12]

Although an inflow of Canadians, both French-speaking and English-speaking, had been constant through the years, they came in greater numbers after the depression of the 1870s. This increased as the extension of Watertown's industrial base during the last two decades of the century attracted thousands of immigrants and rural migrants to the city. During the 1890s, the population almost doubled, reaching 22,000 by 1900. Much of this growth can be attributed to the inflow of immigrants, particularly Canadians, although with only 23.6 percent of the population born outside the United States, Watertown could hardly be classified as an immigrant city. The immigrant presence was nevertheless considerable with 5,119 foreign born present in 1900. Of the city's 5,083 households, 1,499 or 29 percent were headed by foreign born. Of that number, 779 or 52 percent were of English Canadian origin, followed in descending order of size by the Irish (15.8 percent); the English (11.3 percent); the French Canadians (7.3 percent); the Germans (5.1 percent); a group composed mainly of Russians, Poles, Hungarians and other eastern Europeans (4.1 percent); the Scots (2.4 percent); and the Italians (2.0 percent).[13] During this

---

11. While the Black River Valley region is at present an area of high unemployment and population stagnation, the arrival of the Tenth Division at Fort Drum will certainly contribute to the area's economy.

12. E. Hungerford, "A North Country Town in the Nineties," *New York History* 26 (April 1945), 136–40.

13. 1900 U.S. Manuscript Census.

Woodruff's car factory and foundry, on the Black River, was built 1841 and burned in 1853. From Hough, History of Jefferson County *(1854).*

time, it was estimated that nearly one third of the population of Watertown was of Canadian origin or descent.

Watertown's situation along the Black, the second longest river in the state, ensured the development of a power source which provided the spur to this growth. The fall of 112 feet within the city limits in a series of small cataracts and rapids allowed dams and waterwheels to develop power. While the community had been slow to make use of this resource, the 1880s and 1890s witnessed the founding of certain industrial establishments which would produce the city's greatest period of development. Watertown was riding the crest of an industrial boom as it entered the twentieth century. In 1900, 289 manufacturing establishments employed 3,760 workers and they averaged a mere 13 employees per firm (Table 1). Despite this diversity, three large scale industries were dominant: foundries and machine producers with six establishments; pulp and paper, also with six firms; and carriage and wagon makers with four firms. These were the major employers, with a work force that averaged 224, 106 and 115 employees respectively. Together they employed nearly 71 percent of the city's wage earners. New York Air Brake alone employed over 1,200 men, or about one third of the total number of all wage earners in the city in 1900.[14] The rapid tempo of urbanization and industrialization during the last two decades of the century changed the character of Watertown. The city became a bigger and, in the eyes of its citizens, a better place to live. The litany of social facilities enumerated at length in the city directory of 1900 testifies to the progress achieved during the industrial boom:

> Twelve elementary schools, two private kindergartens, one business school, two hospitals, 54 physicians and surgeons, two orphanages, a bureau of charity, 21 churches, 24 blacksmith shops, eight horse and livery stables, seven harness shops, fourteen dealers in wagons and buggies, thirteen wood yards, eight coal dealers, twenty hotels, five commercial

14. Hungerford, "North Country Town," 142; H. Thompson, *Black River in the North Country* (Prospect: Prospect Books, 1963), 116–17.

TABLE 1

MANUFACTURES IN WATERTOWN BY SPECIFIED INDUSTRIES, 1900

Industry	No. of Estab-lishments	Capital ($)	Propri-etors	Average No. of Wage Earners	Average Wage ($)	Average of Wage Earners Per Firm	Total Wages ($)	Value of Product ($)
Blacksmith	22	21,121	22	20	452.05	0.9	9,945	39,092
Bakery Products	13	154,574	13	62	425.77	4.8	26,398	169,178
Carpentering	13	45,792	15	99	553.18	7.6	54,765	218,199
Carriages & Wagons	4	1,236,480	—	463	499.24	115.8	231,150	985,400
Clothing, Men's	20	45,128	20	88	350.11	4.4	30,150	111,938
Clothing, Women's	22	19,865	23	79	207.44	3.6	16,388	85,184
Flour & Grist Mill Products	5	273,634	2	27	479.22	5.4	12,939	329,753
Foundry & Machine Products	6	3,594,582	3	1,347	553.02	224.5	744,924	2,352,945
Lumber Planing Mill Products	5	157,855	9	94	484.56	18.8	45,549	262,345
Masonry	4	28,521	6	58	620.40	14.5	35,983	119,258
Paper & Pulp	6	1,458,304	—	640	479.53	106.7	306,901	1,870,282
Newspapers Printing & Publishing	8	202,839	5	83	590.52	10.4	49,013	149,841
All Industries	289	8,281,845	302	3,760	484.44	13.0	1,821,477	7,881,977

Source: 12th Census of the United States, Census Bulletin #159, April 25, 1902: 76–79.

banks, two savings banks, sixteen restaurants, 31 saloons, 59 dress makers, two large music halls, the City Opera House, 35 fraternal organizations, and a number of unaffiliated social clubs.[15]

There existed a wide choice of facilities for entertainment and social affairs. Two large halls, the music hall in the American Block and Washington Hall in the Y.M.C.A. building, were used for public dances, concerts, lectures and weekly band concerts. The opera hall featured theatrical plays and vaudeville shows. The town also gained a reputation for gambling and prostitution. A prosperous red light and saloon district flourished along River and Court Streets, immediately adjacent to the industrial section of town, and the Watertown *Daily Times* often made reference to laborers being cheated by "tinhorn gamblers and short-card men."[16]

Ignoring the problems of prostitution, gambling and the occasional strike, Watertown's prosperity generated much blatant boosterism in the city's newspaper. At various times during the period, Watertown was labelled in glowing editorials as the "Garland City" and the "Paris of the North." An editorial appearing in the July 2, 1900 edition of the *Daily Times* is an example of this unabashed boosterism:

> We challenge the census-taker to produce another town where there are so many fine homes owned by the same number of population; where business is on such an established basis; where churches and schools are better supported; where public and private enterprise has done so much; to find a town of that population that has so large and complete a newspaper as the Watertown *Daily Times*. Oh, this town has quality and growth too, and more than that its citizens are all proud of it. That is what counts. A great many big cities would be better places to live if a selection of 25 percent of their population could be taken out and drowned.[17]

The editorials were full of confidence, and they had good reason to be proud. The air brakes, carriages, paper-making machines and portable steam engines made in Watertown were sold all over the world.

In addition to its industries, the town was also noted for its citizens. Apart from the contribution of Frank W. Woolworth, it was here that Frederick Eames developed the air brake that was to revolutionize the railroad industry. Watertown could also boast about one of its native sons, Roswell P. Flower, who was elected governor in 1891. An electric trolley system, Public Square (which

15. *Boyd's Directory of Watertown* (Watertown: Boyd and Co.).
16. This information was conveyed to me by local historian Alex Duffy.
17. Watertown *Daily Times,* July 2, 1900.

was said to be the longest continuous block of buildings in the country in the 1890s), and stately mansions were visible signs of prosperity that gave support to this air of confidence and pride.

Watertown at the turn of the century was a thriving community, full of hope for the future. Watertown relied upon industries which, for one reason or another, were soon to disappear or decrease greatly in importance. With the overcutting of the Adirondack forests, the pulpwood supply practically ceased, signalling the demise of the paper mills along the Black River. With the appearance of the automobile came the decline and ultimate end of the carriage industry. The New York Air Brake factory experienced cutbacks as the railroad decreased in importance. And finally, Watertown's rather isolated location relative to other centers in New York State reduced its attraction as a potential industrial site.

At the turn of the century, however, few people could envision the hardships that lay ahead as the city basked in its growing prosperity. Canadians, especially those from nearby eastern Ontario, were very much aware of the opportunities offered in the community, an awareness afforded by their close proximity and by the fact that Canadians formed the largest foreign element in the city, ensuring that affinities were quite strong. James Pappa certainly made the most of the opportunities presented to him and there is little doubt that other Canadians also achieved a comparable degree of success. In 1900, for example, the chief of the Watertown fire department, Fred Morrison, and the publisher of the *Daily Times,* Jeremiah Coughlin, were ex-Canadians.[18] Their stories were not necessarily typical of the Canadian experience in Watertown. Individual accounts that would provide more information about personal experiences, apparently do not exist. Fortunately, the United States manuscript census and various issues of the Watertown *Daily Times* do provide the information that illuminates the experience of the Canadians as a group.

Attitudes expressed in the Watertown *Daily Times* conformed to those widely held in the United States at this time. Local views were generally more favorable towards Anglo-Saxon, Protestant groups coming from northern Europe and English Canada and less supportive of predominantly Catholic and Jewish, non-English-speaking immigrants of eastern and southern Europe. The Italians in particular received several patronizing reviews in the newspaper, including the following:

18. 1900 U.S. Manuscript Census.

A later immigrant is the Italian. It will contribute an element of lightness which is perhaps necessary in our national character. At any rate he fills the need for common labor.[19]

The Italians are viewed as "menial," as contributing a bit of levity and supplying the need for labor, albeit, "common" labor. But little else positive could apparently be said about this group, the use of "it" and "common" underscoring the contemporary judgement of Italians.

Canadians on the other hand were rarely mentioned in discussions of the city's foreign element, suggesting that this group was not thought of in the same terms as other foreigners, although Watertown residents were certainly aware of their neighbors to the north. Many were descended from Canadians who had made the short trip to the city years before and many continued to retain links with Ontario. Several issues of the *Daily Times* reported on trips made by local citizens to such nearby Canadian communities as Kingston and Brockville to visit relatives. News of major Canadian events appeared quite regularly in the paper and mention was often made of friendly competition between local sports clubs and their Canadian counterparts. Indeed, some fifty-eight issues of the *Daily Times* for the year 1900 included references to Canada. Eight items referred to Canadians visiting friends and relatives in Watertown and six to Watertown residents visiting friends and relatives in Canada. These notices barely represent the actual number of visits made by people across the border. Eight different issues carried notices originally published in the Kingston *Whig-Standard*, most of them commenting on some type of interchange between the two communities. For instance, the January 27, 1900 edition of the *Daily Times* printed a notice from the Kingston paper that the Watertown fire chief, Fred Morrison, purchased a team of horses from a farmer in Kingston Township and that "they had been delivered at a Kingston hotel and will be brought across the lake as soon as possible."

The most focussed discussion of Canadian character in the newspaper related to the success of Canadian soldiers in the Boer War:

No wonder Canadians are proud of them. They live much the same and breathe the same air which have made our Americans develop into such good soldiers. They have that strong individuality, power of taking the initiative, quickness of movement and readiness for an emergency which marks men of the west.[20]

19. Watertown *Daily Times*, April 25, 1905.

It is clear that the approbation of the Canadian effort reflects an American ethos. Canadians were perceived as being part of a larger North American community and thus Canadians met the criteria for "good" Americans. The cultural-political context of this sense of community and common identity related more to continental expansion than to welcome accommodation. One editorial commented on the visit of the noted Canadian continentalist Goldwin Smith, who suggested that Canada was a "geographical absurdity":

> Professor Goldwin Smith dislikes the word annexation as applied to the joining of Canada to this country, but prefers 'reunion', because the separation of English speaking people on the continent was only the result of an historical accident, and there is no natural line of separation. Everybody will agree to that. Continental reunion, let it be. Now let the ceremony proceed![21]

Given such views of Canadians, it is not surprising that English Canadians were seldom mentioned in discussions relating to the "immigrant" dimension of the city. The fact that they did not establish ethnic boundaries to differentiate themselves further added to their "invisibility." Only one fraternal organization, the Orange Order, was designed with them in mind, and the local lodge's membership was small and eventually disappeared. While other groups relied to varying degrees upon formal institutions, English Canadians did not have such common denominators beyond kinship, friendship and work relationships.

Nor did English Canadians distinguish themselves in terms of residential congregation. The mapping of residential patterns at the ward level shows a relative lack of concentration among immigrant groups in 1900 (Figure 1). Even at the more specific scale of electoral districts, this same pattern is evident. The index of dissimilarity among Watertown nativity groups for 1900 reveals that the only notable segregation that took place between immigrants and natives was that which existed for the Italians and the "other" eastern European groups (Table 2).[22] Watertown was small enough that ethnic solidarity and identity among immigrant groups were dependent less upon residential clustering than on formal and

---

20. Watertown *Daily Times*, February 28, 1900.
21. Watertown *Daily Times*, March 1, 1890.
22. The index of dissimilarity is calculated according to electoral districts and measures the proportion of one nativity group that would have to change its location in order to be distributed identically with another group. For example, Table 2 shows that only 9.9 percent of other Americans would have to move to be consistent with residential locations of native New Yorkers; but 57.5 percent of the Italians would have to change residence to be residentially identical to New Yorkers. These two examples represent the smallest and largest displacements within the table. A lack of segregation yields a minimum index of 0,

informal associations. Yet English Canadians, as has been noted, lacked the ethnic clubs and churches which catered specifically to the Irish, Italians, Poles, French Canadians and Germans.

Given the favorable attitudes toward English Canadians, their lack of residential segregation from the host community, and their participation in native institutions, one might expect that they would have adapted quite easily and readily to their new environment. Yet a closer inspection of the 1900 manuscript census leads us to question this interpretation, particularly in terms of

---

complete segregation 100; the cutoff point is usually accepted as 25. The formula for the index is:

$$Id = 1/2 \sum_{i=1}^{k} |xi - yi|$$

For further discussion, see K. A. Conzen, *Immigrant Milwaukee, 1836–1860: Accommodation and Community in a Frontier City* (Cambridge: Harvard University Press, 1976), 269.

Figure 1: Distribution of Watertown Nativity Groups Among Wards, 1900

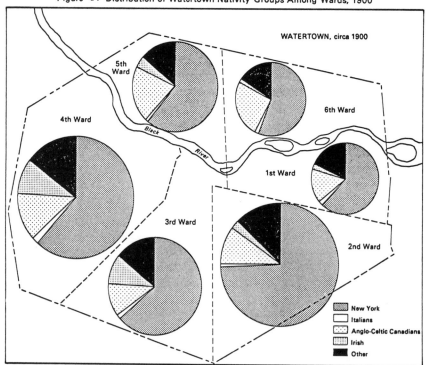

TABLE 2

INDEX OF DISSIMILARITY AMONG WATERTOWN NATIVITY GROUPS, 1900

(12 ELECTORAL DISTRICTS)

Nativity Groups	New Yorkers	Other Americans	English	German	Scottish	Irish	Italian	French Canadian	Anglo-Celtic Canadian	Others
New Yorkers	—	9.9	25.0	23.4	18.7	21.3	57.5	22.6	19.5	34.7
Other Americans	9.9	—	26.5	27.6	24.8	26.0	52.3	23.7	16.6	29.4
English	25.0	26.5	—	37.8	21.2	37.7	49.7	18.9	15.3	31.1
German	23.4	27.6	37.8	—	29.9	44.8	53.6	29.9	16.4	27.4
Scottish	18.7	24.8	21.2	29.9	—	38.8	35.9	25.3	17.4	23.0
Irish	21.3	26.0	37.7	44.8	38.8	—	47.3	34.1	25.9	29.7
Italian	57.5	52.3	49.7	53.6	35.9	47.3	—	48.6	46.1	23.9
French Canadian	22.6	23.7	18.9	29.9	25.3	34.1	48.6	—	13.3	30.5
Anglo-Celtic Canadian	19.5	16.6	15.3	16.4	17.4	25.9	46.1	13.3	—	24.2
Others	34.7	29.4	31.1	27.4	23.0	29.7	23.9	30.5	24.2	—

Source: 1900 U.S. Manuscript Census.

their household, occupational, endogamous and citizenship characteristics.

Generally, English Canadians in Watertown took on certain of the family and household traits of the so-called "New" immigrants from eastern and southern Europe—a stronger reliance on kin and on boarders of the same nationality in the family economy, more living in multiple dwelling units, a greater frequency of extended households, larger households—while the older groups, the English, Germans, and Irish, relied less on kin and boarders, were more likely to live in single dwelling units and lived in smaller households (Table 3). Only the Italians were more likely than the English Canadians to share their homes with relatives, regardless of length of residence. For Canadians, the extended household and the imbedded (boarding) household were major institutions of immigrant adjustment. Almost 65 percent of the English Canadian boarders lived in English Canadian households, which indicates that boarding continued to be important either as a generator of surplus income or as a means to accommodate others.

While they were not segregated residentially from native Americans, the rigid class division in Watertown—where natives composed 84 percent, 82 percent and 88 percent of the clerical, business, and professional occupations respectively—ensured that English Canadians would be congregated in a separate social and economic space. Although they made up over 15 percent of the total number of heads of household, only 7 percent of the English

Pluralism in New York State

TABLE 3

THE COMPOSITION AND ROLE OF WATERTOWN'S FAMILIES AND HOUSEHOLDS, 1900
BY NATIONAL ORIGIN (%)

Characteristics	New Yorkers	Other Americans	English	German	Scottish	Irish	Italian	French Canadians	Anglo-Celtic Canadians	Others
A. *Composition*	(N = 3,286)	(N = 273)	(N = 169)	(N = 77)	(N = 36)	(N = 237)	(N = 30)	(N = 109)	(N = 779)	(N = 62)
1. *Household Size*										
1	4.4	3.0	2.4	0	2.8	6.3	6.7	1.8	2.6	1.6
2	17.9	21.4	18.3	16.9	13.9	21.9	10.0	16.5	16.0	14.5
3–5	57.6	55.8	59.2	53.2	50.0	50.2	40.0	50.5	53.9	62.9
6–10	19.3	19.4	19.5	27.3	30.6	19.4	36.7	28.4	23.5	21.0
>10	0.8	0.4	0.6	2.6	2.8	2.1	6.7	2.8	2.7	1.6
2. *No. of Children in Household*										
0	32.8	37.3	25.4	24.7	27.8	32.5	20.0	26.6	24.9	27.4
1	27.7	23.9	28.4	20.8	13.9	17.3	13.3	14.7	25.0	27.4
2	18.4	19.0	11.8	20.8	13.9	18.6	10.0	22.9	22.6	22.6
3–5	19.0	18.3	29.0	31.2	41.7	26.2	53.3	24.8	23.7	21.0
>5	2.1	1.5	5.3	2.6	2.8	5.5	3.3	11.0	3.7	3.2
3. *No. of Relatives in Household*										
0	77.0	78.7	81.7	81.8	86.1	78.9	76.7	73.4	75.5	85.5
1	16.3	14.9	14.8	9.1	11.1	13.1	16.7	15.6	16.2	12.9
2	4.8	3.0	2.4	6.5	2.8	4.6	0	9.2	5.9	3.2
3–5	1.7	3.4	1.2	2.6	0	2.5	3.3	1.8	2.4	0
>5	0.2	0	0	0	0	0.8	3.3	0	0	0
4. *No. of Families in the Dwelling*										
1	82.8	83.5	85.8	88.3	80.6	93.2	80.0	87.2	81.3	79.0
2	12.1	10.9	12.4	10.4	13.9	3.8	10.0	8.3	13.4	14.5
3–5	3.9	3.4	1.8	1.3	0	3.0	10.0	2.8	3.1	8.1
6–9	0.3	1.1	0	0	5.6	0	0	0.9	1.5	0
>9	0.9	1.1	0	0	0	0	0	0.9	0.8	0
B. *Roles*										
5. *No. of Working Members in the Nuclear Family of the Head*										
0	6.7	9.3	4.1	0	2.8	11.8	0	5.5	2.4	4.8
1	72.6	72.0	64.5	70.1	77.8	44.3	76.7	54.1	74.5	74.2
2	14.8	13.4	19.5	11.7	13.9	22.8	13.3	21.1	14.0	12.9
3–5	5.9	5.3	11.8	18.2	5.6	19.4	10.0	18.3	8.7	8.1
>5	0	0	0	0	0	1.7	0	0.9	0.4	1.6
6. *No. of Relatives in the Household Who Are Working*										
0	89.8	89.2	91.7	89.6	94.4	89.0	93.3	85.3	87.7	87.1
1	9.0	9.3	8.3	9.1	5.6	9.7	6.7	12.8	10.0	11.3
2	1.0	1.1	0	0	0	1.3	0	1.8	2.1	3.2
3–5	0.2	0.4	0	1.3	0	0	0	0	0.2	0
>5	0	0	0	0	0	0	0	0	0	0
7. *No. of Children >14 and Working*										
0	78.5	83.2	70.4	67.5	77.8	51.9	80.0	59.6	75.9	72.6
1	15.0	10.4	14.8	13.0	13.9	19.0	6.7	22.9	14.0	17.7
2	4.5	5.2	10.1	13.0	8.3	18.6	6.7	11.0	6.5	6.5
>2	2.0	1.2	4.7	6.5	0	10.5	6.7	6.4	3.6	4.8
8. *Households with Boarders*										
not present	79.4	82.1	91.5	83.1	80.6	81.9	80.0	83.5	75.5	71.0
present	20.6	17.9	9.5	16.9	19.4	18.1	20.0	16.5	24.5	29.0

Source: 1900 U.S. Manuscript Census.

TABLE 4

OCCUPATIONAL PROFILE OF ANGLO-CELTIC CANADIANS IN WATERTOWN IN 1900:
OCCUPATIONAL GROUPS AND SPECIFIC OCCUPATIONS

	No. of Canadians	% of Canadian Household Heads	Canadians as a % of All Heads Employed in that Position
Occupational Groups			
unskilled	201	25.8	19.4
semi-skilled	254	32.6	22.7
skilled	138	17.7	16.1
clerical	55	7.1	9.7
business	55	7.1	8.5
professional	10	1.2	6.0
private means	66	8.5	9.8
Specific Occupations[1]			
carter/teamster	38	4.9	28.6
labourer	124	15.9	20.3
blacksmith	41	5.3	34.7
carpenter	52	6.7	24.2
mason	13	1.7	18.6
painter (house and carriage)	27	3.5	17.5
paper maker	18	2.3	21.4
dressmaker	12	1.5	17.6
machinist	57	7.3	17.8
moulder	23	3.0	21.9
bookkeeper	8	1.0	14.0
clerk	7	0.9	9.6
salesperson	13	1.7	6.9
grocer	8	1.0	12.1
manufacturer	4	0.5	7.3
merchant	9	1.2	10.8
landlord	3	0.4	4.5
retired	6	0.8	4.1
widow	56	7.2	15.0
woman	14	1.8	16.7

Percentage of Total Heads who are Anglo-Celtic Canadian—15.3%

[1]occupations with the greatest number of employees.
Source: Original Manuscripts, U.S. Census of Population, Watertown, 1900.

Canadians present in 1900 owned a business, only 1 percent were employed in a clerical position, and only 0.5 percent engaged in a profession. They moved to Watertown to find work, and many found jobs in occupations for which their prior experience may have given them an advantage over others. For example, 6.7 percent were working as carpenters in 1900, and another 5.3 percent were employed as blacksmiths (Table 4).

The rural background of many of the Canadian migrants may explain to a large degree their occupational profile in Watertown. Most farm boys learned to use a saw and to shoe a horse and were thus prepared to take up carpentry and blacksmithing. In fact, 34.7 percent of the Watertown blacksmiths and 24.2 percent of the carpenters were English Canadians. As Table 5 indicates, the

English Canadians more closely approximated the structure of a recent immigrant group, with the majority doing manual labor and a large percentage employed as unskilled labor. Both French and English Canadians had over 80 percent of their respective groups employed in manual positions, greater than any other nativity group. In this respect, the difference between the predominantly Northern European groups that came before 1880 and later immigrants was not that significant, as all immigrant groups, with the exception of the Irish, ranged between 69 percent and 79 percent in their representation within the blue-collar positions. Only the Irish diverged from this pattern, a difference attributed to the abnormally large percentage of household heads included in the private means category.[23] The Irish heads in this grouping were predominantly widowed females.

The large representation of the Irish and the Italians in the unskilled occupations supports the traditional argument that both these groups arrived in America lacking industry-related skills. However, both French Canadians with 2.2 percent of the household head population and 2.0 percent of the unskilled labor force, and the English Canadians with 15.4 percent of the household head population and 19.4 percent of the unskilled laborers, were over-represented in this category. Over 25 percent were employed as unskilled laborers, and English Canadians, because of their supe-

23. For further discussion of the classification of class categories used in this study, see Widdis, *With Scarcely a Ripple*, 469–75.

TABLE 5
MEMBERSHIP IN CLASS GROUPS BY NATIVITY
WATERTOWN, 1900[1]

Nativity Group	Unskilled	Semi-Skilled and Skilled	Petty Capitalist	Classes % Large Capitalist	Business Middle Class	Private Means	N
New York	17.6	47.4	12.1	1.7	7.4	11.6	3.311
Other American	6.6	42.9	11.9	1.1	13.1	15.3	273
English	20.1	58.6	5.3	0	4.1	10.7	169
German	16.9	59.7	10.4	1.3	2.6	9.1	77
Scottish	13.9	63.9	8.3	0	5.6	8.3	36
Irish	30.0	22.4	9.4	0	2.5	31.6	237
Italian	46.7	30.0	16.7	0	0	3.3	30
French Canadian	28.4	57.8	2.8	0	0.9	10.1	109
Anglo-Celtic Canadian	25.2	56.4	6.9	0.5	2.6	7.8	779
Others	14.5	54.8	21.0	0	3.2	4.8	62

[1]figures do not add up to 100% because of missing values.
Sources: Petitions for Naturalization; City Directories.

rior numbers, constituted 52.5 percent of the immigrant unskilled labor population. They dominated certain occupations; for example, as teamsters where 5 percent of the English Canadian heads made up 28.5 percent of all household heads in that position.

The large numbers of Canadians employed in the most menial of occupations may be explained by the fact that the majority of the French and English Canadians came from nearby rural western Quebec and eastern Ontario, and like the Irish and the Italians, lacked industry-related skills. What rural skills they did possess may have been adapted to semi-skilled positions, in which both English Canadians (32.6 percent) and French Canadians (32.1 percent) were most represented. The idea that many English Canadians lacked industrial skills is supported by the fact that only 17.7 percent of this group were employed in skilled manual positions in 1900 as opposed to 23.8 percent for the "other" eastern Europeans, 23.3 percent for the Italians, 23.1 percent for the English, 22.2 percent for the Scottish, 22 percent for the French Canadians, and 20.5 percent for the Germans. English Canadians were thus an important source of labor for the city's rapidly expanding industries. While they were largely working class in nature, they demonstrated a considerable diversity in terms of occupations practiced and wages received.

Immigrants regardless of age and length of residence in America were concentrated primarily among the working class, while natives dominated businesses and the professions. The control of capital, jobs, and political decision-making by the native-born ensured a lack of access to real power and prestige for most first generation immigrants, regardless of origin. In addition, the almost annual residential and occupational changes and the departure of many from the city reflect this environment of structural inequality.[24]

Not all English Canadians were willing to be easily assimilated in Watertown. Of all immigrant groups, they were the least likely to give up their former citizenship. Over 40 percent in 1900 were classified as aliens or aliens who had merely declared the intention to become American citizens. They also ranked next to the Italians in terms of endogamy; over 35.1 percent married Canadian spouses. These facts suggest that many retained the idea that one day they would return home; many obviously chose to share their lives in their new home with fellow Canadians.

24. See Widdis, *With Scarcely a Ripple,* chapter 8.

The experience of English Canadians in Watertown at the turn of the century suggests that Canadian immigrants did occupy a distinctive position in their new home in northern New York. In contrast to European immigrants, their homeland was nearby, their language and religion and other cultural attributes provided common bonds with the native-born population. The experiences of James Pappa and other individuals make clear the possibilities of social and economic success for Canadian immigrants possessed of talent and industry. The relatively unencumbered access to local churches and local societies further contributed to the invisibility of the Canadian immigrant. On the other hand, when the Watertown experience is examined on the basis of quantitative evidence at the conceptual level of the family, community, and class, the notion that Canadians underwent a complete and rapid assimilation becomes questionable. Considerations of cultural shock aside, their role in the social and economic life of Watertown, their marriage patterns and family ties, their continuing interest in Canadian life, all suggest that their experience was more similar to that of the great mass of immigrants than has heretofore been implied.

The degree to which their experience was influenced by each of these sometimes conflicting forces is all but impossible to determine. The answer may be that English Canadian immigrants occupied a middle ground: Their new homeland was not a completely alien culture and in many respects was rather familiar, as they too were regarded as a kindred people by the New Yorkers among whom they settled. Yet they were newcomers, conscious of their origins and influenced by the distinct social, cultural, and economic forces of their native province. They were perhaps invisible or not clearly discernable to those around them, natives and European immigrants alike, but never to themselves. It is noteworthy that Ontario attracted American tourists in the 1980s with television commercials that depicted the province as a place of interesting contrasts—friendly, familiar, foreign, and near—where one would be at home, but not quite at home. It may be that these same elements, broadly applied, informed the Canadian experience in Watertown at the turn of the century.

Irish-American Attitudes and the Americanization of the English-Language Parochial School

By HOWARD WEISZ

Introduction by Robert D. Cross

Howard Weisz received his doctorate from Columbia University in 1968. He was revising his manuscript, and teaching at Lehman College, when he was killed in an automobile accident. Robert D. Cross, who directed Dr. Weisz's graduate work, is president of Swarthmore College.

INTRODUCTION

Howard Weisz was one of the most scrupulous and diligent graduate students that it was my pleasure to work with. If he had a fault, it was that he did ten times more research than was required for his dissertation. He was also an effective teacher. It was therefore doubly tragic that he was the victim of a traffic accident in Europe the summer after he had completed his dissertation. The following article represents the careful scholarship and thorough research that characterized Weisz's work. It throws great light on the development of parochial schools, a subject just now beginning to get some of the scholarly attention it deserves. Free of political bias, the article suggests how deeply American the parochial schools in fact were; that is, how much they incorporated, consciously or unconsciously, the patterns of American culture. As such, the article illustrates an important aspect of American pluralism.

New York History April 1972

DURING the last several decades of the nineteenth century many Irish-Americans devoted themselves to the creation of a separate school system for Catholic children. They thought that separate schools were necessary to protect the faith of their children and would, they believed, help to build a rich Catholic culture in the United States. They also justified educational separatism on the grounds that parochial schools would provide an education different from and superior to that of the public schools. In addition, they argued that children were not learning because of serious weaknesses in the public schools.[1] Irish-American propagandists of the English-language parochial schools had proclaimed that they employed more able teachers, used superior instructional methods, and had a better selected course of study than public schools. In time, the Irish-Americans were successful in building a parochial school system, but the building process was paralleled by the erosion of the educational independence of the parochial schools. As the parochial schools gradually adopted the ways of the public schools their reason for being was inadvertently jeopardized.

An important weapon in the arsenal of those opposed to separate Catholic schools was the argument that they were un-American. Parochial schools patronized by Irish-Americans were, from the start, American in that they taught in English and made efforts to instill loyalty to the United States in their pupils. But to the enemies of the parochial schools, and even to some who supported them, this Americanism had to be measured against the practices of the public schools. Advocates of English-language parochial schools were faced with the difficulty of arguing both that the schools were American and that they were very different from all other American schools. If parochial schools were not demonstrably American, then they could not survive pressure from their enemies, and if they were not different, then they had no reason to exist. Yet, as we shall see, the American Irish who worked to create parochial schools, were, in fact, responsible for making them increasingly like public schools.

[1] Howard R. Weisz, "Irish-American and Italian-American Educational Views and Activities, 1870-1900: A Comparison" (unpublished Ph.D. dissertation, Department of History, Columbia University, 1968), Chapter VI.

The American Irish approved of the loyalty to Catholicism shown by Germans and others in establishing church schools. But their opinion of foreign-language parochial schools was tinged with doubt that they were appropriate in America. Generally the Irish ignored foreign-language schools. In fact, they had more contact with public schools than with foreign-language church schools.

Irish-Americans were pleased that English-language parochial schools made a special point of inculcating American patriotism. When the tensions of the school question led to the establishment of the anti-Catholic National League for the Protection of American Institutions, Patrick Ford, an Irish nationalist who owned and edited the weekly *Irish World,* found that he agreed with its professed position, but he could see no reason why anti-Catholicism should be thought to be implicit in those principles. Ford maintained that Catholics wanted "no foreign schools with doctrines, ideas, and methods at variance with our constitutional principles, disturbing, instead of conserving, the national harmony. . . ."[2]

To combat what they saw as a decline in patriotic feeling, the members of a New York City post of the Grand Army of the Republic began in 1888 to give flags to schools for display. The practice spread rapidly and by the mid-Nineties most public schools flew the national flag.[3] The Irish-run parochial schools adopted the use of the flag with alacrity. There had been incidents in which the Catholic clerics had objected to the display of the flag in or on churches, but there seems to have been no such opposition with respect to the schools. In 1889 the *Catholic News* observed on the adoption of this practice in Pittsburgh: "That the Stars and Stripes has not received its glories from Protestants alone is a fact that will be duly emphasized in this diocese by the uprearing of the national standard over the parochial schools."[4]

A high point of the dedication of Father Morgan Sheedy's school in Pittsburgh the next year was the presentation of an American flag by a G.A.R. member, Nicholas Brady.[5] In an-

[2] *Irish World and American Industrial Liberator,* May 24, 1890; hereafter cited as *Irish World.*

[3] George J. Lankevich, "The Grand Army of the Republic in New York State" (unpublished Ph.D. dissertation, Department of History, Columbia University, 1967), pp. 264-271.

[4] *Catholic News,* March 3, 1889.

[5] *New-York Freeman's Journal and Catholic Register,* February 22, 1890; hereafter cited as *New-York Freeman's Journal.*

An exhibition of calisthenics on opening day of the public schools, New York City, September 5, 1881. From Frank Leslie's Illustrated Newspaper, *September 17, 1881.*

other instance, Father Patrick F. McSweeny declared in defense of the Americanism of his parish school, St. Brigid's in New York City: "We have no flag but the stars and stripes, which we fly on every public occasion over school and rectory, speak no other language than United States, and when we sing, you can always hear Hail Columbia, America, the Star Spangled Banner, etc. . . ."[6] When State Superintendent Charles R. Skinner asked the public schools of New York to observe Flag Day 1896, the *Catholic Review* urged Catholic schools to celebrate with appropriate exercises.[7]

Irish-Americans further defended the establishment of parochial schools as acts of patriotism. Bourke Cochran, New York politician and orator, asserted that he was never so proud of his Church as when she was "preparing the minds of the youth of this country for the work and duties of citizen-

[6] Patrick D. O'Flaherty, "History of St. Brigid's Parish in the City of New York Under the Administration of Rev. Patrick F. McSweeny" (unpublished Master's thesis, Department of History, Fordham University, 1952), p. 97.
[7] *Catholic Review,* June 20, 1896.

ship."[8] A strong statement of a like position was made by Father James Loughlin of Philadelphia, who argued "that the parochial school, established freely by American citizens, [was] the most genuinely American institution in the United States."[9]

Nevertheless, critics accused the Catholic schools of trying to indoctrinate children so that they could be manipulated by priests with monarchial or authoritarian ideas, though some supporters of the parochial schools praised them for producing shy, docile children.[10] In reply to such attacks Father John Mullany, a Syracuse, New York, pastor and writer, admitted that Catholic educated children, especially the Irish, might well be more "modest" and "diffident," but doubted that this lowered their value as citizens or lessened their chance for success in the world.[11] On the other hand, another cleric,

[8] *American Herald and Catholic School Advocate*, May 21, 1894; hereafter cited as *American Herald*.
[9] *Catholic Review*, May 27, 1893.
[10] *Catholic Review*, June 7, 1890.
[11] See sermon of Father Mullany in *Catholic Review*, September 26, 1896.

Charles R. Skinner. From Hills, New York State Men.

Bishop B. J. McQuaid. From Peck, History of Rochester and Monroe County.

Father John Murphy thought that Catholic secondary schools were often too paternal. Since the students did not have enough opportunity to exercise self-control and self-respect, they did not develop "self-government and initiative."[12]

Those who believed that the establishment of separate schools on religious grounds was an act of good citizenship argued that those schools were significantly different from the public schools in areas other than religious instruction. Bishop Bernard McQuaid of Rochester, for example, thought that Catholic schools remained unique and superior institutions, free of all the weaknesses of the public schools and owing nothing to them. McQuaid found differences in all aspects of schooling:

It is true the parochial schools are not victims to the vagaries of cranks. The latter are not permitted to run our schools, nor are they under the domination of school-book publishers. Nor are they "loaded down" with music, modern languages, the mechanical arts, savings banks, and military drill.[13]

[12] John T. Murphy, "Catholic Secondary Education in the United States," *American Catholic Quarterly Review,* XXII (July, 1897), p. 457.
[13] Bernard McQuaid, "Religious Teaching in Schools," *Forum,* VIII.

These assumptions of the special character of the parochial school were largely divorced from reality.

Others, more realistic, admitted that the parochial schools strayed from the narrow path of the four R's. In 1880, the proprietor and editor of the *Catholic Review,* Patrick Hickey, maintained that the worst thing that could be said against the parochial schools was that they were like the public schools. He thought it unfortunate that the two types of school were similar. In 1886 he argued that the progress of parochial schools had been hindered by the "insane attempt" to imitate the public schools. Near the end of the decade an editor of the *Catholic Review* chided pastors for being too "servile" in following the public school system, which he thought too young to have been really tried, and noted it was already beseiged by determined opponents who thought it an unfit system.[14] When asked to comment on the proposed course of study of a new Catholic school, Maurice Francis Egan, who later made a reputation as a professor and literary critic, stated: "It savors too much of the pretentious system of brain stuffing and stifling adopted in the public schools." He added:

In answer to this objection, we are told that numbers of young girls at this school are preparing themselves to be teachers in public schools, and that the Sisters must keep this end in view. This is unfortunate. The evils of the public school system are forcing themselves into our schools. And yet there is no remedy of it proposed just at present. School teaching in public schools offers the prospect of respectable employment to many young women who would otherwise have to remain idle or secure distasteful work in large and overcrowded shops.[15]

The Reverend Michael Walsh, an immigrant priest and journalist, also looked with displeasure on the expansion of the parochial school curriculum in response to the public school example. He thought that when Catholic schools added studies, it was "more the fault of the parents than the teachers."[16]

In contrast to these complaints were the efforts by parochial schools to attract pupils by advertising their similarity to the public schools. Father Richard Shortell of St. Augustine's Church, Bridgeport, Connecticut, boasted in 1891 that his

[14] *Catholic Review,* July 1, 1880; September 25, 1880; October 2, 1886; September 14, 1889.
[15] *New-York Freeman's Journal,* April 2, 1887.
[16] *American Herald,* July 1, 1895.

school was organized on the same basis as the public school, so that a child leaving a certain grade in public school would fit in the same grade in parochial school.[17] Sacred Heart school of Bridgeport announced in 1896 that "there should be no hesitancy in sending children to the parochial schools, as the line of work followed in the public schools is copied entirely by the Sisters, even to the smallest detail."[18] Both the *Freeman's Journal* and the *Catholic News* in 1900 reprinted without comment a secular paper's statement that, except for the study of religion, the curriculum of Brooklyn parochial schools varied only slightly from the one adopted by the local board of education.[19]

The course of study for parochial schools of the Archdiocese of New York published in 1887 provided for secular instruction similar to that in public schools. In the sixth of the eight grammar grades both public and parochial schools concentrated on percentage problems in the study of arithmetic. They both continued penmanship practice begun in earlier grades. Public school geography focused on North America, and parochial schools on South America and Europe. The public schools taught American colonial history and the parochial schools were expected to teach the history of the United States from the Revolution to the Mexican War. Both continued lessons in reading, composition, and grammar. But the public schools required as part of practice in the use of language oral lessons in "simple facts of natural philosophy," that is, the fundamentals of science. Public grammar schools required a course in drawing, while the parochial schools gave lessons in Christian doctrine and Church history.[20]

In 1889 St. James' school boasted of being the only parochial school in New York City offering studies that included trigonometry, philosophy, rhetoric, bookkeeping, and geometry. By the mid-Nineties the most respected parochial schools in New York City, all with mostly Irish pupils, had followed the public schools in expanding their course of study. The *Catholic*

---

[17] Arthur J. Heffernan, *A History of Catholic Education in Connecticut* (Washington, D. C., 1937), p. 93.

[18] Heffernan, *Catholic Education in Connecticut,* p. 93.

[19] *New-York Freeman's Journal,* September 15, 1900; *Catholic News,* September 15, 1900.

[20] The Catholic course of study appeared in the *Catholic Review,* August 27, 1887. Compare with New York (City), Board of Education, *Annual Report of the Board of Education* (New York, 1887), p. 225.

"A Picture Without Words." Puck comments on Catholic requests for a share of public school funds. From **Puck**, *January 16, 1884.*

News reported that St. Joseph's school gave all the courses usually taught in the primary and grammar grades in the public schools. The curriculum included algebra, geometry, physiology, hygiene, bookkeeping, ancient and modern history, free hand and mechanical drawing, and vocal and instrumental music. The girls at St. Mary's studied astronomy. At St. Gabriel's, presided over by Msgr. John A. Farley, pupils studied, in addition to the usual subjects, surveying, navigation, analytical geometry, conic sections, plane and spherical geometry, and algebra.[21]

Irish spokesmen naturally wanted certain special courses to be added to the parochial school curriculum. Supporters of parochial schools admitted that religious instruction was a function of the family, but they argued that parents who worked long hours away from home could not attend to it properly. Parochial schools were also asked to teach additional skills marginal to the practice of Catholicism. John Talbot Smith,

[21] *New-York Freeman's Journal,* July 6, 1889; April 28, 1894. *Catholic News,* March 11, June 17, 1894.

editor of the *Catholic Review,* wanted sacred music, especially singing, to be taught. When a reader, one John J. McEvoy, replied that the schools of 1890 were in the midst of a difficult effort and that vocal training could wait until they were well organized, Smith countered that music should start with the school. He found many virtues in singing: it "soothes the savage breast, it refreshes and calms; it brings attention to prayers."[22]

In the elaboration of one educational frill of the time—military training—parochial schools sometimes went beyond their public counterparts. After the Civil War repeated efforts were made to have schools introduce military drill. Its advocates often confused military training with physical training, and militarism with the traditional virtues of the gentleman soldier. When the *New York Tribune Monthly* interviewed all of the principals of the city's grammar schools in 1896, the reporters found some opposed to the idea and others ready to turn their charges into miniature soldiers. Several schools had units of the American Guard, begun in 1893 with G.A.R. encouragement. Usually the unit enrolled only a minority of the boys. Several of the principals, especially in the poorer neighborhoods, forbade uniforms.[23]

The fever for marching, drill, and having schoolboys play soldiers infected the parochial schools. Cadet corps named for Catholic schools paraded on holidays and went through their drill routines at school exhibitions and commencements. One parade in 1892 featured the Assumption Fife and Drum Corps of St. James Cathedral school, Brooklyn. This corps of over three hundred boys drilled under the direction of the teaching brothers. Military drill was part of the annual exhibition put on by the boys of St. Bridget's school, Jersey City. Cadets of the Holy Cross school in New York City performed at graduation exercises in 1895.[24] At Father Patrick McSweeny's school, St. Brigid's, in New York City, the cadet corps wore uniforms modeled on Civil War styles and was drilled by a sergeant of the Sixty-Ninth Regiment. Father McSweeny complimented the St. Brigid's cadets after their performance at the graduation ceremony:

[22] *Catholic Review,* February 13, 22, 1890; March 22, 1890.
[23] *New York Tribune Monthly* (March, 1896).
[24] *Catholic Review,* October 22, April 16, 1892; *American Herald,* July 1, 1895.

Reverend Patrick F. McSweeny. From King, Notable New Yorkers.

I read in the papers, that there is a great dispute going on in Congress whether we shall have a standing army or no. However this may be, the Brothers are preparing to send a good battalion from St. Brigid's. Another praiseworthy feature of your performance was the love it showed for poor old Ireland, the land of your fathers, and whence your faith, your Catholicity has come.[25]

Military training programs were primarily a response by both parochial and public schools to pressures from patriotic organizations, especially the G.A.R.

Demands that the public schools add new activities, raise standards, save money, and organize more efficiently led to the systematization of the schools. By 1870 the public schools of large American cities were being drawn into centrally administered systems. In most places, the parochial schools were, as the *Catholic Review* later described them, "little more than a congeries of fortuitous atoms."[26] The eventual systematizing of the parochial schools was done in conscious imitation of the public schools. Proponents of order and uniformity in the parochial school system pointed to the public school

[25] O'Flaherty, "History of St. Brigid's," pp. 43 & 99.
[26] *Catholic Review,* March 19, 1881.

example. "An Experienced Teacher" wrote to the *Catholic Review* in 1890 to call for removal of defects in the parochial schools by imitation of the public schools: As an example of unsound practices in ungraded or poorly graded-schools he noted that in some Catholic elementary schools history was taught in the form of a catechism—rote memorization of questions and answers. To the arguments of "An Experienced Teacher" Father John Talbot Smith added that the appointment of school boards and superintendents might be a way of bringing parochial schools up to the level of public schools in temporal studies.[27]

Anxious over the future of the parochial schools, Father Daniel McDermott, pastor of St. Mary's Church in Philadelphia, attributed many of their faults to a lack of system. In an 1889 article he described many advantages of public school organization. A uniform system of grading made transfer easy. Standards, he thought, could be maintained better and raised if schools were more closely coordinated. Organization also made possible general development rather than the piecemeal reform that might be carried out by individual schools. McDermott's plan for the church schools was never fully implemented in any diocese. He wanted a complete system of Catholic schools organized under a single control. School districts would not follow parish lines.[28]

The parish school has remained the pastor's castle, but most American bishops took steps toward diocesan organization in the last years of the nineteenth century. The offices and institutions that were established reflected the influence of the public schools. Bishops appointed diocesan school boards, boards of school examiners, and superintendents of schools.[29]

There were relatively few Catholic secondary schools (in the 1890s) and most of them were private, select institutions.[30] If Irish Catholics wanted secondary education for their children, they had to send them to public high schools.

[27] *Catholic Review,* May 31, 1890.
[28] Daniel I. McDermott, "Roman Catholics and the Parochial Schools," *Independent,* XLI (October 31, 1889), pp. 1420-1421; *Catholic Review,* November 16, 1889. For a similar analysis of the problem of school organization see Joseph V. Tracy, "Is the Catholic School System Perfect?" *Catholic World,* II (July, 1890), pp. 427-32.
[29] James A. Burns & Bernard J. Kohlbrenner, *A History of Catholic Education in the United States* (New York, 1937), Chap. VIII.
[30] Mary O'Brien, *History and Development of Catholic Secondary Education in the Archdiocese of New York* (New York, 1941).

Melvil Dewey. From Hills, New York State Men.

This was the case, for example, in Connecticut. Some towns in that state placed the additional burden on Catholic schools of requiring that graduates of private schools take high school entrance examinations. In Kansas there were no Catholic high schools until Catholic students began to attend the public high schools and the state demanded a high school education for rural teachers.[31] Even in the cities of the northeast, where there were many Catholic schools, large numbers of Irish-American children had either to go to the public schools or get no secondary schooling. At the end of the century parochial schools in New York City boasted of the number of their graduates admitted to public high schools.[32] Maurice Francis Egan thought that the public schools were particularly attractive to girls, who were likely to consider teaching as an occupation. He saw the parochial schools becoming "feeders" for the public secondary schools which would, in turn, prepare the girls to be teachers in the public system.[33]

In New York the activities of the Board of Regents and the State Department of Education fostered similarity be-

[31] Heffernan, *Catholic Education in Connecticut,* p. 90; Richard J. Bollig, *History of Catholic Education in Kansas* (Washington, D. C., 1933), pp. 65-66, 84.
[32] *American Herald,* February 12, 1900.
[33] *New-York Freeman's Journal,* August 4, 1888.

tween public and private secondary schools. Increasing numbers of Catholic institutions sought the prestige associated with a Regents' charter.[34] Graduates of Regents accredited schools had advantages in entering colleges and professional schools. In order for St. Gabriel's school, in New York City, to meet the Regents' requirements Msgr. James Farley, vicar-general of the Archdiocese of New York, arranged for modern languages and science laboratory work to be added to the curriculum.[35]

Of this effort of Catholic schools to qualify for state charters, Melvil Dewey, Secretary of the Board of Regents, commented in 1895: "We are Americanizing the parochial school with the assistance of the broader-minded Roman Catholic clergymen; and when we have done that there will be no excuse for these ill-advised i.e., anti-Catholic societies."[36] A committee of priests recommended in 1897 that the parochial schools be incorporated under the Regents to insure uniformity and a high standard of instruction.[37]

An 1895 New York statute that required candidates for state teaching certificates to have completed a high school or academy course approved by the state superintendent had an effect on Catholic secondary schools similar to that of Regents regulations. Since many of their students expected to work in the public schools, the Catholic schools had to meet the state requirements. Even the diocesan academy of Bishop McQuaid, a champion of independent Catholic education, adjusted its curriculum, in order to receive state approval. The school, Nazareth Academy in Rochester, added a course in zoology and lengthened its drawing course to fulfill the requirements set by the state.[38]

Irish-American spokesmen continued to voice doubts about the value of widespread secondary education. But experience with public high schools caused the adoption of new positions. In 1890 Brother Azarias, an Irish-born member of the Brothers of the Christian Schools, called for central Catholic high

---

[34] The report of the Board of Regents listed no Catholic schools in 1885, nine in 1890, and thirty-seven in 1895. New York (State), University of the State of New York, *Report of the Regents* (Albany, 1885); (Albany, 1890); (Albany, 1895).

[35] *Catholic News*, April 1, 1894. *Irish-American*, April 5, 1894.

[36] *School Bulletin*, XXI (January, 1895), p. 73.

[37] *New York Times*, December 10, 1897; *Irish World*, January 15, 1898.

[38] Frederick J. Zwierlein, *The Life and Letters of Bishop McQuaid* (Rochester: The Art Print Shop, 1926), Vol. II, pp. 108-110.

schools in cities.[39] Writing in the *American Catholic Quarterly Review,* Father John T. Murphy warned in 1897 that Catholics must find a way to establish high schools. If not, they would either fall farther behind socially and economically or suffer the consequences of giving their children non-Catholic schooling. He found that without a high school education young men could seldom get good jobs. Because of this he criticized the Catholic secondary schools which had to exclude many because they could not pay the fees.[40]

Father James A. Burns, historian of the American parochial school, praised the public high school as "the people's college" and as the response to a popular demand for more and better education. In a 1901 article he criticized current Catholic secondary education and called for central Catholic high schools. He thought the number of students in Catholic secondary schools was often too small to be efficient. Burns marshalled statistics to show that Catholic children were not getting as much education as American youth generally and that Catholic parents were sending their children to public high schools. Father Burns thought that both these problems could be attacked by establishing a system of Catholic high schools. Secondary schooling would have to be taken out of the hands of the preparatory departments of Catholic colleges, which enrolled most of the boys receiving Catholic schooling, and of the female academies, which were often elementary schools with a few secondary students. Burns thought the main obstacle to the establishment of Catholic high schools was lack of faith in the utility and desirability of such schools rather than lack of means. Pastors who zealously supported parochial elementary schools seemed not to see the need for high schools. Administrators of Catholic academies and colleges looked coldly on changes that might hurt their institutions. Yet Burns believed that the expansion of public schools and the attendance of ever larger numbers of Catholic children made Catholic high schools a pressing need.[41]

Despite the long history of the Catholic teaching orders, the public schools, through the Irish, had an influence on the

---

[39] Patrick Francis Mullany (Brother Azarias), "Lessons of a Century of Catholic Education," *Catholic World,* L (November, 1889), p. 147.

[40] Murphy, "Catholic Secondary Education," pp. 449-464.

[41] James A. Burns, "Catholic Secondary Schools," *American Catholic Quarterly Review,* XXVI (July, 1901), pp. 485-499.

Thomas Nast's famous cartoon, "The American River Ganges." From Harper's Weekly, *September 30, 1871.*

training of parochial school teachers. Irish supporters of parochial schools pointed out proudly to the praise given by disinterested observers to teachers in the best schools of the Christian Brothers and the Jesuits. Yet people hoping to improve the many poorly-prepared parochial school teachers often turned to the public school as a model. Parochial schoolmen naturally found it difficult to admit flaws in institutions they had struggled to build; they found it even harder to admit they could learn anything from the public schools. But, as one priest asked his fellows in 1892: "What boots the pastor's *ipse dixit* [unsupported statement] of a teacher's capacity when the advanced scholars from under the trained masterhand of the neighboring public school, who have come to supply the greater need of religious instruction, discover the 'breaks' and deficiencies of the Catholic teacher."[42] Even Father John Talbot Smith, later to be historian of the Archdiocese of New York, wondered whether there were too many "half-fledged neophytes" teaching in Catholic schools. Be-

[42] J. Price, "Our Parochial School System," *Ecclesiastical Review,* VII (July, 1892), p. 56.

cause of competition he believed the schools could not afford a reputation for low standards. Father Smith advised that the religious should not be too secluded, or too bound by traditional rules or methods "which are not in harmony with the spirit of American ideas and institutions." He suggested that each teaching order have a training school whether or not it was a part of the design of the founder.[43]

Orders of teaching sisters had to struggle to supply needed teachers. In communities where the schools were in the hands of an order with international branches, some shortages were filled, even in the English-language schools, with Europeans who knew no English. Hard-pressed religious superiors also placed novices with no preparation as teachers.[44]

Father Richard Shortell admitted that the parochial school sisters were at a disadvantage because they lacked normal school training and had no opportunity to meet in conventions or institutes, which were popular with public school teachers. He thought these techniques for educating had wrought a "wonderful change" in the public schools. Since it seemed to him unlikely that Catholic normal schools would be built rapidly, Father Shortell called for conventions of religious teachers. He recognized that the parochial schools had learned from the public schools, but believed that by the 1890s they were no longer dependent on them.[45] Yet, when the practice of holding institutes for parochial school teachers did develop in the middle of the decade, it was public school teachers who served as instructors.

The movement started with a series of lectures given to nuns in New York City by Mrs. B. Ellen Burke,[46] an experienced teacher who for several years had worked for the New York State Education Department. To give similar courses, she assembled a group of teachers, whom the *American Catholic Who's Who* described as "some of the ablest Catholic teachers in the country."[47] Most of the ladies were Irish-Americans. All had secular pedagogical training. Mrs. Burke

---

[43] *Catholic Review*, April 18, 1891.

[44] Burns & Kohlbrenner, *Catholic Education*, pp. 218, 222-223.

[45] Richard E. Shortell, "Conventions for Our Teachers," *Ecclesiastical Review*, IX (July, 1893), pp. 42-43.

[46] James P. Kiernan, "Institutes in the Catholic Educational System," *New York Education*, I (October, 1897), p. 74. For a biographical sketch of Mrs. Burke see *American Catholic Who's Who* (St. Louis: B. Herder, 1911).

[47] *American Catholic Who's Who*, p. 64.

and her staff held the first diocesan institute for the teaching sisters of Rochester in 1896. The next similar institutes were held in six other cities. Eventually Mrs. Burke's group reached at least some parochial school teachers in most states.[48] Clerical educators praised this enterprise. One priest, writing in *New York Education* attributed some of the progress he saw in the parochial schools to the institutes.[49] The rector of the Rochester Cathedral described the growth of teachers' institutes as a "great movement" and gave credit for it to Mrs. Burke.[50]

Teacher training was just one aspect of the competition Irish Catholic schoolmen perceived between public and parochial schools. Each advance in what educators of the time called the "efficiency" of the public schools was seen by Irish spokesmen as another battle in the struggle for the children. Patrick Hickey of the *Catholic Review* attributed improvements in the public schools to "animosity to the growing parochial schools and a desire to cripple their usefulness."[51] *The New York School Journal* warned its readers in 1888 that to save their jobs they must make the public schools so good that Catholic schools could not measure up. The editor told the teachers that the future of the public schools depended on their quality, since Americans "know a good thing when they see it."[52]

Many changes were, however, undertaken without reference to the religious issue. Other spokesmen expressed, without Hickey's peevishness, awareness of the burden competition with public schools placed on Catholic institutions. Father Shortell described candidly the position of the parochial schools: "It is true that the Public Schools have to a great extent served us as a pattern of excellence, but it is also true that the existence of that system which is already more than a century old, has raised the demands from us and forced us to greater exertions in secular training than would be neces-

---

[48] Kiernan, "Institutes," p. 74. In 1898 Mrs. Burke directed a five-day course for teachers of the Archdiocese of Boston. Louis S. Walsh, *Archdiocese of Boston; Growth of Parochial Schools in Chronological Order, 1820-1900* (Newton Highlands, Mass.: Press of St. John's Industrial Training School, 1901), p. 15.

[49] M. W. Hollands, "The Growth of the National Catholic Teachers' Institute," *New York Education*, II (March, 1899), pp. 395-396.

[50] Kiernan, "Institutes," p. 74.

[51] *Catholic Review*, September 29, 1877.

[52] *New York School Journal*, XXXVI (September 22, 1888), p. 151.

sary if our aim were simply to educate good American citizens who are at the same time good Christians." Similarly, Father John Murphy realized that the parochial schools must aim high because the public schools did. He thought the latter had gone a long way towards attaining their goals "if we are to judge by the intelligence of the average American citizen who has received none but a common school education."[53]

The parochial schools, however, remained distinct from the public schools. Their concentration on religious subjects was the most obvious difference. There were also variations in substance within similar forms. The parochial schools emphasized Catholic literature and the role of Catholicism in history. Nevertheless, the direction of change was to bring the parochial schools closer to the public schools. The dream of creating a pure Catholic culture on the base of the parochial schools was doomed. The parish schools came into existence not only to further the Catholic faith, but also to serve as a surrogate for the public schools. Pressure to emulate those public schools came from parents jealous of the educational advantages of others. Parochial systems vied with public systems in raising their percentage of graded schools. In Boston, for example, the parochial school followed public school hours and vacation schedules.[54]

The entrance of parochial pupils into non-Catholic secondary schools and colleges for career training forced the parochial schools to approximate the offerings of the public schools. State control of professional requirements, especially those for teachers, put pressure on the parochial schools to follow the public school model. Pastors accepted changes that would help their schools compete, if they felt the changes did not endanger the religious nature of the schools. Thus the English-language parish schools, American in their origin and character, became even more like other American schools in their attempt to compete.

Compulsory schooling laws were not so rigid that they prevented private schools from following their own course. Yet the English-language parochial school joined the ladder of

[53] Richard E. Shortell, "How Can Our Schools Be Improved?" *Ecclesiastical Review*, V (December, 1891), p. 461.
[54] John T. Murphy, "The Idea of a Parochial School," *American Catholic Quarterly Review*, XVI (July, 1891), p. 450.

American education—elementary school, high schools, and college—which was in the process of formation. The parallel was not perfect, but neither were the public schools yet nationally uniform even in the number of years of the elementary or high school. From the bitterness of the Irish-American critique of the public school one might have expected the parochial school to make its own way, but even men who assailed the public school cheered the parochial school's successive approximations to it.

By the beginning of the twentieth century, the only substantial reason for the maintenance of Catholic parochial schools was that they aimed to provide their pupils with knowledge of their religion and inculcate in them devotion to it. They were too much like the public schools in other ways to justify a separate system. Irish-American advocates of the church schools played an essential role in bringing them to that point.

The Assimilation of the Welsh in Central New York

By DAVID MALDWYN ELLIS

David Ellis, a distinguished historian of New York State and a fellow of this Association, discusses the Americanization of the Welsh in upstate New York, with some interesting personal observations stemming from his Welsh ancestry. He is P. V. Rogers Professor of History at Hamilton College.

THE PROCESS of Americanizing the immigrant is a phenomenon which never ceases to intrigue foreign observers and to interest each generation of citizens. St. John de Crèvecoeur, who lived in 1770 along the lower Hudson, wrote that the "American" was a "new man" shaped by the free institutions under which he lived. "Here individuals of all nations are melted into a new race of men, . . ."[1] It is unlikely that Israel Zangwill, a Jewish immigrant, borrowed the title of his play, the *Melting Pot* (1908) from the obscure writings of Crèvecoeur, but from his own experience and aspirations he noted "how the great Alchemist melts and fuses them [immigrants] with his purging flame! Here shall all unite to build the Republic of Man and the Kingdom of God."[2]

American society and culture—operating through such agencies as the school, the job, the playing field, political parties, and television—have had a massive effect upon the life style of newcomers, their institutions, and even their values.

[1] Michel Guillaume St. Jean de Crèvecoeur, *Letters from an American Farmer* (Everymans Library edition, n. d.), p. 43.
[2] Quoted in Oscar Handlin, ed., *Immigration as a Factor in American History* (Englewood Cliffs, 1959), p. 150. This work is a convenient source for selections from commentators on the melting pot thesis.

New York History July 1972

Choral competition in the Welsh National Eisteddfod, Scranton, Pennsylvania, 1880. From Frank Leslie's Illustrated Newspaper, *July 10, 1880.*

Most immigrants learn to speak English more or less well, abandon native dress for American garb, take a keen interest in American sports, and imitate the customs of this country. In fact the immigrant press, fraternal societies, and even churches are often more similar to American models than to foreign institutions. Nevertheless ethnic consciousness persists, with millions identifying themselves as of Irish, English, German, Italian, Spanish, Polish, and Russian descent.[3]

In the late 1960s political observers popularized the term "ethnics" to describe Americans who belong to the second generation, such as the Poles of Buffalo, the Italians of Newark, New Jersey, and the Hungarians and Slovaks of Gary, Indiana. Deeply conscious that the WASPs (White Anglo-Saxon Protestants) among the urban elite, the suburbs, and the countryside did not fully accept them, they also felt their

[3] The Census Bureau in 1971 reported that 75 million Americans still consider themselves as members of seven major nationality groups. All but 11 million of them were born in this country. The groups are: German 19,961,000; English 19,060,000; Irish 13,282,000; Spanish 9,230,000; Italian 7,239,000; Polish 4,021,000; Russian 2,152,000. This report was summarized in *U.S. News and World Report,* August 9, 1971.

neighborhoods threatened by the massive influx of Blacks. The rise of the Italian American Civil Rights League and the Jewish Defense League in the late 1960s registers this upsurge of ethnic feeling. No doubt Black separatism and militancy, with its emphasis on "soul" music and food, the Afro-style hairdo, and the *dashigi,* stimulated ethnic self-consciousness. The ethnic associations hope to protect their neighborhoods and schools from the change involved in the busing of school children for racial integration.

Clearly people prefer to associate with those who are like themselves. Milton Gordon has described it well.

. . . the characteristic ethnic group experience is this: within the ethnic group there develops a network of organizations and informal social relationships which permits and encourages the members of the ethnic group to remain within the confines of the group for all of their primary relationships . . . From the cradle in the sectarian hospital to the child's play group, the social clique in high school, the fraternity and religious center in college, the dating group within which he searches for a spouse, the marriage partner, the neighborhood of his residence, the church affiliation and the church clubs, the men's and the women's social and service organizations, the adult clique of "marrieds," the vacation resort, and then, as the age cycle nears completion, the rest home for the elderly and, finally, the sectarian cemetery—in all these activities and relationships which are close to the core of personality and selfhood—the member of the ethnic group may if he wishes follow a path which never takes him across the boundaries of his ethnic structural network.[4]

Before 1914 and even today in the South and parts of the West, the American cultural pattern has been British in stock and Protestant in faith. At first even English, Scottish, Welsh, Ulster Irish, and Anglo-Canadian immigrants did not always receive a cordial welcome from the older native stock. For example, Scotch-Irish Presbyterians, who settled in colonial New Hampshire, met criticism by Yankee Puritans. Similarly the Yankees met much distrust when they settled in New York, Pennsylvania, and the Old Northwest. The inhabitants of those regions criticized them for their nasal speech, sharp business methods, meddlesome consciences, greed, and parsimony.

When the currents of immigration swept in more newcomers from Ireland after 1840 and from southern and eastern

---

[4] "Assimilation in America: Theory and Reality," *Daedalus* XC (Spring 1961), 280.

Europe after 1890, British immigrants found the welcome somewhat warmer. Irish Catholics despite their English speech were greeted with suspicion and occasional violence primarily because their religious loyalty revived old fears and hostilities. A rival Irish Catholic society, fully equipped with churches, schools, fraternal associations, saloons, and aristocracy, developed in New York, Albany, and other urban centers.[5] Although other Catholic immigrants did not accept Irish domination of the church and the local Democratic party with enthusiasm, they distrusted the WASPs even more. After all it was the Protestants who were trying to prohibit the consumption of alcoholic beverages, who passed immigration restriction laws through Congress, and attacked their institutions and way of life.

Scholars from several disciplines have approached the ethnic problem from various viewpoints. Anthropologists have sought to explain the process in terms of acculturation and assimilation.[6] The first term describes the acquisition by an ethnic group of the culture of the dominant group. Most immigrants to America have had the desire and the capacity for acculturation. Many had cut the umbilical cord when they left their native village and boarded ship for America. In contrast some French-Canadian communities in northern New England, Spanish-speaking communities in the Southwest, and closely-knit religious groups, notably the German Amish, have stubbornly resisted acculturation.

Assimilation may be defined as the disappearance of group identity through association with outsiders and exogamy (marriage outside the tribe or blood group). Note that in this instance another step is necessary, namely, acceptance by the dominant group. The old native stock has drawn the line sharply against persons of other races whether red, yellow, or black. Furthermore, it has greeted newcomers from southern or eastern Europe with suspicion. The crusade for Americanization of the immigrant during World War I and Wilson's attacks on hyphenated Americans demanded that immigrants should adopt "American" values. The National Origins Act of

[5] For Albany, see William E. Rowley, "The Irish Aristocracy of Albany, 1798-1878," *New York History* LII (July 1971), 275-304. For New York City, see Robert Ernst, *Immigrant Life in New York City, 1825-1863* (New York, 1949).

[6] Melford E. Spiro, "The Acculturation of American Ethnic Groups," *American Anthropologist* LVII (Dec. 1955), 1243-1248.

1924 assumed that individuals from Northwest Europe would become good citizens faster than Italians, Poles, Greeks, and Jews.

Each nationality group has its own rate of acculturation and assimilation.[7] To complicate matters these rates vary according to educational and economic levels, the size of the immigrant community, and its location. For example, Italian musicians were lionized in drawing rooms while Sicilian ditch-diggers were often treated with contempt even by their co-religionists, the Irish. Ethnic enclaves on the land and linked together by a religious loyalty resisted acculturation easier than urban dwellers. Good examples are the Pennsylvania "Dutch," the French in the bayou country of Louisiana, Dutch, German, Norwegian, and Swedish communities in the Middle West.

Sociologists have shown surprise at the survival of ethnic groups long after the passing of the great wave of immigration.[8] Andrew M. Greeley holds that these groups, however, are "best conceived as something entirely new" and not mere survivals of migratory waves.[9] Nathan Glazer and Daniel Patrick Moynihan in 1963 analyzed the Negro, Puerto Rican, Italian, Jewish, and Irish communities of New York City in a study significantly entitled *Beyond the Melting Pot*. And yet the melting pot has its defenders and modifiers. For example, Will Herberg has advanced the thesis of the triple melting pot in his 1961 study, *Protestant-Catholic-Jew*.

Historians have also observed how ethnic groups maintained a sense of group consciousness for generations. Robert Ernst described in great detail the creation of separate institutions among the Irish and Germans of pre-Civil War New York. Another New York study, *The Concept of Jacksonian Democracy as a Test Case* by Lee Benson, asserts that ". . . at least since the 1820's, . . . ethnic and religious differences have

---

[7] W. Lloyd Warner and Leo Strole, *The Social System of American Ethnic Groups* (New York, 1946).

[8] *This U. S. A.*, a penetrating analysis of our population by Ben J. Wattenberg and Richard M. Scammon, the latter Director of the Census, 1961-1965, confirms the continuation of a high degree of religious endogamy. Of all married couples, 94 percent are spouses of the same religion. See Pocket Book edition, 1967, pp. 70-71. The latest group to show ethnic feeling may be the *White Protestant Americans*, the title of a study by Charles Anderson published in 1970 in Englewood Cliffs, New Jersey.

[9] "American Sociology and the Study of Ethnic Immigrant Groups," *International Migration Digest* I (Fall 1964), 107-113.

tended to be *relatively* the most important sources of political differences."[10] Studies of New York politics in the twentieth century reveal a similar importance of the ethnic vote. David Burner, *The Politics of Provincialism: The Democratic Party in Transition 1918-1932* has informative tables on the variations in the Jewish, Italian, German, Irish, and Negro vote in selected New York neighborhoods.

A study of the Welsh settlements in central New York is interesting in its own right but it can also tell us a good deal about the process of acculturation and assimilation. We can observe this immigrant group over a span of 175 years in both a rural and urban setting. The record is fairly abundant although hidden behind the formidable language barrier of *Cymreig*. Fortunately almost all the Welsh are bilingual, and scholars with a command of the Welsh language have analyzed this subgroup at different times.[11]

Welsh emigration was stimulated by bad harvests which plagued the rural areas of Wales between 1789 and 1802. As a result small bands of farmers left the land, some heading for America.[12] Pennsylvania was the main attraction, partly because more ships called at Philadelphia than at New York in that period. Furthermore William Penn had earlier encouraged hundreds of Welsh Quakers and Baptists to settle the Welsh Tract. No doubt a region bearing names such as Bryn Mawr, Llanerch, Merion, Haverford, and Dyffryn Mawr had considerable appeal to Welsh emigrants. In 1795 about fifty emigrants left Montgomeryshire for lands purchased by the Cambrian Company in western Pennsylvania. The first settlement was at Ebensburg from which place Welshmen mi-

---

[10] (Princeton, 1961), p. 165.

[11] The best study remains Paul Demund Evans, "The Welsh in Oneida County," (M. A. thesis, Cornell University, 1914). Emrys Jones, now of the University of London, utilizes the methods of cultural anthropologists in his analysis of Utica Welsh, "Some Aspects of Cultural Change in an American Welsh Community" *Transactions of the Honourable Society of Cymmrodorion* (London, 1952), pp. 15-41. Hereafter cited as "American Welsh Community." For comparative purposes, see Daniel Jenkins Williams, "The Welsh of Columbus, Ohio: A Study in Adaptation and Assimilation," (Ph.D. thesis, Ohio State University, 1913).

[12] I rely for some information in my article, "The Welsh in Oneida County in New York State," *Transactions of the Honourable Society of Cymmrodorion* (London, 1961), pp. 115-124. A useful account is Erasmus Jones, "The Early Welsh Settlers of Oneida County, N.Y.," *The Cambrian* IX (Feb. 1889), 38-40; IX (March 1889), 78-80.

grated to Paddy's Run in southern Ohio. Substantial Welsh colonies grew up near Gomer and Jackson, Ohio. But Oneida County in the 1790s was also a booming frontier region which was drawing hundreds of settlers each year, especially from New England.[13] It enjoyed good transportation since settlers could move their goods by keelboats up the Mohawk River or by wagons through the Mohawk Valley. Land was cheap, especially north of Utica, then known as Old Fort Schuyler. The fresh lands with their rich covering of vegetable mould produced good yields of wheat. The rolling countryside naturally appealed to persons brought up in New England or in Wales. Furthermore backwoodsmen had already made the first clearings, a necessary step before the more stable farming community could be established.

In 1786 Baron Von Steuben received a grant of 16,000 acres from New York State for his great services in the organization of the Continental Army. The Baron made his selection from state land which he believed would be near the portage of Fort Stanwix (present-day Rome). Unfortunately his tract lay some five miles to the north of the Mohawk River and in hilly country. In the spring of 1787 James Cockburn surveyed the tract, laying out 160 lots of approximately 100 acres each.

Steuben decided to adopt the leasehold policy, which probably fitted in with his memories of landholding in Prussia and the Hudson Valley. But he found difficulty in attracting Yankee settlers, who disliked the leasehold and who found the land in southern Oneida County more fertile. By 1791 Steuben decided to sell half his lots for one dollar an acre or $1.25 an acre with three year's credit. In 1791 he had 3,446 acres under lease. Three years later the old soldier died leaving his estate to his Revolutionary aides, Benjamin Walker and William North. In the following year North sold his interest to Walker for $5,000. We know little of Walker's management of his holdings, but his will in 1818 reveals 2,800 acres under lease. Walker also sold farms for cash.

Neither Paul Evans nor I found Steuben township deeds to persons bearing Welsh names before 1803.[14] Lacking funds

---

[13] For an account of the land pattern and settlement of Oneida County, see David Maldwyn Ellis, *Landlords and Farmers in the Hudson-Mohawk Region, 1790-1850* (Ithaca, 1946), pp. 46-54.

[14] Evans, "Welsh in Oneida County," p. 44. An inventory of Walker's

for purchasing land, many if not all of the earliest Welsh settlers took up leases under Walker. During the 1790s thousands of upstate pioneers who lacked funds (and most belonged to this category) became tenants of Stephen Van Rensselaer in Albany and Rensselaer counties, James Wadsworth in the Genesee Valley, James Duane near Schenectady, and dozens of large landholders in the Hudson Valley and in Delaware County.[15] To substantiate these inferences, we also have the statement of Llewellyn Howell that it was Benjamin Walker who induced the Welsh to settle in Steuben.[16]

The first group of Welsh settlers, five heads of families, reached Steuben on September 15, 1795 where they found five or six families of Americans.[17] They had traveled from New York City by sloop up the Hudson River, by bateau up the Mohawk River to Utica, and then by wagon for four days to Steuben. They set to work felling trees and building log cabins. Apparently these pioneers liked their new homes and they wrote to their friends in New York City and Pennsylvania to join them. By 1812 one observer estimated that there were 700 Welsh people in the neighborhood of Steuben.[18]

The Welsh did not settle the Remsen township until after 1800. The main landholder was the Holland Land Company, an association of Amsterdam banking houses, which owned about 5,000,000 acres in New York and Pennsylvania. In 1792 Gerrit Boon, their agent, bought the Servis Patent which contained some 30,000 acres stretching northward from Utica to beyond the present village of Remsen. In 1795 Boon arranged for surveys of the tract which was divided into 120-acre lots. New Englanders bought over thirty lots in that year and over 6,000 acres. The settlers received only five to six

---

estate in 1826 shows that half of the twenty-four rent payers in Steuben bore Welsh names. Another list of mortgages includes some Welsh purchasers buying the farms in 1806. B. Walker Papers, Oneida Historical Society, Utica.

[15] For a survey showing the extent of leasehold tenancy in the period 1790-1810, see Ellis, *Landlords and Farmers*, pp. 26-65.

[16] Llewellyn Howell, *Traithawd ar Ddechreuad a Chynydd y Cymry yn Utica a'i Hamgylchoedd* (Rome, N.Y., 1860). A translation is available in *Utica Morning Herald*, April 29, 1879, and most of it is quoted in Dr. Moses M. Bagg, *Pioneers of Utica* (Utica, 1877).

[17] Griffith O. Griffiths, son of one of the original five pioneers, has written an account of the early settlement of Steuben. It is quoted in Daniel E. Wager, ed., *Our County and Its People A Descriptive Work on Oneida County* (Boston, 1896), pp. 547-549.

[18] Iago ap Owain in *Y Cyfaill*, 1839, translated and reprinted in *The Cambrian* VII (Nov. 1887), 334-335.

Chapel Cerrig (Presbyterian), Remsen, New York. Photo: William Pritchard.

year's credit but Boon found it necessary to make many extensions and to accept payment in kind. Evans found that Welsh names began to appear in the deeds of the Holland Land Company in 1804 and thereafter.[19]

Remsen was destined to become the capital of the Welsh community in Oneida County for many decades. By 1850 people of Welsh descent in Remsen and Steuben constituted over three-fourths of the population.[20]

Meanwhile a few Welshmen had made their home in Utica before 1800.[21] In 1801 a small group met in the log house of John Williams and formed the Welsh Baptist Church, which in 1899 merged with Tabernacle Baptist. Another group in 1802 founded Bethesda Congregational Church, the oldest religious association in the city.

Probably the peak of Welsh settlement came in 1855 when over 4,000 Welsh-born were listed in the census for Oneida County. Table 1, based on the state census, gives a good idea

[19] Evans, "Welsh in Oneida County," p. 44. Pomroy Jones, son of an immigrant, stated that the Welsh settled Remsen in 1808. See his *Annals and Recollections of Oneida County* (Rome, N.Y., 1851), p. 306.

[20] *Ibid.* L. Howell, *Traithawd ar Ddechreuad*, p. 18 put the percentages somewhat higher in 1859.

[21] Wager, *Oneida County*, p. 549; Evans, "Welsh in Oneida County," p. 38.

of how the Welsh had spread into various sections of the
county and spilled over to Madison, Lewis, Herkimer, and
Otsego counties.

TABLE 1

WELSH-BORN IN SELECTED TOWNSHIPS

	1855	1865
Oneida County		
Boonville	67	46
Bridgewater	95	85
Deerfield	143	107
Floyd	176	155
Lee	50	17
Marcy	263	178
Marshall	85	82
New Hartford	189	135
Paris	90	111
Remsen	537	331
Rome	181	158
Sangerfield	69	37
Steuben	365	224
Trenton	456	296
Utica	860	811
Western	134	95
Westmoreland	61	28
Whitesboro	256	159
Madison County		
Eaton	154	139
Nelson	158	160
Otsego County		
Plainfield	24	100
Lewis County		
Turin	105	82
West Turin	151	94
Herkimer County		
Frankfort	124	60
Russia	64	37
Schuyler	74	42

The founding dates of churches and other evidence indicate that the Welsh were filling in the region between Remsen-
Steuben and Utica during the period, 1820-1850. In general
they were moving south and west by mid-century, making
small settlements in Paris, Bridgewater, Marshall, and New
Hartford. A few moved over the line into Plainfield in Otsego
County and a somewhat larger group found the hilly country
around Nelson in Madison County to their liking.[22] A handful
slipped eastward into Herkimer County. To the north Lewis

---

[22] *History of Otsego County New York* (Philadelphia, 1878), p. 293;
Benjamin L. Jones, "History of Peniel Church, Nelson, N.Y.," *Y Drych,*
Nov. 6, 1902. For churches in Lewis County, see Lewis Williams, *The
Cambrian* XXV (Sept. 1905), 372, and G. Gyron Bowen, ed., *History of
Lewis County New York 1880-1965* (n.p., 1970), p. 536.

County attracted a few hardy souls who, in the 1840s, established five of their six churches. The Welsh were buying up farms from native (largely Yankee) farmers who were moving to the more fertile Middle West or to the rising commercial centers along the Erie Canal.

The countryside attracted the great majority of Welsh immigrants before the Civil War.[23] The typical farm had 100 to 160 acres, much of which remained under forest cover. Farmers supplied much of their own food, clothes, fuel and tools. To raise money for such necessities as ironware and salt, the settlers desperately sought a cash crop. At first they turned to potash and wheat. Winter-killing, pests, and western competition forced them to give up wheat raising after 1830. The Welsh were among the first to turn to dairying. The housewives of Steuben were noted for their fine butter as early as 1813.[24] In 1851 Jessie Williams developed a cheese factory near Rome. Several cheese factories were built in Steuben, Remsen, and Trenton in the next few years. The Welsh naturally turned to sheep raising, which reached its peak in the 1830s. After 1845 practically all New York farmers gave up sheep raising because of the competition from Ohio and the prairie states.

Other Welshmen became craftsmen and shopkeepers in the villages such as Remsen and in Utica and Rome. A few found jobs in the small textile mills in New York Mills and Oriskany. Some Welshmen worked on the locks of the Erie Canal which was under construction between 1817 and 1825. On December 11, 1818 David Richard of Utica wrote to his brother in Wales,

> . . . William Thomas and myself are working on the arches under the canal. . . . Wages on the canal are one dollar a day and thirteen to fourteen dollars a month with food and washing and half a pint of whiskey a day. Those who provide their own food, wet and dry, get twenty-two to twenty-three dollars.[25]

Several of the immigrants were shocked, or pretended to be, at the amount of heavy drinking in America. Their comments

---

[23] Rural life is described in Millard F. Roberts, *A Narrative History of Remsen* (Syracuse, 1914) and Ellis, *Landlords and Farmers*, pp. 184-224.

[24] Horatio Gates Spafford, *A Gazetteer of the State of New York* (Albany, 1813), p. 306; Alan Conway, *The Welsh in America Letters from the Immigrants* (Minneapolis, 1961), p. 55.

[25] Conway, *Welsh in America*, p. 62.

were no more lurid than those of native Americans who were
appalled at the widespread drunkenness. Other Welshmen deplored the lack of Sabbath observance. Hugh Jones in Utica
in 1818 noted, "There is no difference between work days and
Sundays here. They do every kind of work on a Sunday; even
the Welsh work on a Sunday."[26] Both of these observers would
have welcomed the strong campaign for temperance and Sabbath observance which had one of its most active centers in
Utica during the period following the Finney revival of 1826.

The Welsh-American community in central New York began
to decline even before the Civil War. Few newcomers chose
Oneida County farms after 1850 when they could secure better land in Wisconsin, Iowa, and Minnesota. Indeed, hundreds
of Oneida County farmers of Yankee descent, and to a somewhat lesser degree Welsh descent joined the westward procession.[27] Furthermore fewer immigrants arrived in this country after the panic of 1857 set in and the Civil War opened
in 1861. The 5,586 Welsh-born in the five central New York
counties in the 1855 state census dwindled to 4,890 ten years
later.

During the next half century the Welsh population in rural
New York steadily declined, while the urban centers—Utica,
Rome and the Herkimer County cities of Frankfort, Ilion, and
Herkimer—attracted most immigrants and large numbers of
the second generation. Two exceptions to this trend were the
small rural settlements in Nelson and Plainfield which had
their peak Welsh population about 1890. Meanwhile the
Welsh-born in Oneida County outside Utica fell from 3,335
in 1855 to 1,792 in 1890. Table 2, based on federal and state
censuses, shows the decline in Welsh population after the mid-
nineteenth century.

Rural decline affected upstate New York, and especially
the eastern half of the state, in the period after 1840. For example, the number of farms in Oneida County fell from 8,390
in 1880 to 4,420 in 1945 and by 1969 had dropped to 1,629.
The hills towns of Steuben, Remsen, and Trenton with their
high percentages of submarginal land suffered most severely
from abandonment.

26 *Ibid.*
27 Ellis, *Landlords and Farmers,* pp. 220-222. Evans, "Welsh in Oneida
County," p. 62, read the obituaries of scores of Oneida County Welsh who
had moved to Wisconsin, Minnesota and Iowa.

TABLE 2

WELSH-BORN, CENTRAL NEW YORK AND UNITED STATES

Year	U.S.A.	Utica	Oneida Co.	Madison Co.	Lewis Co.	Otsego Co.	Herkimer Co.
1850	29,868						
1855		860	4,195	467	417	46	431
1860	45,763						
1865		811	3,746	424	346	116	258
1870	74,553		y				
1875							
1880	83,302		y				
1885							
1890	100,079	1,314	3,106	333	166	134	310
1900	93,586	1,165	2,536	259	89	126	199
1910	82,448	1,188	2,314	175	52	110	173
1920	67,006		y				
1930	60,205	1,186	y				
1940	35,360	800	y				
1950	30,060						

y Combined with England

The decline of the Welsh community of Utica began in 1914, if one were forced to pick a date. World War I not only cut off immigration but it also tended to disrupt the Welsh-American community. Conscription and the war boom accelerated the process of Americanization. During the 1920s enough immigrants arrived to balance the losses. The census of 1930 showed 1,186 Welsh-born, about the same figure as in 1900 and 1910. But a closer check would show that the average age in 1930 was much higher than the youthful population of 1900 or 1910.

During the 1930s the Welsh-American community was hard hit not only by the depression but by the end of immigration. The census of 1940 revealed only 800 Welsh-born in Utica. After World War II immigration resumed but on a very small scale. I would estimate that since 1945 fewer than thirty Welsh people, or approximately one a year, have settled in Utica. In the same period Moriah Church in Utica has averaged more than ten deaths a years. At least half of these people were born in Wales.

The growth of Utica before World War I provided plenty of jobs for immigrants from Wales. They were particularly active in the construction trades. The unskilled found jobs as janitors or went into the textile mills. Newcomers could find room and board at boarding houses where news about work was quick to circulate. Contractors were eager to hire craftsmen, especially those who knew how to handle stone or slate. Table 3 reveals the extent of employment at different times.

TABLE 3

OCCUPATIONS OF UTICA WELSH, 1817-1948

Occupation	1817		1865		1915		1948		1948
	No.	%	No.	%	No.	%	No.	%	Utica %
Professional	3	7.8	9	2.9	18	3.3	9	5.4	6.7
Clerks	—	—	20	6.5	56	10.4	16	9.5	21.8 (inc. Sales)
Retail	9	23.2	36	11.6	21	3.9	10	5.9	8.9
Craftsmen	14	35.6	122	39.4	157	29.2	40	23.8	} 13.0
Skilled Workers	—	—	17	5.4	27	5.0	9	5.4	
Factory Workers	—	—	31	10.0	34	6.3	26	15.5	26.0
Labourers	7	17.8	53	7.1	46	8.5	4	2.4	5.7
Miscellaneous	6	15.6	22	17.1	46	8.5	21	12.5	9.0
Janitors	—	—	—	—	79	14.7	21	12.5	—
Transport and Service	—	—	—	—	55	10.2	12	7.1	8.9
	39	100.0	310	100.0	539	100.0	168	100.0	100.0

Source: Emrys Jones, "Some Aspects of Cultural Change in an American Welsh Community," *Transactions of the Honourable Society of Cymmodorion* (1952), p. 37.

Table 3 shows a high percentage of craftsmen and skilled workers, the majority of whom were carpenters and stone masons. The Welsh were consistently higher in this category. It also shows that they were less numerous than average among factory workers. A considerable number worked in the textile mills, notably at New York Mills, west of Utica, but after World War I most drifted into white collar work. Although few were laborers, a considerable number were janitors. Older men, often semi-retired, took care of large houses on Genesee Street or commercial buildings. The Welsh entered the ranks of salespeople and clerks in about the same proportion as the rest of the population. Few were professionals except, of course, the ministers and a few musicians. Overall, these figures show that the Welsh-born belonged to the middle class and their relatively high economic status made them more ready for assimilation.

An examination of the *Utica City Directories* for 1850, 1865, 1875, 1885, and 1900 reveals the eastward and southward movement of the Welsh community. In 1865, over two-thirds lived in the old houses and flats near the Erie and Chenango canals. Whitesboro Street had the highest concentration of families, with the name "Jones" appearing seventeen times. A decade later almost half of the Joneses were living east of Genesee Street, about equally divided between the districts north and south of Rutger Street. Some of the most aristocratic families, including U. S. Senator Roscoe Conkling, lived on Rutger. Many Welsh girls became domestics in the big houses on Genesee, Park, John, and Rutger streets. The area south of Rutger all the way to Pleasant Street and bordered on the west by Oneida and on the east by Mohawk Street is locally known as Corn Hill. The name derives from the corn fields which covered most of the district in 1860 and a good portion as late as 1890. Gradually the city laid out streets and contractors put up houses which made the area attractive for upwardly mobile Welsh, Irish, and Germans. German Catholics in 1871 built St. Mary's Church on South Street and the Irish Catholics in 1877 built St. Francis de Sales on Eagle Street.

Moriah Church in 1882 sold its building on Seneca Street and erected a new structure a block from Genesee Street on Park Avenue, a fashionable street. Membership kept rising and children thronged the Sunday School.[28] The Session,

[28] Useful information on Moriah Church in Utica is found in *Moriah Presbyterian Church (Welsh) 1830-1930* (Utica, 1930).

therefore, set up a chapel (Peniel) on Miller Street in 1890 which served as a center for both children and adults until 1924 when Moriah built a large churchhouse next to the sanctuary. The Cymreigyddion Society bought an old church on South Street and turned it into St. David's Hall. Here its members could play shuffle board, billiards, and cards. The auditorium was used for meetings, concerts, and smaller *eisteddfodau*—competitive festivals of poetry and song.

A large minority of Welsh still lived in the old district west of Genesee Street. No doubt Bethesda Church on Washington Street anchored some people in that neighborhood. The Methodist Church on the corner of Hopper and Union streets was conveniently located for Welsh in all sections of the city but it never attracted many members and died in 1918.

The majority of the Welsh lived on Corn Hill until World War II. In the late 1940s Dr. Emrys Jones made a survey of the population and found the Corn Hill district still a desirable one.

Most of the rents here are above average, especially in the newer section; houses are for one or two families, never multiple dwellings; it is also away from the commercial-industrial strip near the river and railroad. A high proportion of the Welsh also live in south Utica, the newest district, which is predominantly upper class.[29]

Corn Hill during the past two decades has lost some of its desirability as a residential area. Some streets and blocks have become "blighted" or, to use a more euphemistic term, "transitional." Most of the houses, which were built before 1900, needed repairs and modernization. Some lacked space for a driveway or a garage—a great disadvantage in the automobile age. Families of every background preferred to move into detached houses in south Utica or the suburbs.[30] Using their wartime savings and utilizing cheap credit guaranteed by the government, they built or bought new homes on the outskirts. The widespread ownership of automobiles speeded the movement from the older districts. The influx of blacks into Corn Hill, whose numbers in Utica rose from about 1,600 in 1950 to over 5,500 in 1970, hastened or followed this shift.

Only a handful of the older Welsh lived on Corn Hill in

[29] "American Welsh Community," p. 38.
[30] William C. Morris and family of New Hartford erected the largest shopping center in Oneida County and opened up a residential tract of detached houses.

1971. A rundown of the membership in the 1970 annual report of Moriah Church shows only 55 out of 369 members (15%) still living in that area. Most of these individuals are over sixty-five years of age.

The scattering of the Welsh population in Utica followed the pattern of the Welsh in Columbus, Ohio, who by 1913 had migrated to various parts of the city. In brief, individuals were making their housing decisions with little consideration of their proximity to church, club, or neighbors. Isolated individuals (some critics use the adjectives, "atomized" and "rootless") were more ready for complete assimilation than those clustered around the church.

A sidelight for the curious! In 1875 the *Utica Directory* listed 75 men bearing the typically Welsh name, John Jones, which must have created confusion in the post office, not to mention church records. Fortunately this figure dropped to 43 by 1900. Strangely enough, the number of William Williamses rose from 16 to 35, a statistical movement which seems to contradict the trend for the Joneses. The 1971 phone book, which covers a population well over three times that of the *Directory* for 1900, reveals that the John Joneses have fallen to 13 and the William Williamses to 9. Indeed, Remsen lists only one William Williams and no John Jones!

These trends force one to conclude that modern parents have shown more imagination in selecting names than their predecessors. Might this trend indicate, albeit indirectly, another sign of assimilation? Hollywood stars, I suspect, have had more influence on American parents in naming their children than either the Bible or grandparents. One must doubt, however, that a shift from Gwladys to Shirley is a sign of progress!

The immigrants and their children kept ties with the *Hen Wlad* (Old Country) by letters, subscriptions to papers, and by visits. A large number managed to make at least one visit to the home parish where they usually met with a warm welcome. And they generally tried to attend the afternoon session of the National Eisteddfod in which the Welsh from overseas were welcomed to the stage. Members of the second and third generations inspected Caernarvon Castle, rode up Snowdon, and looked for cousins. Discovering the right gravestone bearing the name of John Jones was not the easiest task. Invariably returning immigrants reported that conditions in the Old Country had changed since their youth and not always for the better. This complaint is familiar among most ethnic groups who find it hard "to go home again."

The upsurge of Welsh nationalism after World War II had a slight impact upon the Oneida County Welsh. A handful of immigrants wanted to keep memories alive and to bring the older generation more current information on Welsh life. They organized a branch of *Undeb y Cymry as Wasgar* (Welsh in dispersion) which held monthly meetings from 1950 to about 1964.[31] But deaths, removals and old age caused its decline and disbanding by 1965. This organization, like the church clubs, the lodge, the theater, and even the saloon, could not overcome the competition of television in the evening.

Interestingly enough in 1970-1971 a group from the second and third generations organized a class to learn Welsh.[32] Over a score of attendants did their homework faithfully and attended weekly classes for several months. This development illustrates the observation of Marcus Lee Hansen, the historian of immigration, who stated that the third generation often seeks to revive the ties with the Old Country. He noted, "the almost universal phenomenon that what the son wishes to forget, the grandson wishes to remember."[33]

Not all Welshmen found a pot of gold in America. In fact, some found poverty, disease, and unemployment. In 1831 a Utica group formed the Welsh Charitable Society, which later merged into the Welsh Benevolent Society. This society had a small fund from bequests and from collections in the churches. About 1945 it disbanded and divided its funds equally between Moriah and Bethesda Churches. Many immigrants joined the American Order of True Ivorites which had several chapters in the country. Its object was partly social and partly to provide a certain amount of social security for its members. Like most fraternal associations formed by immigrant groups it suffered from the fact that its members grew old together. Consequently, the officers have had to cut the benefits. The

---

[31] I am indebted to Vaughn Jones of Utica for information about this organization.

[32] Mair Lloyd who majored in the Welsh language at the University of Wales in Aberystwyth taught this class.

[33] The Problem of the Third-Generation Immigration," from Augustana Historical Society *Publications* (1938), reprinted in Edward N. Saveth, ed. *Understanding the American Past* (Boston, 1965), p. 472.

Ivorites sponsored the annual banquet on St. David's Day for many years in Utica.

Welsh life in upstate New York, as in Wales, revolved around the church. Practically all the rural churches were small with from twenty-five to seventy-five members. Settlers wanted a neighborhood church, one within walking distance of home. The roads were tortuous, blocked with snow in winter, muddy in spring, and pocked with holes in summer. Furthermore, the immigrants brought with them fierce denominational loyalties and strong theological convictions. As a result, members of each denomination established their own church. For example, Utica and the Remsen area each had a Welsh Presbyterian, Congregational, Baptist, and Methodist church. Congregations sometimes split over dogma, forms of church organizations, and the selection of leaders.

Most churches in Wales and rural Oneida County relied less on regular full-time ministers than has been customary in American Protestantism. A small group of believers would elect elders (*blaenoriaid*) to arrange worship services and classes.[34] They relied upon itinerant ministers who eked out a spare living by farming or running a small business. The ministers married the members, baptized their children, and buried the dead. The elders conducted the services when no minister officiated, which was often the case.

The larger congregations in Utica and Rome followed the American practice of calling a clergyman. They often called clergymen from Wales and did so as late as the 1940s. Bethesda Church in 1940 called Rees T. Williams who originally came from Wales. In 1946 Moriah Church extended a call to Dr. R. Glynne Lloyd who was then serving a Welsh church in Liverpool, England.

The young men in the Welsh-American churches who decided to become ministers attended seminaries such as Princeton which were operated by the American denominations. Because few of the churches could afford to employ a full-time clergyman, most of these men found it necessary to take pulpits in American churches, and a few became distinguished clergymen. William H. Roberts, the son of Rev. William Roberts, pastor of Moriah Church from 1877 to 1887, became the Stated Clerk of the General Assembly of the Pres-

---

[34] *Moriah Presbyterian Church,* pp. 50-51.

byterian Church, U.S.A. William Pugh, another of the Oneida
County Welsh, held the same post in the 1940s. A consider-
able number of preachers from Wales left Welsh churches in
Oneida County for other assignments. Thus, in the 1960s,
Rees T. Williams of Bethesda Church became pastor of the
Congregational Church in Oswego and Dr. R. Glynne Lloyd
of Moriah became a professor of philosophy at Utica College.

The churches introduced the class meeting and Sunday
school which in Wales had provided elementary education
long before the British government established public schools.
These schools preceded the American Sunday schools which
began in Connecticut about 1816 and spread to New York
in the 1820s.[35]

The Welsh churches resembled sects, that is, associations
of believers characterized by strict qualifications for membership as distinguished from the more inclusive churches. In
practically all European countries there existed a national,
state-supported church: Lutheran in Scandinavia and Prussia;
Roman Catholic in Italy, Spain, and many other nations;
Greek Orthodox in pre-Revolutionary Russia and the Balkan
countries; Church of England in England and Wales. But only
in Wales did the great majority abandon the established
church.[36] In so doing the Welsh learned how to organize and
support the voluntary church associations which became the
American pattern after the colonial period. Furthermore, the
momentum of the Methodist revivals led to a somewhat ex-
travagant denominationalism in Wales. Religious pluralism,
so characteristic a feature of American society, was also the
pattern in Wales. No other European country had the same
spectrum of religious pluralism which matched so closely
evangelical Protestantism in America. Every Welsh county
and most parishes had chapels belonging to the Calvinistic
Methodists (Presbyterians), the Congregationalists, Wesleyans
(Methodists), and Baptists. The Church of England retained
most of the Anglo-Welsh aristocracy, the publicans, and the
uncommitted. The Anglican rector had a good living from the
tithes but few duties to perform.

---

[35] Whitney R. Cross, *The Burned-Over District: The Social and Intellectual History of Enthusiastic Religion in Western New York, 1800-1850*
(Ithaca, 1950), p. 128.

[36] The religious revival is described in David Williams, *A History of
Modern Wales* (London, 1950), pp. 140-157.

The teachings of John Calvin penetrated as deeply into Wales as in early New England. Welsh immigrants, thereafter, found familiar the religious climate of upstate New York whose members of Presbyterian and Congregational churches dominated the business, cultural and political life. Furthermore, immigrants who were Baptists or Methodists found churches of their persuasion nearby.

A listing of Welsh churches in central New York presents many difficulties.[37] Some churches were little more than pious hopes. Others were preaching points or places for class meetings. Some lasted only a few years with intermittent reopenings. For example, Bethel near Alder Creek has held services only during the summer. Others were yoked with other churches. The Presbyterians were the most numerous followed by the Congregationalists. The Methodists had four churches and the Baptists had possibly seven.

Welsh Baptist churches showed a tendency toward contention and division.[38] An observer noted in 1831 that delegates from several churches unsuccessfully tried to settle a controversy between two of the Steuben township churches. In Steuben there were Capel Ucha, Capel Isaf, and Capel Coch (Zion). Bardwell, north of Remsen, also had a Baptist church.

---

[37] I have begun with the list in Edward G. Hartman, *Americans From Wales* (Boston, 1967), pp. 175-176. The churches are Presbyterian unless otherwise indicated. Dates and names are uncertain. Some churches with a cemetery maintained a corporate existence long after the end of services. ONEIDA COUNTY—*Bridgewater:* Bethel 1851-1900, *Deerfield:* Bryn Mawr 1841-1870, Cong. 1831-1898; *Floyd:* Camroden 1834-1971, Cong. 1843-1920; *Marcy:* Rehoboth 1848-1920, Bethany Cong. 1840-1913; *New Hartford:* Zion (ended about 1955 and members joined Moriah Church, Utica); *New York Mills:* Salem Cong. 1847-1930?; *Oriskany:* Pres. 1850-1900; *Remsen:* Bardwell Baptist 1809-1917, Bethel Cong. 1838-?, Cerrig 1831-1971 (federated with Baptists for years), Coch Baptist 1823-, Peniel Cong. 1838-1937, Pen-y-caerau 1824-1907, Ninety-six 1841-1900?, Enlli 1837-1965; *Rome:* Bethel 1841-1971; Cong. 1851-1927; *Steuben:* Baptist 1806-1896, French Road 1828-1928, Nant 1828-1941, Pen-y-graig 1828-1937, Pen-y-mynydd Cong. 1832-1910, Ucha Cong. 1805-1946; *Sangerfield:* Waterville Cong. 1852-1910, *Trenton:* Holland Patent Cong. 1842-1956, Pres. 1840-1905, Trenton Cong. 1854-1906, Prospect Cong. 1856-1896, Pres. 1857-1900; *Utica:* Moriah 1830-, Bethesda Cong. 1802-1963 when it merged with Plymouth, Baptist 1801-1899, Methodist 1850-1918; *Western:* Webster Hill 1832-1920. HERKIMER COUNTY—Frankfort Hill 1849-1920; Ilion 1850-1935; Newport 1842-1860; Salisbury 1855-1865. LEWIS COUNTY—Collinsville 1846-1900?; Gomer Flats 1842-1850; *Tug Hill:* Zion 1846-1881, Cong. 1843-1886; *Turin:* Pres. 1842-1849, Cong. 1861-1886. MADISON COUNTY—Farmersville, Siloam Cong. 1856-1900?; *Nelson:* Cong. 1850-1971 (only one Sunday in summer for many years), Pres. 1855-1932. OTSEGO COUNTY—*Plainfield:* Cong. 1861-1941, Pres. 1855-1900?.

[38] Roberts, *Remsen,* p. 135.

Cylchwyl Lenyddol

Cyfrinfau
IFORAIDD
GORONWY a
GWENFRON
UTICA, N. Y.

Nos Gwyl
Dewi Sant
1923

Buddugol

St. David's Day prize ribbon awarded at a regional literary contest (Cylchwyl Lenyddol) in Utica, 1923.

In both Utica and Trenton the Welsh Baptists in 1831 had two societies, no doubt because of some quarrel mercifully forgotten over the years.

Paul Evans counted twenty churches in the Steuben-Remsen area in 1914, but only one full-time pastor served in this district and his services were shared by Cerrig and Nant churches. Meanwhile, in Utica, Moriah Presbyterian and Bethesda Congregational were expanding rapidly. The Congregational churches in New York Mills and Holland Patent had passed their peak as had Zion Presbyterian in New Hartford.

By 1971 the Welsh churches had become "American" churches or had disappeared. Bethesda discontinued Welsh services in 1960 and three years later merged with Plymouth Congregational Church. Moriah Church in Utica in 1960 had Welsh vespers once a month but by 1965, after the resignation of Dr. Lloyd, these services ended. In 1967 Moriah called Rev. Richard Weld as its minister—the first non-Welshman in its history. Over half the members of the Board of Deacons of Moriah Church in 1960 and again in 1970 were not of Welsh descent. Throughout the 1960s over half of the children in the Sunday School did not bear Welsh names. Bethel Presbyterian in Rome in 1960 was still offering Welsh services to a dwindling congregation. But the departure of the Rev. Carodog P. Williams ended Welsh services and a disastrous fire in 1971 forced the congregation to give up.

No doubt the language question was the most severe issue for the Welsh churches to face. The Welsh leaders had a passionate loyalty to *Cymreig,* which many believed was, is, and ever shall be the language of paradise. As Rowland Berthoff has noted, "Of all the British-Americans they were the most anxious to preserve the culture—particularly the language— of their fatherland."[39] But the forces of assimilation—the job, store, school, press, street—were relentless and insidious. Most vulnerable were the children, who sought the acceptance and approval of their teachers and playmates. Often children rebelled against speaking Welsh and some insisted on speaking English even with their parents. The oldsters, however, controlled the churches and insisted upon keeping Welsh in

[39] *British Immigrants in Industrial America* (Cambridge, 1953), p. 170.

French Road Presbyterian Church, Steuben Township. Photo: William Pritchard.

the Sunday services. They allowed English to creep into the Sunday School and other societies in which young people had more influence. No doubt young people took advantage of this stubbornness as an excuse to leave the church, which some felt was too censorious of dancing, drinking, card playing, and Sunday excursions.

Each generation had to face this problem but as long as immigration balanced losses, the church fathers could avoid the issue. Rev. J. Eldred Jones, pastor of the Welsh Baptist Church in Utica in 1877, stated:

> The children of the old citizens are growing up in the English and when they profess religion they join one of the English churches. They feel above doing anything with the Welsh. . . . In order to keep our young people we are holding an English service every second Sunday night . . . but after all we have no legitimate right to expect the church to grow in numbers, power and influence unless many of those Welshmen, who are today members of the English churches but who are much better versed in the Welsh language than they are or ever can be in the English, return to the old fold where they ought to be for their own personal advantage as well as for the honor of the church of the living God.[40]

Welsh churches throughout the country were facing much of the same problem. Between 1900 and 1914, the Utica newspaper, *Y Drych,* ran dozens of letters dealing with the issue.[41] Of course, the main argument for change was the defection of most young people because of the insistence upon the use of Welsh in the services.

Church leaders tried to postpone the issue or compromise it. For example, in Columbus, Ohio the Calvinist Methodist church in 1900 authorized one English sermon a month on Sunday evening. Within seven years the elders found it advisable to permit English services every Sunday night. By 1913 the annual report of the church and the minutes of the trustees were kept in English. We find a similar story in Remsen.[42] The minister of Capel Cerrig in 1914 preached Sunday

---

[40] *Y Wawr,* II (1887), p. 84, quoted by Evans, "Welsh in Oneida County," p. 72. In 1856 a writer noted that the children with few exceptions were uninterested in talking, reading, and writing Welsh. J. Hughes, *Hanes Methodistiaeth Cymru* III (1856), p. 16, cited by Emrys Jones, "American Welsh Community," p. 28.

[41] Williams, "The Welsh of Columbus, Ohio," p. 127. Immigration from Wales to Columbus virtually ended by 1860. Subsequently most new members of the Presbyterian and Congregational churches were recruited from rural churches.

[42] Evans, "Welsh in Oneida County," p. 66. Evans' father was a minister in the Calvinist Methodist Church.

morning in Welsh but offered two English sermons a month. For some oldtimers these concessions smacked of Satan. Moriah and Bethesda churches in Utica could afford to postpone the issue because of the fairly heavy influx of Welshmen to the city after 1903. In Wales the revival of 1904–1905 stirred many individuals to seek a better land to raise their children. Furthermore, a considerable number of Welsh families migrated to Utica from Granville and other Vermont quarry towns because of strikes and hard times in those communities. The Welsh contractors in Utica were eager to employ skilled stoneworkers and carpenters.

The language problem finally came to a head in Moriah Church during the 1920s. Llewelyn Jones, a young minister from Wales, arrived in 1924. Although he was an ardent Welshman and later a strong nationalist, he urged the Session to introduce one English service each Sunday. When the Session brought this proposal to the congregation, the opponents used parliamentary maneuvers and impassioned speeches against it. Few who were present will forget the heated denunciations and the calming prayer by the minister. A half dozen diehards out of a congregation of over six hundred stalked from the church.[43] However, Bethesda Church in 1920 had instituted a Sunday service in English without any difficulty.

A content analysis by Emrys Jones of the annual reports of Moriah shows a few items in English after 1907, a shift to a majority after 1920, and an almost complete takeover in 1937 and thereafter. The last item to go was the pastor's address, which was changed to English in 1945.[44]

The process of Americanization or acculturation, if one wishes to be more precise, influenced the Welsh churches in many areas: architecture, order of service, ritual, the choir, prayer meetings, and financing. Hebron Church and Capel Cerrig in the Remsen area, the latter of stone, are two remaining examples of Welsh-American church architecture.

[43] My account is based upon early memories aided by those of Margaret Ellis Blabey of Slingerlands, New York. I am grateful for details to Arthur M. Roberts, financial secretary of Moriah for many years, and also to John R. Thomas, an elder for more than forty years.

[44] "American Welsh Community," pp. 22-23. A survey of Moriah membership in 1932 showed that approximately 400 attended the Welsh and an equal number the English services. Seventy-one attended only the Welsh services while seventy-eight attended English services only.

The internal arrangement featured a raised pulpit at one end. Directly in front of it was the *Set Fawr* (big seat literally) where the elders sat. A precentor led the singing of the hymns but enthusiastic singers would often repeat the last chorus of *Cwm Rhondda* and other hymns. One of the elders announced the order of service and the activities of the week.

The sermon was the high point of the service and ministers were rigidly judged for their adherence to Scripture, their imagery, and oratorical ability. The preacher usually constructed his sermon around three points and approached his climax on a rising note of intensity, sometimes referred to as *hwyl*. The finest compliment a minister could receive was that he had good *hwyl*. Several times a year a *gymanfa pregethu* or preaching service was held in one of the churches of the circuit or synod of New York and Vermont. Most of the ministers, many of the elders, and several members attended several sessions of preaching. The final session was assigned to the most eloquent or to a distinguished preacher from Wales.

The gradual decline of the Welsh Calvinistic Methodist Church to about 14,000 persons led to its union with the Presbyterian Church in the United States of America in 1920.[45] This action forced the Oneida County churches to associate more closely with the American churches in the Presbytery of Utica. No doubt these associations and the governmental directions of the General Assembly and the New York Synod offices accelerated the process of turning the Calvinist Methodist churches into regular Presbyterian congregations. In 1921 Moriah Church, a year after union, adopted a fixed budget as well as the Every Member Canvass. Shortly thereafter, the church erected a three-story church house for its Sunday School program. In the basement was a kitchen and a large dining room. Interestingly enough, the men of the church erected a stage at one end. Fifty years earlier the elders would have raised their hands in horror at the thought of a theatrical production in the church. During the late 1920s the young people pushed through improvements to the interior of the sanctuary. The old *Set Fawr* was eliminated and in its place appeared a massive Gothic pulpit flanked by a Gothic choir rail enclosing seats for fifty choris-

[45] The standard account is Daniel Jenkins Williams, *One Hundred Years of Welsh Calvinistic Methodism in America* (Philadelphia, 1937).

ters. In 1928 the Session authorized a vested choir which took a regular part in the Sunday services. Throughout the 1930s and 1940s this choir was the only unpaid church choir in Utica which presented the *Messiah* and other oratorios.

During the 1920s Moriah and Bethesda churches reached their greatest heights in terms of membership, contributions, and activity.[46] In Moriah, the Men's Club attracted as many as three hundred to its monthly meetings. The Sunday School flourished with many adult classes. The losses of young people were made up by continued immigration.

The decade of the 1930s and the war years that followed brought many problems to Utica Protestant churches. Among them were a falling off of attendance, a drop in revenues, and the emigration of young people to other communities with better employment possibilities. The two Welsh churches lost membership because of many deaths, the end of immigration, and the defection of young people. World War II brought prosperity, but mainly in war industries in which few Welsh were employed.

The next major change in the structure of Moriah Church came in 1955 when the congregation voted for a reconstruction of the interior including a divided chancel.[47] The organ which had formerly stood in the front center was placed on one side with the pipes relegated to the rear balcony. A chancel was formed with a new communion table (no Welsh on it) surmounted by a cross. The Session voted that robed acolytes should open and close the services by lighting and extinguishing the candles on the altar.

The above changes illustrate trends in American Protestantism and are mentioned to illustrate how these trends reached an ethnic, or former ethnic, church. Observers have noted the tendency for churches to move from a "low" to a "high" form. A visitor to Moriah or Bethesda Churches in the 1950s would have been hard put to distinguish the order of services from their American counterparts. Needless to say, the congregational singing was infinitely better.

The manner of election to the various boards of Moriah was changed in the annual meeting of 1955. Thereafter mem-

---

[46] *Moriah Presbyterian Church,* p. 41, includes a chart of membership and contributions.

[47] *A Decade of Achievement, 1948-1958* (Utica, 1958). This pamphlet describes the high points in that transitional decade.

bers of the Session, Trustees, and the Board of Deacons were elected for three-year terms. This procedure, which was recommended by the General Assembly, was quite a contrast with the old system in which elders were elected for life.

All these changes—architectural, organizational, ritualistic—were a radical departure from the chapels of rural Wales and rural Oneida County.

The *Gymanfa Ganu* became popular after 1860 and has remained the most popular expression of Welsh life. It is basically a religious service devoted to the singing of hymns. What makes it distinctive is the ability of the congregation to sing the four parts in harmony. Throughout the 1950s and 1960s some four to six hundred people came together in the fall for this singing festival.[48] The *Noson Lawen* (merry evening) on Saturday night is devoted to good fellowship. The National *Gymanfa Ganu* which meets around Labor Day always attracts a delegation from Utica. In 1971, the 3,000 attendants at Salt Lake City included a half dozen from Utica. The Welsh Church in Nelson opens up for one service each summer and people of Welsh background pack the small chapel. Once a year the Methodist Church of Remsen sponsors a Sunday evening devoted to singing Welsh hymns.

No group of foreign-born showed more interest than the Welsh in becoming American citizens.[49] Although most of the Utica Welsh came from the quarry districts of Caernarvonshire, a bastion for Lloyd George's Liberal party, in the United States they usually lined up with the Republican party, which was thought to be the main defender of the business and social establishment of New York.

The early Welsh settlers did not take an active part in politics. Before 1840 they split between the Whigs and the Democrats, with the majority supporting the Whig candidates.[50] Remsen had the lowest percentage of Democrats of any town in Oneida County in 1844. Only a handful followed Dr. Robert Everett, Congregational editor who joined the abolitionists about 1840. Although few Welshmen became abolitionists,

---

[48] The program for Sept. 18-19, 1971 was held in Tabernacle Baptist Church, Utica. Soloists were drawn from Binghamton and Toronto. The Rev. J. Humphreys Jones of Toronto preached a Welsh sermon in Moriah Church.

[49] Berthoff, *British Immigrants in Industrial America* p. 140. Over ninety-three percent of the Welsh-born had become citizens in 1900.

[50] Evans, "Welsh in Oneida County," pp. 125-140.

most of them came to oppose slavery. Consequently, when the Republican party was organized in 1855 with its platform opposing the extension of slavery into the territories, it appealed to many Welshmen and their children. Soon it became almost an article of faith for Welshmen to vote the straight Republican ticket. In 1869, Forestport, which contained a large number of Irish Democrats, was set off from Remsen. Whereas Remsen in 1868 voted Republican 62.5 percent, four years later its reduced portion voted Republican 95.4 percent.[51]

Other factors, however, reinforced this habit. Most Welshmen were farmers or members of the urban middle class. The Republican party in New York has built its strength on these groups although its leadership and direction have come from the business groups. Furthermore, the Democratic party had few attractions for the Welsh. Its main support came from New York City. It was crowded with Irish Catholics and later with immigrants from Italy, Poland, and southern Europe. The Welsh as ardent Protestants joined the native stock Americans who welcomed them as allies against the Catholic immigrants. The Republican leaders eventually recognized the importance of the Welsh vote by naming Welsh-Americans for local office. During the 1930s some Welshmen deserted the Republican ranks, partly because its leadership was isolationist, partly because Roosevelt's social program attracted them.[52]

Oneida County became the intellectual center for Welsh immigrants in America.[53] The Welsh press was centered in Utica and Remsen. Several printers, notably T. J. Griffith, published hymnbooks, tracts, and journals. The Presbyterians established *Y Cyfaill* (The Friend) in 1838. Its highest circulation was about 2,000. In 1933 it discontinued publication. Not to be outdone, the Congregationalists set up the *Y Cenhadwr* (The Messenger) which Dr. Robert Everett of Remsen ably edited for many years.

In 1861 *Y Drych* (The Mirror) moved to Utica from New York City where it had been founded ten years earlier. At one time *Y Drych* had a circulation of 12,000. Prior to 1910 this

[51] Benson, *Jacksonian Democracy*, p. 169.

[52] Welsh-born William R. Williams of Clayville represented central New York in the House of Representatives for several terms in the 1950s.

[53] The best source for Welsh publications is Evans, "Welsh in Oneida County," pp. 81-119.

newspaper was entirely in Welsh. During the 1920s a few English items crept in because the Welsh subscribers and correspondents in Pennsylvania did not know Welsh very well. Many miners in Scranton-Wilkes-Barre came from South Wales where the majority did not speak Welsh. In the next decade the editor tried to reach the second generation by turning the paper into an English language journal. This move could not reverse the steady decline in circulation as the older generation died. In 1960 Arthur Roberts, the publisher and editor of *Y Drych,* announced that it would cease publication. Horace Breese Powill of Milwaukee, Wisconsin, however, bought control and continues publication to this date.

Another journal, *The Cambrian,* 1880-1920, began in Cincinnati but moved to Utica. This was designed for persons who could not read Welsh but were interested in the history of Wales and its people. It contained several historical sketches and biographies of notable Welshmen.

In the nineteenth century ministers published nearly two hundred books in Utica. These were mostly collections of sermons, editions of hymnbooks, or commentaries on Scripture. They were offered for sale in *Y Drych* and the pages of the denominational journals. A few authors like Dr. Everett actually made a modest income from their writings.

Literature in the lighter vein was not encouraged although a favorite sport was telling stories about the witticisms of Welsh ministers and the eccentricities of certain local characters. In 1913 Sam Ellis, a grocer on Elm Street, Corn Hill, wrote *Ann y Foty yn Myn'd i'r Mor,* a series of sketches of an old peasant lady on the way to the seashore. Mr. Ellis won dozens of prizes in essay and short story competitions offered in *eisteddfodau* in Warren, Ohio, Salt Lake City, and Scranton. In the late 1950s, some half century after he left Montgomeryshire, North Wales, he won an essay prize in the National Eisteddfod of Wales.

Some mention should be made of the writing of Howard Thomas, a teacher who retired after World War II to Prospect to write books. Thomas wrote two novels about Welsh life in the Remsen area. *The Singing Hills* (1964) tells the story of an orphan who was brought up by a strict but kindly Welsh farmer. Two years later he published *The Road to Sixty* which centered around a farmhouse overlooking the French Road in the Steuben hills. This novel stresses the strict sectarianism prevalent among the Welsh. Thomas, who knew no Welsh, had a sympathetic and sentimental attitude toward the Welsh farmers and preachers.

The *eisteddfod* is perhaps the most famous Welsh institution. Individuals compete for prizes in music, poetry and crafts. This institution took root mainly in the large Welsh community in Utica. Beginning in the 1850s, the Cymreigyddion Society sponsored an annual *eisteddfod* for over a century. For decades it was held on the last day of the year and New Year's Day in the Armory building on Rutger Street. The *eisteddfod* in 1926, which was "national," attracted thousands of visitors to a large tent on the Parkway. Dr. Daniel Prothero, an eminent composer of Chicago, for years was the musical adjudicator and his decisions were eagerly awaited. Choirs from Scranton, Wilkes-Barre, Toronto, and other cities competed for handsome prizes. Smaller *eisteddfodau* were organized by the young people of Moriah and Bethesda churches.

Before 1918 almost all the items in the *eisteddfod* program were Welsh, but by 1930 English selections constituted almost half of the contests. By 1948 there were no Welsh items. The literary competitions had been dropped largely because few residents in America had the necessary command of the language. In fact, the *eisteddfod* became in the 1940s and 1950s a sort of community activity with a majority of prizes carried off by singers of non-Welsh extraction.[54]

The Welsh passion for singing made an impact upon Oneida County. Choral groups sprang up, the most famous of which was the Hadyns, a male chorus. This organization sang at the Chicago World Fair in 1894 and at the inauguration of President McKinley. Welsh musicians provided many of the soloists and choir leaders in the Protestant church of central New York. Utica's Grace Episcopal Church hired outstanding organists and choirmasters such as Tertius Noble and paid its choir members. A high percentage of the boys and men in the choir were of Welsh stock before 1940.

Exogamy is of course a "final solution" for an immigrant group. Dr. Daniel Williams found that the Welsh of Columbus, Ohio by 1913 were rapidly assimilated through mixed marriages. With each generation the percentage rose until in-

---

[54] Emrys Jones, "American Welsh Community," pp. 24-26.

dividuals were paying little attention to the ethnic factor in selecting their marriage partners. Among the Columbus Welsh-born, 39 percent of 108 marriages were between persons of Welsh blood. Among the native-born of foreign parents, only 10 percent were within the group. Among the native-born of native parents (third generation), only 6 percent were between persons of Welsh stock.[55]

Similar trends are apparent among the Welsh population in central New York. William Owen Williams of Utica, who remembers trends in Bethesda Congregational Church, concludes that the young people married other persons of Welsh descent until about 1945-1950. Thereafter, they married "anyone they could find."

The statistics for Moriah Church confirm the trend, especially of the second generation, to marry outside the group. Between 1909 and 1931 out of a total of 160 marriages, 46 (29 percent) involved a non-Welsh partner; between 1932 and 1954, out of 165 marriages, 128 (78 percent) involved a non-Welsh partner; between 1954 and 1970, out of a total of 84 marriages, 79 (94 percent) involved a non-Welsh partner.[56]

The crucial years were those around 1930 when a majority began to marry "outside." This period also coincided with the trend for some young people to attend college. Few graduates returned to Utica and very few of them married persons of Welsh descent.[57] Clearly by 1930 any restraints against marrying "outside" had vanished.

The Welsh story in central New York is coming to a close after almost two centuries. Intense loyalty to the language combined with a sectarian suspicion of "worldly" evils outside church circles slowed acculturation for many immigrants. Moreover, an elaborate social system of church activities many evenings a week and all day Sunday, clubs, fraternal societies, concerts, *eisteddfodau,* newcomers and visitors from the *Hen*

---

[55] "The Welsh of Columbus, Ohio," p. 85.

[56] These statistics were graciously provided to me by Arthur M. Roberts who served as secretary of the church for decades.

[57] A personal example may be pardoned. My grandfather, John Brymer Jones, a quarryman in Caernarvonshire, brought his wife and eight children to Oneida County in 1887. His children entered eleven marriages, seven of them with individuals of Welsh descent. Of the 26 grandchildren only four took Welsh partners out of 31 marriages. None of the 11 college graduates married a Welsh partner, which confirms the findings of sociologists that persons of higher educational levels tend to marry "outside" more often..

Wlad reinforced kinship ties and created an ethnic enclave. But once immigration ceased, and the young left for college or jobs outside the city, the Welsh community disintegrated. Assimilation by the Welsh was comparatively painless because the American community accepted them, or at least their children, with few, if any, reservations. Not many could distinguish the Welsh from the dominant stock which was mainly British, or more broadly, Northwest European. Secondly, the strong Protestantism of the Welsh made them the allies of the old stock. The numerical superiority of the Roman Catholics in Utica and even in Oneida County hastened the consolidation of the various groups in the Protestant minority. Thirdly, the Welsh stood fairly high in economic status with a large number of skilled craftsmen, farmers, and later, white collar workers. Like other folk stressing knowledge of the Bible (one can cite the Scots and of course the Jews), the Welsh in both the motherland and in this country placed a high premium upon education. It is my impression that the number of second generation Welsh attending college in the 1920s and 1930s was higher than average for persons in their socioeconomic background.

The rural citadels Remsen-Steuben, Nelson, and Plainfield were too small and isolated for a permanent community to continue. Furthermore, rural decline which was pushing farm families off the land hit the Welsh farmers particularly hard since they had picked the rockiest uplands. Their children on the whole slipped into the urban middle class without keeping the ethnic identification. A second generation Welsh person from Remsen probably found it easier to join WASP society than to enter the strident Welshiness of Moriah and Bethesda churches, which before 1920 made few concessions to the use of English in worship services.

The economic decline of Utica after 1920 had an adverse effect upon the Welsh community of Utica and Oneida County.[58] Hundreds of individuals, especially the second generation, left the area to seek employment in Syracuse, New York City,

---

[58] For a more detailed analysis of the economic difficulties of Utica, see Virgil Crisafulli, *Economic Development Efforts in the Utica-Rome, New York Area.* This study is included in Committee for Economic Development, *Community Economic Development Efforts Five Case Studies* (December, 1964). See also John Thompson, ed., *The Geography of New York State* (Syracuse, 1966), for a sketch of Utica by Sidley MacFarlane who dates the decline from the early 1920s.

California, Florida, and elsewhere. The few individuals of Welsh descent who settled in Utica were not likely to affiliate with Welsh churches or organizations.

Finally, acceptance by the American community was no doubt influenced by the fact that the Welsh had helped develop the area since pioneer days. As early as 1850, Pomroy Jones, a judge and local historian, and Ellis H. Roberts, the editor of the *Utica Herald* and a power in state Republican circles, were second generation Welsh who had entered American society. The upstate Welsh took great pride in Governor Charles Evans Hughes, the son of a Welsh minister of Glens Falls. Each generation produced a few leaders in the business, political, and cultural life of the era. Perhaps some significance of "acceptance" can be attached to the present composition of the Board of Trustees of the Munson-Williams-Proctor Art Institute, the most prestigious institution in Utica and the area. Two of the five trustees are of Welsh descent.[59]

The Welsh imprint on central New York is still discernable. In the Steuben-Remsen district the stone walls, stone farmhouses, and churches, and a few place-names carry on memories similar to those of the Welsh Tract near Philadelphia. Utica College has set aside a Welsh collection in its new library and efforts are being made to create a Welsh museum in Capel Cerrig in Remsen. The Oneida Historical Society in the summer of 1971 collected materials on the Welsh and Italians in its new program of ethnic studies for which it received funds from the State Council on the Arts and assistance from the New York State Historical Association in Cooperstown.

Emrys Jones expressed the lingering Welsh influence as he observed it in 1949,

This generation is conscious of some kind of cultural heritage which is different. The culture has not been entirely absorbed. What is left—and it will soon be no more than a remnant—is real enough and has been adapted to the new cultural values in a way which will ensure its continuance in a new guise. The Saint David's Day celebration is an example of this. It is, like most festive occasions, centred on a dinner and followed by speeches and dancing. The sentimental note is struck in the speeches, and in a few Welsh folk songs—the singer is effective although she does not understand the words; but the eve-

[59] Arthur Evans is an attorney. James Hughes is President of the Savings Bank of Utica.

ning has begun by swearing allegiance to the American flag, and ends with the singing of "America." No exiles these. It is true that they are proud, in a land where history is recent and traditions meagre, of a "different" tradition which they will preserve in part. But they are prouder still to be Americans.[60]

[60] "American Welsh Community," p. 40.

LIVE AND LET LIVE IN RUSSIA.

"Your money, Jew, or your life!"—*The cry for ages.*

This pictorial comment by Thomas Nast suggests the conditions that stimulated emigration of Jews from eastern Europe. From Harper's Weekly, *February 11, 1882.*

In Their Image: German Jews and the Americanization of the *Ost Juden* in New York City

By SELMA C. BERROL

Jews whose families had been in the United States for generations felt it in their interest to hasten the Americanization of the new immigrants from eastern Europe. Selma Berrol is a member of the Department of History at Baruch College of the City University of New York.

URING THE PERIOD 1880 to 1914, when the United States was receiving hundreds of thousands of immigrants each year, Americanization was an important issue. There was little controversy about the need to Americanize the newcomers; indeed some contemporary statements said that the fate of the republic rested on the foreigners learning English and civics immediately upon arrival! There was also little disagreement about the best agency for Americanization. By consensus, the assignment went to the public schools. Questions did arise about the ability of the schools to do the job alone, and in those areas where the immigration impact was heaviest, such as New York's Lower East Side, settlement houses shared the workload. Almost without exception, especially in the 1880s and 1890s, the teachers and residents who worked with the urban immigrants were WASPS, Irish or Germans. Their clients were most likely to be Jews, Italians or other people from southern and eastern Europe.

So far the story is familiar and for most of the ethnic groups arriving in these years, complete. For the East European Jews, however, especially those who settled in New York City, the public schools and WASP settlements were only the beginning of the Americanization process. In addition to the lessons they learned at places like Public School

62 and the College Settlement, they were subjected to powerful assimilative pressures from the already established
Jewish community of New York. These German Jewish
businessmen and their wives, products of an immigration
that took place in the 1840s and 1850s, were determined to
reshape the *Ost Juden* in their image in the shortest possible
time and were willing to spend large amounts of time and
money to accomplish their goal. Their efforts represent an
important difference between the experience of eastern
European Jews and that of most other immigrant groups
whose established members played a casual role, if any, in
their Americanization.

Why did the German Jewish bourgeoisie donate large
sums and form a myriad of organizations to do "missionary"

*A fair in aid of the Montefiore Home for Chronic Invalids, held in 1886 at the New
Central Park Garden. From* Frank Leslie's Illustrated Newspaper, *December 18,
1886.*

Mr. and Mrs. Jacob Schiff. From Moses King, Notable New Yorkers; Frank Leslie's Illustrated Newspaper, *December 18, 1886.*

work among the new arrivals from Russia, Poland and the Balkans? Among the reasons behind their desire for the quick and total Americanization of the new immigrants, anti-Semitism heads the list. Most members of the New York City German Jewish community had grown up in an era that was relatively free of overt bigotry. Because their numbers were small and they were dispersed throughout the United States, the Jewish immigrants of mid-century had not experienced great prejudice.[1] Following the national pattern, in New York City the German Jews were scattered. The largest group and also the poorest, lived in Kleindeutschland, the German enclave on the Lower East Side. A smaller number of Jews in better financial circumstances lived in Chelsea,

1. John Higham, "American Anti-Semitism Historically Reconsidered," in Leonard Dinnerstein, ed., *Anti-Semitism in the United States* (New York, 1971), pp. 69–70; Higham, "Social Discrimination Against Jews in America," *Publications of the American Jewish Historical Society* XLVII (September 1957), 3.

centered around Seventh Avenue and Nineteenth Street. Many other families were scattered throughout the city. In language and culture they were often indistinguishable from non-Jewish Germans and this may help to explain the absence of hostility to them.[2]

In the Gilded Age, however, this changed. From the late 1870s to the end of the century, anti-Semitism in the United States was on the rise, its growth marked by populist rhetoric, prejudicial literature and exclusionary policies at universities, private schools and resorts. At the same time, Jewish immigrants from eastern Europe were arriving in the United States in ever increasing numbers. Not surprisingly, the older Jewish community blamed the newcomers for jeopardizing what had seemed to be a relatively secure position. They were mistaken in this belief, but their actions were based on their perceptions of the situation, regardless of their accuracy.

By the Gilded Age, many German Jews had achieved prosperity in manufacturing, trade, real estate speculation and, for a few famous families, investment banking. As their economic position improved, they also sought certain social gains. Thus, they tried to send their children to elite private schools and Ivy League colleges and to escort their wives to deluxe resorts. In most of these places they were unwelcome, especially when they came in sizable numbers. Upper middle-class WASPs saw them as "mercenary, unscrupulous and clamorously self-assertive — tasteless barbarians rudely elbowing their way into genteel company." Hotels, such as the Grand Union in Saratoga, refused to admit them, private schools turned down their children's applications, and quotas appeared at colleges.[3]

Only the desire to preserve the image of the United States as a haven for the oppressed combined with a grudging admiration for the way Jews had adopted American competitive values, kept anti-Semitism from being even stronger. The bigotry that did emerge was enough to make the German Jews puzzled and resentful. After all, had they not followed the rules and achieved economic mobility through hard

2. Robert Ernst, *Immigrant Life in New York* (Port Washington, N.Y., 1949), p. 46.

3. John Higham, *Send These to Me: Jews and Other Immigrants in Urban America* (New York, 1975), pp. 149, 150, 152; Higham, *Strangers in the Land: Patterns of American Nativism, 1860–1925* (New York, 1963), p. 27.

work? Seriously troubled, the German Jewish community looked for the cause of their problem and found the fault to lie not in themselves, but in the "backwardness," poverty and strangeness of their eastern European brethren.

Following a trickle in the 1870s, two million eastern European Jews arrived in the United States between 1880 and 1914. Since there were fewer than a quarter million American Jews in 1880, the impact of the newcomers was considerable. For most of the period, however, they were not targets of anti-Semitism. They lived and worked in self-contained enclaves like the Lower East Side and did not impinge on the lives of the larger society to any great extent. Not until they followed the path trod by the German Jews earlier and achieved considerable upward mobility did they also become objects of prejudice. Long before this happened, however, they were very much feared and disliked by many in the existing Jewish community, who shifted the onus for increased anti-Semitism from bigots in the gentile world onto their poor and foreign kinsmen.[4]

As the German Jews saw it, the new arrivals, whether wearing caftans and side curls, carrying *Das Kapital,* or just terribly poor, were unwelcome in the United States. Before any sizable number of East Europeans had settled in New York, German Jews feared that "strange looking, penniless Orthodox Jews would be a financial drain and a stimulus to prejudice." When the pogroms that followed the assassination of Czar Alexander II in 1881 sent waves of Russian Jews to the United States, most of the established community urged that immigration be restricted.[5]

Even those most opposed to the new arrivals, however, did not suggest that they remain in Russia. The need for emigration was accepted but not the final destination. The German Jewish solution to what was termed the refugee problem was resettlement in western Europe. There Jews of really great wealth, such as the Baron de Hirsch and the Rothschilds could help them start a new life. Help was forthcoming from these great families but the funds they gave were to be used to ease the journey across and out of Europe and for relief and Americanization in the United States. In contrast to

---

4. Higham, *Send These to Me,* p. 144.

5. Myron Berman, "The Attitude of American Jewry Toward East European Immigration" (Ph.D. diss., Columbia University, 1963), p. 27.

those already here, the western European Jewish community saw removal to the United States as the best solution to the refugee problem.[6]

Unable to influence their own government or their wealthy brethren overseas, the German Jews in America accepted the fact that an unknown but large number of Russian and Polish Jews would soon be living in the United States and set about taking steps to ease the difficulties. Acceptance, however, in no way assumed friendliness. Indeed, one of their first steps was to disassociate themselves from the newcomers as much as possible. Until this point, most American Jews had practiced a modified Orthodoxy but the coming of the truly Orthodox sent them headlong toward Reform Judaism. In New York, for example, the central rabbinical organization became the Board of Jewish Ministers, *yarmulkas* disappeared and choirs appeared in synagogues.

In one important way, the German Jews were already separated from the eastern Europeans, and this also accounted for their hostility to them. To a great extent, the two groups were economic adversaries. Russian Jews were tenants and German Jews their landlords. Even more important, German Jews were the employers of the eastern Europeans. The garment industry offers the best example. In 1885, 97 percent of the garment factories in New York City were owned by German Jews, and it was in these factories that the greatest number of Russian and Polish Jews worked. This relationship was also true in the hat, cap, fur, jewelry, textile or trimming trades. Since most of the tenements that housed these workers were also in the hands of German Jews, conflict was inevitable. At this stage in their development, each group had very different interests.

The dichotomy that separated the uptown Jews from their downtown brethren was an enlargement of class antagonisms already present within the German Jewish community. Not all of the immigrants from central Europe had moved into the ranks of the bourgeoisie. Many remained workers and some of them were radicals. Long before the eastern Europeans arrived, German workers, some of whom were Jews, had formed a number of important craft unions. There were also specifically German Jewish unions, such as the United Hebrew Trades. In general, working-class Ger-

6. *Ibid.*, p. 519.

Newly-arrived Jewish exiles from Russia leave Castle Garden for temporary quarters. From Frank Leslie's Illustrated Newspaper, *March 4, 1882.*

man Jews were not hostile to the eastern European newcomers. Socialist ideals assumed unity among all workers and practical considerations made it essential. In the Gilded Age, even the strongest unions had an uphill fight and German Jewish labor activists needed all the recruits they could find.

As it turned out, they found many. A sizable portion of the Polish and Russian Jews were veterans of the socialist movement in Europe. Others, socialist or not, were willing to join the struggling garment unions of the Lower East Side. The radical rhetoric of these labor leaders and socialists caused great alarm in the bourgeois German Jewish community. It directly challenged their economic interests and at a time when labor struggles drew very little support from the majority society, it seemed to threaten the security of all Jews.

From the vantage point of today, we can see that much of the East Side's radicalism was indeed rhetorical; as a group, the eastern Europen Jews were capitalist to the core, willing to endure self-exploitation and privation to amass the reserve that would enable them to become bosses and landlords themselves. But this was not how it seemed to the *Yahudim*, the wealthy German Jews. Insecure about their own place in society, the established Jews greatly overestimated the radicalism of the eastern European Jews and the danger it posed to them. The German Jewish-owned *New York Times* spoke of "hatchet faced, pimply, sallow cheeked, rat eyed young men of the Russian Jewish colony who, weaned on nihilism and dynamite throwing, long to demolish law and order.... Such individuals damage the image of Jews as a group."[7]

Other members of the Jewish establishment expressed alarm on different grounds. Oscar Straus said, "Hoarded together as they are, [the refugees] constantly breathe the atmosphere of the ghetto and do not become Americanized." The *American Israelite*, weekly organ of the Reform Jewish community, was more direct: "These newcomers must be turned into useful American citizens or they will upset our position before the community." William Rosenblatt begged the readers of *Galaxy* magazine not to judge all Jews by the "ignorant ... and vicious Poles and Russians who cluster around Chatham Square and Broadway." Julia Richman, a member of the German Jewish establishment and later to be the superintendent of schools for the Lower East Side, sounded the tocsin: "The condition of affairs in that little corner of the 7th and 10th wards which is frightfully overcrowded with Jewish refugees ... is not only fraught with the direst evil for those who live there, but is full of menace to the entire Jewish community of New York."[8]

The threat was clear but what was the remedy? Public education would turn many of the "little aliens" into "little citizens" but what of their older siblings and parents? The settlement houses, even if their number was doubled, could not fill the gap and in any case, there was some doubt that the Orthodox segment of the community would utilize their serv-

7. Jesse E. Pope, *The Clothing Industry in New York* (Columbia, Mo., 1905), p. 7; Ronald Sanders, *The Downtown Jews: Portraits of an Immigrant Generation* (New York, 1969), p. 48n; *New York Times*, August 21, 1893.

8. Straus and the *Israelite* are quoted in Berman, "Attitude," p. 85; Julia Richman's statement was in a typewritten letter of invitation to join the Ladies Auxiliary of the YWHA, October 10, 1888, archives of the YMHA and YWHA, New York City.

ices. There seemed to be no help for it. If the eastern European Jews were to shed their foreign garb and Yiddish "jargon" and be turned away from Orthodoxy or radicalism, the German Jewish community would have to do the job.

And so they tried. Between 1870 and 1893, new organizations were created to minister to what the German Jews saw as the needs of their downtown brethren. The first of these was the Hebrew Emigrant Aid Society, which was founded in 1881. Representatives of the society met the immigrants at Castle Garden and steered them through the formalities of arrival. They also administered the Schiff Refugee Center, a temporary shelter on Ward's Island for those whose medical condition was being evaluated. Their major function, however, was to keep the new arrivals moving. HEAS agents helped them begin their journey to communities in the South and Mid-West and to agricultural colonies the society had founded in New Jersey.[9]

The desire to resettle the eastern Europeans away from east coast cities was an important aspect of German Jewish policy during the immigration crisis. It had several rationales. As had been true for their own group, geographic dispersion would make the Russian and Polish Jews less noticeable and thus less likely to create or exacerbate anti-Semitism. Resettlement would also relieve the established New York Jewish community of an embarrassment on its doorstep. On the positive side, removal to places where Jews were few would force the newcomers to become Americanized more quickly than if they remained in a familiar, if not very comfortable, enclave like the Lower East Side. In general, however, the stubbornly urban eastern European Jews resisted resettlement and those agricultural colonies that were created were not very successful.

In any case, underfunded for the magnitude of its task, the Hebrew Emigrant Aid Society collapsed in 1883. The United Hebrew Charities, outgrowth of a charitable organization founded long before the eastern European immigration began, reluctantly took over the responsibilities of HEAS, but were not successful. Several smaller organizations, with Russian Jewish participation, stepped into the vacuum thus created and in 1902, combined to form the

9. Bernard Postal and Lionel Koppman, *Jewish Landmarks of New York* (New York, 1978), pp. 32, 33.

Hebrew Immigrant Aid Society. With more money and a leadership committed to the permanent settlement of eastern European Jews in New York, the Hebrew Immigrant Aid Society was far more successful than its predecessors. In addition to providing the most recent arrivals with temporary shelter, location of relatives and employment advice, HIAS also conducted naturalization classes and Saturday afternoon children's services.[10]

The latter activity competed with the work of another group sponsored by the German Jews, the Hebrew Free School Association. It had been organized in 1864, well before the onset of eastern European immigration, and its original purpose was not Americanization. A Christian mission school on East Second Street was offering food and clothing as well as lessons from the New Testament to the children in the area, many of whom were the offspring of Jews from Prussian Poland. These families had arrived somewhat later than the majority of German Jews, and with less capital and fewer skills. As a result, they were desperately poor and for practical reasons were attracted to the charity school.

Confident that the children would abandon the Christian school if they had one of their own to go to, the Association opened its first building a few doors away. Eventually they came to operate five schools which taught Bible, Hebrew prayers, jewish history, English, and arithmetic.[11] Christian proselytizing never completely disappeared from the Lower East Side, but after 1880 it ceased to be the Association's major concern. Instead, their anxiety was now focused on the hundreds of Orthodox religious schools, called *chedarim*, which opened all over the East Side following the influx of Russian, Polish and Galician Jews.

The objections of the Hebrew Free School Association to the continuation of these old-world schools were many: Classes were held in damp cellars, backyard shacks, and sometimes in the teacher's kitchen. The instructors, known as *melamdim*, were often poorly trained and were harsh disciplinarians. Instruction was in Yiddish and Hebrew, a

---

10. Moses Rischin, *The Promised City: New York's Jews, 1870–1914* (Cambridge, Mass., 1962), p. 106.

11. Jeremiah Berman, "Jewish Education in New York City, 1860–1900," *YIVO Annual* IX (1954), 253, 255, 262, 264.

practice which was thought to retard assimilation. The absence of history and ethics from the curriculum would perpetuate what the established Jewish community saw as the ignorance and immorality of the East Side. Worst of all, the kind of religious education offered in these schools was inappropriate to the American environment and was likely to turn native-born Jewish children away from Judaism entirely.

To combat the spreading influence of the *chedarim*, the Hebrew Free School Association began a multifaceted Americanization program which included kindergartens to reach the very young and manual training classes for adolescents.[12] Learning to sew, cook and use hand tools might seem to bear little relationship to Americanization but in the eyes of the Association's leaders, it did. Such skills would make it easier for East Side children to find work and this would alleviate both their poverty and the burden on German Jewish pocketbooks. In addition, and in view of their mission, training for "honest" labor would dispel the image of the crafty, scheming Jew who lived by his wits and whose bad reputation injured all Jews.

The Shylock stereotype had been applied to the German Jews when they arrived in the United States. Indeed, it was a familiar charge against Jews in many countries. What is interesting in this case, however, is that the trustees of the Hebrew Free School Association had internalized the unfavorable image held by bigots and were now applying it to the East Europeans. Although they hoped to make them ethical and moral, they believed that the *Ost Juden* were basically cunning knaves, perfectly willing to lie, cheat and break the law to gain their ends. This view led to a heavy emphasis on moral and ethical teaching in the religious classes they sponsored.

Money from a fund established by the De Hirsch family was used for an extensive English program which also included civic education. Hoping to expand their good works, in 1890 the trustees accepted a generous offer from philanthropist Jacob Schiff and joined two other groups doing similar work on the Lower East Side. Together with the downtown branch of the YMHA and YWHA and the Agui-

12. "Minutes" of the Hebrew Free School Association, December 1885, May 1887, June 1887, November 1888, April 1889.

lar Free Library they created the Educational Alliance.[13]

On the surface, the Educational Alliance was a settlement house much like the University and College Settlements. In reality, it had a different *raison d'être*. Unlike the idealistic WASP residents who were their neighbors, the German Jewish leadership of the Alliance rejected the notion that immigrant cultural traditions should be respected. They wanted their clients to discard their old-world cultural baggage entirely. At the Educational Alliance, clubs, sports, theatres and study groups were directed to one end: to reform the eastern European Jews into the kind of people who would be acceptable to the majority society.

Thus Yiddish, the language of the East Side, was con-

13. "Minutes" of the HFSA, August 1888; Berman, "Jewish Education," p. 263; "Annual Meeting of the Hebrew Free School Association," *Menorah* II (January 1887), 34.

Russian Jews at Castle Garden. From Frank Leslie's Illustrated Newspaper, *August 5, 1882.*

sidered a "piggish jargon" and a reminder of the ghetto. It was argued that because it was a language no other group could speak, it made Jews into pariahs. In the early years of the Alliance, Yiddish was absolutely prohibited. Such rigidity created considerable hostility among the residents of the East Side. Indeed, some Russian and Polish Jews equated Alliance Americanization tactics with the forced conversion policies of the Russian Czars. Anger at the hostile and patronizing attitudes of the Alliance leadership led a group of Russian Jews to an abortive attempt to found a competing organization, the Educational League. Much of the antagonism declined in later years as the board of directors came to see that if they were to have any influence on the East Side, they would have to curb their hostility to eastern European culture and habits.[14]

Among its many programs, the Educational Alliance offered recreational and cultural pursuits, coaching for civil service examinations, lectures on a variety of subjects and, of course, classes in basic English. Whenever possible, even in some instances where it seemed farfetched, they preached their message of Americanization. Debate topics are a case in point: The affirmative side of the question, "Will Reform Judaism Win Students of Russian Parentage"? won the approval of the judges. The negative position, "Does Yiddish Have a Future in America"? was similarly rewarded. When the matter was very serious, the debate format was abandoned. "The Degeneracy of the Yiddish Stage," for example, was presented as a lecture, without opportunity for discussion.[15]

In addition to its own program, the Alliance rented space to other organizations whose mission resembled its own. The National Council of Jewish Women was an example of this. The Council was an outgrowth of an organization formed to speak for Jewish women at the Parliament of Religions conducted at the 1893 Chicago exposition. Although the national organization had several different purposes, philanthropic

14. Education Alliance, "Minutes of the Board of Directors," January 1903, February 1903, at YIVO, New York City; Isaac Rubinow, "The Jewish Question in New York City," *Publication of the American Jewish Historical Society* XLIX (December 1959), 110, 113; Irving Howe, *World of Our Fathers* (New York, 1976), p. 234.

15. Education Alliance, "Minutes," September 1902, November 1902, March 1905, November 1910.

The Hebrew Orphan Asylum on 136th Street in Manhattan. Opposite page: Mayor Edson addressing The Friends of the Institution at its dedication, October 23, 1884. From Frank Leslie's Illustrated Newspaper, November 1, 1884.

and educational work on the Lower East Side became the main activity of the New York section. Its organizer was Minnie Louis, a wealthy woman who had done volunteer work on the East Side since the early days of the Hebrew Free School Association. Her attitude toward the eastern European Jews was expressed in a poem she wrote, entitled "The Eternal Jew":

> To wear the yellow badge, the locks
> The caftan long, the low bent head
> To pocket unprovoked knocks
> And shamble on in servile dread
> Tis not this to be a Jew

This poem went on to describe the strong and noble "modern Jew" as the *real* Jew.[16]

In an attempt to transform East Siders into "modern Jews," the Council offered "mission classes" at the Educational Alliance and thus added their bit to the ongoing at-

16. *American Jewess*, November 1896; *Papers of the Jewish Women's Congress*, Chicago, September 4–7, 1893, p. 3; Minnie Louis poem is quoted in Stephen Birmingham, *"Our Crowd": The Great Jewish Families of New York* (New York, 1967), p. 291.

tempts to Americanize the East Siders. Many council members were at the same time active in the Temple Emmanuel
Sisterhood of Personal Service, and their husbands were part
of the Brotherhood. These groups provided additional volunteers for missionary work on the Lower East Side.[17]

Uptown money and personnel were also used for a group
of organizations whose primary purpose was to meet the
social problems of the eastern European Jews. The Hebrew
Orphan Asylum and Clara De Hirsch Home for Working
Girls were founded to save children and female and adolescents from lives of crime and prostitution. The Jewish Pro-
tectory and Lakeview Home for Girls was to salvage those
who had already run afoul of the law and the Jewish Big
Brothers and Sisters worked with those placed on probation.
With some reluctance, a Jewish Prisoners Aid Society was
established in 1893 to help adult criminals, and a National
Desertion bureau was formed to deal with a major symptom
of East Side social pathology, missing husbands.[18]

17. Temple Emanuel Brotherhood, "Minute Book," 1904, *passim.*

The Americanization function of these social work organizations, especially those that dealt with children, was indirect but present nonetheless. Each of the institutions maintained by German Jewish dollars taught basic English, arithmetic, and various trades, and attempted to instill a civic and moral conscience. Their primary goal was to alleviate immediate problems, but part of their reason for caring about maladjusted Jewish children at all was to keep them from dishonoring and thus injuring the community as a whole. Again, what they saw as the tenuous place of Jews in American society led them to try to strengthen their weaker links.

Jacob Schiff, the most important single source of funds for work on the Lower East Side, constantly deplored duplication and urged the various missionary groups to unite. In a formal sense, especially after each group developed its own bureaucracy, this proved difficult to accomplish. In another sense, however, the entire missionary effort *was* united by means of a device better known to big business, the interlocking directorate. The same names appeared repeatedly on the rosters and boards of trustees. Whole families were often represented. The Schiffs, Warburgs, Loebs and Strauses are only the most famous. Others, less well-known, include Judge Samuel Greenbaum, Albert Hochstadter, William Popper, Meyer Isaacs, Jesse Seligman, Charles Bernheimer, Joseph Silverman and Isadore Levy. Louis Marshall, perhaps better known for other activities in the Jewish community, was also part of the group and one woman, Julia Richman, was active in all.

The leaders of such groups as the Hebrew Free School Association, Educational Alliance, YMHA, and National Council of Jewish Women were thoroughly linked by social, family and business relationships. It is therefore not surprising to see them working together as missionaries on the East Side. Their common background led them to the same anxieties and therefore to the same goal. It also accounts for the similarities in the programs of the various organizations they funded and administered. Each tried to reach the children of the immigrants and all attempted to teach the language and government of America. They were also united in trying to

---

18. Rischin, *Promised City*, pp. 103–04.

get the new arrivals to exchange their old-world cultural baggage for the values and behavior patterns of the new.

Were they successful? Behavioral assimilation was relatively quick for the eastern European Jews as a whole, radicalism diminished with prosperity and until the Holocaust, Orthodoxy did not flourish in the American milieu. By the 1920s and even earlier, eastern European Jews were virtually indistinguishable from German Jews. But this was not the result of the missionary effort of the established group. Americanization would have occurred at just about the same pace if the German Jews had behaved like the first arrivals of other ethnic groups, or as the Sephardic Jews had behaved towards them; that is, done nothing except be themselves. It is probable that many eastern European Jews paid little attention to the assimilative message of the uptown missionaries, but they certainly noted their comfortable economic position. The older community as a whole had set a most attractive example for the new arrivals. German Jewish success in business, trade and real estate led many Russian and Polish Jews to try to become bosses and landlords themselves. It was not as teachers and preachers, therefore, but as role models for the newcomers, that the German Jews hastened the Americanization of the eastern Europeans.

The American Jewish community that finally emerged, however, owed as much or more to the public schools, day and evening, and to unions and settlement houses. Most of all, it was a happy economic match that speeded the eastern European adjustment. Russian, Polish and Galician Jews provided skills that were needed in New York at the time that they arrived. This, combined with their ambition and capacity for hard work led to economic mobility, and assimilation flowed from that. In hindsight, it would seem that German Jews undervalued both the adaptability of the *Ost Juden* and the capacity of an open society to absorb them.

This 1923 cartoon from The Evening News *of Glasgow, Scotland, indicates one British attitude toward American immigration policies.*

A Modern "Black Hole of Calcutta"? The Anglo-American Controversy Over Ellis Island, 1921–1924

By BENJAMIN D. RHODES

No one could have enjoyed the Ellis Island experience, but various British subjects found it so appalling that their complaints reached the highest diplomatic levels. Benjamin Rhodes is Professor of History at the University of Wisconsin in Whitewater, Wisconsin.

O N DECEMBER 28, 1922, at the invitation of the Harding administration, Sir Auckland Campbell Geddes, Britain's Ambassador to the United States, visited the immigration facilities at Ellis Island. His tour was an attempt to resolve a year-old Anglo-American controversy over the treatment of British citizens unfortunate enough to be detained there by American immigration authorities. Probably the most vivid impression carried away by the British visitor was the presence of a "flat stale smell" combined with "the pungent odour of unwashed humanity." "Indeed," reported Geddes, "the compound smell of old dirt and new immigrants is so nearly universal there that I should not be surprised if it were no longer noticed by members of the staff. After leaving the island, it took me thirty-six hours to get rid of the aroma which flavoured everything I ate or drank."[1]

The controversy over Ellis Island began soon after World War I as large scale European immigration strained the dilapidated New York facility. In 1920, 225,206 newcomers entered through Ellis Island, with the total rising to 560,971 in 1921. During the war, Congress had taken the first steps to end the nation's tradition of allowing unrestricted immigration by imposing, over the veto of President Woodrow Wilson, a weak literacy test. When this measure proved ineffective in limiting the flow of immigrants, a new law was rushed through early in the Harding administration. The

---

1. Sir Auckland Geddes to the Marquess Curzon of Kedleston, January 18, 1923, *Parliamentary Paper* (1923, XXV, Cmd. 1940), 4.

Immigration Act of 1921 restricted each country to a yearly quota of 3 percent of its foreign born listed in the census of 1910. No more than 20 percent of a country's quota could be admitted in any one month. On paper the plan looked workable enough, but in practice the result was chaos. One unforeseen problem produced by the quota system was that it frequently became necessary to confine cabin class passengers at Ellis Island in facilities which were designed for immigrants who had crossed the ocean in steerage. Since the Ellis Island station compared favorably with steerage accommodations, there were few serious complaints from the poorer immigrants. But wealthier passengers from the British Empire found the sanitary, social, and racial conditions to be totally unacceptable. Moreover, the crush at Ellis Island came at a time when, as an economy measure, the number of government employees there had been sharply reduced (from 780 to 520). And the greed of shipping companies, which sought to pile in as many immigrants as possible before the start of the quotas on June 3, 1921, contributed to the general mismanagement.[2]

In 1921, when the Ellis Island situation became an issue of dispute between the United States and Britain, Anglo-American relations were in some need of improvement. Both countries were somewhat disillusioned by their collaboration in the recently concluded war. The British, on the one hand, were disappointed by the Senate's rejection of the League of Nations, while many Americans felt that the moral and material results of the conflict had fallen far short of expectations. The single most divisive matter concerned the repayment of Britain's war debt to the United States of $4.6 billion, an issue which remained unsettled until 1923. Other sources of disagreement included naval rivalry, the high tariff policy of the Harding administration, and the existence of the Anglo-Japanese Alliance of 1902, which many Americans suspected was directed against them. Then there were what Sir Auckland Geddes called "lesser differences, each by itself unimportant, but collectively an irritation."[3] And in this category fell British smuggling of liquor into the United States and immigration troubles.

2. The most detailed survey is Thomas M. Pitkin, *Keepers of the Gate: A History of Ellis Island* (New York, 1975), 129–157. The author briefly (147–148) discusses Sir Auckland Geddes' report and its stormy reception. For the general background see John Higham, *Strangers in the Land: Patterns of American Nativism, 1860–1925* (New York, 1965), 300–330. A brief mention of the Anglo-American disagreement over Ellis Island is contained in Ann Novotny, *Strangers at the Door: Ellis Island, Castle Garden, and the Great Migration to America* (Riverside, Connecticut, 1971), 125–126.
3. Sir Auckland Campbell Geddes, *The Forging of a Family* (London, 1952), 334.

Sir Auckland Campbell Geddes, who was appointed as British Ambassador in May, 1920, was uniquely qualified to deal with the congested Ellis Island situation. Only forty years old, Geddes had been trained as a medical doctor at the University of Edinburgh and had risen to become professor of anatomy at McGill University in Montreal. During World War I Geddes left his medical career permanently as he was called to service by the War Office. From 1916 to 1917 he was Director of Recruiting and for the next two years held a position in the Cabinet as Minister of National Service. Next Geddes was president of the Board of Trade and it was his intention to become Principal of McGill University when Prime Minister David Lloyd George offered him the post at Washington. His outstanding accomplishment during his three and one-half year tenure was the settlement of the British war debt to the United States in 1923. But his career came to a premature and tragic end in 1924 when he was forced into retirement at age forty-four by a detached retina in his right eye. Twelve years previously the vision in his left eye had been severely damaged in a laboratory experiment. His inability to continue as British Ambassador was sadly confirmed during an interview with Secretary of State Charles Evans Hughes when Geddes realized that "with a blind left eye and a right eye centrally useless, the impossibility of seeing facial expression, made conversation more than difficult."[4]

Geddes was first called upon by the Foreign Office to protest the conditions at Ellis Island in the fall of 1921, which happened to coincide with the height of immigration congestion and confusion. Foreign Secretary Lord Curzon objected specifically to the lack of governmental machinery for warning travelers that they might be denied admission to the United States if the quota for their country had been exhausted. Moreover, complained Curzon, travelers to the United States were not warned in advance that they might "be subjected to detention in conditions unworthy of a civilized country."[5] In support of these claims, Geddes was instructed to present to Secretary of State Charles Evans Hughes a number of statements by British subjects relating their experiences while detained at Ellis Island. Graphically and plaintively these well-written testimonials summarized the human tragedy which affected all, whether immigrant or employee, who were associated with Ellis Island.

Not all of the detained travelers had run afoul of the quota

4. Ibid., 292–333.
5. Curzon to Geddes, September 16, 1921, FO414/248/A6238, Public Record Office (hereafter cited as PRO).

system. Miss Harriet L. Porter, employed as a governess, was confined at Ellis Island because she lacked a notarized affidavit stating that the parents of the two children she accompanied were willing and able to support them. Arriving at New York on May 25, 1921 as second class passengers on the *Olympic,* Miss Porter and her two charges were ferried to Ellis Island where they were "herded and counted like animals." The most objectionable features of her two-day stay were the confinement in close proximity with 2700 southern and eastern Europeans and, above all, the lack of sanitation. The recreation area, she recalled, "was absolutely filthy; the tiles which formed the floor were simply sticking with dirt. When I saw it there was not as much as a square yard of it fit to stand on; it was a case of picking one's steps to avoid the loathsome expectorations and general filth of the ground." Porter objected also to the "evil-smelling lavatory" which lacked privacy, and to crowded, rodent-infested sleeping quarters. "It is nearly impossible," she concluded, "to give an idea of the awful indignities we suffered whilst at Ellis Island; one has got to spend a day there as an immigrant to realise the horror of it all. . . . These facts are the bare truth without any exaggerations, and it is incredible that such a state of affairs should be allowed, or such treatment accorded anyone, be he second-class passenger or other immigrant."[6]

The statements of other British citizens mirrored the account of Miss Porter. A British family detained in July, 1921, because their child had been born in South Africa and the South African quota was exhausted for the month, reported that the immigration facility was jammed "by a seething mass of humanity, filthy in the extreme—Europe's worst, negroes, Asiatics, dregs of humanity." According to the account of Mark Glanvill, the officials were uniformly insolent, the blankets gritty and infested with lice, and the general atmosphere resembled that of a police state. "Guards are everywhere," he wrote. "Prison conditions existed throughout. The whole experience was cruel, revolting and humiliating. For one night Mrs. Glanvill went to hospital, baby not being well. She and the baby were treated in a shameful way. The nurses shook their fists in her face when she appealed for food for baby. She returned the next day on the point of collapse." After four days the Glanvills' ordeal ended when they decided to return to England at their own expense.[7]

6. Statement of Harriet L. Porter, June 21, 1921, enclosed in Curzon to Geddes, September 16, 1921, ibid.

7. Statement of Mark Glanvill, no date, enclosed in Curzon to Geddes, September 16, 1921, ibid.

British Foreign Secretary Lord Curzon. From Mid-Week Pictorial, *November 2, 1922.*

The experiences of two other South Africans, Percival W. Elliott and his son Bruce, were depressingly similar. Arriving a day after the Glanvills, Bruce Elliott, who intended to study mechanical engineering in Kansas City, was denied admission owing to the filling up of the South African quota. His father Percival, who planned a three-week American tour, was admissible but chose voluntarily to accompany his son to Ellis Island. Characterizing the conditions he encountered to be "absolutely degrading and humiliating," Percival Elliott found the noise and confusion to be the most objectionable aspects of the island. The facilities, he observed, were badly overcrowded "with men, women and children of various nationalities, unkempt, dishevelled, and dejected, and the babel of noise, shouting and screaming was terrible." One British couple in their seventies who "sat in a corner looking utterly apathetic and spiritless," told Elliott that they had been in detention for five weeks. The confusion continued at meal time: "The jabbering, din and uproar of the mob around us, and clattering of crockery, etc., gathered by waiters was indescribable. It seemed as if we had strayed into a lunatic asylum. We could not eat. The thought of eating in such intolerable conditions was revolting and repulsive. . . . . The loathsome confinement, callous conduct of the warders, spitting and filthy habits of some of the immigrants, were torture to any person of refinement." The next morning, July 24, 1921, Bruce Elliott's request to be admitted having been rejected by an appeal board, the Elliotts, their passports now stamped "Deported," returned to England on the *Aquitania,* the same liner which had brought them to America two days before.[8]

In South Africa the press reacted indignantly to reports of "truly appalling conditions" at Ellis Island. One newspaper remarked:

8. Statement of Percival Wilfred Elliott, July 30, 1921, enclosed in Curzon to Geddes, September 16, 1921, ibid.

A dining-room scene at Ellis Island in 1923. From The Literary Digest, *August 4, 1923.*

"The experiences of Mr. and Mrs. Glanvill on Ellis Island read more like an account of a Hun war prison than that of a presumably modern station for the reception and examination of immigrants."[9] A letter from Mrs. Glanvill to her father was printed under the headlines: "'Black Holes' of Ellis Island; Revolting Revelations of South Africans; Herded Like Pigs in a Pen; Lady Bullied and Cursed by Guards; Indescribable State of Filth; American Travesty of Justice." According to Mrs. Glanvill, the experience had left a mark for life upon herself and her husband. "The horrors were unbelievable," she wrote her father, "and you could never believe that such a hell existed on earth, and that free British subjects could be treated like that."[10]

Racial conditions at Ellis Island produced additional complaints from South Africans. A woman detained under the quota system related that a black employee rudely stated to her: "You are not in England now and you are not an American subject. If you were the King of England you would have to stay here."[11] Even more offended was a South African dental student who was confined for ten days at Ellis Island. In a letter to his parents, David Monk complained bitterly about the lack of segregated eating facilities: "My God, I never wish to go through that again. It broke my heart ... For the first time in my life I sat at the same table with niggers and ate with them. You can imagine my feelings. The disgust and anger of the other English-speaking people cannot be expressed."[12]

No formal notes were presented by Geddes regarding matters of race, but the ambassador did file a protest in the case of an employee of the British Government, A.J. Pharaoh, who had been sent to the United States in March, 1921, in charge of a former prisoner of war. The man, who was insane, was being returned to relatives in the United States at the expense of the British government. For over two months Pharaoh was detained at Ellis Island while commitment proceedings were completed for his insane charge. And, upon his release on May 30, he recounted that he had

9. Monnett B. Davis, American Consul, Port Elizabeth, South Africa, to Secretary of State Charles Evans Hughes, September 7, 1921, RG 59, General Records of the Department of State, File No. 150.08/96, Washington National Records Center, Suitland, Maryland (hereafter cited as WNRC).

10. Davis to Hughes, September 6, 1921, RG 59, 158.08/96, WNRC

11. Fred D. Fisher, American Consul, Johannesburg, South Africa, to Hughes, November 7, 1921, RG 59, 150.08/129, WNRC.

12. Alfred A. Winslow, American Consul General, Cape Town, South Africa, to Hughes, January 9, 1922, RG 59, 150.08/144, WNRC.

been detained with immigrants of "a very undesirable class" who were "very dirty in their habits." Moreover, said Pharaoh, he had been subjected to "very serious discomfort owing to dirt, vermin, lack of air, exercise, etc."[13] Even less fortunate was a young Australian, Ormond J. McDermott, Jr., who came to America as an employee of the Studebaker Corporation to study salesmanship at South Bend, Indiana. When he arrived at New York on February 17, he was denied admission under the contract labor clause of the immigration law, which prohibited aliens from possessing employment prior to their entry. While the Studebaker Corporation was appealing the case, McDermott contracted scarlet fever and died two days later in the Ellis Island hospital. "It is an outrageous injustice to a worthy foreigner," declared the New York manager of the Studebaker Corporation.[14]

For Secretary of State Charles Evans Hughes the controversy over Ellis Island could not have come at a worse time as he was in the midst of preparations for the November, 1921 Washington Conference on naval disarmament. Demonstrating his formidable legal ability (he was a former member of the Supreme Court), Hughes set out to disprove each and every allegation advanced by the British. And, in the process, he barely concealed his irritation over the timing of the British protests. Stating that he regretted "the many inaccuracies and the unusual phraseology" of the British protests, Hughes contended that the British charges were characterized by an "utter lack of foundation." It was Hughes' contention that the congestion at Ellis Island was primarily the fault of private steamship companies which sought to transport masses of immigrants to New York prior to the effective date of the 1921 Immigration Act (June 3, 1921). Later, when the quota system was in place, the steamship companies engaged in a "deliberate attempt ... to discredit a law which the United States deemed to be necessary for its own protection."

The worst offender, in Hughes' view, was the Cunard Line which "repeatedly caused great hardship by deliberately bringing to the United States ports many ignorant and innocent people who were inadmissible under the laws." That the steamship companies were guilty of "deliberately overcrowding" Ellis Island was demonstrated by the fact that once a day statistics were published at New

13. Curzon to Geddes, September 27, 1921, FO414/248/A6702, PRO.
14. Ormond J. McDermott, Sr., to the Acting Prime Minister of Australia Sir J. Cook, June 30, 1921, and extract from the *Brooklyn Daily Eagle*, March 6, 1921, enclosed in Curzon to Geddes, September 27, 1921, ibid.

York stating the exact status of each country's quota. By monitoring the figures the companies could "readily avoid" bringing persons to New York who were inadmissible. (Cunard officials in New York, however, maintained that information concerning the open balance of the quotas was not readily available and that American consuls abroad greatly confused the situation by issuing visas to immigrants without regard to the status of the quotas.) Hughes'

"That Awful Geddes Boy." From The Evening Express *(London), in* The Literary Digest, *September 22, 1923.*

sole concession was that the physical conditions at Ellis Island were "not satisfactory." But they were not, he maintained, as objectionable as stated by the British and "they are to be put in better order very shortly."[15]

The Anglo-American diplomatic controversy over Ellis Island continued to simmer even as the two powers cooperated at the Washington Conference. As usual the focus of British protests centered upon the dormitory and sanitary arrangements at Ellis Island—which Hughes had admitted were in need of improvement.

15. Hughes to Curzon, October 3, 1921, RG 59, 150.08/92, WNRC.

"DRAIN IT BEFORE YOU SHOVEL IN AND MAYBE I CAN KEEP THINGS CLEANER OVER HERE OLD MAN"

The Pittsburgh Sun *suggests "One Remedy for that Clogged-Up Condition."* The Literary Digest, *September 1, 1923.*

"Further statements of the same character continue to reach me," observed Curzon, "and the close similarity of the complaints make it almost incredible that they should be without serious foundation."[16] Yet, at the same time, the Foreign Office made it plain that the disagreement would not be permitted to interfere with the progress being made on disarmament. Although he was "constantly being pressed" to publish the Ellis Island correspondence, Curzon informed the Washington Embassy that such a course of action "would not be opportune during the sittings of the Washington Conference."[17]

As the congestion at Ellis Island subsided during the winter of 1921–1922, so did the diplomatic furor. With the disarmament conference successfully completed, Secretary of State Hughes now adopted a less irritable tone in replying to the British protests. It was his "earnest desire," Hughes assured Curzon, that British citizens be subjected to "the least possible inconvenience at Ellis Island." Owing to overcrowding, which he still blamed on the shipping companies, Hughes conceded that conditions at Ellis

16. Curzon to Geddes, November 23, 1921, FO414/248/A8442, PRO.
17. Curzon to Geddes, November 23, 1921, FO414/248/A8443, PRO.

Island "have not been so good as the American authorities desire them to be." However, relying upon a memorandum from the Department of Labor, Hughes maintained that the complaints were "so grossly exaggerated as to make them largely untrue." In nearly every case, he suggested, the basis for the complaint was the fact of the detention itself. And, Hughes asked that before further diplomatic protests were filed, British representatives make an unannounced inspection of Ellis Island.[18]

This proved to be a shrewd request as a visit to Ellis Island by two British officials on January 21, 1922, confirmed the accuracy of many of the points raised by the Secretary of State. The Third Secretary of the British Embassy at Washington, A. Yencken, accompanied by Frederick Watson of the British Consulate-General in New York were "most cordially received" by Robert E. Tod, the Ellis Island Commissioner. A wealthy Scottish-born banker, yachtsman, and philanthropist, Tod made "a most agreeable impression" upon his visitors. Having made "a full and careful inspection" of the facilities, Yencken concluded that the American officials at Ellis Island were making "an honest endeavour to cope with very real difficulties." Concerning the protests made by British citizens, Yencken expressed the view that the root cause was "not so much maladministration as the question of their being obliged to mix with the lowest classes of Eastern Europe, Latins, Jews and Russians." To which Ambassador Geddes remarked: "As is well known, the habits of these latter classes of people will not bear description."

To improve the physical conditions at Ellis Island Yencken recommended, with the support of Geddes, that the ventilation and toilet facilities be altered. Above all, it was urged that a system similar to that used by the shipping companies should be devised so as to segregate Western European immigrants from Eastern Europeans. "Under the existing system," noted Yencken, "it would undoubtedly be a severe hardship for any delicately nurtured person to spend even one night upon Ellis Island."[19]

Yet, in the opinion of the British Embassy, conditions at Ellis Island did improve slightly for a few months. In response to the intervention of Columbia University Professor Edwin R. Selig-

18. Hughes to Curzon, February 10, 1922, RG 59, 150.08/145b, WNRC; Hughes to Geddes, February 3, 1922, enclosed in Geddes to Curzon, February 18, 1922, FO414/249/A1397, PRO.
19. Memorandum by A. Yencken, January 21, 1922, enclosed in Geddes to Curzon, February 18, 1922, ibid.

man, the Labor Department agreed to improve the system for treating foreign students arriving at Ellis Island. As Professor Seligman pointed out, foreign students—through a defect in the 1921 Immigration Act—were not exempted from the quota system and were thus frequently detained for lengthy periods. In order to relieve what was termed "the rather embarrassing situation concerning bona fide students" the Labor Department agreed to expedite hearings for students so as to speed their admission. And, in another conciliatory gesture, the Labor Department admitted that it had made a mistake in the case of A. J. Pharaoh the previous year and remitted to the British Embassy £114.11.0 as compensation for expenses incurred in connection with his detention.[20]

By the fall of 1922, however, a familiar litany of complaints from British subjects detained at Ellis Island descended upon Sir Auckland Geddes. Now, recalling that his past written protests had had the effect of provoking the State and Labor Departments into determined defenses of the administration of Ellis Island, Geddes "thought it best to try a somewhat different line." First of all, the ambassador outlined to Hughes the distressing experiences of an English woman and her niece while in confinement at Ellis Island, but he refrained from leaving a written protest. Instead, explained Geddes, "I invited him to look at the matter from a more general point of view." America, he suggested, should consider Ellis Island as essential to the nation's desire to encourage the immigration of "better-class people." Such persons, especially women, were likely to be discouraged and subjected to "an almost intolerable mental strain" by being confined "cheek-by-jowl with the sort of individuals who formed the bulk of the immigrant traffic, to whom the habit of cleanliness is almost unknown." The remedy which occurred to Geddes was to place each nationality in separate quarters or to give immigrants the option of paying for private accommodations. Hughes seemed sympathetic and promised once again to take up the Ellis Island question with the Secretary of Labor.[21]

Throughout the controversy, Sir Auckland Geddes had advocated changes in American immigration policy without the benefit of having visited Ellis Island. An opportunity to make such a tour

---

20. Edwin R. Seligman to Hughes, April 3, 1922, RG 59, 158.08/155 WNRC; W.J. Pixon, Acting Commissioner General, Bureau of Immigration to Seligman, May 3, 1922, RG 59, 150.08/165, WNRC; E.J. Henning, Acting Secretary of Labor to Hughes, May 2, 1922, RG 59, 158.08/163, WNRC.
21. Geddes to Curzon, October 27, 1922, FO414/250/A6739, PRO.

suddenly presented itself as the result of critical statements in the House of Commons about alleged maltreatment of British citizens at Ellis Island. In early December, 1922, in answer to a parliamentary question, Ronald McNeill, the Under-Secretary of State for Foreign Affairs, made the statement that conditions at Ellis Island were adapted primarily to a low standard of conduct and constituted a serious hardship for persons of refinement.[22] American congressmen leaped to the defense, maintaining that the Ellis Island facilities and methods were ideal. The chief objection of the British, claimed Representative John L. Cable of Ohio, was that America had failed to provide immigrants with "separate rooms and baths."[23] Soon afterward Secretary of Labor James J. Davis, no doubt hoping to quiet the debate, invited Geddes to tour the Ellis Island facilities.

The Ellis Island visit took place on December 28, 1922, a day marked by rain, hail, and freezing temperatures. During his three-hour tour Geddes, according to the *New York Times,* "searched into nooks and crannies with as many questions and as much perseverance as a customs inspector going through luggage." To the *New York Times* correspondent, Geddes was a "tall envoy with [an] impassive face," but the ambassador came away from the tour of Ellis Island with very definite impressions, most of them unfavorable.[24]

First of all, Geddes was struck by the inefficient arrangement of the buildings. The ground floor of the immigration station had much space which was practically useless because of inadequate ventilation. Even more illogical was the arrangement of the toilets which were located directly adjacent to the sleeping and living rooms. Geddes found this "an inevitably unpleasant arrangement, especially in view of the fact that many, perhaps a majority of the immigrants, are unfamiliar with the pattern of conveniences in use in North America. Some of the immigrants are, I was told by the Secretary of Labor, apt to mistake the sanitary hoppers for drinking troughs, and the floor or some drainage channel in it, for a latrine pit." Moreover, it was evident that the maintenance of the facility had been neglected for years as the paint and the roof had fallen into disrepair.

Under the circumstances, Geddes conceded that maintaining

22. *Parliamentary Debates: House of Commons,* Fifth series, vol. 159, 1728–1729 (December 6, 1922).
23. *New York Times,* December 17, 1922.
24. Ibid., December 29, 1922.

"cleanliness" was a monumental challenge. In many of the corners Geddes observed the presence of "impacted greasy dirt." This problem was apparently attributable to the method of cleaning the floors and walls with long-handled mops and cold water. In Geddes' judgment, "nothing but hot water, strong soda and soap freely and frequently applied with a scrub brush" would dislodge the chronic dirt and offensive odor of the place. Cleanliness was also a problem in the sleeping quarters, which consisted of double-

A government inspector searches immigrant baggage for typhus. The Literary Digest, *August 4, 1923.*

Welfare workers teaching cleanliness and child care at Ellis Island. The Literary Digest, *September 1, 1923.*

decked bunks enclosed by wire "cages" with locked doors. Because of the crush of humanity, neither the canvas cots nor the blankets were cleaned between uses. Imagining himself in the position of an immigrant, Geddes dreaded the thought of occupying the lower berth "when ill-luck places a brutalized sort of creature in the berth above. The Secretary of Labour informed me that cases have been known where the different calls made by nature on the upper berthholder are responded to without his or her rising from the 'bed.'" While such cases were not numerous on a percentage basis, Geddes personally felt he would prefer detention at Sing Sing to Ellis Island.

As a physician and former Director of Recruiting, Geddes paid particular attention to the facilities and procedures provided for the mandatory medical examination. Noting that he had observed many medical boards in Britain during World War I, many of which labored in conditions that were "far from perfect," Geddes reported that he had never seen any British examining board "quite so badly accommodated" as those on Ellis Island. No separate dressing rooms were provided. Instead, observed the ambassador, the men stripped to their trousers jammed between coat-racks, piling their clothes on the racks, "higgledy-piggledy—the clean clothes of the washed on the foul clothes of the unwashed. Personally I thought it disgusting for the washed." Then came the most unpleasant part of the experience:

> The line of male immigrants approached the first medical officer with their trousers open. The doctor examined their external genitals for signs of venereal infection. Next he examined the inguinal canals for hernia. The doctor wore rubber gloves. I saw him "do" nine or ten men. His gloves were not cleaned between cases. I saw one nice, clean-looking Irish boy examined immediately after a very unpleasant looking individual who, I understood, came from some Eastern European district. I saw the boy shudder. I did not wonder. The doctor's rubber gloves were with hardly a second's interval in contact with his private parts after having been soiled, in the surgical sense at least, by contact with those of the unpleasant looking individual.

From a purely professional point of view, Geddes conceded, the medical examinations were "thorough and effective." But from the perspective of a "sensitive immigrant" the experience must have been "distinctly unpleasant."

Finally, Geddes was highly critical of the procedure devised for housing immigrants who were temporarily detained—those who were stowaways, awaiting diagnosis of tuberculosis, or ordered deported for illiteracy, violations of the contract labor clause, or because they were over their nation's quota. Many of the detained had been rejected for admission by one of the appeal boards at Ellis Island, several of which were observed in session by Geddes. The proceedings appeared "decorous and seemly," but in practice the system was "nothing short of diabolic." Every immigrant rejected had the right to appeal to the Secretary of Labor in Washington, but since days and weeks could elapse before a final decision was reached, the mental anguish was frequently excruciating. In Geddes' judgment, the only logical solution was to delegate the appeal decision to an official on the spot so that the process could be expedited in no more than twenty-four hours. Finally, Geddes objected to the "quaint custom" whereby "well meaning, kindly people, with heads softer even than their hearts," entertained the deportees with "Americanisation" addresses and films. "The purpose of these," he related, "is to tell immigrants how great a country America is and to make them good citizens. A 'Red' under sentence of deportation has possibly views of his own on the subject of the United States. So, too, possibly have those who are to be deported because they are in excess of their national quota."

In Geddes' opinion, "the very heart of the tragedy of Ellis Island is in the room of the temporarily detained."

Nevertheless, Geddes did observe a few bright spots during his visit. Commissioner Robert Tod impressed Geddes as humane, energetic, and kindly. "Any country might be proud to point to him as one of its officials," noted the ambassador. Tod's staff also appeared to Geddes as "suitable and efficient." And he was impressed with the "good quality and well cooked" food served in the dining room. Geddes personally saw the dinner served and pronounced the meal to be "excellent." But the ambassador felt that the "tablemanners" of the guests, who used the floor "as a universal slop bowl and refuse can" constituted an aesthetic drawback. Also receiving favorable comment was the efficient system established for arranging the railroad transportation of the immigrants to their destinations. He observed baggage being "skillfully and expeditiously handled," and the immigrants were able to purchase "at surprisingly low cost" excellent food for the journey which would take them away from Ellis Island forever. "All the arrangements for handling admitted immigrants are efficient and reflect high credit on those concerned. They are, in fact," he concluded, "a very good example of American business administration." Finally, a brief examination of the hospital arrangements left the impression that these facilities were at least adequate if in need of new paint and minor repairs.

Before his visit to Ellis Island, Geddes had advocated the segregation of immigrants according to their country of origin. But afterwards, he concluded that such an idea was actually impractical. First of all, the flow of immigrants from each country was too irregular. And, Geddes saw that the sheer volume of immigrants made separation according to nationality unworkable. "As a matter of fact," he reported, "what Ellis Island needs, in my judgement is to be relieved of the presence of about one-half of the people who are poured into it." Concerning the future of Ellis Island three alternatives were open to the United States. The "line of least resistance" was to maintain the existing facility with a few minor repairs and improvements. Another possibility was to develop a procedure either at Ellis Island or elsewhere for separating the stream of immigrants "into its Jewish and non-Jewish parts." Geddes stressed that his suggestion was advanced without animus toward Jewish immigrants, but as a practical method of lessening Ellis Island's chronic congestion. Since segregation by nationality was unworkable, Geddes felt that separation on the basis of food might be a workable alternative. The final option, and the one preferred by the ambassador, was "to abandon Ellis Island and build a completely new station somewhere else in New York Harbour or on its shores."

Nevertheless, as a practical man, Geddes saw that even under the best of circumstances Ellis Island would have to be continued for some time to come. Therefore, he recommended that the existing facility be thoroughly repainted and thoroughly cleaned. At the same time he would alter the toilet facilities, improve the ventilation, expedite the handling of immigrant appeals, and establish a new facility for Jewish immigrants ("or alternately, let Ellis Island be the 'kosher' station and provide a new station for the rest.") Geddes also sensibly recommended that a system be devised under which immigrants would be finally approved or disapproved for admission to the United States by American consuls in Europe thus eliminating the "tragedy and hardship" of possible rejection by the inspectors at Ellis Island. "In conclusion," observed Geddes, "I noticed a desire upon the part of officials to say that Ellis Island is as good as any immigration station in any land. It may be. Still, it is quite certain that no other nation's principal immigration station has the same problem to solve for the reason that the laws of the United States are not the same as those of any other nation."[25]

For half a year the existence of this thoughtful report remained unknown to the general public. However, in the latter part of June, 1923, in answer to a parliamentary question, Ronald McNeill, the Under-Secretary of State for Foreign Affairs, alluded to Geddes' visit and report. Responding to questions about the number of Englishmen "incarcerated" in "cages" at Ellis Island, McNeill disclosed that Geddes had made an inspection and communicated his findings to the State Department.[26] Following press reports that fifty English citizens had been deported for being in excess of the English quota and after further hostile parliamentary questions, it was decided to make the report public as a Parliamentary White Paper. A brief newspaper controversy then ensued in which a hostile American press attacked Geddes for having unjustly depicted Ellis Island as a "modern Black Hole of Calcutta."[27] But the furor proved short-lived largely because the American press was

25. Geddes to Curzon, January 18, 1923, *Parliamentary Paper* (1923, XXV, Cmd. 1940), 1–12.

26. *Parliamentary Debates: House of Commons,* Fifth series, vol. 165, 1400–1401 (June 20, 1923).

27. *New York Times,* August 16, 1923; *Literary Digest,* 78 (September 1, 1923), 17–19, and 78.

fundamentally less concerned with reforming Ellis Island than with speculating about the policies and personality of President Calvin Coolidge, who had taken office only two weeks before, following the death of Warren G. Harding. Furthermore, Geddes was absent from Washington while undergoing eye surgery in London and was therefore unavailable for any comment upon his controversial report. Unfortunately, the attempt to reattach Geddes' retina through electrical cautery failed when his surgeon slipped and by accident burned a hole in the ambassador's eyeball permitting a portion of the vitreous humor to slide down his cheek.[28]

Probably Geddes' report did more good than harm as several of his suggestions ultimately bore fruit. Commissioner Henry H. Curran, who replaced Robert E. Tod in the summer of 1923, promptly mounted a campaign for the modernization of the Ellis Island facilities. No doubt the Geddes report, which Curran had denounced as "grossly misleading," was helpful in prying a $326,000 appropriation from the Coolidge administration.[29] But the replacement of Ellis Island, as Geddes had recommended, was never a serious possibility. Faced with a choice between building expensive new facilities or reducing immigration through more restrictive quotas, Congress was inclined to follow what Geddes termed the "line of least resistance."

In its handling of the matter the Foreign Office was almost as coldly realistic as the Harding and Coolidge administrations. At the same time that Curzon and Geddes were denouncing Ellis Island as a "bear garden," care was taken to ensure that the controversy was handled discreetly so as not to interfere with Anglo-American negotiations in more vital fields such as naval disarmament and the settlement of Britain's war debt to the United States. Nevertheless, the repeated British diplomatic protests and the occasional visits to Ellis Island were no doubt a factor influencing the Harding and Coolidge administrations to make modest improvements in the physical condition of the facility. Had Sir Auckland Geddes toured Ellis Island in July, 1921, instead of a year and a half later he would have witnessed an even more distressing situation. By 1924 the controversy all but ended with the passage of more restrictive quotas. The new law also adopted Geddes' recommendation that immigrants be examined at American consular offices in Europe rather than at Ellis Island. Consuls were to fill the

28. Geddes, *Forging a Family,* 333.
29. *New York Times,* August 17, 1923; Pitkin, *Keepers of the Gate,* 153.

quotas slowly so as to ensure an orderly flow of immigrants and thereby eliminate the need to detain immigrants who were in excess of their nation's quota.[30]

To record that the two governments moved efficiently and humanely to resolve the Ellis Island dilemma would be satisfying but inaccurate. In reality, most of the improvements in facilities and procedures were undertaken grudgingly only after repeated protests or after Congress had in 1924 substantially reduced the flow of immigrants. Between American procrastination and administrative bungling, the greed of British shipping companies, and the desire of both governments to assign the dispute a relatively low priority, it is hardly to be wondered that the immigrant was often caught in the middle.

30. Pitkin, *Keepers of the Gate*, 154.

Anna

By CHRISTINA S. GODSHALK

Christina Godshalk presents a memoir of her mother, Anna, in her own words and in Anna's, as recorded by tape and memory. Their words touch upon several generations of an American family. Mrs. Godshalk is a writer who lives in Dover, Massachusetts. Anna Carcich Soccolich now lives in Huntington, New York.

ANNA

On an early October afternoon, looking out on a freak snow storm, on still-green leaves cupped with the heavy snow that is ruining our hike and picnic with the children, I find I am listening, truly listening for the first time, to stories half-heard all my life, stories told to me so many, many times by my mother, of her life as a child. She stands next to me now, wearing my green and white striped apron, watching through the glass. Why, after thirty-seven years of blocking out the known, the mundane, the stories hackneyed the first time they were uttered because they were "family" stories, not new, not bright, not better, do I now suddenly hear her. Perhaps the freak snow has fractured some tiny dam in my auditory canal. For today I hear her like a bell.

Are they maudlin, these remembrances of hers? Is the tragedy laughable? "The string of villains," "the strength of youth" seem to ripple by on matinee organ music. But truth has no style, no balance, no credibility. It never did.

They are haphazard, these memories, they skitter, they drift into nothing, then reappear brilliantly in some dark corner. The snow. What was the snow like? The flivvers would cross the frozen Hudson in winter, in steamy puffs. My mother would cross it, too, on foot, muffled up tight, a baked potato in each pocket, going to school.

I have slipped her words into their chronological slots and they sit in these boxes laughing at me. But so be it, they are corralled. For what? I don't know. I like to hear them, I guess, now that I am not young, and not old. I will read them someday to the small head on which my mother now rams a hat. But it's not important. It's not important if they are locked in a box or float down a river to shred and melt. Things happen in a certain way, and the story is told, and heard. Once, maybe, is enough.

Now, half way through my life with my own children, my own husband, my own home, my own education, my own tastes, my own beauty—mine—all of it, I can somehow open doors, doors on that person, that awkward girl in white with all the roses, that woman with peppery hair in the starched house dress, that beauty in muted red velvet in the luminous phototype, my mother. The angry, loving, frightening, comforting individual I am introducing myself to for the first time.

PAPA

For my mother, things, life, began with her Papa. She speaks of him as a child speaks, with the overwhelming love and awe of a small daughter. There are no pictures of my grandfather as an old man, or even in middle age. He did not live to be an old man, and in middle age I suppose he had no time for photographs. All my mother has is a picture of a very young man, perhaps twenty-five, with carefully parted blonde hair and crystal colored eyes, almost a dandy. I look at this picture and think I would not have liked him then. "Who was he?" I ask my mother. "Why did he come to New York from so far away?" "What did he do with his youth?" She knows very little of her Papa as a young man. He came as an immigrant, but not as the immigrant comes, for something better, for something to build. He came, she says, "to visit." "To see what it was like." And to fish. He liked very much to fish, and would go, obviously, great distances to try a new place. He did not intend to stay. In fact, he didn't. After a few years doing no one remembers what, he went back to Europe, again to fish in his old favorite places. He told her he had a little boat and a little dog. For the man in the photo, resplendent in boiled collared perfection, the picture was incongruous. Dominic Carcich was in fact, not one, but two men. And he remained this way all his life. He came from one of those islands, strung out along the Yugoslav coast in the Adriatic Sea. Small, jagged protuberances in eye view of their sisters, each holding her children close, suspecting all the other little islands of inferiority, of treachery. They are immensely beautiful, and so are the people when they are young, looking more than anything else like lean, handsome birds of prey. But they have that disconcerting

*Elvera (left) and Anna—a First Communion photograph. Courtesy of
Christina S. Godshalk.*

habit common among Eastern Europeans of skipping the middle
part of their lives. They are children one day, ripe and clear-eyed,
and the next they are old, black clad sticks bent against the wind. It
is like that.

  These people are jacks-of-all-trade as only poor island people
can be. Farmers, herdsmen, weavers, wine makers, and most of
all, and best of all, seamen. These islands lie where blood mixed
freely over the centuries, through sea commerce, through invasion.
A new flag flew over my grandfather's head every three years of his
youth. It may have lent him that strangely cosmopolitan air they say

he had, the jauntiness that put off and at the same time attracted his friends. The lesson of the child was adaptability. Sail when the wind was favorable, speak the language of the highest flag on the pole. In middle age my grandfather returned to New York, to begin and to end the life my mother remembers.

First this was in the city itself, the impoverished, fecund New York of the immigrant. Later, joining the mass exodus of consumptives to clear, high country places, it was the Hudson Valley. In New York it was the era of great banquets in public places. My grandfather worked as silver steward at the Waldorf, and the shimmering fantasy of those grand rooms, the spit and polish, suited him well. Later, he left his heavy plate, his epergnes, his candelabras; he left Sara Bernhardt in the green room and Queen Marie of Rumania at lunch; and he went to milk cows and grow vegetables on another man's land. He did this for a dark-haired, consumptive girl named Angela, my grandmother. And he did it well and uncomplainingly, as an island man can turn his hand and heart to a different thing and not look back.

Dominic Carcich was forty when he married. He loved his family deeply, as a man who marries late often does, and he cherished his young wife, perhaps to his own extinction. And yet this same man, they say, walked away from a ship that carried a girl, another girl, over half the world to join him. He had seen her through the crowd at dockside, and had changed his mind. He simply walked away.

"At any rate," my mother says, smiling at a face I cannot see, "he was a striking man. Quiet but quick tempered, with a peculiar sense of the comedic in life." Lastly, and for his small daughter the best, he told stories. Not lies, "stories." It is an art that no longer exists, except perhaps in uneducated backwaters in the land, but to hear it practiced by one gifted in the medium is a rare experience. In those days, fame for it soon spread through the tenements of the city, the gifted one was sought after, was looked upon as a cool draught after a week's labor in hell. Small children were sent to fetch him in the evening; cakes were set out. "The story teller"— my grandfather was one of these.

"When Papa died," my mother says, gazing at the white shifting world outside, "strangers would say, 'Welcome to my house. Your father was a friend of mine and a good man.'" "But it was his fault," she adds with strange bitterness. "It was too much, too much. Seven children in so little time. Mama was so frail and quiet. Like a wren. She was like a little wren." And my mother's mind has now switched, as it always does, to the true center of her childhood universe, a center dissolving too soon, and therefore missed forever.

MAMA

"She was supposed to come on the Titanic," my mother says, frenching beans in a shaft of sunlight. "It had been overbooked and at the last minute she had to take another boat. She told us of passing the area where the liner went down, and of the wailing of her ship's whistles, like a great animal lamenting, and the quiet weeping all around her. It was a memory that stayed with her all her life." Angela Piljurovich, a slender, quiet girl with a cloud of black hair, came to New York in 1912 to stay with her married sister in a tenement walk-up. "She hated it," my mother says, plunging the beans under cold water. "She didn't want to stay, and she didn't know how to go back. She came from Dubrovnik, and she would often tell us about it, a lovely city of white walls and blue water and palm trees, although I never believed her about the palm trees. Fifty years later I saw them for myself, and I remembered how she always told me the truth."

My grandmother's sister in New York was named Elena, and she was said to be beautiful with auburn hair. There were four sisters in all: Angela, Elena, Christina, who married an Italian coffee planter in South America, and Saveta, who never married. There were also two brothers, Luca and Todor, great giants with black hair who took after their mother in size but not in temperament. Of this woman, my great grandmother, not much is remembered, or at least not much is said. There is a photo somewhere of a ramrod straight woman with a great yellow dog at her feet, hair drawn back tightly, the fierce eyes of a survivor. When this woman materialized in their conversations, the faces of her children would go blank, registering nothing. She died at ninety-five, long after the last of her children was dead. Her husband, my great grandfather, is remembered just as scantily but in another way. "A little man with curly hair," they said, "powerfully built, chopping wood in winter and coming into his house with pains in his chest, dying young. A wonderful little man."

When Angela was twenty-eight, six months after she arrived in New York, not able to speak English, not able to find work, not belonging in the small rooms of her married sister, she met my grandfather. By then he was forty, still handsome, "never without work," as his friends would say afterwards, "and never with a nickel in his pocket," meticulous in dress, merry-eyed. They were a strange, unlikely combination, the handsome, light figure of a man who even at forty would never quite grow up, and the dark, frail column of womanhood who must have been ancient as a child. She never changed, but he did. He put himself, his bachelor needs, his aspirations, his elite aloneness, into a drawer and simply never opened it again. He saved money. He loved her.

Anna, my mother, was their first child. She was born in 1914 on East Fifty-seventh Street in an area of Manhattan still known as Yorkville. Six more babies followed in close succession: Mary, Philip, Charlie, Elvera, Victor, and the last, a long-legged, curly-haired bud of a child that was never to open.

"Yorkville," my mother says, "was very nice then. It was a German area. We lived near the Paulist Fathers' church.[1] Later we moved to Forty-fifth street and this wasn't as nice, but it was closer to our people."

This was so important, to be close to one's people. I try to imagine why, why these enclaves of special dialects and foods and smells and songs and superstitions and ways to tell a story, and ways to love, and to honor, and to dishonor, were so important. I try to compare it to me and my young family living as we did recently in an Asian city, hooking up with western friends, clubs, shops, cultural activities, but it doesn't stand comparison. For us finding other Americans, plugging into "Americanisms," was a convenience, a respite from a foreign city in which we had enough knowledge and money to move freely. For them, this folding in among one's own, was more. Much more. A bulwark against the unknown, the enemy, to be thus enfolded among one's own.

"There were many Yugoslavs in the Forty-fifth street area," my mother continues, "although they didn't call us Yugoslavs then. It was only after the war that there even was a Yugoslavia. Our people were all born under the Emperor of Austria, and technically were Austrian immigrants."

Immigrant New York was a patchwork of clear, bright colors pushed up against the two rivers. People took pride in their

---

1. Yorkville extends roughly from East 59th Street to East 96th Street. The Church of St. Paul the Apostle is actually west of Broadway on 60th Street. See *New York City Guide*. American Guide Series. (New York, 1939), 243, 281.

"place." You lived as close to where you came from as possible, and your people took care of their own. Nobody was on welfare; there was no welfare. The smells, the textures, the drawing together were, despite the poverty, nourishing and safe. My mother does not say this, she only says that it was nice, that I may be surprised, but it was.

"I don't remember everything," she says, and there is a round sadness in the sound. "I was thirteen when it all ended, and a child doesn't remember everything." Bits and pieces, like colored shards, gleaming here and there over so many years. This is what she has.

"Mama was a very quiet woman," my mother says, "she simply didn't say much. Her family was everything in the world to her, and she was always careful that we were safe and didn't cause trouble, as if her life and ours was one long probation. I don't know why, but it was this way with her. My clearest memory of Mama comes always at Christmas. It must be like this for other children left alone. She would take me, only me, with her on Christmas Eve and leave all the smaller children home with Papa. We'd go early in the morning. I can see myself walking down the street with her, she always held my hand tightly. She had her big, cloth shopping bag; it was almost as long as me. And we'd head down to Paddy's Market in that cold morning air. It was the grandest thing in the world, to shop with her like that on Christmas Eve. Paddy's Market was a huge, open air market.[2] You could buy anything you wanted, everything was fresh, and for the least amount of money anywhere, and you could pick it out yourself. Mama would never buy from the first stall, she would always walk to the very end and then back, only then deciding where to buy. Everything was so fresh. The fragrance coming out of our bags on the way back, mixed with pine from the last-minute tree dragging behind, was so heady you could walk on it! 'I spent too much, I spent too much,' she would say, and I waited for this, too; it was part of the magic. Her bag was filled with ingredients for 'fritta' and for the special cakes. One was a sweet bread that I have seen in dreams all my life. It was very, very high and bright yellow. Mama would fill it with candied citrus, huge sultanas, Papa's thick smooth apricot brandy, pounds of butter and eggs. It shook gently when it was finished and it's aroma

2. Paddy's Market was a pushcart market located for about fifty years at Ninth Avenue between 39th and 42nd Streets. The pushcart merchants were evicted in 1938 when the construction of the Lincoln Tunnel increased traffic in the area. *New York City Guide*, 157–58.

has lasted in my memory, my 'nose' memory, for fifty years. Of course, to be made something special to eat by someone who loves you is the ultimate joy of small children, and I guess the very old, and perhaps idiots.

"Mama had been cook to a sea captain in Dubrovnik and she said his wife had taught her to make this cake. Do you know," my mother says, her eyes glistening as she checks the frozen window for my small daughter's sled, "my father made it for us when we were alone in New York, just little Victor and me after she had died. I said, 'Papa, you know, for Christmas.' And he said, 'Don't worry. I'll make it.' And he did. He was a wonderful cook just like Mama, and he made this cake appear again. My memory of those times is a child's memory, not of things, but of tastes and smells and how things felt. Maybe that's why they have lasted. Even in the streets, it is the wonderful velvet taste of sweet potatoes, stolen and baked by street children, not 'starving' children, but somehow 'always hungry' children—baked in small fires by the Hudson docks. 'We'll tell! We'll tell!' we shouted, 'Give us some or we'll tell!' And one of these children would break off the front or back of his steaming orange boat and hand it to us. It tasted good on a cold day. There was the salty, sweet fragrance of the prosciutto I would buy for the longshoremen, 'our people,' courteous, rough men with bad English who would ask a small child, 'If you please Anna, buy me a little prosciutto with this.' And I would bring back the thin delicate pink sheets wrapped in waxed paper, like the inside of shells. These things are clear for me. Other things, 'great events,' are not.

"Papa loved us with the love of a man who has started a family late in life, a life devoted until that time to himself. Instead of the last encumbrance, we were for him 'the saving grace.' He worked very, very hard for us."

"What," I ask her, "did he do? What kind of work did your Papa do?" And my mother reaches back in silence. "Papa's work." What does a small child remember of her father's work? "He worked in a very long coat, to his ankles, in a room filled with glittering things," and she is reading it off from a thin fragile page in her head. "Once Mama was very sick. It was morning, and I went to find him to bring him home." She had walked across New York, a nine-year-old, counting the street signs in panic, crossing the great city that morning in June, walking, half running, crying, to find her father, the silver steward at the Waldorf. "She was of course not dying," my mother smiles, "she was having a baby."

"Papa would tell us stories of the Waldorf. I think I imagined it as a great palace at the far end of the city, cold and sparkling, where people glided on little wheels, under fur and jewels, and ate strange wonderful foods in the middle of the night."

In reality, it was close to the truth. A place of endless banquets in pastel rooms, each with its own appointed cache of silver and gilt, matching candelabras, epergnes, and livery. Where Queen Marie of Rumania sipped asparagus soup at two o'clock. And all was supervised by the stern presence of "Oscar." "Oscar of the Waldorf, cook to kings."

"'You know something,' Papa would bend down, his eyes dancing, 'there is no Oscar! Only a lot of little Oscars, all running around doing his work. A sip here, a sip there, but he can't boil an egg! Oscar of the Waldorf, pah!' This was probably untrue, but it made us laugh wildly.

"Papa was a superb cook himself, and his wines were even better. Rich deep burgundies, fruit brandies, and the best, a fragrant baked wine. Upstate, it was dandelion wine, pale golden and delicate; we children didn't like this wine because we picked endlessly for something we couldn't drink. He made a silky brandy from apricots and one from Dalmatian cherries that left a dull flame on the tongue. It was Prohibition then. In New York he kept a little copper still and Mama stored the big yellow and tan demijohns under their bed. She was so frightened that someone might find out, she made sure to lock all the doors before he started. And my sister Mary with her mass of brown curls and mischievous turn of mind, would stand in the middle of the small tenement kitchen and shout at the top of her lungs, 'My Mama makes whiskey and wine! My Mama makes whiskey and wine!' loud enough to be heard in New Jersey and driving poor Mama to distraction. We children would watch in wonder as Papa fiddled with the fragile copper wires. If it leaked a bit, he would melt Octagon soap and wrap it around the pipes. The liquor would drip slowly down a little cloth into a container. Then he would test the proof, lighting a match and somehow measuring it with a thermometer. It meant nothing to us really, and yet everything because it was Papa's magic. After he died, someone came and quietly took the little copper still.

"When Mama began to be sick in New York, Papa would give her doctor, Dr. Prentice, a glass of his wine each time he came. In those days they were not the way they are now; in those days the doctor was your friend and you offered him hospitality. Dr. Prentice would hold up the ruby glass and say 'Dominic, if this is what you make, you can tear up that prescription. This is a wonderful tonic for someone who will not eat.'

"Papa would take me with him when it was time to go down to Canal Street and select barrels. They were special oak barrels, and he would knock them and roll them around and steer them into the light, to get perfect ones for his wine. He would never go off without at least one of us, no matter where he was going.

"Because he was a hotel man, Papa always had one day off in the middle of the week to make up for the Saturday or Sunday when he worked. On that day he took all the children to Central Park. We were all scrubbed and marshalled into line and walked happily into that green world with a carousel at its center. Somewhere along the way we got ice cream. All the children were given two-cent cones, but I was the oldest, and mine was three cents. On our way home Papa would stop at a big store on Ninth Avenue and buy jelly. Yes, the kind you spread on toast. It was loose like soft cut rubies, and they would dish it out into a wax-coated container. Papa would buy one pound. In those days most things were sold 'loose' and it was nice, for you could take as much or as little as you liked or you could afford. And of course you saw what you were buying. Food stores were filled with odors and fragrances and tastes; they were rich, pleasurable little rooms—more than now." "Now," my mother says vehemently, "entire food stores are wrapped behind plastic and cellophane or worse, 'frozen'—you might as well be buying paper or nails for all it matters. Of course, then it wasn't sanitary. But sanitation, like some other American virtues, can be overrated!

"Milk was like this, too. Mama would give me the dipper and a pail and send me for ten cents of milk. The stores had big cans, people fill them with flowers now, but then they were full of milk. Later they had milk bottles. I remember once collecting a bunch of those bottles, I was six years old, and two older girls told me to get a deposit for them at the local saloon. They pushed me through those swinging doors with all these bottles and I walked up to the bar and said, 'I want a deposit!' and the bartender looked over the bar and said, 'How would you like to be arrested?' Boy, those bottles crashed and did I fly out that door! Mama had driven it into all our heads that we mustn't make trouble. This was her only true obsession. And of course there was one of us, there always is one child, who recognized this fear in Mama, who teased her merrily with it, and sometimes used it as a weapon. Mary, my young sister with the halo of ringlets, standing in the kitchen shouting 'My

Mama makes whiskey and wine!' Mary handing the old Italian iceman a button instead of money and running madly down the street with her lemon ice. Mary, leaping upstairs, the old man in hot pursuit, calling to him over the landing, and when he looked up—dropping the ice on his nose. Mama suspected the bright, mischievous nature of this child would develop into a merry, madcap disposition. It didn't.

"Mama always worried. Once, at Halloween, someone put a sign on our door saying we must stay out of the house or something terrible would happen. That evening, Papa found us all outside when he came home, gathered around Mama in the cold, waiting for him. She of course did not believe in hobgoblins or ghosts, but she was afraid of strangers, of their pranks, of the pain they might cause her children. 'You are such a fool,' he said, putting his arm around her, and she said nothing. My brothers would try her sorely when they became a bit older. Upstate once I watched transfixed as she tried to beat fire out of a field with wet blankets, her skirts licked by the glow as she twisted and bent. They had set it accidentally and had run away. She would never touch them, but Papa certainly did. He'd come home from work and Mama would have some quiet things to tell him. And Papa would go to punish the boys and Mama would get in between. 'I shouldn't hit them, I should hit you!' he'd shout at her furiously. But he loved this in her, too. We feared him as children, and we loved him to distraction. I don't know why except perhaps that he didn't treat us like children, but more like small people, worthy of respect—and with funny bones that had to be tickled regularly for health's sake. He'd stretch himself on the floor and we'd walk all over him, and he'd tell us the most amazing stories. Stories of hunchbacks and people carrying statues of Christ across the sea and big storms coming up, and there was always laughter weaving in and out, and it was heavenly. One child, my brother Philip, has this gift, and it has saved him many times and marked a sad life happy in the summing up. To be a story-teller in ethnic New York was to have identity and respect. People would politely come to our little apartment to listen to him in the evening. And courteous invitations would come by word of mouth from a child to go and tell stories, and he would sometimes take us with him.

"There were three other men in my childhood. And still, though I am looking back through so many years, I see them as they were for me then, not men but three great bears, friendly and gruff and warm: my uncles Luca and Todor, and my Mama's cousin Dushon. All were over six feet, and all had jet black hair. Uncle Luca worked at a granary, a huge place owned by the New York Central Railroad on the west side of the city by the Hudson. Most people do not believe there was such a place in the city, but there was. Todor was kind and silent and the most bear-like. Dushon was the closest and dearest to us all. I believe he was a communist and, at eight years of age, I thought this was probably very special. He drove one of the electric trucks for Horn & Hardart. He had a uniform with nice leather leggings, and a matching hat. He used to bring us the grandest pies each time he came. He often came for Mama to write his letters. She could write the 'cyrillitza' for him, the Cyrillic letters. She was one of the few people then who could write in both ways. He was very fond of Mama; they had grown up together as children in Europe. When we moved upstate, Uncle Dushon would spend his vacations with us at the farm. He would get up early on those mornings and say to Mama, 'Nothing to eat but milk and eggs. Fresh from the land!' and then he'd go outside and put his huge fists on his chest and bellow, 'Ah, fresca aria!' with all my little brothers behind him beating their small chests and giggling wildly. At Christmas, a five-pound box of Schrafft's chocolates would appear on the kitchen table, always we knew—from Dushon. After a long while, he met a Russian lady named Maria and they married. They had one daughter and I've often thought she must have been a happy little girl with such a father.

"For Mama, though, Papa was the world. When he was late from work she would make us all sit quietly and pray for him to come home safely. The city was an alien world for her in an alien universe, and she sat as so many other immigrant women must have sat innumerable times, waiting and hoping in fear for the city to send a loved one back unscathed. There was one evening, an evening I will never forget, when Papa didn't come home. Mama paced and paced and then finally said in her quiet way, 'Your Papa is a good man, he works hard, we don't want to lose him.' Very late that night, we finally heard his step on the stairway. He had emerged from the Waldorf Hotel after work and dropped into a roiling mass of hysterical people. He found quickly that to survive he must go, without fighting, whichever way the crowd was shifting. 'The world,' he said, 'was in the streets, laughing and crying.' Armistice had been declared and World War I was over. A friend of mine said she worked for Bonwit Tellers on that day and all the salesgirls swept into the street when they heard the news and they had to hurriedly lock the store for no one was left. All the ships in the harbor were blowing their whistles and sirens and church bells were ringing madly, everything that could make a sound was going full blast and I remember putting my hands over my ears and crying 'If this doesn't stop, I'll go mad Mama!' and Mama saying 'Don't say that Anna, this is the happiest day, the happiest day!' And then, of course, Papa didn't come home. People were wild, they didn't care about anything, there was such joy."

And listening to her, I find my own mind slips back to memories of another armistice, another peace, another day of wild cacophony, of sitting on a fire escape with my own mother, a black frying pan and spoon in my hands, banging them and laughing—for then it was the second great war that had run out of steam. In my mother's face I can see that she too has skipped to this time, something we've often been able to do in tandem. "I hope," I say, "there's not another one. There won't be any pots left to bang."

Soon after the Armistice, the soldiers began returning through New York in great numbers, and with them something called the Spanish flu. In one year, 1918, the city soared through days of joyous elation and then plunged into bitter despair.

"It killed and killed and killed," my mother says simply. "There was no medication for it, no penicillin for the pneumonia which so often followed. They would nail a wreathe on the door of an apartment house when somebody died inside. They were circles of fresh flowers intertwined with black artificial leaves. I remember absently counting them as a child, one on top of another, on the doors. In the streets, black funeral carriages drawn by horses would go by endlessly, sometimes plumed in black. It raged in the city for so long, and as children will, we learned to accept it and worked it into our child's daily pattern. Then one winter day I saw a dead horse on the side of Fifty-seventh Street. It was a big white horse. This wasn't unusual, they would sometimes die in the street and the public works or some department would carry them off. But on that day, with the snow falling on that great white flank, I said to myself as a child with a child's inner eye, 'Everything, everything in this city is dying.' Mama finally caught it, and when Dr. Prentice came to see her he put his hands on our heads and said, 'Poor children.' And my father took me into the little room where the children slept and he said 'I don't think Mama will be with us for very long.' She had a raging fever for days, and her lungs became badly infected. But she was a very slender person with a very strong heart, and she pulled through. It left her weak for the rest of her life. The three babies she had after that did the rest. She finally developed tuberculosis or 'consumption' as they used to call it. This, too, was everywhere. The only treatment was fresh air, and sanatoriums sprung up all over the country in cool, dry, elevated areas.

"The tiny tuberculosis bacillus threw a switch and as a family our life was never the same again. We were 'on the move,' joining the shifting consumptive masses of Americans seeking higher ground, cleaner, dryer air, most often in vain. First Papa took us all to New Jersey because he was told that it was a little more elevated, and the air was supposed to be better. But Mama wasn't any better. The words I used to hear spoken in the kitchen after we children were put to sleep—plans for a little store, a little business, a shiny bright nugget of hope they took out and held to the light when we were asleep—were heard no more. When someone was ill in those days, the money just went."

My mother doesn't remember the details, but somehow, somewhere my grandfather learned of the Hudson Valley, not down where the river disappeared into the ooze and muck of the great city and harbor at its feet, but farther up, cutting through green hills in a clear pure swath. Up where it had, according to a Protestant clergyman two centuries earlier, "a climate of a sweet and wholesome breath." He decided this was the place for my grandmother. He left his silver stewardship in the great hotel in the great city, he placed his boiled collars and his three-piece suits in a trunk, closed the lid, and turned his mind to different work. To work as a farmhand, a handyman, milker, gardener, switchman, all the things he had spent his life getting away from.

This move seems as clear and fresh to my mother now as if she had just brushed the train dust from her small brown coat. "First Mama, Papa and I traveled up and found a small clean house to rent in one of the pretty valley towns. We left my younger brothers and sisters behind in the care of 'our people' until Mama felt stronger. 'Your Mama needs rest,' Dr. Prentice said, 'and packing up six children and taking them all up there in one fell swoop is not the way to get it!' Later, one by one, they came to join us.

"This was the beginning of the second part of my childhood, the best part, the 'country' part. It was filled with the most beauty and love it could hold, and also with sorrow—of a kind that even now, as an old woman, I cannot bear to think on except lightly, on the wing."

THE HUDSON YEARS

"We left on a chill, colorless morning in early spring. Papa in the one boiled collar he had left out for the journey, our bags neatly strapped on either side of him, Mama's face a pale oval above her dark dress. I was eight years old, the eldest, and the only child allowed to go with them. The others were left behind with friends and cousins, the baby with an 'agency lady,' to follow when Mama was better.

"To leave that gray, sick city with the two best-loved human beings in my world was a very pleasant thing. I don't remember much about that day except the rush of colors from the train window. After awhile the gray softly muted to green, a timid gray-green at first, then a pale tender green, and finally, rushing north-ward along the river, a vibrant emerald blur of trees with water sparkling here and there through the new leaves. Mama unpacked ham sandwiches and the three of us ate in silence through that green vibrating world. Who would have imagined the flat, stale water separating our city blocks from the Jersey shore had flowed down from such loveliness. I wondered why we had waited so long to follow this river. I knew Mama would bloom up here! She would have a garden. We children would play in green fields and hear her voice coming over the air calling us home. It would be a new beginning, a wonderful new beginning for all of us. I remember thinking these things.

"We went to Germantown.[3] Papa found a little house to rent owned by a stout, friendly woman named Mrs. Lasher, and as soon as he settled Mama and me inside, he went to look for work. I looked for work too, and I found a job carrying milk at ten cents a bucket from Mrs. Lasher, who had a cow, to Mrs. Saulpaugh who did not. Mama shook her head and said, 'You'll wear out more in shoe leather than you'll ever earn,' but I did it anyway and she'd take me down to the general store to spend my 'pay.' I always bought the same two things—Teaberry gum and Delmonte canned pineapple. To me these were ambrosia—to this day I don't re-member ever enjoying the fruit of my labor so much.

"Papa did not find work. He finally moved us to Hudson where he did farm chores here and there. For the Orland T. Moores, the Spankenburgs, the Piries. Why do I persist in remembering these names!" my mother says in wonder, more to the bunch of zinnias

3. About ten miles south of Hudson in Columbia County.

she has crammed into my broken creamer than to me. "After so many years."

"After harvests were in that year, Papa found work as a switch-man for the New York Central Railroad at Linlithgo, a name which amused and exasperated him no end.[4] Then, one by one, the other children started to join us. Mary, darkly smiling in her too big coat, holding the small hand of Elvera—a pale little owl in gold-rimmed glasses. Victor standing fearfully in mismatched socks, tall quiet Philip, and finally the baby Charlie. Only after we were all gathered round her did Mama start to look better. In the country she had a Dr. McCormick to care for her, a bald-headed man and very kind. He would come to our house with his horse and buggy, and later, when we moved away to the farm that was really to be our Hudson Valley home, he came, to our great delight, sputtering up the road in a flivver.

"These were still hard times for Papa. He was good at patching enough jobs together to feed and shelter us all, it is an island man's area of expertise, but even at eight, I knew how difficult and demeaning it was for him. He asked endlessly here and there to be farm hand, milker, gardener, switchman, anything. It was good for Mama, this pure river country, and we would stay.

"Finally, after a year of moving over the countryside to follow bits of work, someone's suggestion, or a chance letter, I can't remember, drew Papa to the small Hudson town of Greendale—and us to the beginning of our true 'country life.'[5] On a clear spring morning we all rode up to a neat white house sitting above a small stream, a caretaker's house, one of several owned by Herman and Emmeline Livingston. It was here that the second half of my childhood, the good Hudson years, began. And it was this woman, Mrs. Livingston, who opened this new world to me with a loving hand, who made a child truly welcome. I came to dance on small feet down her polished halls, to walk with her under maple leaves to the ferry, to travel with her to Albany, to sip Spanish velvet in her kitchen, to love her, without ever knowing who she was until I was an old lady and she was long dead."

The Livingstons. It is worth knowing more of this old river family to understand the valley itelf, the world that my mother, the young child Anna, entered so happily. To an immigrant Yugoslav

4. Linlithgo is in the Town of Livingston, Columbia County.
5. Greendale was the unincorporated community located at the ferry landing on the east shore of the Hudson, opposite the village of Catskill. My thanks to historian Mabel Parker Smith for this information.

family, the Livingstons meant work, livelihood, fairness and kindness. No more nor less than this. But to the Hudson Valley, they were much more. They were there before anybody else and it seemed they'd be there long after everyone else had gone. My curiosity to know more about this family my mother 'chanced upon,' went beyond what a child could remember. It brought me, at my leisure, to books and historical treatises, and I read with fascination—to learn, in time, that the Livingstons dominated and profited by most of the history and growth of the Hudson valley. Yet to look on these lives as all greed and grasp is to miss the mark. Much of the progress and commercial expansion enjoyed by the valley was spawned and supported by Livingston wealth and planning. The great manor house sat there, swinging its weight at the right time and in the right direction through the young country's history—patriotic, beneficent, usurous, beauty-bestowing, ever turning a profit on commerce, politics, and labor, and always converting it to land.

The Livingstons of my mother's childhood, those resting atop these acquisitions, these seasoned traditions of a manor house, were good and kind and fair-minded people. Some would argue that they could afford to be at this stage of the game. But it was so nevertheless.

"A tall woman," my mother says of Emmeline Livingston, her eyes warming to an image I cannot see, "a big hat, long nose, high clipped voice, the kindest woman I ever met in my life. She wore beautiful oxfords that were sent from New York, she had them in several colors. Isn't it ridiculous to remember someone's shoes?" my mother laughs. "But children are close to the ground, I guess, they notice things like that. She was a Hopkins and her family lived across the river in Catskill. She took me there to meet them all.[6] We

6. Emmeline Cornell Hopkins (1869–1940) was probably descended from Caleb Hopkins, a New Englander who became a merchant in New York City and retired to Catskill, New York, in the 1860s. During the years that Anna describes, the family included Samuel and Charles Hopkins, both of whom attended Yale, as did Emmeline's husband, Herman, and his sons. Charles had no children. Samuel's sons sold the family's Catskill holdings and no member of the family lives in Catskill today. I am grateful to two generous and interested individuals who shared their knowledge of the Livingston and Hopkins families: Henry H. Livingston of New York City and Oak Hill, grandson of Emmeline and Herman Livingston, and Ruth Piwonka of Kinderhook, guest curator for the Friends of Clermont, who is at work on projects for the observance of the tercentenary of the founding of Livingston Manor. See also James D. Pinckney, *Reminiscences of Catskill: Local Sketches* (Catskill, 1868), 40; Clare Brandt and Arthur Kelly, *A Livingston Genealogy* (Rhinebeck, N.Y., 1982), D8, G21; Edwin Brockholst Livingston, *The Livingstons of Livingston Manor* (privately published, 1910), 484–87.

were friends, we two, I don't know why for I was only a child. But I was interested in everything, and she liked that. She was a lovely feminine being with three grown sons and no daughter.[7] Over the years I became her little companion, and afterwards, when it became time for us to leave, she asked Papa to let me stay with her.

"Her husband, Herman Livingston, Papa's employer, was a very stern man. He was vice president of the Sinclair Oil Company, I think, and he had a big tank on his land.[8] He was a direct descendant of Robert Livingston, a signer of the Declaration of Independence," my mother adds proudly. "His house stood on a hill over the river, it was old and cool and lovely.[9] He had about a dozen men to run the farm; there was a dairy barn, turkeys, and horses. Papa helped with all of these, and with gardening, too. When autumn came there was always less to do, so he would work again for the railroad, usually as a switchman, and then help with milking on weekends. He took pride in his work for the Livingstons. The only time I remember him unhappy with his work, sad and angry at the same time, was the day he had to help with Mr. Livingston's horse. It was a great spirited animal and apparently it threw Mr. Livingston hard. He called my father and another man, and he tied the horse with stakes and had him shot. It was wrong to begin with and it was done poorly, Papa said, so that the animal pulled up the stakes and ran and they shot and shot. He said Mr. Livingston's eyes were rimmed with red and terribly angry, and this was not good in a man.

"But it was a good place to be. Greendale is thirty-five miles from Albany," my mother explains, something she had to look up now to remember, but it doesn't matter. "The river is quite wide up there. I'd walk across in winter to go to school, and in summer we'd ride the ferry. The river was always there, quietly, in the middle of our lives. I think perhaps if you were born next to it, you would be haunted with a longing to have it near you all of your life.

7. The sons of Emmeline and Herman Livingston were Herman Livingston (b. 1883), Henry Hopkins Livingston (b. 1887), and Edmund Pendleton Livingston (b. 1889). For biographical sketches of the latter two, see *Columbia County in the World War* (Albany, 1924), 486–87.

8. Herman Livingston (1856–1936) was the son of Herman Thong Livingston and Susan Bard Rogers. He had a variety of financial interests but became involved in the Paramount Oil Company only at the urging of a local businessman in Columbia County. Paramount was a distributor of petroleum products in Dutchess and Columbia Counties. Its trucks did bear the statement, "Sinclair Oil," which would suggest to the young Anna that Herman's company was Sinclair. Mr. Livingston finally divested himself of Paramount in the 1930s.

9. The house, Oak Hill, was built in the 1790s by John Livingston, great-grandfather of the Herman Livingston whom Anna knew. See Livingston, *The Livingstons of Livingston Manor*, 485–87.

It was a living thing. Silent under snow, sometimes it whispered, and then in spring it groaned through its ice, and finally it gurgled like a baby all summer.

"There were other houses besides ours on the Livingston land," my mother continues, following a thread I cannot see. "There was Jessie Cole's house, he was the chauffeur. There was also the white house where Henry Livingston, the middle son, came with his family all summer and every holiday. Our house was by the little stream. Mama loved it. Even now, if I close my eyes, I can see her in that clean, fragrant kitchen.

"She was still thin and pale after that first year, but she was happy. She kept chickens and we always had eggs to throw away, and lots of milk and apples. Papa kept great barrels of apples in our cellar, fifteen of them. The cellar was cool and sweet-smelling and dark and I liked to go down to fetch things, except that one time I reached in an apple barrel and grabbed a mouse! It could be a fiery hot summer day, but down there it was cool. Mama had a cabinet suspended from the ceiling in the middle of the cellar; you could slide it back and forth. It had a screen door and inside she kept slabs of butter between huge leaves that came from a round umbrella-like tree. She would wash these leaves carefully and slip them in between the butter. Milk, butter, cheese, everything kept beautifully. It was only much later that we had an icebox. Mama would make barrels of sauerkraut and they would sit down there too, sharp and delicious. And all the sparkling jars she put up, fruits and vegetables and jams, and the special ones for Christmas, brandied peaches, white cherries. She learned how to can in this country, but I don't know who could have taught her because she kept to herself always. I remember we children begged her once to make a pie, 'an American pie.' She tried, and her pie crust was like a rock. And she said in that low, melodious voice, 'Anna, go to Mrs. Cole and ask her please how to do this.' Mrs. Cole, the chauffeur's wife, wrote down the ingredients and Mama started to make pies in her big roasting pan, great square pies with lattice tops. They came and they came out of the oven and they were superb. Mama wasn't friends with any of the women, though. She used to say 'I have no time for a silk blouse.' We children and Papa were everything, although she was always kind and courteous with other people, and very, very nice to animals. If an animal, any kind, were not acting well, she would bundle it in her apron and place it in a warm spot by the stove, and feed it brandy with a dropper if it seemed worse."

My mother has stopped talking now, but I hear her still. I hear the question radiating from the glistening eyes, the question. "Pies baked in love and eaten in love so long ago and the baker and the eater no more on this earth? This earth?" Her words come again. It is a ripple now followed by another for she is seeing it all faster than she can tell it.

"On Saturday the 'mastela,' the huge tub, was placed in front of the kitchen stove and each small body was washed carefully. The boys snickered and carried on. But we would all be squeaky and slick afterwards. Then Mama would sit down, her hair combed nicely and her dress pressed, and lean her head back and close her eyes with a cup of coffee in those beautiful long fingers.

"With rain"—my mother watches the dripping pine bough outside my kitchen window—"would come the click-click-click sound, six irons heating all over the stove. Mama would click the handle onto a hot one, then click, another, and another. But sometimes, especially when it was good weather for outdoor work, the ironing did not get done. 'All right not ironed,' she would say on these days, 'but it can't have a hole.' You know, I don't think of these things for a long time and then, usually when the seasons start to change, a red leaf, the first thin rim of ice on a pond, the bright green tips of skunk cabbage, they come rushing back, these child-hood things—the colors, smells, the cold the quiet, the warm arms lost somewhere in time. And always, the river.

"In winter the river would freeze and the flivvers would cross—jiggling black bugs with puffs of smoke behind. We would cross, too, to go to school in Catskill, with baked potatoes in our pockets if it was a real cold day, and lunch pails filled with apples and ham sandwiches. It was so still on those cold mornings, all you could hear was the crunch of snow under our boots, and occasionally a bird. It was two miles to the door and we were little, but strong and happy. On very windy days, Mama would pack the front of our coats with newspaper. Newspaper is wonderful insulation.

"The coal in winter was beautiful. Yes, the coal—children look at things like that, low down and beautiful. It was hard coal and it burned long and evenly with beautiful blue and red and yellow flame. We had a copper water tank alongside the fire and Mama polished it until it mirrored all the little flames. Everybody had a tank like this. Everybody had copper water tanks, kerosene lamps, outhouses, chamber pots in the bedrooms. I don't remember them as inconveniences. They were decent, friendly things. There was no stove in the children's rooms upstairs, and I remember sometimes leaving a pitcher of water on the little wooden dresser and finding it frozen in the morning.

"Yet we were almost never sick. When we did develop a cold, Mama took care of it herself. For chest congestion, she made poultices of goose fat on flannel. For an upset stomach it would be sage boiled in milk. This was awful. It was also our 'spring tonic.' And 'schlez.' Mama said everyone in Europe knew how to use this little weed, but in this country nobody recognized it. It made a bitter tea which she sweetened with honey. Your own father knows this herb," my mother adds, for my father is one of our people. "Wild camomile grew all over and Mama cut this too and dried it in fragrant small bouquets from the rafters, also basil, and lutzmarine which is a form of rosemary.

"Winter of course meant school, and this I loved best of all. Mama kept me back a year to wait for Elvera, a pale, fragile little girl who clung to her skirts like a small shadow. My sister Mary, however, was the next child in age and more robust and gay. We did everything together, joining ranks against Victor, Philip, and a particularly devilish little boy named Charlie, my youngest brother. While we were in the country, Mama had another child, her last, an extraordinarily pretty and cheerful baby with light curly hair. They named her Angela after Mama, but we called her Julie—and sometimes 'Jelly' because she loved it. We had a big orange cat who would spit and claw at my brothers viciously, but the baby girl could sit on him and punch him into a pillow and all he did was purr. They would play in front of the fire like this, the big cat and the baby, and bother no one.

"If there was snow, Sundays were wonderful. The three Livingston boys, Herman Jr., Henry and Edmund, would take out their huge toboggans and we would all ride down Clay Hill shrieking and bumping and tumbling to the bottom until the light started to fade and the snow turned a pale lavender. But the river in winter was the most fun. It was very wide up there, and Mr. Livingston would bring out his ice boat. He had two boats, the *Armadillo*, a huge yacht with a personal crew to tend it (fifteen people could fit into it easily), and the ice boat. You had to lie back flat, you couldn't sit, and the snowy banks would start to turn blue and blur as you gathered speed, and then the tears would streak out over your hair and freeze into two long icicles.[10] All my life I've been afraid in boats," my mother says wonderingly, "because I can't swim, but I guess this didn't matter in an ice boat.

10. Henry Livingston remembers three boats—the *Amarilla* and two ice boats.

"There were so many good times then, and some of the best were not in playing or holidays, but in work. I always had jobs, as far back as I can remember—carrying milk, picking fruit, selling greeting cards or soap. They always made me feel important and useful as a child. The one job I had that I loved best of all, though, that opened a whole new world to me, was caring for the small chapel on the Livingston farm. It was a lovely cool and quiet place, and it had one magical room filled with hundreds and hundreds of books, books by the ancient Greeks, and Julius Caesar, and Charles Dickens, and Melville, and I could take any one and read it and keep it with me and return it and take another.

"I began to read then," my mother says, "and I guess I've never stopped. Although I was quite small, Mrs. Livingston gave me two dollars a month to keep the chapel clean and tidy. I also had to make certain everything was neat and ready for Sunday service, and in winter this meant a fire in the grate. I always had trouble with this. I had begged Papa to let me take the job and he grumbled but finally relented on the promise that I would do it entirely on my own. I remember one cold Sunday—flying back to our house and begging him to come help me start the fire for it was always going out and the people had already started up the hill for morning service and he hurried over with me, cursing the Protestants for needing a Catholic to start their fire, and he built it for me and it lasted. The bells were also part of the job, and they were a problem, too. I was a little too small and I would go up with the bell rope sometimes. Once I really got stuck and luckily an early worshiper pulled me down by the ankles. But the job got done and I made my two dollars each month. Mama had an old coat hanging in the pantry which she put on to get wood or hang out clothes. And this coat had a hole in the pocket and each month I secretly dropped my two dollars into this hole, down into the lining. At the end of December, at Christmas, I knew I would have twenty-four dollars, and all year I planned on what I would do with that money. All my school friends had bicycles, two-wheelers. I used to lie in bed and imagine myself gripping the handlebars and pumping my own bicycle. I could almost feel the wind rushing by. At Christmas I would have enough. And when December came, Mama started to prepare us as she always did in her quiet way for the 'fritta' and oranges that were to be our presents instead of toys. 'Your Papa works so hard,' she would say, 'and we don't have very much.' Every year it was the same. 'We don't have money for presents.' We would find the little fritta, fried sugar balls with candied citrus in our stockings, fritta and oranges, and I would think 'My God, does Santa Claus know we're foreigners too?' I'd say, 'Mama, why does he give us fritta, I'm choking on them! Gracie at school got dolls and carriages and everything!' And she'd say, 'Shhh! Her father drinks and we have a good Papa.' And I'd never figure out what that had to do with Santa Claus. Anyway, at the end of the year I had my twenty-four dollars, and I guess I knew by then what I would do. A few days before Christmas I said 'Mama, please give me a dollar. Just one. You won't be sorry. Just give it to me for a little, little while.' She looked at me as if I was crazy, but she gave me a dollar. And I took it and put it with the twenty-four and on Christmas morning I gave her twenty five dollars. She held it in her hand and cried. I never got that bicycle, but after awhile, I stopped wanting it.

"After Christmas, the cold, short days of real winter edged on and on until they were stopped, abruptly, by the river. It was the Hudson that gave the most certain sign of winter dying. The ice began to break up, sometimes in a long, shattering groan that continued for miles. It was a strange thing for the human ear to experience, clean, frightening, and joyous at the same time. They used to cut the ice, you know, many men working fast before the temperature dropped and made it too thick to cut, or rose and made it too thin. Sometimes they'd work through the night, by torchlight, pushing great crystal blocks into little canals and on up to the ice houses on shore. They would stack the blocks in sawdust and even in high summer it would be there ready to use.

"The upper part of the valley is a great fruit-growing region and at the start of spring, after school, I would go around to the farms to line up picking jobs. I would say we had a big family and the farmers would say, 'We don't want children stepping all over our berries and eating them, sorry!' And I would say, 'Mr. Schatler (or Mr. Jorgenson or Mr. Pirie)—just try me out. I guarantee no one is going to eat your berries and no one will step on them.' A guarantee from a nine-year-old. 'All right,' they'd say, 'We'll try you.' And the next year they'd come by and say, 'Picking time!'

"Mama would wake us at five A.M. to pick strawberries and then we'd go home for breakfast before school. Grown-ups didn't like to pick strawberries, I guess because they're so low to the ground. Later it was cherries—Oxhearts, and golden Montmorencies and sour cherries and the dye cherries they sold to companies to dye fabric. Cherries had to be picked very early. Afterwards, when the sun was up, it was too hot, and the heavy ladders were hard to move around. I always wore the same thing for picking: knickers, and canvas shoes with two crisscross straps and buttons, and a khaki shirt with my hair pulled back tight. In summer, if it wasn't too far, Mama would bring our lunches and we'd sit together under the trees. Wonderful lunches of thick bread and butter and fresh ham.

"Summer was berry time. Blackberries, raspberries, red caps, black caps, loganberries, blueberries, currants, gooseberries. Mama made little gloves for the gooseberry picking, there were no fingers in them, but they protected our arms from the big thorns. She'd show us how to lift the branches and pick from the inside so the thorns didn't get us. She always found a way to make it nicer. Gooseberries have inch-long thorns; they are beautiful pale green globes with stripes. When they're ripe they're yellow, but you can't pick them yellow. People don't seem to grow them much anymore, but they make the best pies and jam you ever tasted.

"We were little children," my mother says, letting her memories recede for a time, "and we worked hard, but it was a good part of our lives. Papa picked, too, when he had the time, heavy dark grapes for his wine. We picked dandelions for his pale golden wine, and we griped all the way, for we got nothing out of this crop, not even a sip. By the end of the summer, the seven of us made five hundred dollars. That was quite a lot in those days, especially for children!

"Apples started in late summer. There was one wonderful apple that always arrived first and it was the tastiest of all. 'Wealthy' they called it. It was pale green and soft—not hard like a Granny Smith. Then the Macs and Gravensteins and tiny Hyslop crabs in their deep pink skins.

"And the pears!" my mother swoons. "Bartletts were Mama's favorites. And not just to eat; she picked them green and tied them in the corner of the sheets in the linen cupboard. They would dry and fill every nook with their lovely fragrance. She slipped quince between the sheets too. There was always a spray of some sweet-smelling thing in her pocket. Spearmint, camomile, lemon balm— she'd reach in and sniff it and put it back. Even fresh blades of grass. Easter eggs were tenderly wrapped in these which left a delicate green filigree on their shells. Onion skins left gold tones, and if we had a red one, they were ruby.

"Summer was the time of Papa's garden, and people would actually go out of their way to pass by and look at it. It was a wonderful, lush tapestry of vegetables set like flowers in circles and squares and little hills. He never planted in rows, it seemed against his nature. Great arcs of lettuce, cauliflower and cabbages spun out from a heart of smaller herbs. There isn't any flower on earth more beautiful than a cabbage sparkling with dew," my mother confides. "And melons! From the palest pink to peach to deep coral inside, and the best one always for Mrs. Livingston. She never went to chapel in summer that she didn't stop to admire Papa's garden.

"He worked in it only in the evening, after his regular work was done. He would stand in the moonlight and run the dark cool earth through his fingers. 'Anything can grow in this, Anna,' he would say. 'This will grow anything for anyone no matter how they plant.' And I knew then he was remembering the sand and rock of those islands, and how much sweat and misery the land took, and the poor, warped fruits it gave.

"Sometimes on summer evenings, Papa would fish. All his life he loved to fish, and sometimes he would take me along. Then it was Hudson shad, lashing flashes of silver in the dark, and sometimes sturgeon. He would never say much, we just sat there in the little boat for hours. Mama would do wonderful things with the fish, and a good portion would always be potted or salted for the winter. Winter made a heavy claim on summer. Mama would prepare for it endlessly and everywhere, even on the roof. Little bell tomatoes were set in long rows to dry up there in the sun under a thin veil of cheesecloth. At the end of summer, she would can right up through evening. Then she would come out and call us in for a late supper, always with Elvera, a dark small shadow at her skirts. Often it would be a big bowl of rice, yellow with beaten eggs and butter and cheese, a special 'children's dinner' we loved. She would call us with a beautiful little bird sound. It was extraordinary how Mama could imitate birds. At first you'd think she was whistling, but it was happening deeper down in her throat, a sweet and melodious trill. I couldn't do it, none of us could. I loved to sing, though, when I was little, in church mostly, and at school. Mama liked to hear us sing, I knew, because she would smile. Once, at Christmas time, one of the older girls named Edith Warburg was chosen for the lead voice in our pageant. I wanted to sing those songs so badly and every day, as she practiced, I would sing along in my mind, twisted up with envy. Well, Edith Warburg came down with laryngitis three days before the pageant, and they picked me to substitute because nobody else knew the words. I was ecstatic! My teacher, Miss Duntz, if you can believe it, told me I must have a pretty white dress for the role and I went home and told Mama. She was happy for me but she said, 'Anna, where am I going to get you a white dress? Where?' But on the day of the pageant, she mixed me the yoke of an egg and sugar 'to clear the throat' and I paraded out the door in a lovely white lace pinafore. I could see Mama's face clearly in the window, where there were no curtains to block the view.

"On Sundays Mama sent us all to the Roman Catholic Church across the river. She was an 'orthodox' Catholic and never went to this church, and Papa never went to church at all. He did believe that we children should go, and we received Communion every Sunday. I received my First Communion with Elvera. We had huge bouquets, mine mostly roses, Elvera's mostly leaves. I remember one of the things Papa did not care for was Confession. He did not believe in this for anyone. Later, it was the simple act of crossing the river each Sunday, this child's contact with the mystery of worship, which held together for me when the whole world began to crumble.

"Towards the end of each summer a neighbor would return from his travels round the world, and somehow we children always sensed when he was home again. His name was Doug Hill and he owned a huge farm near the Livingstons. He was a solitary man, a bachelor, and he loved children. He always brought things with him. One summer it was kites, box kites from China and I can still see all those clear bright colors floating in the summer sky. Mama especially enjoyed them. She looked so small looking up, as if the wind could take her, too—anytime it wanted. I believe only Papa and I looked at her in those days and saw the tired eyes, the paleness, and were afraid.

"Sometimes, now that I'm old, I truly wonder if those Hudson summers ever really happened at all. They were so full and sweet, and few. Those special mornings, walking down, down under a deep canopy of green, down to the ferry, my hand in the cool, slender grasp of Emmeline Livingston. 'Your mother is a good woman, Anna,' she would say out of the blue. Mrs. Livingston would take me with her on the little ferry, across to Catskill to visit her family. And Mr. Haynes always waited for us on the other side with his taxi. We would visit with the Hopkins, and then she'd take out Lizzie's grocery list and we'd do the marketing. Lizzie was the cook and my great friend. Sometimes we'd go all the way to Albany and spend a day shopping and browsing. Just we two.

"Occasionally we would visit the Churches. Louis Palmer Church lived about three miles away from the Livingstons, and the families were old friends. He was the son of Frederic E. Church, the well-known member of the Hudson River School of painters. In

View of Olana. By Frederic E. Church. Courtesy of the Cooper-Hewitt Museum, the Smithsonian Institution's National Museum of Design.

fact, one of his paintings was recently dug up in some obscure part of the world and sold in New York for millions of dollars! "Oh well, that's neither here nor there," my mother says. 'Olana,' the Church place was called. There is no real way to describe it. It was a maharajah's palace on a hilltop overlooking the Hudson. On sunny days you could see the marquisite patios and walkways sparkling through the trees. They say Samuel Clemens wrote his stories there in front of the fireplace. I believe the state of New York has taken it over now, and perhaps one can visit, I don't know.[11]

"They said you could see seven counties from Olana. It was a special place to visit, for I had many friends there, including my best friend, Helen Wilsey. Her father, Louis Wilsey, was chauffeur for the Churches.[12] A black man by the name of Bryant was their

11. Frederic E. Church began acquiring property in Columbia County in the 1860s and built Olana in the 1870s. Louis P. Church, who died in 1943, inherited Olana after Frederic's death in 1900. The New York State Office of Parks and Recreation bought Olana in 1966 and operates it as a historic site museum.

other chauffeur and he had three daughters who became my good friends, Tessie, Essie, and Ida. Their mother was the cook. Then there was another family working on the Church land, the Junes— Eston June and Stanley June. These were friendly, openhearted people and they made Olana a lovely place for a child to visit.

"But for me, next to home, the best place in all the world was the Livingston kitchen. Lizzie's kitchen. There was always something wonderful being mixed and measured, or in the oven, or ready to be tasted. Lizzie couldn't wait for an open mouth to slap something into. My favorite concoction was a dessert she called 'Spanish Velvet.' I would watch her take out the oval copper mold and measure out amber drops of some fragrant liquor into the fine cornstarch pudding.

"Oh that Lizzie!" my mother laughs. "How she could cook! She was an ageless white lady who had never been married. Poor Lizzie. I never tasted pancakes like Lizzie's. She'd rub her great black skillet with a grease cloth and clothespin and flip these thin golden miracles into the air. Bread was almost always baking, and I would go down there after school and have my thick slice with butter and a glass of milk. She always made extra everything, and Mrs. Livingston would come into the kitchen and in her high, clipped voice say, 'Lizzie, put this in a basket and Anna will take it home.' Strawberry shortcake with lovely yellow biscuits split in two and great dollops of sweet cream, all to turn sour in the hot summer kitchen unless someone ate it fast. And Elvera's pale little face appearing in the kitchen door each evening for her eggnog, for Emmeline Livingston insisted that 'this' particular child have an eggnog before bedtime. It was a grand home of tapestries and paintings and inlaid cabinets and crystal glinting down the long cool halls, but for a child it all surrounded a kitchen.

"This was not part of Mama's world, this grand white house on the hill. She had her work, and it was endless and kept her where she was. Sometimes Mrs. Livingston would stop on the path in front of our house and call in, 'Angela, come out, come out so I may talk with you!' And Mama would appear quietly and prettily at the door. But she stayed to home.

"She did come to church the summer two of us were confirmed. It was quite an occasion for the little Catholic church across the

---

12. Reuben Louis Wilsey, Sr., became the Church's chauffeur and superintendent of the estate in 1920. A photo of his quarters as they appeared in 1928 is in Aileen W. Stevenson "Preliminary Restoration Report for the Stable-Coachhouse Complex, Olana Historic Site, Greenport, New York." (M.A. thesis, State University of New York-Cooperstown Graduate Programs, 1973), 24, 131.

river. All the girls were ordered white dresses with box pleats and a middy top, black stockings and black shoes, and it all came in big boxes from 'the city.' There is a picture somewhere," my mother says, half laughing, half embarrassed.

I know this picture because it is so strange. Two girls, one about thirteen, long dark hair, pretty; another younger with a little pinched face and gold-rimmed glasses, both dressed in white with wreathes in their hair, and a little boy shyly seated in front. Elvera, Anna, and Victor.

"And then that summer, that particular summer, was over and the fall began and school began and it was never the same again," my mother says, her eyes narrowing as if to catch the last glimpse of a receding dream. "Mama became very ill. She grew steadily worse through the autumn. We saw it, Papa and I, but the words were too painful to speak.

"Sister Josephine, the sister superior from the Catholic school, traveled across the river to see her that last fall. They were so kind to us and gave the children huge breakfasts at the convent after Mass each Sunday. I remember those vague, vacant days at the end of autumn only as spreading darkness. We started to embroider Christmas presents for our mothers at school. 'Bucilla Needlework,' the label said. The big girls had to embroider their own and also do one for the little children who came there because, of course, they couldn't do it themselves. I knew my mother was dying, and I said to the teacher, 'Miss Loomis, I have to make my mother's pillow cases very early.' And I made them, and I brought them to her and how she cried when she saw them. She was forty years old on the first of December, and she died on December fourth. It was 1927 and they say she died of tuberculosis. I went back to school those few days before Christmas and made more pillow cases. They were for Earl and Eddie O'Connor, two little boys.

"You know," my mother says softly, and it is the child Anna whispering, "there is such a thing as a death rattle. I remember when she was dying I kept saying, 'Keep your eyes open, if only you do that you won't die.' And she said, 'I'm trying, I'm trying!' At the last, she began to sew. She kept on sewing, very fast, she put the needle in and stretched her arm to pull the thread through— only there was no needle or thread. And she said, 'Cut the thread! Cut the thread!' I didn't know what to do. I was a child. 'There is no thread, Mama,' I said, but she kept on saying it and holding it up for me to cut. So, I don't know, I made a kind of clipping motion with my fingers,and that was it. She went over.

"After Christmas I stayed home from school to help Papa. Victor and I would wash the clothes in Mama's big tub and hang them out on the line like she did. All the little hands—always too short, too small. I cooked beets one night and I cooked them so long I made a hole in her big pot. The one child who took it the worst was Elvera, she simply fell apart when Mama died. She was so close to her all her little life, and now she was so afraid. She was afraid she was going to die, too. She would feel her heart and say 'Kabeat, kabeat, kabeat'—so it wouldn't stop, and my brothers would laugh at her.

"After awhile, some men came to the house, authorities from the school department, and they told Papa I could not stay home any longer. And I went back to school, two miles there and two miles back, all winter, carrying little Julie with me. It was Swamp School, a little red schoolhouse in a swamp. Miss Loomis, my teacher, was a hunchback lady, God love her. She was a wonderful woman. She put two little desks together and fixed it all up so Julie could have her naps. She was three years old. I carried her back and forth to school through all kinds of weather and she was wonderful. She slept, she ate, everything was fine. It would get very cold sometimes, to this day when it's cold I feel it first here on my cheek from one of those walks, and yet that rosy baby would never complain.

"I graduated from grade school in June and I went to Hudson to try the Regents and I did very well. But we couldn't continue. Papa tried, we all tried, but seven children, some so small, were too much to keep together without Mama. A social worker from Hudson talked to Papa and it was decided that Victor and Julie, the two littlest, would go to the Little Angels Home in Troy. But Victor cried and cried on the day he was to go and so Papa bribed my brother Charlie, he was six, with a box of cookies and he went instead. Julie was almost four when she went off, a pretty golden-haired little girl with blue eyes. She already had long legs and was going to be tall like Mary. Charlie would tell us how she cried. The home was run by Sisters, but there were many black people to take care of the children and Julie had never seen black people before and she was very afraid of them.

"Mama had died of tuberculosis and so they took all of us to be checked at a sanatorium. The nurse who took us was a lady named Gertrude van Netten—why, why do I remember these names? All the children were all right but Elvera. She had no lesions, they said, but she was very weak. She was eleven years old and she was the first one sent to the sanatorium to stay. She went by herself. Miss van Netten and I left her in a little room and all she did was take a window shade and pull it up and down, up and down. She didn't say anything. We had been so close as children, Elvera, Mary and me. We slept in the same big bed. And that day as I sat in a car with Miss van Netten I heard her screams after us. I kept saying, 'Miss van Netten, I have to go back for her, I have to, if I don't she won't be there when I come back!' But the car kept going, away from that place. Later Philip and Mary were sent together to the same sanatorium.

"And finally, on a dismal morning, Papa, little Victor and I left that beautiful river valley, that white house still filled with Mama, and returned to New York City. Papa felt he could find better work there and make enough money to pull the children together again. Before we left, Mrs. Livingston came to Papa and asked him to leave me behind. She promised I would have everything, and the best education. And Papa looked at her and said, 'Why don't you take my right arm?' I never saw her again."

JULIE

My mother wears the same green and white striped apron that she wore watching the early October snow; it seems so long ago that I first began listening. We have come and gone through a winter and summer solstice, and she stands now cutting the sturdy stems of black-eyed Susans and Queen Anne's Lace, the wild flowers of high summer, the time of both our births.

"When we returned to New York after Mama died it was 1930," she says, and both our minds pick up the fragile thread. "The Depression had already set in. It was difficult to get any kind of work. There were employment offices all over Sixth Avenue and they had jobs listed outside, one on top of the other, on index cards. You would go into one of these 'job brokers' and apply, and they knew very well that they had already sent several men out for the job, but they would send you, too, and you had to give them a fee. Five dollars, six dollars, it was a lot of money and if it was all you had—well, what could you do? Whether the job was there or not, you couldn't get back your fee.

"Papa was fortunate. Almost immediately he found a job with

the Barclay Hotel and went to work. My brother Victor and I went to school and kept house, a tenement I suppose it was, smaller than we had before. Papa worked long hours. His dream was to get us all together again. But he was not the same Papa anymore, and this perhaps even more than Mama's death, frightened us. He was a shadow. He had developed ulcers and he used to have horrible pain. I would get dressed and go out to get the doctor for him in the night. But he never stopped working. He missed Mama so much. He was a man with a strong, powerful presence, a handsome face and a deep-rooted sense of humor, but when Mama died he 'disappeared.' He would wake up at night and cry her name. To me the whole world had come to an end then, for I felt that if a man like that fell apart, there was nothing left. Nothing to look forward to. He became gray and old very quickly.

"The other children were still upstate, Elvera alone, Philip and Mary in a sanatorium in Belmont, and little Charlie and Julie at the Angel's Home in Troy. After awhile, Papa received a letter from the nuns in Troy saying that Julie was not well. When we went up, Charlie told us she had been crying for so long and would say that her tooth hurt her, but no one listened. 'And then,' he said, his small face reciting from memory and misery, 'all of a sudden she stopped crying.' We never had word of this and of course they were both too little to write themselves. When Papa and I got there, she wasn't at the home for they had taken her to the hospital. We went there. The doctor who had seen her said that the Mother Superior brought this little child to his office. She was six years old then. It was around Saint Patrick's Day. The winter, I remember, was over, and it was just beginning to be spring. And he told us he said to the Mother Superior, 'You have brought this child to the wrong place. Why didn't you go around the corner to the funeral home.' He said her infection had burst, it was in her bloodstream. I stayed with a family in Troy to be near her, and Papa had to go back to work. I was fifteen then. Everytime I thought she got worse, I would send a telegram to Papa, and he would come up. He would go back when she seemed to improve. He was up three times. One day the Mother Superior came into her room and she said, 'Well, Anna, the only thing we can do is go to the chapel and pray.' I turned around and took my fists and pounded her chest with all my strength. 'Pray?' I said, 'Pray? You killed her!' She never came back but always sent another nun. She was such a beautiful little child, so rosy and healthy when I carried her to school that last winter on the Hudson. Her heart was so strong, like Mama's, and it took her over a month to die. It was around Easter, I know, for she asked me for jelly beans. She loved them." My mother says no more.

This was the last child, the littlest, the most lighthearted. She died three years after her Mama, but perhaps for them it was a twinkling, the slow, heavy foot, and the little light foot passing over right after, into "heavenliness," into "nothingness," it doesn't matter. Together.

Unlike her mother's death, the death of the little girl is one thing my mother's words, her mind, seem not to touch, beyond the bare recital of events. A point in space and time traveled once and not for all the world to be traveled again, at least not willingly, given the reality of the words, never to draw on memory to relive those days, those days of a child's dying. And what is remembered of this child? The hair, gold and curly. And pretty, with long legs for someone just out of babyhood, yes. And pink cheeks, yes, and a love for jelly. Yes.

"One tragic thing," my mother says, and it is something that even now transforms her face in to a mask of remorse and suffering. "I had a box. A tin box of powder, a prize for selling the most Christmas cards. And she took it and emptied it out and I caught her and spanked her and she cried and cried." And I know this of all the things in her life, my mother would like to reverse, to erase.

THE CITY

"When we first moved back to New York, Victor and I shared the housekeeping after school. He was such a good little boy, he did everything he was told to do, quietly and well. I don't remember him ever laughing, but he had a shy little smile sometimes. It was hard on him in the beginning; he loved the country and he missed it terribly. 'I can't breathe, Anna,' he would whisper in the night. 'There's no air.' Finally Papa fixed a safe little sleeping place for him on the fire escape, for it was still summer, and he slept out there until it became quite cold.

"Victor went to a school near our home, and I went to Washington Irving High School where they gave me a scholarship. It was for music, but when I realized I couldn't do much to earn a living with music, I changed to 'business.' Vic and I did everything together. We kept house, we went down to Paddy's Market to buy food. I would say, 'Vic, you will get home before I do. Have the potatoes peeled and in the pot.' He was six. When I got home, they

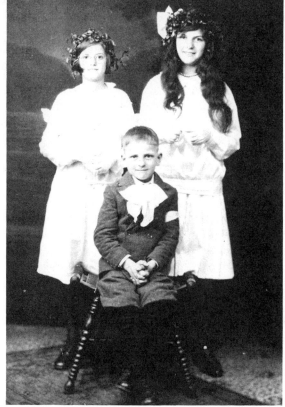

*A Confirmation photo of Elvera (left), Anna, and
Victor. Courtesy of Christina S. Godshalk.*

would be all ready. We made fried pork chops almost every night.
Papa would get mad to see the same dinner all the time, but we
loved them. On his day off, Papa would make us a big hearty dinner
and it would last for a couple of days. Then back to pork chops. Vic
and I would do the dishes and wait for Papa to get home. He used to
come in late. We would sleep together in a big bed until he came
home, then he would wake me and I'd go to a little cot and he
would sleep with Vic.

"Papa would turn over his whole salary to me each week, and I
was very careful with it. I put some aside, it wasn't much, and I
kept it in the house. The more we saved the sooner we could start
bringing the smaller children down to us. Victor knew where the
money was kept. I don't know how, but some bigger kids in the

neighborhood found out about it, perhaps they asked him and he was an honest little boy. They hit him and hit him and made him get the money. There was a couple of hundred dollars. I almost lost my mind when he told me. I asked him who they were, and he was so afraid to tell me. I went with him to the families and they told me to go home. But I wouldn't. I held Vic's hand and I said, 'Your children beat my brother and took our money. Give it to me and I'll go.' And I got most of it back. Some was spent.

"On the weekends when Papa was off, the three of us would take the train and visit the two little ones in Troy. When Julie died, it was only Charlie. These trips were hard on Papa. He was sick and aging before our eyes and finally they put him in the hospital. Bellevue. I would visit him there after school, and he was in a great deal of pain. I remember him holding my wrist tightly and asking me to take care of the children, asking, asking, over and over. And I said, 'Yes! Why are you asking like this?' And he said, 'I'm just asking, Anna.' He was fifty-nine and he died on December 28, Vic's birthday. I took the trolley car back home that day, and when I got there, there was a telegram from the hospital. I went back and a young doctor there put his arm around me and told me he could not have lived the way he was.

"Little Julie died in April of that year, and Papa in December. I remember I called up Dr. Post at Philmont where Mary, Philip and Elvera were together. I told him Papa had died and I wanted my brothers and sisters with me. And he said, 'Anna, I'm very sorry, but you're only sixteen. I can't let these children come down. I will do my best to console them, but I must keep them here.' So they never saw Papa again. Elvera, as long as she lived, could never understand this. That she never saw her Papa again.

"There was a funeral and many of our people came to the apartment to pay their respects. Victor and I stayed close to each other, there were so many faces we had never seen before. After everyone left, I realized that the money Papa left us was gone. His citizenship papers were gone, too, and the small copper still for his brandies and wine. Uncle Dushon walked through the door and found me crying and he was wonderful. He asked me how much money it was, and he replaced it. He said, 'Anna, you must have a black coat now,' and he gave me thirteen dollars more for a black coat. He was a bachelor, of course, and could not take care of us. I went to stay with cousins of my father, and Vic went with another one of our people. The two of us had been through so much together, and when that little boy left, I felt suddenly invulnerable, like steel. I was sixteen, and there was nothing—nothing they could take away anymore.

"I stayed with Papa's cousins for almost a year while I went to school. I did the laundry and cleaning and I slept in their living room on a little cot. They finally went back to Europe and I stayed for awhile with the woman's sister. They did not want me, and I did not want to be there.

"Victor went to a woman named Sharcovitza. She was a person who came from the island my father came from, but she was not a relative. She bought a farm with a second husband somewhere upstate, and she took this little boy up there with her. I did not find out until it was too late what she was doing to him. I had finished school and had found a job and a place to live with a wonderful Yugoslav woman named Maritza. I would get these awful letters in a child's big printing. Victor would say that I had forgotten him, that I was a terrible sister, that I must send more money. Maritza read these letters and she said, 'Anna, I don't know who this lady is, but no child writes like this.' I planned to go up on my next day off from work. It was hard to leave work for it was the Depression and a job meant so much, and I couldn't get there and back in one day. Then there was another letter from a young man named Miro Carcich. He said he had seen what this woman was doing to the little boy who was my brother, she taught him to steal for her, and beat him terribly. He said he was afraid for the child, and had reported her to the authorities in Hudson and they had taken him away.

"I went up immediately and found they had put Victor with my other brothers, with Philip and Charlie who were staying with a woman who took care of orphans. Her name was Miss Connolly, a wonderful big Irish woman who took care of six little boys. Her house was next to the Shaker Village in Lebanon, and the Shaker people were very nice to the children. Miss Connolly had them organized to do the chores in the house. She told me it was one whole year afterwards before she could get Victor to talk. He was a little robot, she said. He ate, he worked harder than any other little boy, he would do anything she asked. He never answered back, but he wouldn't talk.

"At that point in my life," my mother says in half wonderment, "I had great faith. I felt I was being looked after and that nobody would hurt me and I knew I would make it. I remember when I went looking for a job during the Depression, I went with a friend, and there was one opening at Horn & Hardart and when we got to the store I said to her, 'Don't go in with me.' I knew if there was a job in there, it was going to be mine. She looked at me strangely, but she waited outside. And when I came out I said to her, 'I have to go to church.' And she said, 'What for?' I had to go and thank God for this job. And ten years later, Mr. Farley, the man who hired me, remembered that day. He said, 'You weren't going to leave my office without that job. We asked you how old you were because you had to be bonded. "Are you eighteen?" And you said, "Honest to God I am!" And I knew then of course that you were not eighteen and that we had to hire you.'

"Because of youth," my mother says, "you are so strong when you're young, you turn, turn always to something new, something needing you right away, you cannot be buried. All the agonizing, the sorrow, still can't darken those years for me. When I remember sorrow and disappointment, the clearest memories are still a child's sorrows and disappointments. Jello! That was one. A shimmering pyramid in a cut glass bowl in the window of Schrafft's. I longed to try it when I was four feet high. There couldn't possibly be anything more wonderful in the whole world. And at some point, I did—and it turned to sugary nothing in my mouth. This simply was a disappointment to be ranked with the worst."

I listen and yet I know, I am her child and I know, that to be small and to experience death upon death upon death does not leave you unmarked. It shapes an adult who still calls a parent when in pain, who fears to let the wind whip too freely about her, who has an undying need to be soothed, and who has a deep rage, ready and full-blown when called upon.

There was one other thing. Before my grandfather died, he contrived, by some magical, maniacal bending of will in that sad time, to give a party, a light and merry moment, for Anna on her sixteenth birthday. And at this party she met a young man, an island man, of dazzling beauty and sweetness of nature. This man was my father. When they married three years later, they spent their honeymoon visiting her brothers and sisters in their orphan homes and sanatoriums upstate. And slowly, one by one, they brought them down, and put them in school, and later found them jobs, until one day all Angela Piljurovich's children but one, her cherished, cherished ones, were grown and on their own.

Victor married early, a pretty child bride who bore him three children and left one day never to return. Philip drifted through the world, touching lives lightly. He has a daughter, a tall child like himself who lives in England—she on one continent and he on another, yet a man who sees the humor of life, a "storyteller," marked for salvation. Charlie, who after his small sister died was placed through windows by bigger boys, the right size to steal; who stayed with Anna and her young husband, a rash child, a scrapper, to find and marry a good woman and work hard and well. Mary, curly-haired, mischievous, continued down a narrowing path.

And the last, the one I myself knew best next to my mother—Elvera. Elvera with the gold-rimmed glasses and the leaf bouquet. Alone always, a sad life and short, they say. But for me, a small child, she spread love and magic in such abundance that to take her out of my childhood would leave it infinitely more arid and flat a place. "Aunt Elvera," the sound of tinkling bells. She was a child's nursemaid, and her life was a long string of best-loved children, other people's children, with desperately empty gaps in between. For the two of us, Elvera and me, it was matinees and tea, endless still afternoons on a lily-rimmed pond in Vermont, morning pancakes in the shape of turtles and elephants and yes, you could place your order for any form of animal life, secret jokes, tiny boxes, and an endless parade of wrong buses, subways and trains we took together, our eyes meeting in half-panic, half-adventure. Why did they turn out so differently, Angela's children? Questions really worth asking never have answers.

Next spring, we plan a little trip. We will go, my little son and my little daughters, with Anna, the still beautiful and vigorous Anna, to the Hudson Valley. We will try to find the white house above the stream. We will walk with her under the maples down to the river. The ferry? Who knows. The big cool houses—Clermont, Olana? Perhaps. But the river and the valley, yes. It has, they say, "a climate of sweet and wholesome breath."

A Comparative Perspective on the Ethnic Enclave: Blacks, Italians, and Jews in New York City

This article contributes to the growing literature maintaining that the ethnic enclave represents a distinct, third alternative to a dual economy. The data are interviews with 45 elderly, immigrant blacks, Jews and Italians from New York City. Two facets of the enclave are explored: determinants of job outcomes for employees and factors responsible for entrepreneurial viability. With regard to employees, the analysis shows enclave workers obtain job security and job status equivalent to openings in the primary sector. Investigation of the organization of ethnic entrepreneurship reveals that the mobilization of several factors unique to ethnicity enhances the competitiveness of minority firms.[1]

I t has long been recognized that many minority groups have been highly segregated occupationally (U. S. Immigration Commission, 1911; Hutchinson, 1956). Yet, until relatively recently, the meaning of the distinctive job environments of ethnics received scant scholarly attention. Currently, the term "ethnic enclave" is enjoying popularity among stratification researchers. The term refers to an occupational niche in which an ethnic group has secured some activity and influence. The role of ethnic enclaves in both individual and group achievement is now a central research question.

Theories about enclave processes provide an alternative structural explanation for an upward mobility that neither classical Marxist nor contemporary segmentationist thinking accurately pre-

Reprinted from *International Migration Review* 19 (Spring 1985), 64-81.

Suzanne Model is a member of the Sociology Department at the University of Massachusetts at Amherst. In researching and writing this article, she was associated with the Russell Sage Foundation.

1. Support for this project came from a Rackham Dissertation Grant from the University of Michigan. A previous version of this paper was presented at the 1984 annual meeting of the Eastern Sociological Society in Boston, Mass. The author wishes to thank Joel Leon, Vincent Parrillo, Patricia Roos, Charles Tilly and three anonymous reviewers of this journal for their helpful comments on earlier drafts. The responsibility for errors, of course, rests with the writer.

dict. Early structural analysis focused only on the significance of class membership. Later, revisionists uncovered important variations within the laboring class. These new theorists proposed that those workers who gained access to capital intensive and monopolistic enterprises (called primary industries) succeeded in establishing strong labor organizations, which in turn secured attractive wages and benefits for their members. Conversely, workers confined to small, labor intensive and competitive environments (labeled secondary industries) were unable to develop strong unions. Their employers simply could not afford the price of job stability and high wages (Edwards, *et al.,* 1975; Gordon, *et al.,* 1982).

This theory of a segmented labor market has implications for ethnic mobility because many of the workers absorbed by the large, profitable industries were white ethnics. These ethnics obtained security and opportunity along with other primary sector workers. But, the segmentationist theory goes on to predict that employees relegated to the competitive secondary sector remain disadvantaged and dependent.

Nevertheless, some ethnics who did not concentrate heavily in primary sector jobs also achieved substantial upward mobility. Asians, Jews, and Southern Europeans, for example, frequently labored in the small competitive industries traditionally associated with secondary employment. According to labor market segmentation theorists, these opportunities yield only dead-ends and revolving doors. Some writers have since proposed that the ethnic enclave constitutes a third alternative to this bifurcated vision (Portes and Bach, 1980; Wilson and Portes, 1980).

This article is designed to explore the empirical bases for such a proposition. The research reported here examines two sets of individuals: workers and entrepreneurs. First, it documents that ethnic employees who labor in an enclave environment receive rewards in some ways superior to those available to their counterparts in the secondary sector. The results indicate further that most of these benefits accrue to workers who have obtained their positions through personal contacts. This finding suggests that the social relations of employment have something to do with the economic advantage of the enclave. Then, the economic organization of ethnic entrepreneurship is explored. This investigation reveals special linkages between ethnic businesses that facilitate the prosperity of these companies in an aggressive and competitive market place. Thus, there is a structural as well as a social basis for the benefits of enclave employ.

THEORETICAL AND EMPIRICAL GROUNDING

The theory of middleman minorities, those groups that specialize in self-employment and working for the self-employed within the ethnic collectivity, furnishes a foundation for understanding the social and economic construction of small ethnic firms (Bonacich and Model, 1980). As Reitz, *et al.* (1981) points out, the allocation of job rewards may depend on both social factors and employment qualifications. Applicants may secure jobs through bonds of ethnicity, friendship, and family. Indeed, Bonacich (1973) argues that ethnic economies function less as modern capitalist settings than as traditional, personalized communities. Paternalism often blurs the boundary between employer and employee, and an atmosphere of mutual obligation prevails.

For these reasons, many investigators have hypothesized that the enclave holds the potential for special, non-monetary rewards. In particular, enclave employees may enjoy greater opportunity for skill development and more secure employment. Waldinger (1983) cites the willingness of enclave employers to invest in the training of new workers, as well as to permit immigrant employees to assume managerial tasks. Light (1972) has credited the strong ascriptive bonds within the Asian enclave for the low rates of unemployment exhibited by the Chinese and Japanese during the Depression. It is also reported that some Asian employers have lent assistance in their employees' efforts eventually to become entrepreneurs (Light, 1972; Wong, 1974).

However, if enclave firms do provide their labor force with some advantages, these advantages need have root in a secure economic foundation. For, if the efforts of labor market segmentationists have validity, differences in rewards between sectors are an outgrowth of differences in the profitability of these sectors.

Researchers have suggested a number of processes that could promote the viability of the enclave. One competitive advantage that the small ethnic employer may enjoy is cheap information about the quality of future workers. The tendency to recruit labor through personal ties may screen out undesirables (Sowell, 1981). Moreover, because many enclave workers enter the firm via personal sponsorship, they may feel especially obliged to perform well.

Another frequently cited reason for enclave profitability is that enclave employers pay lower wages than their counterparts in the majority economy. Employees who are migrants may be willing to accept inferior wages because they are accustomed to lower living standards (Piore, 1979). Enclave workers may also be more pliant because they are socially embedded in their jobs and isolated from the larger labor market (Waldinger, 1983). To date, the low wage hypothesis has received mixed empirical support. Bonacich and Modell (1980) cite some historical data showing that Japanese farm workers in California earned less when working for Japanese employers than when employed by other groups. A more recent study, this of Hispanics in the New York garment industry, suggests that enclave employees received wages below union scale (Waldinger, 1983). On the other hand, research on the Cuban immigrant population of Miami indicates that Cuban workers in the enclave did not suffer financial disadvantage (Wilson and Portes, 1980; Portes and Bach, 1980). Still, these studies are far from conclusive and more research is needed.

Middleman minority thinkers posit an additional foundation for the economic survival of enclave employers, their propensity to establish valuable intra-ethnic economic linkages. Three types of linkages can be conceptualized: horizontal, backward, and forward. Horizontal linkage describes the tendency among middleman minority groups to limit their economic activity to a few spheres of endeavor. Such specialization provides the minority with an area of expertise which is easily transmitted within the group.

The market gardening practiced by Japanese Americans before World War II is an ideal example of this strategy. For some twenty selected crops raised in Los Angeles County in 1941, from 75 percent to 99 percent of tilled acreage lay in Japanese hands (Bonacich and Modell, 1980). Jewish domination of the clothing industry or Greek preponderance in the restaurant trade are other, more obvious illustrations (Rischin, 1962; Lovell-Troy, 1980).

Another dimension to economic linkage is vertical integration, both backward and forward. In the enclave context, backward linkage refers to the dependency of ethnic producers on co-ethnic suppliers. If business transactions are also intra-ethnic transactions, the interpersonal bonds between the participants heighten the likelihood of conducting business with reliable parties and doing so on favorable commercial terms.[2]

Thus, Chinese hand laundries turned to Chinese washing and pressing plants for their demanding chores, while Jewish real estate agents chose Jewish painters and plasterers to refurbish their apartments

---

2. Research into the effects of personal relationships on economic decisions suggests that social bonds are not only important in the ethnic world, but in the larger economy as well. Even bureaucratic firms rely on particularistic forms of business transaction to a much greater degree than sociologists had originally thought (Granovetter, 1974, 1983).

(Wong, 1976; Moore, 1981). A comparative study of inter-business linkages among Cuban and Afro-American enterprises in Miami documented the potential for strong ties within the former and the near absence of links within the latter (Wilson and Martin, 1982).

But vertical integration may also proceed in a forward direction, from producers to customers. In particular, some early writers on minority enterprise argued that ethnic entrepreneurship was stimulated by demand from specific ethnic markets. Specialized requirements in food stuffs, foreign language newspapers, and so forth encourage the emergence of ethnic businesses to fill this demand (*cf.,* Light, 1972). However, the evidence to follow will suggest that forward linkages alone are insufficient for profitable business, a conclusion other research has likewise confirmed (Aldrich, *et al.,* 1984).

There are, then, several processes that could explain the extraordinary viability of the enclave. First, the labor force may be superior; second its price may be lower; and third, intra-ethnic economic linkages may promote expertise and cut operating costs.

This article examines the enclave experience from a historical perspective. Detailed information on a small sample of elderly blacks, Jews, and Italians, in a variety of economic settings is analyzed. The results indicate that enclave opportunities are indeed a function of the social and structural processes outlined above.

SAMPLE AND DATA

This project is part of a larger study investigating the historical roots of ethnic mobility in New York. Three minorities were chosen that represent varying extremes in ethnic enclave participation. Job histories were obtained from a total of 45 black, Jewish, and Italian elderly, immigrant males who entered New York City from the South, Eastern Europe, or Southern Italy respectively. Fifteen members of each group were included.

Restricting participation to migrants permits insight into the early process of ethnic stratification, a critical determinant of the differences in adjustment that we observe today (Duncan, *et al.,* 1972; Lieberson, 1980). Resource constraints dictated that the research effort be limited to males, although the neglect of females may constitute a serious omission in the understanding of the black experience. Similarly, for reasons of efficiency, it was decided to draw the sample from social and medical programs for the elderly: nursing homes, health care facilities, senior citizen centers and the like. With the exception of a few blacks who arrived in the thirties, all respondents came to New York before the Depression.

Interview locations were chosen from the telephone book by a procedure that involved purposeful inclusion of places in known ethnic neighborhoods, such as Harlem and Little Italy, and a random sample of the remaining agencies. Approximately two-thirds of the sample were obtained from facilities in Manhattan, the remaining third having been recruited from the borough of Queens.[3]

To determine how well the participants represented their respective populations, their occupational pursuits at mid-life were compared to published census data on these groups for the year 1950 (U.S. Bureau of the Census, 1952, 1954). In the case of Italians and Jews, the sample is somewhat younger than the census group; among blacks the age compares quite well, but the census fails to distinguish Northern from Southern by birth. The 1950 census divides the labor force into seven categories ranging from professional and technical work to service pursuits. The comparison revealed that respondents differed from their 1950 compatriots on no more than two of the seven occupational categories. The general trends in the occupational distributions of the three sampled groups were the same as that of their census counterparts.[4]

The survey instrument was developed in consultation with similar schedules and field tested on seven pilot subjects. The core of the schedule consisted of detailed information on the occupational experience of respondents at three points in their lives: first job, job at age forty, and last job. Extensive information on any business ventures undertaken by respondents was also secured (cf. Model, 1985). Interviewing took place in the Fall of 1982.

The empirical analysis is divided into two sections, a formal study of the determinants of job outcome for individuals and a more general discussion of potential factors that promote the viability of firms established by informants. The major focus of the employee analysis is limited to positions held at midlife. The effects of all independent variables were strongest at this point. Comments about and comparisons between midlife job and first and last positions appear in several footnotes. The analysis of entrepreneurship includes all business efforts, but the major emphasis rests on first venture, the undertaking for which the case base is the largest.

3. Of the 28 facilities contacted, 5 refused on the grounds that they did not serve the relevant populations. Eight were eliminated for other reasons. This left 15 programs that contributed an average of three informants each (cf. Model, 1985).

4. The match is particularly surprising in the Afro-American case because black respondents were an average of 10 years younger (74.6 years) than white (84.9 years). This difference, largely an outcome of the differential mortality rates between the races, raised the suspicion of an upward bias in the black occupational distribution, a concern that the data did not substantiate.

ANALYSIS OF INDIVIDUAL JOB OUTCOMES

Variables

Two measures of occupational adjustment, job length and job status, serve as dependent variables in the analysis of the respondents' employment.[5] The length of each post was obtained directly.
This measure is especially relevant because labor market
segmentationists have made short tenure one of the hallmarks of
the secondary sector.

Job status is measured on a scale of 1.00 (highest) to 5.00 (lowest)
developed for historical studies by Stephan Thernstrom (1973). The
use of such a narrow scale sets rather rigorous limits on the range
of values available, but is appropriate to the small sample size.
Thernstrom's index is especially sensitive to differences in authority and independence.

The associated independent variables reflect influences from several perspectives. Status attainment models have demonstrated that
the individual attributes employees bring to the work place affect
job rewards (Blau and Duncan, 1967; Duncan *et al.,* 1972).
Representing this tradition are the following variables: ethnicity,
age at migration, size of previous residence, father's status, and
respondent's educational achievement. Research on class distinctions has suggested that employers enjoy substantially better job
outcomes than employees (Wright and Perrone, 1977). Because of
the small size of the sample, the index of respondent's class aggregates all business owners, whether or not they engaged subordinates. Network analysts have demonstrated the value of
intermediaries in obtaining jobs (Granovetter, 1974; Lin, *et al.,* 1981).
Thus, the method of job access and the role of the agent in recruitment were also obtained.[6]

---

5. Income data were not solicited for two reasons. First, given the changing value
of the dollar and the age of respondents, the possibility of error was great. Second,
income usually changes within jobs, and it was unlikely that interviewees could
recall figures that were comparable across cases.
6. The following coding procedures were used. Father's status was indexed on a
four point scale based on the research of Wright and Perrone (1977). Their measure
focuses only on levels of ownership and authority and is hence more appropriate to
the diverse family origins of these respondents. Fathers who were employers received
a code of, 1. Employees with subordinates are coded, 2. Self-employed without
subordinates are 3. And employees with no subordinates are 4. Educational achievement was dichotomized at the mean of 7 years to facilitate cross-tabulation. Three
methods of approaching jobs were distinguished: advice of kin, suggestions of friends,
and appeals of a more formal nature. Among the latter were grouped together
employment agencies, want ads, anonymous direct application, and impersonal

Attention also needs to be directed at the sector of employment. Sectoral determinations were limited to the employee class to maintain analytic clarity. Theoretically, three distinct sectors were possible: primary, secondary, and enclave. Because the New York economy has a dearth of the large, capital intensive firms typical of the primary sector, union membership or government employ was utilized as a rough proxy for employment in the primary sector. The secondary sector was defined as all the remaining opportunities, provided that the employers were not compatriots of the respondent. The enclave was thus defined as those jobs in which the employee reported a co-ethnic superior.[7] A problem developed, however, because several respondents indicated the existence of a co-ethnic superior in unionized environments. These individuals were assigned to a separate, fourth category because of the impossibility of determining whether job outcomes for these persons resulted from union or enclave forces.

Job Length

Average job length at midlife was a fairly generous 17.2 years. Table 1 presents the effects of the major independent variables, with the exception of sector, on job length and job status.[8] Looking now only at the first of these outcomes, we see that the only factor from status attainment models that was significantly associated with length of tenure is education.[9] Men with seven or more years of schooling

recruitment. This collapsing was necessary in order to have large enough cells. Personalized contacts to facilitate jobs were further subdivided into direct hiring of the respondent and referral to a prospective employer. In the case of referrals, note was made of whether or not the contact was employed in the same firm as the respondent. The emotional strength of the tie was not determined, again because time might dim reliability. Size of previous residence was assigned to one of six levels.

7. All respondents assigned to the enclave also reported that the majority of their co-workers were compatriots, further evidence that they indeed labored in an enclave environment.

8. The variables age at migration and size of previous residence had no effects on outcome and, therefore, are deleted from the remaining discussion.

9. The use of significance testing in this study is questionable since the observations are not independent. This difficulty occurs because respondents were recruited not randomly, but from fifteen specific settings. When cases are not independent, there is the danger that their associated errors are correlated. Such correlation violates the basic assumptions of statistical inference.

Nevertheless, it is not uncommon for social scientists to undertake significance testing even when the data do not completely warrant such procedures. In this paper, the reported measure is a one-directional t-test, since the hypotheses predict the direction of the effect. The results give some idea of the magnitude of the relationships involved. However, the reader should judge statistical findings with caution, keeping in mind that the data do not fully justify the methods.

TABLE 1

Selected Measures and Midlife Job Outcome

Measure	Mean Job Length	Mean Job Status	N
Father's Status 1	12.0	2.78	9
Father's Status 2/3	21.6	3.05[a]	19
Father's Status 4	11.9	4.14	14
Education ‹ 7 yrs.	14.2[b]	3.55	31
Education ›=7 yrs.	23.6	3.07	14
Owners	18.6	1.90[c]	10
Employees	17.6	3.83	35
Blacks	17.6	3.87[d]	15
Jews	15.5	2.93	15
Italians	13.6	3.40	15
Personal Networks	21.6[e]	3.62	16
Formal Means	12.7	4.00	19

Notes: [a] $P < .05$ that job status for sons of fathers with status 2/3 differs from sons of fathers' status 4. (Three respondents were not able to supply data on father's status.)

[b] $P < .05$ that job length differs by educational level.

[c] $P < .05$ that job status differs by class.

[d] $P < .05$ that Jews and blacks differ on job status.

[e] $P < .05$ that job length differs by method of job access.

held midlife jobs for an average of 23.6 years, while those with less than seven years of education lasted only 14.2 years. Father's status exhibited a curvilinear relation, while the differences within classes and within ethnic groups are not significant. Finally, another significant result is that those employees who found jobs via network ties report an average job length of 21.6 years while those using formal means remained only 12.7 years.

The central question of this research, however, concerns the effects of sector on employee outcome. Table 2 reports these statistics. Here we see that even without unionization, co-ethnic employment provided significantly longer positions (20.1 years) than did secondary jobs (4.14 years). Although positions in the primary labor

market of the majority economy were longer than those within the
two co-ethnic possibilities, they were not significantly so.[10]

With so small a sample, the introduction of further controls is
problematic. However, attempts to cross-classify sector with additional factors of potential importance unearthed a particularly interesting pattern with regard to method of job access. Separating the
two factors yields very small cells, but the figures suggest that long
tenure was associated with the combination of networks and enclave
posts. Non-unionized enclave employment without contacts was
very short (3.5 years), while contacts did nothing for secondary
workers (2.5 years). In fact, here the figures reverse themselves in
favor of formal means (4.8 versus 2.5 years). In the two unionized
sectors, a similar but less dramatic trend obtains. Although job
length in these two arenas was respectable regardless of means of
entry, those applicants using formal methods suffered some
disadvantage.[11] To summarize, the data on job tenure suggest that
co-ethnic employment obtained through a personal referral offers
substantial stability.

Job Status

For these respondents high status was elusive. By age 40, they
achieved an average status of only 3.40, not a very high rating on
the Thernstrom scale, where 1.00 is the most favorable and 5.00
the least favorable outcome. Turning back now to the right side of
Table 1, we note that men whose fathers were employees without
subordinates (4 on Wright and Perrone's scale), experienced
significantly lower prestige themselves (4.14 versus 3.05 and 2.78
for men with some discretion over their own or others' labor power).
That the self-employed displayed higher status than employees is
hardly informative, since this advantage is inherent in the construction of the measure. But, ethnicity too claims an influence, with
blacks having lowest (3.87) and Jews highest (2.93) prestige. While

10. The results for job length at first and last jobs display a weaker version of this
pattern.
11. The results at first job revealed an even more complex phenomenon. Those
men who were directly hired (all by relatives) experienced either very short (0.58
years, N=3) or very long (49 years, N=1) mean tenure. The information supplied
by these respondents suggests that the brief situations involved the exploitation of
family members in the manner suggested by the writings of Bonacich (1973). On the
other hand, employment gained through personal referral appeared more strongly
associated with opportunity. This process could not be explored further because by
midlife the practice of direct hiring by a contact had all but disappeared. Still, at
last job, personal referrals continued to lead to longer employment in all but the
secondary sector.

TABLE 2

STATISTICS ON JOB TENURE AT MIDLIFE FOR EMPLOYEES BY SECTOR AND MODE OF ACCESS

STATISTIC	SECTOR			
	Coethnic Non-Union	Coethnic Union	Union Govt	Secondary
Total Mean				
Length	20.1[a]	16.4	22.6	4.14[a]
Stand Dev	20.0	14.2	8.82	4.10
N	8	9	11	7
Mean Length Via				
Personal Access	25.7	18.7	27.7	2.50
Stand Dev	20.3	20.0	8.77	0.707
N	6	4	4	2
Mean Length Via				
Formal Access	3.50	14.6	19.7	4.80
Stand Dev	2.12	9.66	7.99	4.82
N	2	5	7	5

Note: [a] Difference between columns 1 and 4, $p < .05$.

the direction of the effects for education and for job search strategies is the same on job status as it was on job length, these two factors do not prove statistically significant predictors of the former measure.

Table 3 records the sectoral contributions to job status for employees. We see a continuum of growing prestige associated with increasingly ethnic positions. (Note that low numbers reflect high status.) This result indicates that jobs in the primary, union/government sector, while long on security, were short on prestige, at least for these respondents. It seems likely that men were reluctant to abandon these positions because they offered substantial stability and benefits despite their low status. However, there is no reason to believe that either type of enclave position was inferior to opportunities in the primary sector. The jobs in the co-ethnic non-unionized sector were significantly higher in rank (3.25) than those in the secondary arena (4.43).

Attention to the influence of networks within sectors also duplicates the findings for job length. Co-ethnic jobs at midlife in the non-unionized sector that were facilitated by contacts were higher

TABLE 3

STATISTICS ON JOB STATUS AT MIDLIFE FOR EMPLOYEES BY SECTOR AND MODE OF ACCESS

STATISTIC	SECTOR			
	Coethnic Non-Union	Coethnic Union	Union Govt	Secondary
Total				
Mean Status	3.25[a]	3.78	3.91	4.43[a]
Stand Dev	1.04	0.834	0.701	0.787
N	8	9	11	7
Mean Via				
Personal Access	3.00	3.50	4.00	5.00
Stand Dev	1.10	1.00	0.826	0
N	6	4	4	2
Mean Via				
Formal Access	4.00	4.00	3.86	4.20
Stand Dev	0	0.707	0.690	0.837
N	2	5	7	5

[a] Difference between columns 1 and 4, p‹.05.

in average status (3.00) than posts in that arena secured by formal means (4.00). This effect reverses to a slight degree in the primary labor market (4.00 versus 3.86), probably because status does not vary very much in this setting. But in the secondary environment, personal sponsorship became a real detriment (5.00 versus 4.20). Thus the value of personal as against formal means of job entry again seems a function of the type of job environment involved, a finding noted also by Anderson (1974) and Calzavera (1983).[12]

These results, even more than those on job security, substantiate the thesis that co-ethnic employ offered advantages commensurate with those in the primary sector. Indeed, when co-ethnic employ was secured through personal means, the resulting average job status was above all other options.

12. The findings at first and last job also showed higher status associated with co-ethnic employ. The patterns of interaction between methods of access to jobs and sector at these two points in time were the same as at midlife, except in the case of co-ethnic first jobs. There formal entry did not depress job status.

But why did enclave participants fare so well? The discussion so far has said nothing about the structural viability of the ethnic enclave. A solid financial foundation is necessary if a substantial number of workers are to obtain such benefits as job security. But how does the enclave achieve a solid resource base? To the extent that interview data reveal the economic organization of the enclave, this structure is the necessary next topic.

ANALYSIS OF ENTREPRENEURIAL SUCCESS

Although only ten respondents were self-employed at midlife, Table 1 has already described these positions as relatively stable and tautologically prestigious. However, looking across the careers of respondents, there were a total of twenty entrepreneurs. Between them they undertook forty separate enterprises. Several men from each group gave independence a try at least once. Even among the black respondents, whom many would anticipate were exclusively employees, four of fifteen entered some form of self-employment. The level of drive among these men is communicated by the remark of one Afro-American respondent: "When you stop pushing, you're dead."

At the same time, business was precarious. The line between owner and worker was very thin, and enterprises toppled as quickly and as easily as they rose. Two restauranteers began and ended as kitchen workers. A butcher held his own shop only a few years. Most particularly among Afro-Americans, commerce was fragile and easily discouraged.

That Jews are a vigorously entrepreneurial group is widely recognized and clearly borne out in this study. Comprising only 33 percent of the sample (N=45), Jews were 45 percent of the men with one or more business efforts (N=20), 55 percent of those with two or more (N=9), and 80 percent of those assuming three or more undertakings (N=5). On the most reliable indicator of prosperity that the data provide, duration of the enterprise, Jewish first attempts averaged 2.42 years above the grand mean of all efforts (10.6 years).

There is no denying the contribution that a long history of mercantilism has made to Jewish success. Still, attention to the structural differences between Jewish and non-Jewish endeavor furnishes additional clues to the causes of differential ethnic achievement. For example, 89 percent of Jews beginning their first entrepreneurial venture had some experience as employees in the same industry, compared to 71 percent of Italians and 25 percent of blacks. Moreover, this experience paid off. The establishments of first time entrepreneurs who had employee experience in their field survived an average of over 13 years (N=14), compared to only 4 years (N=6) for their novice counterparts.

Another mechanism aspiring entrepreneurs utilized to enhance their viability was to rely upon partners, kin, or friends with relevant backgrounds. For example, a respondent who obtained ownership of a hat store had a wife who had previously worked as a trimmer in a millinery factory.

This reliance on co-ethnic support to enhance business prosperity is a major characteristic of the successful enclave. Almost 20 percent of the enterprises used kinsmen in some laboring capacity, while 45 percent of all endeavors utilized some capital beyond what the respondent brought to the undertaking himself. About half of these contributors were kinsmen, the remainder being partners who in only one case did not share the respondent's ethnicity. In no instance did a businessman report assistance from a former employer. Rather, family ties were exploited for ethnic entrepreneurship, and migrants also attempted to mobilize the resources of friends and co-workers.

Another way of documenting the benefits of collective endeavor is to categorize types of intra-ethnic business linkages and relate these linkages to economic outcome. Recall that the term horizontal linkage refers to the concentration of a group in a small number of endeavors. Backward linkages mesh producers to suppliers, while their forward counterparts join ethnic consumer goods to the corresponding customers.[13]

In pursuing these distinctions, it is necessary to control for the experience of the entrepreneur because experience extends the longevity of the enterprise. Those entrepreneurs who succeed best often have previous attempts behind them. Thus the analysis is limited to the largest pool of data, first undertaking. At this stage there were ten cases of co-ethnic suppliers, eleven situations of co-ethnic customers, and fourteen examples of co-ethnic concentration. Obviously these overlap, so heavily in fact, that the independent effect of each is hard to gauge. Yet, there were five examples of concentration only, four instances of customers only, and one case of suppliers only.

The impact of these categories is best illustrated in relation to

13. One informant was engaged in an enterprise that held none of these qualities. This effort might best be categorized as not of the ethnic enclave, at least on structural counts. It is probably not accidental that his business lasted less than one year.

the longevity of the enterprise. The respondents experiencing occupational concentration alone averaged 11.2 years in business; those with only co-ethnic customers lasted merely 2.0 years. Leaving aside the one case of co-ethnic suppliers as too small for interpretation, these results suggest that a pool of co-ethnic customers alone is an inadequate foundation for vigorous enterprise. An Italian beautician explained the importance of customers even more definitively. "I always chose Jewish neighborhoods for my shops", he declared. "Jewish women have the money and they always want to look nice."

A close relation between horizontal and backward linkages is suggested by the finding that two-thirds of the businessmen located in endeavors displaying horizontal links reported obtaining the major portion of their supplies from co-ethnic sources. Thus, concentration occurs not only at the level of an occupation (horizontal), but throughout the broader industry (backward). Moreover, the opportunity for employees and failing entrepreneurs to obtain valuable experience for the future is surely enhanced by the industrial concentration of an ethnic labor force. For, as already shown, prior experience in the same field improves the probability of later entrepreneurial success.

The ability of each ethnic group to forge the three types of linkages followed predictable lines. Almost every Jewish enterprise participated in all three parameters. The Italians were less solid, 43 percent of their enterprises met two of the enclave's linkage patterns. Interestingly, it was co-ethnic customers that were least typical of Italian undertakings, with only two of seven first businesses catering to other Italians. Conversely, the only linkage present in 75 percent of the black enterprises was their black customers.

A black fruit vendor vividly portrayed the disadvantages of non-co-ethnic suppliers when he described automatic price increases that he suffered when buying at the wholesale produce market. On occasion he could circumvent discrimination by commissioning white acquaintances to purchase fruits and vegetables on his behalf. In contrast, an Italian informant in the same line of work told of learning the business from an Italian boss. Later, he went out on his own, but by then he was well versed in the art of haggling with his Italian compatriots at the market.

This discussion has emphasized the collective nature of white ethnic entrepreneurship. The disadvantages suffered by black entrepreneurs directly follow from an individualistic economic organization. While some observers explain collectivism in terms of culture (Light, 1972), structural factors are also involved. Most importantly, Afro-Americans are not a significant number of butchers or bakers. They produce nothing they sell, and what they sell they offer only to themselves. These limitations, partly the result of racism and partly the result of the lack of an ethnic legacy in industry or craft, set up a vicious circle by reinforcing the propensity for blacks to eschew co-operative endeavor. Thus, in their study of Pittsburgh ethnic groups, Bodnar, *et al.* (1982) observe a staunchly individualist economic strategy among their black informants.

The additional possibility that the survival of these ethnic employers was enhanced by the payment of exceptionally low wages could not be systematically explored. The few who reported engaging non-family labor, however, generally claimed to have procured their employees through the appropriate union, a practice that implies a union wage.

What the data available here do indicate is that prior experience, interpersonal resources, and economic linkages are valuable to ethnic enterprise. Unfortunately, the small sample size prohibits quantification of the net benefits contributed by each of these variables. Yet, the essentially "ethnic" quality of all the relevant factors is unmistakable.

CONCLUSIONS

The survey described here provides more clues than conclusions, a shortcoming already anticipated at the outset. Still, some patterns appear more than spurious. Among the most important findings are the greater stability and higher status of enclave employment compared to labor in the secondary sector, the suggestion that these rewards are limited to recruits personally sponsored by co-workers, and the association of successful minority enterprise with the mobilization of ethnic resources.

The trends observed for the two worker outcome measures are consonant with prior research on the effects of personal characteristics on occupational rewards. Studies of labor market structure have also concluded that primary sector employment outranks secondary sector participation (Beck, *et al.*, 1978). The major finding of this project is that there were some advantages to enclave jobs. In fact, because unionization per se is a weak proxy for sector, segmentation theorists would also relegate to the secondary sector many of the jobs categorized here as co-ethnic union positions. These likewise were distinctly better than the comparison group of non-co-ethnic, non-unionized secondary posts. Thus, the findings for this sample both support other studies critical of the dualistic nature of segmentation theory and confirm the hypothesis that enclave employment delimits a viable alternative sector.

The possibility that personal contacts were necessary to reap rewards in the enclave casts some doubt on whether the general phenomenon of shared ethnicity is sufficient to promote worker benefit. Perhaps more direct personal ties are required to fuel the mechanisms of mutual obligation. One hypothesis already suggested is that ties between employees encourage a feeling of social belonging and a faster acclimation to the job. Waldinger (1983) has proposed that a socially cohesive co-ethnic work group may diminish incentives to leave the job. A related possibility is that co-worker bonds could lead to obligations about performance that are absent in more anonymous situations. Greater initiative and diligence could, in turn, enhance the opportunity for promotion. If this reasoning is correct, further research is needed to determine if this phenomenon is exceptionally strong under conditions of co-ethnic employment or is simply an outgrowth of more general interpersonal processes, as the findings in all but the secondary sector suggest.

Yet, how to explain the disadvantage associated with personal sponsorship in the secondary sector? Perhaps interpersonal bonds produced different results in different surroundings. Labor market segmentation thinkers maintain that an oppressive and arbitrary atmosphere characterizes job conditions in the secondary sector. In such an environment, relationships between workers could promote consciousness of job dissatisfactions. Indeed, one reason that early factory owners integrated ethnic groups was to defuse just the sort of disaffection associated with secondary positions (Edwards, 1979). Workers of many languages were less likely to seek collective redress for their malaise. Hence, within the secondary sector isolated workers may have fared relatively better than employees who were part of an interpersonally attached, and potentially more alienated labor force.

Regrettably, it was impossible to obtain firm level data on the economic stability of employee environments. Thus, the possibility that market factors, not social relations, determined worker opportunity cannot be ruled out. While controlling for sector mitigates this danger, the analysis of ethnic entrepreneurship suggests that differences in firm viability certainly obtained within that sector.

In particular, the longevity of minority businesses was enhanced by the mobilization of a variety of ethnic resources. These included collective financing, concentration in one, frequently "ethnic" specialty, and backward linkages to co-ethnic sources of supply. Location in a predominantly co-ethnic market appeared least responsible for a favorable outcome. These findings should encourage policy analysts to re-evaluate current strategies for minority business development, especially decisions to place minority firms in ghetto locations.

But more studies are still needed, and in this regard, a word of caution. Ethnic enclaves are not economically independent of the majority sector. This researcher has simplified considerably by ignoring the many contextual variables that affect economic survival: markets, technology, capital, credit. Critics have taken segmentation theorists to task for oversimplifying the organization of work (Wallace and Kalleberg, 1982). Similarly, enclave thinkers tend to sweep away complexities with generalization and selective attention. The main excuse for doing so here is that the period and industries covered were prosperous during the time we took a look. An eventually more complete understanding of the ethnic enclave cannot permit such casualness.

REFERENCES

Aldrich, H. *et al.*
1984   "Ethnic Advantage and Minority Business Development", In *Ethnic Communities in Business.* Edited by R. Ward and R. Jenkins. Cambridge: Cambridge University Press.

Anderson, G.
1974   *Networks of Contact: The Portuguese and Toronto.* Waterloo, Ont.: Wilfrid Laurier University Press.

Beck, E. M. *et al.*
1978   "Stratification in a Dual Economy: A Sectoral Model of Earnings Determination," *American Sociological Review,* 43:704-20. Oct.

Blau, P. and O.D. Duncan
1967   *The American Occupational Structure.* New York: The Free Press.

Bodnar, J. *et al.*
1982   *Lives of Their Own.* Urbana: University of Illinois Press.

Bonacich, E.
1973   "A Theory of Middleman Minorities", *American Sociological Review,* 38:583-94. Oct.

Bonacich, E. and J. Modell
1980   *The Economic Basis of Ethnic Solidarity.* Berkeley: University of California Press.

Calzavera, L.
1983   "Social Networks and Access to Job Opportunities". Paper presented at the annual meeting of the American Sociological Association, Detroit.

Duncan, O.D. *et al.*
1972   *Socioeconomic Background and Achievement.* New York: Seminar Press.

Edwards, R.
1979   *Contested Terrain.* New York: Basic Books

Edwards, R. *et al.*
1975   *Labor Market Segmentation.* Lexington, Mass.: D.C. Heath.

Gordon, D. *et al.*
1982   *Segmented Work, Divided Workers.* New York: Cambridge University Press.

Granovetter, M.
1974   *Getting a Job.* Cambridge, Mass.: Harvard University Press.

1983   "Economic Action and Social Structure: A Theory of Embeddedness", Dept. of Sociology, S.U.N.Y. at Stony Brook. Mimeo.

Hutchinson, E.
1956   *Immigrants and Their Children, 1850-1950.* New York: John Wiley.

Lieberson, S.
1980   *A Piece of the Pie.* Berkeley, University of California Press.

Light, I.
1972   *Ethnic Enterprise in America.* Berkeley, Calif.: University of California Press.

Lin, N. *et al.*
1981   "Social Resources and Strength of Ties: Structural Factors in Occupational Status Attainment", *American Sociological Review,* 46:393-405, August.

Lovell-Troy, L.
1980   "Clan Structure and Economic Activity: The Case of the Greeks in Small Business Enterprise". In *Self Help in Urban America.* Edited by S. Cummings. Port Washington, N.Y.: Kennikat Press.

Model, S.
1985   *Ethnic Bonds in the Workplace: Blacks, Italians, and Jews in New York City.* Unpublished Ph.D. dissertation, University of Michigan.

Moore, D.
1981   *At Home in America: Second Generation New York Jews.* New York: Columbia University Press.

Piore, M.
1979   *Birds of Passage.* New York: Cambridge University Press.

Portes, A. and R. Bach
1980   "Immigrant Earnings: Cuban and Mexican Immigrants in the United States", *International Migration Review,* 14:315-41, Fall.

Reitz, J. *et al.*
1981   "Ethnic Inequality and Segregation in Jobs". Research Paper No. 123. Center for Urban and Community Studies, University of Toronto.

Rischin, M.
1962   *The Promised City: New York's Jews, 1870-1914.* Cambridge, Mass.: Harvard University Press.

Sowell, T.
1981   *Markets and Minorities.* New York: Basic Books.

Thernstrom, S.
1973   *The Other Bostonians.* Cambridge, Mass.: Harvard University Press.

U.S. Bureau of the Census
1952   *U.S. Census of the Population: 1950.* Vol. II, *Characteristics of the Population,* Part 32, *New York.* Washington, D.C.: Government Printing Office.

1954   *U.S. Census of the Populations: 1950.* Vol. IV, *Special Reports,* Part 3, *Nativity and Parentage.* Washington, D.C.: Government Printing Office.

U.S. Immigration Commission
1911   *Reports,* Part 23, *Immigrants in Industry.* Washington, D.C.: Government Printing Office.

Waldinger, R.
1983   "Ethnic Enterprise: A Critique and Reformulation". Paper presented at the annual meeting of the American Sociological Association, Detroit.

Wallace, M. and A. Kalleberg
1981   "Economic Organization of Firms and Labor Market Consequences: Towards a Specification of Dual Economy Theory". In *Sociological Perspectives on Labor Markets.* Edited by I. Berg. New York: Academic Press. Pp. 77-117.

Wilson, K. and A. Portes
1980   "Immigrant Enclaves: An Analysis of the Labor Market Experience of Cubans in Miami", *American Journal of Sociology,* 86:295-319, Sept.

Wilson, K. and W. Martin
1982   "Ethnic Enclaves: A Comparison of the Cuban and Black Economies in Miami", *American Journal of Sociology,* 88:135-160, July.

Wong, B.
1974   *Patronage, Brokerage, and Entrepreneurship and the Chinese Community of New York.* Unpublished Ph.D. Dissertation, University of Wisconsin.

1976   "Social Stratification, Adaptive Strategies, and the Chinese Community of New York", *Urban Life,* 5:33-52, April.

Wright, E. and L. Perrone
1977   "Marxist Class Categories and Income Inequality", *American Sociological Review,* 42:32-55, Feb.

Three Generations of Greek Americans: A Study in Ethnicity

By ALICE SCOURBY

This study proposes to measure ethnic identity among three generations of Greek Americans living in the New York metropolitan area.
New York City has the largest Greek community in the United States.
Although the evidence reveals variation from generation to generation, the majority of Greeks still have a relatively strong attachment to
their ethnic culture, in spite of identification with American society.

A cursory look at the literature dealing with Greek ethnicity
only disappoints those who are looking for a clear and simple
definition of what constitutes ethnicity for the Greek American.
One reads, on the one hand, that the Church has been remiss in
providing its parishioners with an understanding of Hellenism and,
as a result, has led Greek-Americans to view Hellenism in parochial and tenuous terms. Because of this, runs the argument, Americans of Greek descent have been so brainwashed as to regard
ritualistic religion, along with Greek music, Greek cuisine and Greek
dances, as comprising the alpha and omega of Greekness. On the
other hand, one also reads that the Church has provided the solidarity and inspiration, without which a Greek American community would be impossible (Saloutos, 1973:395-407). Its supporters
maintain that the Church has succeeded despite the inveterate factionalism that has plagued it throughout this century. In 1970, when
the delegates to the Clergy Laity Congress approved the substitu-
tion of English for Greek in the Liturgy, it was viewed by many as
the only realistic action that could be taken in the light of the fact
that a new generation of Greek Americans was emerging without a
competent knowledge of the Greek language. It was regarded as a
genuine effort to reconcile Hellenism with the demands of American society.

This seemingly innocuous attempt to salvage the younger gener-

Reprinted from *International Migration Review* 14 (Spring 1980), 43-52.

Alice Scourby is chairman of the Department of Sociology at C. W. Post Center of
Long Island University.

ation by making the Church more relevant to them represented a long delayed response to the grievances lodged by the second generation who found the Church's role alien to their secular experiences. The recent introduction of English in the Church was spurred by the belief that this alienation could be overcome by providing a basis for communication on a variety of social issues including abortion, birth control and mixed marriages. The underlying rationale was that the application of long held concepts such as the "logos" were no longer viable in a society dominated by scientific modes of thought.

Simultaneously, one also reads articles which report that the third generation of Greek Americans feel affinity neither for the Church, nor with their Greek heritage, and does not identify strongly with folkloristic values. These authors suggest that the locus of identification for the younger generation has changed, that they have opted for "class" rather than religion or nationality as the locus of belonging. They have done this, runs the thesis, because they are far more psychologically secure in their Americanism than were prior generations. As a result of this, "class" and "status" have become the *sine qua non* of their identification (Kourvetaris, 1971:34-38).

Some Greek Americans identify ethnically with a popular fair of music, dance and food, only to have it demeaned as trivia by others who impose a hierarchy of values that alienates most of the population of Greek descent. Since a pecking order functions to affirm one's own worth in most societies, this need to rank groups from Brahmins to Untouchables should not strike us as too unusual. It is true that the cultural appurtenances that are deemed trivial are, in and by themselves, meaningless. Yet, in the collective sharing they are transformed from something profane to something sacred by providing the *esprit de corps* so essential to a collective sense of belonging and community.

Clearly, ethnic identity is extremely difficult to pinpoint. The concept is a fluid one and changes along a continuum of such variables as generation, education, occupation and class. For example, the first generation of Greek immigrants who came to this country in the early part of this century viewed nationality and religion as part and parcel of their identity. For this reason the Church became the major vehicle through which the immigrants' world was protected. Language, religion, old world customs and endogamous marriages were the accepted indices of Greek identification (Stycos, 1978: 24-34). Any deviation by their children constituted a threat to their security, self-image, traditional roles and well-being.

Their children, the second generation, experienced the parents' definition of ethnicity as a liability. Despite this, the Greek Church, the Greek school and the Greek language became integral parts of the self-image of these reluctant participants. They became the hyphenated Greek Americans bordering two worlds. The collision of these two worlds reversed the natural order of things so that the children became the culture bearers and the social arbiters for their parents. This paper is not the place to analyze the demeaning experiences and rejections suffered by the second generation in their efforts to adjust to American surroundings within the ideological framework of the "melting pot" (Anonymous, 1950:41-42; Saloutos, 1964:310-325). The English language, one of the most important indices used in measuring adjustment to American culture, was hampered by the fact that, for the second generation, Greek had to be spoken at home, albeit limited by a vocabulary dictated by the exigencies of day-to-day living. Nevertheless, ethnicity for this generation was still identified with language, tradition and religion, but was altered in conjunction with the American ethos of success and upward mobility.

By the 1950s a third generation of Greek Americans was emerging, and a new definition of ethnicity was in the wind. This new definition as articulated by social scientists who believed that ethnicity based upon nationality and language was gradually being replaced by religion in the lives of all Americans. They measured religiosity by a belief in God and attendance at religious services. Belonging to a religious institution was not only a new way of determining one's ethnicity, it was a legitimate way of being an American, because while one was expected to give up the ways of the "old world", one was never expected to give up one's religion. However, the three religions having institutional status were Protestantism, Catholicism, and Judaism (Herberg, 1950). Obviously, Greek Orthodoxy was excluded. What did this mean for the third generation of Greek Americans? Was being Greek different from being Greek Orthodox? Given the above thesis, it would seem not.

In the mid-1960s we sampled seventy-one third generation Greek Americans in the New York metropolitan area and found that religion continued to provide the context of self-identification for them. Indeed, while identification with language, customs, and a preference for endogamous marriages persisted, it was with a marked ambivalence. For example, on the one hand they wanted the Church to substitute English in the sermon, but on the other hand, they did not want all Orthodox Churches to merge (Scourby, 1967).

In a recent study of first, second and third generation Greek Americans, totaling 160, it was found that there was less Greek school attendance wtih each subsequent group; fewer of the third generation spoke Greek; and increased identification as Americans was noted among the younger generation, as was a significant increase in the number who approved of non-Greek marriages as compared to those of the first and second generation.

THE STUDY

The following data are derived from a sample of 160 individuals of Greek descent living in the New York Metropolitan area. The sample was fixed by circumstance. The questionnaire in this study was prepared in English and in Greek. The first part was a personal data sheet on which the subjects were asked to designate their age, sex, education and other census information.

The second part of the questionnaire consisted of items measuring the rate of assimilation. Indices included language, church attendance, religious attitudes, identification with cultural values and exogamy which would permit the respondent to be placed in either of two categories: Ethno-Religious or Ethno-Cultural. The former reflects the ethnic identification associated with the first generation, i.e., religion, language and nationalism, while the latter reflects a wider range of cultural values, i.e., Greek history, dance, music, cuisine and social organizations.

The sample was drawn from several sources including religious and secular organizations. Of the 160 individuals, 46 percent were males and 54 percent females. The age groups represented are 13-22 years (N-76), 23-45 years (N-40), and 46-68 years (N-33). Of the total sample, approximately two-thirds were either in high school or completed it. The remaining one-third completed one to four years of college or postgraduate work.

Forty-two percent of the sample were students, 18 percent professionals, while 32 percent were equally divided between white collar workers and housewives. Six percent were blue collar workers and two percent were unemployed. Thirty-eight percent of the professional category were found in the first generation, 35 percent in the second generation and 27 percent in the third generation.

Forty-two percent of the respondents' fathers were white collar workers, 30 percent blue collar, 16 percent professional and 12 percent other than the above. The greatest concentration of blue collar workers was found in the second and third generations. The white collar group was equally divided between the second and third generations, while two-thirds of the professional group was found among fathers of the third generation.

Sixty-seven percent of the respondents' mothers were housewives. They were the largest number in each of the three generations. Eleven percent were white collar, ten percent professional and eight percent blue collar. The remaining four percent were either unemployed or deceased.

These findings were consistent with the 1970 Census (U.S. Department of Commerce, 1976:114) which reports that 27,949 males of Greek ancestry who were 25 years old and over completed high school from a total of 87,143. Of these, 22,115 or 82 percent had completed four years of college or more. In contrast, only 9,613 or 20 percent of native born women of Greek background totaling 42,396 completed high school and went on to complete four or more years of college. Less than half of the women who entered college graduated, revealing the persistence of traditional attitudes regarding role expectations of male and female. It should be noted, however, that the 1970 Census data indicated a significant rise of native born females of Greek ancestry in the professional category: 8.3 percent in 1950, 17 percent in 1970. As of 1970, the largest number of native born women of Greek descent were in the category of clerical and kindred workers, whereas the largest number of native born males of Greek ancestry were in the professional, technical and kindred category, followed by the category of managers and administrators. These data are consistent with the occupational distribution in our study. Of the 75 males and 85 females in our sample: 31 comprise the first generation, 62 the second generation and 67 the third generation. They responded as follows to the questionnaire.

GREEK LANGUAGE

A significant index of assimilation is the declining use of the ethnic language. The answers were coded as follows: Do you speak Greek? 1) Yes; 2) No; and 3) No, but understand it. We found that erosion took place across the second and third generations. Of the second generation, 96.7 percent indicated they spoke Greek while 57.8 percent of the third generation spoke Greek. In the "No" category, the second generation comprised 3.3 percent of the total and the third generation 21.9 percent (Chi Square = 35.119, 2 d.f., Sig. @ .005).

Should English Replace Greek in Church

The individuals in the first generation unanimously responded in the negative. The second generation was divided and the third generation was unanimous in wanting the sermons delivered in English. Both the second and third generations, however, demonstrated a more traditional response when asked if English should replace Greek in the Liturgy. Of the second generation, 58.3. percent preferred the Liturgy in Greek while the third generation was divided. One explanation for their split attitude toward the Sermon and the Liturgy may be that the latter represents the sacred, the transcendental aspect of the religious experience and does not require knowledge of the language, while the sermon represents the Church's position on issues ranging from religious to secular (Chi Square = 16.7375, 4 d.f., Sig. @ .005).

Attend Greek School

The Greek school has traditionally been a most important vehicle for transmitting ethnic identity. First generation parents knew instinctively that their children would be quickly Americanized without supportive institutions to counteract it. Attendance in Greek school was significant between the second and third generations. Ninety percent of the second generation had attended, while 70.3 percent of the third generation did (Chi Square = 15.715, 2 d.f., Sig. @ .005).

Intermarriage

The ethnic background of one's friends is an indicator of prospective mates from which one will choose. The respondents were asked if they would marry someone who was not of Greek extraction. Responses were coded as follows: 1) Yes; 2) No; and 3) Indifferent. With each successive generation there was a tendency toward marrying outside the group. Of the first generation, 51.6 percent reported that they would prefer to marry someone who was Greek, 30 percent of the second generation expressed similar sentiments compared to 25 percent of the third generation (Chi Square = 10.4402, 4 d.f., Sig. @ .5).

Contact with Greek Mass Media

The question of involvement with Greek mass media indicated a decline from first to third generation. Of the third generation, 55.2 percent expressed no contact, while 7.4 percent in the first generation reported similar response. Statistical significance was found between the first and third generations (Chi Square = 12.4316, 2 d.f., Sig. @ .005).

Attend Church

Respondents were asked if they attend church: 1) Every Sunday; 2) Every other Sunday; 3) Several times a year. Thirty-eight percent of the first generation, 61 percent of the second and 65 percent of the third generation go to Church at least every other Sunday. The second generation is inclined to go to Church more often than the first generation. When education is kept constant, those in the first and second generations seem to attend Church less frequently (Chi Square = 18.342, 4 d.f., Sig. @ .005).

Attitude Toward the Church

The respondents were asked to indicate their attitude toward the Church, coded as follows: 1) Strongly favorable to the Church; 2) Neutral; and 3) Strongly against the Church (Thurstone and Chave, 1932). The three generations were strongly favorable to the Church or at least neutral. Of the first generation, 35.5 percent were strongly favorable, 51.6 percent were neutral and only 3.2 percent were strongly against the Church. In the second generation, 78 percent were strongly favorable while 20 percent were neutral and none were strongly against the Church. The third generation indicated 56.3 percent as strongly favorable, 39.1 percent as neutral, while 3.1 percent were strongly against the Church. Ten percent failed to respond. The second generation was significantly more favorably inclined toward the Church. Only three individuals in the sample were strongly against the Church: one from the first generation and two from the third generation.

The first generation college graduates tended to be more critical of the Church than their second generation counterparts. They were opposed, however, to the use of English in the Church, did not support an American Orthodoxy, and chose friends of similar ethnic background. Sixty-one percent indicated their friends were Greek compared to 25.3 percent of the second generation and 14 percent of the third generation.

Ethnic Identity

The respondents were asked to identify themselves as either: 1) Greek; 2) American; 3) Greek Orthodox; 4) Greek American. The second and third generations tended to identify as either Greek American or Greek Orthodox, but a trend was discerned for third generation to identify as American. The first generation identified as Greek or Greek Orthodox.[1] A further inquiry was made as to whether there was a difference between being Greek and being Greek Orthodox. Fifty-eight percent of the first generation, 55 percent of the second and 64 percent of the third generation feel there is a distinction. As for a merging of all Eastern Orthodox Churches: the first generation is opposed, the second generation is divided and the third generation is strongly opposed to a merger.

A final question dealt with impressions held by Greek people. The responses were coded as follows: 1) Positive; 2) Negative; and 3) Indifferent. No generation had negative attitudes, although a hint of indifference was discerned in the response of the third generation.

The findings of this study show that both U.S. born and foreign born Greek Americans have retained a relatively strong attachment to their ethnic background. It also indicates that the attainment of higher occupational status among the second generation did not result, as might be expected, in a denial of ethnic identity or an abandonment of the Greek community.

The results have demonstrated that there is an association between ethno-religious identification and generation that is significantly different at the one percent level.

The first generation is still strongly identified with an ethno-religious dimension, while the third generation showed a greater identification with the broader cultural values of the Greek American community. Confusion as to precisely what constitutes Greek ethnicity was reflected in the younger generation who, while they expected both the sermon and the Liturgy to be in English, were negative in their response to becoming part of an American Orthodox Church which would unify all Eastern Orthodox Churches. A myriad of inconsistencies were revealed. Clearly, so much of ethnic identity is an unconscious experience as well as an ambivalent experience. The individual is reacting to judgments and responses of people within the group as well as those outside. Judgments, both positive and negative, can operate to pull the person toward or away from the group into which one was born. How these positive and negative forces are transmitted to the third generation vis-à-vis the second generation is something about which little is known. One thing is clear, more studies that will take us beyond the anecdotal and the descriptive narrative are essential for an understanding of the complex phenomenon of ethnicity.

Complicating the picture even further has been the influx of new immigrants since the Immigration Act of 1965. According to

1. Multiple answers obviated Chi Square.

the Annual Report of 1975 (U.S. Department of Justice, INS 1976:65), 125,924 Greeks came to the United States between 1966 and 1975. In the year ending June, 1975, a total of 1,864 males in the age category 20-29 emigrated to the U.S. as compared to 1,170 for the female population. It is interesting to note that during this same period, 5,719 Greeks were classified as housewives, children and other, with no occupation reported. The other largest category of 1,223 were in the category of craftsmen and kindred workers, while only 421 Greeks were listed as professional, technical and kindred workers. If it can be agreed upon that ethnicity is affected by generation, occupation and education, then the figures would lead us to expect the persistence of traditional attitudes regarding ethnicity, the role of the Church and family size. Since the new arrivals are mainly young, this may portend a high birth rate for the next decade, while the second and third generations continue to have low fertility rates following the population trend of Americans generally. The demographic imbalance between the old immigrants and the new immigrants produces needs and demands from different vantage points. The Greek American community has been and will continue to be fractured by the different rates of adjustment each group makes to the surrounding environment. Therefore, Greek ethnicity can only be understood within a specific social context.

For the majority of new immigrants, identification is rooted in nationality and the Church. If they do not find a Greek church, they build one. An unestimated number of Greek churches, not affiliated with the Greek Archdiocese of North and South America, have already been founded in the New York metropolitan area. It should not be surprising that the recent arrivals from Greece expected a Hellenized Church, thus repeating the pattern of earlier immigrants who sought continuity of experience and solidarity within the Church. They view the introduction of English in the Church as part of a conspiracy to "de-Hellenize" it. If the Greek language and Greek values are not the focal points of the established Church, then other avenues for maintaining self-esteem and security will be sought as, indeed, they are. In time, the children of

TABLE 1

Generation	Ethno-Religious Number	Percent	Ethno-Cultural Number	Percent	Total Number
1	24	75.0	8	25.0	32
2	38	57.5	28	42.4	66
3	26	41.9	36	58.0	62
	88		72		160

NOTE: $X^2 = 9.62$ d.f. = 2   Sig. @ .01

the new immigrants may react against the ethnic church their parents hold on to so tenaciously and, if so, a new ethnic identity will take form to be determined, in part, by the structure of the larger society.

REFERENCES

Anonymous
1950 "The Forgotten Generation", *Athene,* 10:23-24, 41-42. Winter.

Greeley, A.M. and W.C. McCready
1974 *Ethnicity in the United States.* New York: John Wiley & Sons.

Herberg, W.
1950 *Protestant, Catholic, Jew.* New York: Anchor Books.

Kourvetaris, G.
1971 "Patterns of Generational Subculture and Intermarriage of the Greeks in the United States", *International Journal of Sociology and the Family,* Pp. 34-48. May.

Saloutos, T.
1973 "The Greek Orthodox Church in the United States and Assimilation", *International Migration Review,* 7(4):395-407. Winter.

1964 *The Greeks in the United States.* Cambridge, Massachusetts: The Harvard University Press.

Scourby, A.
"Third Generation Greek Americans: A Study of Religious Attitudes". To be published by Arno Press Inc., New York.

Stycos, M.J.
1948 "The Spartan Greeks of Bridgetown: Community and Cohesion", *Common ground,* 8:24-34. Spring.

Thurstone, L.K., and E.J. Chave
1932 *The Measurement of Attitude.* Chicago: The University of Chicago Press.

U.S. Department of Commerce, Social and Economic Statistics Administration, Bureau of Census
1971 *1970 Census of Population Subject Reports: National Origin and Language.* Washington, D.C.: Government Printing Office.

U.S. Department of Justice, Immigration and Naturalization Service
1976 *1975 Annual Report Immigration and Naturalization Service.* Washington, D.C.: Government Printing Office.

Yancey, W. L., *et al.*
1976 "Emergent Ethnicity: A Review and Reformulation", *American Sociological Review,* 41:391-403. June.

Reflections of an African American on his Life in the Greater Buffalo Area, 1930s – 1960s

By JAMES D. BILOTTA

An American historian interested in the African American experience, particularly in black/white relations, has available a wealth of secondary material to pursue. However, for the researcher, there is little secondary material that can replace a first hand account, especially in the study of racialism. What better way to learn about a black perspective of life in the Buffalo area and of the struggle for basic civil rights than to have face to face discussions with an African American who lived in the area during the time period under discussion. This paper is based on a conversation with Mr. Harold Brown, who was born and lived in the Greater Buffalo area all his life.[1] Mr. Brown was the first African American to move his family into a previously all-white area of the Tonawandas (a suburban community north of Buffalo).

Born and raised in the City of Lackawanna, Mr. Brown grew up in the Ridge Road area in the late 1920s and 1930s era. At that time there were very few blacks in Lackawanna (located to the south of Buffalo). As he recalls, the area at that time was perhaps 95% white. The community had an international flavor, as Americans of German, Polish, Irish and Italian extraction mingled in Lackawanna. Economically, times were tough in the 1930s and for blacks conditions were unusually harsh. Added to economic woes were the effects of racial prejudice. Mr. Brown remembers that while white children seemed somewhat colorblind and were willing to mingle and play with him, their parents were usually opposed to this "mixing." On one occasion a white mother snatched her child away, simply

Reprinted from *Afro-Americans in New York Life and History* 13 (July 1989), 47-55.

James D. Bilotta is an historian and a resident of North Tonawanda, New York.

[1]The surname "Brown" is an alias. The subject wishes to keep his identity confidential. However, his name is known to the editor of this journal. Material for this paper was gathered from a taped conversation with the subject.

because she didn't want him talking to a black child. Incidents such as this stuck in his mind as he tried to understand the nature of white prejudice. As he attended the basically white public school system and later graduated from Lackawanna High School, he generally kept to himself. He received his degree at about the time of the outbreak of World War II in Europe.

As a result of the approaching United States involvement in the War, and the increasing demand for steel, Mr. Brown was hired at Bethlehem Steel's Lackawanna plant, one of the largest in the country. Here again his experience is revealing. He noted that after the war began Bethlehem would hire anyone, even grandma. He remembers sitting in the Bethlehem employment office as numerous white applicants were interviewed and offered employment. The personnel manager conducted the interviews in an open office, where conversation could easily be overheard. He recalled that he had to wait until the whites were processed, and that the interviewer would ask applicants if they graduated from high school and what job they wanted in the plant, i.e., skilled or semi-skilled jobs. Even white dropouts were offered these options. When his turn finally came, the manager never asked him if he had graduated from high school, never asked him what area he would like to work in, etc. Instead, he was told that they only had yard work available, the lowest unskilled bull work, work that most whites would not accept and, of course, this work was the lowest paying union scale labor. The memory of the way this manager conducted that interview still rankles Mr. Brown. Once employed, he found himself working with a crew that was about 90% black, but he was happy to have work. His experience at Bethlehem convinced him that the union, the company and the government worked hand-in-hand to keep the black man down economically. He recalls that he received no help or encouragement from the union.

After working there several years, Mr. Brown was drafted into the armed forces in 1943, and he found himself serving 3½ years in the Navy. Most of his recollections of life in the Navy were positive. In contrast to the other services, Mr. Brown believes that it was more difficult to practice discrimination in the Navy, especially when on shipboard, because men on board are dependent on one another in the operation and safety of the ship. The crew is isolated and each man has a particular job to do which benefits the entire crew. He remembers that his close friend during these years was a very light-skinned Negro from Virginia, named Leon. Leon, in fact, had blond hair and blue eyes. Mr. Brown asked Leon why he simply didn't cross over into the white world, which was routinely done by many Negroes who were able to pass. Life would certainly have been easier, as Mr. Brown believed that blacks in the United States faced a double-standard. Requirements for their advancement were usually higher than for whites. Leon replied that he knew who he was, where his roots were, and he was proud to be black.

After the Navy Mr. Brown returned to Lackawanna and to employment in the yard gang at Bethlehem. He was living with his father, who rented a home in Lackawanna. It was at this time, 1947, that he married, and in order to save money with which to eventually purchase his own home he worked another job, as manager of a cooperative store. Homes were being sold in Bethlehem Park, at this time, as the postwar building boom was getting under way, and Mr. Brown was interested in purchasing one. He remembers a telephone conversation with the realtor, who at first seemed more than willing to sell him a home. However, at one point the realtor wanted to speak to the store clerk, to ask if Mr. Brown was black. After "beating around the bush," the realtor finally got up the courage to ask Mr. Brown directly. Mr. Brown was aware of the question before it was asked. After being informed that Mr. Brown was of African descent, the realtor informed Mr. Brown that he could not sell to blacks because a white home owners association in the Park had decreed against this. It was at this point, when he had just about had his fill of Lackawanna, that a young black friend of his had acquired a 2 family home on Adams Street on Buffalo's East side. Mr. Brown decided to rent the upper half.

Mr. Brown thought it was a beautiful apartment, and the Browns had their first of four children there. It was also at this time that he had heard that the Post Office Department was hiring. He took the required civil service exam, passed it, and was given a position in the Buffalo Railway Mails division, which was later merged under the regular division when a new central office was built on Williams Street.

Mr. Brown continued to work full-time at Bethlehem as well as full-time at his post office job. With the extra income he bought new furniture. He always resented hand-me-downs of any kind, especially second-hand furnishings, and wanting to build a better life for himself and family he worked over 16 hours per day.

He lived in the apartment for several years until his father bought an older home from a German family on Glenwood Ave., in the Humboldt Park area of Buffalo. Mr. Brown recalls that in the 1950s it was very difficult for blacks to purchase new homes anywhere. Suburban developers would not sell to blacks. Therefore, African Americans usually had to take what was available, providing owners and/or realtors (who practiced redlining) would sell. In an effort to save money to eventually purchase his own home, and in order to help his father maintain and repair the home he had just purchased, Mr. Brown moved his family to his father's Glenwood house. That area was mainly white in the 1950s. Mr. Brown remembers coming home after working the 4 to 12 shift at Bethlehem and having to go down the cellar and stoke two coal fired furnaces. He eventually convinced his father to install a more modern and efficient gas furnace. At that point he was more determined than ever to purchase his own home, one that would fit his budget and suit his needs. He and his family spent a year looking and finally found such a home in the Town of Tonawanda, an all white suburb north of the City.

Mr. Brown recalls his first attempt at buying a new home in the Millstream Village subdivision of the Town of Tonawanda. At first the builder agreed, over the telephone, to show him the home he was interested in. However, when they met and the builder saw that Mr. Brown was of African descent, he quickly came up with a cover story that this was the last house he had and it was sold. Shortly thereafter, Mr. Brown found another home that he liked in the all white town, off Sheridan Drive.

Again Mr. Brown first contacted the builder by telephone and the latter, not knowing Brown's color, agreed to accept a down payment. Mr. Brown, meanwhile, had had enough experience with these situations, and he retained an attorney and kept careful records of all proceedings, just in case. Only after the down payment for the house was accepted did the builder learn that he had sold a home to a black family. At first the builder tried to back out of the deal; then he tried to get Mr. Brown to accept a house in another area. There were other attempts to side-track the deal, the thoughts of which still infuriate Mr. Brown. For example, the survey was deliberately botched, the contract was incorrectly drawn, etc. as the builder's attorney became involved. The bank gave Mr. Brown the runaround and delayed his mortgage application. This was at a time when whites had little trouble securing mortgage money on new homes. Almost every device was used to break the deal, but to no avail. After a year of legal wrangling, Mr. Brown was finally able to move into his new home in 1962. By this time he had given up his "second" job at Bethlehem.

Besides his lawyer, Mr. Brown notes that he received moral support from a white ladies group in the Glenwood Avenue area. The ladies group wrote letters on his behalf. Although not able to recall the name of this particular organization, he remains grateful to this day. He also believes he was one of the first to receive assistance from HOME (Housing Opportunities Made Equal). Eventually, his case was taken to the New York State Commission for Human Rights, which ruled in his favor. He notes that at that time, the Commission could only hear cases which involved builders of 10 or more houses. In effect, small builders were exempt and hence could continue to discriminate. Fortunately the builder of his home fell within the Commission's guidelines. The builder received harsh criticism after neighbors learned that a black family had purchased a home in their community.

The day before he was set to move in vandals painted the previously white house black. The Town police investigated and identified the teenagers responsible, but Mr. Brown declined to press charges. However, Mr. Brown relates that when the minister of the local Presbyterian church learned of the incident, he and his congregation came to his house and repainted it white. Mr. Brown fondly remembers an older lady of the congregation who personally apologized to him for being late (she apparently had trouble locating the house), and she hoped that there was still some work for her to do.

Mr. Brown recalls that when he first moved in his neighbors were generally not very friendly. That was particularly true of a Town police officer and his family who lived several houses away. Mr. Brown notes that this officer and his children "lorded it" over the entire neighborhood, and set the tone for the community. After approximately a year of ostracism, some neighbors slowly began to speak to him. They usually did this at night, apparently so the police officer and others wouldn't learn of their "treason." Mr. Brown says that at the time, i.e., before the full impact of the Civil Rights movement, this behavior was not unusual. He refers to it as "nighttime integration, daytime segregation." At one point his neighbor immediately next door came up to him and told Mr. Brown how proud he was to have him there. Since that time they have been close friends.

The same, however, can not be said for two of Mr. Brown's white friends at the Post Office, who also lived in the Town of Tonawanda. He notes that for almost 15 years they had gone out together, twice a month or so, to have a few beers. Shortly after he moved into his new home, Mr. Brown telephoned to tell them the good news on acquiring his home. Instead of congratulating him and coming over, they gave him the cold shoulder: they didn't associate with him anymore. Evidently, Mr. Brown could be their friend only if he lived in the City of Buffalo, where blacks were supposed to live.

In 1963, a year after moving in, tragedy struck; the Brown's first born, a daughter, died, apparently of a head injury sustained several years before, as a result of being pushed down a flight of stairs at school. The death of his daughter may have caused some of his white neighbors to show some compassion, to be more friendly. He notes, however, that his children suffered greatly from the move.

While Mr. Brown and his wife could bear the situation by essentially keeping to themselves, the same could not be said for the children. Children are by nature more outgoing than adults. While he had prepared his children for the experience, the principal at the local elementary school and white parents had done little or nothing to prepare the white children in the neighborhood. As a result, his children were being constantly beaten up by white youths. Even though Mr. Brown told his three sons to defend themselves, they were still coming home bloodied. Seeing his children mistreated was one of his worst recollections of the move. On several occasions he went to speak to the female principal, but he received no cooperation from her office. He finally took the matter to the school board and shortly thereafter the situation at school began to improve slightly. However, that was not the end of racial prejudice in the community.

Mr. Brown believes that prejudice is not inborn, i.e. that it is learned behavior, and that all children (and later adults), could be more tolerant, if they were not taught the wrong lessons at home. In effect, racial stereotyping and prejudice are most often the fault of parents. For instance, he remembers that his and the police officer's two children were playing in his back yard, when an argument and shoving incident occurred. One of the white children pushed one of his children, and called him "nigger." The other white child immediately admonished his brother to "remember what daddy said: never call them that to their faces." As Mr. Brown observed this he chuckled, for at that time the incident had a funny side. However, it also had a serious side, and he notes that it was and is indicative of the double standard of white society. He had always taught his children to respect all people, and in particular adults. He also taught his children that if they couldn't say something to a person's face, then they surely shouldn't say it behind that person's back.

While children can sometimes be cruel and blunt, the way some adults treated his children disturbed him even more. He recalls that his children would come home and tell him that they said "hello Mr. Doe" to a neighbor, or asked a question, but received no reply. Naturally they wanted to know why they were being ignored.

How, Mr. Brown asked, does one go about explaining to a child that some people will not speak to him because of the color of his skin? Mr. Brown would usually come up with something to the effect that "Oh, Mr. Doe probably didn't hear you."

Once his sons began to attend Kenmore West High School, the situation improved considerably. Fellow students, teachers and administrators were more tolerant and his children began forming white friendships and were being accepted. His sons went on to graduate and presently 2 of them live in Washington, D.C., and the other is a police officer in the City of Buffalo.

Today, almost 30 years after moving from Buffalo, Mr. Brown still lives in the same home and is retired from the Post Office. Children from the neighborhood respectfully call him "Mr. Brown," and most of his neighbors have accepted him. When the opportunity arises he enjoys traveling. I asked him if he thought the situation for blacks is better today than before the Civil Rights movement, and he said that in some respects it is. Discrimination is not as open. For example, blacks can vote and, income constraints aside, can usually choose where they will live. However, he sees Affirmative Action as basically tokenism brought up-to-date, akin to modern T.V. advertising, which pictures the typical black as upper middle-class, three piece suit, briefcase, Mercedes and all, the executive image. While he readily admits that some blacks have done very well for themselves, especially in professional sports, one is only speaking about a very small, if highly visible, group. In reality, the typical black has to struggle at a low paying job, if he or she is fortunate enough to have employment at all. In effect, one still has two different societies today: a white, economically prosperous society, and a black under-society.

Mr. Brown believes that whites want to maintain the status quo because they do not really want to share economic wealth with blacks. In that regard, I asked him if he saw any major difference between the two political parties and he said that he did not. He prefers to vote for the candidate, not the party. I then asked him how he compares black/white relations in Buffalo and its suburbs to other areas he has visited, and Mr. Brown believes that relations are not as good in the Buffalo area compared to places like Cleveland, Chicago and especially cities on the West Coast. He remarked that Buffalo is quite conservative, showing little in the way of racial progress and cooperation; hence prejudice is more prevalent than in other communities.

As noted, Mr. Brown believes that prejudice is learned behavior, and that it is up to each individual to essentially unlearn stereotypes, to reach within themselves to eradicate racism. Like the abolitionists of old he maintains that each individual must first reform himself, before he can reform others. Once hypocrisy is removed, once people are honest with themselves, attitudes in the country will change, and the economic situation for blacks will improve.

Lebanese-Americans
in Cortland County

By LAURICE DARWEESH BURKE

M ost of them thought he was Italian. Several dark-haired foreigners had come to Cortland in the late 1800's and they had
been Italians. But a few Americans saw something different about
him, and they asked, "What is your nationality?" And he never
knew what to answer.

What was he? Maybe he was a Turk. His passport officially labeled
him an Asian-Turkish subject of the Ottoman Empire. But how
could he be loyal to that oppressive Sultan in distant Constantinople?
Maybe he was Syrian. That's what his fellow peddlers and farmers
in Solon and Homer claimed. The Province of Greater Syria which
stretched from the borders of Persia across vast dry flatlands to the
southern border of Palestine, included Beirut, from which they
had sailed.

Certainly, all inhabitants of Greater Syria spoke Arabic, and all
have similar Semitic features. But the cool, green hills of Cortland
were more familiar to the mountaineer immigrant than the empty
deserts of most of the Arab world. There, only the perennial snow-
capped Lebanon mountains provided this same lifegiving green-
ness. So, he thought of himself as Lebanese.

The word "Lebanon," in Arabic, means "Milky-white," referring
probably to the white mountain peaks; or perhaps to the "land of
milk and honey" of the Bible. In any case, its unique climate gave
its pre-historic settlers more than mere subsistence and it became
part of the "cradle of civilization." Just as the narrow green river
valley of the Egyptian desert is the "Gift of the Nile, " so is Lebanon
the gift of its two mountain ranges. But while the Nile tends to
unify Egypt, Lebanon's hills and valleys tend to divide its inhabitants into separated, independent village-states, each ruled by a different family, clan, or religious sect.

Reprinted from Louis M. Vanaria, ed., *From Many Roots: Immigrants and Ethnic
Groups in the History of Cortland County, New York* (Cortland County Historical
Society, 1986), 75-83.

When this essay was written, Laurice Darweesh Burke was an art teacher at Cortland
High School.

Agriculture on terraced slopes at the different altitudes produces a variety of crops, making each village self-sufficient. The prevailing westerly sea winds first strike the 10,000 foot heights of the coastal mountains, condensing 33 inches of rain annually on the shoreside. Passing over the Bekaa plateau and a deeply fertile river valley that legend calls the "Garden of Eden," the cooling winds also water the inland range, leaving only ten inches of rainfall annually for Damascus behind the rain barriers of green Lebanon.

Farming was what Joseph Abdallah knew best, and extraordinary courage was his greatest possession. In 1989, with very little money and a few words of English, he and his sister Minnie pioneered into Solon where hired farm hands were needed and where comparatively inexpensive land was available. After several years of working for room and board and peddling dry goods and notions on foot to area farms, enough money was saved to purchase their own farm. Thus, they secured an anchor hold in Cortland for the connecting chain to Lebanon used by subsequent immigrants.

Akil Calale, Michael Nauseef, Joseph Yaman, and about thirty other men and women soon followed the difficult trail blazed by the Abdallahs. The ordeals of the peddlers, unaccustomed to the harsh climate, irregular meals, and unhealthful sleeping conditions, took their toll. A few perished, often from tuberculosis, some found regular jobs, and others returned to their families and homeland.

Some of their escapades seem funny now. One thirsty non-English-speaking peddler approached a native farmwife gesturing the usual Arabic hand signal for "water jug" with jutting thumb as its spout. Thinking he was thumbing his nose at her, she screamed at his insulting motion, causing her husband to run the stranger off with his shotgun.

One of the original settlers, Akil Calale, soon prospered in his new life, accumulating enough cash from peddling to open a general store on Main Street in Homer. By providing employment to new immigrants and giving them shelter in his own home behind the store, he strengthened the new Lebanese community in traditional fashion. A generation later, his son Holley, who owned a thriving chicken farm business, continued the custom by hiring unemployed landsmen during the Great Depression. In 1986 his wife Selma still volunteers her services to local organizations, and his son Harry Calale, elected mayor of Homer in 1967, gives unstintingly toward the village's betterment.

James Yaman, owner of Cortland's largest real estate firm, expressed his family's gratitude to Cortland County by donating land for a public park. Dedicated in his father's name, Yaman Park's facilities and upkeep still benefit from his financial support.

The family name Abdallah, (whose son Charles founded the well-known Abdallah Dairy) Calale, Nauseef, and Yaman are perpetuated locally into the fourth generation. Thoroughly Americanized now, an instilled appreciation for their adopted country remains undiminished. They understand how different their lives might have been had their forefathers remained in the Old World.

The First World War had finally ended and passenger ships were sailing to America again. In 1920 Joseph Darweesh was only an adventurous teenager, but the established network of relatives in the United States offered him room and board and told him that unskilled factory work was available. Since his inheritance of fields and orchards were still in his father's and older brother's control, he decided to sail to the New World, make fast money, and return triumphantly in a few years as a man of means.

For a time, only good things happened to him and his savings in the stock market grew steadily. Then something bad called the "crash," and something even worse called the "depression" struck down his golden America and with it his simple happy plan.

Cortland's small group of Lebanese reacted with ages-old mountain survival tactics. Combining resources, caring, and sharing together, they could proudly state that no Lebanese ever asked for government relief or welfare assistance.

When war raged again in Europe, Joe had steady defense work in Wickwire's steel mills, as did most of the more recent immigrants of his age. Thankful for the financial security of his growing family, he no longer yearned to return to the land of his boyhood.

Sometimes, though, when the noise of the machinery drowned out the small talk of his co-workers, or when they playfully called him "Turk," he'd brood about the days of the First World War under the Turkish military. He would recall that at eleven years of age, he was sent on the family's last remaining donkey to deliver fruit to the Beirut market. A Turkish soldier commanded him at gunpoint to halt, in order to requisition the animal for the army. Reacting without thinking, he instead spurred the beast into galloping away. A loud shot, a burning pain in his leg, and then he remembered nothing, until he opened his eyes surrounded by his tearful family calling him a hero. But they laughed through the tears, as they rated the intelligence of the ass higher than that of its rider, because it had found its way home without direction from its unconscious burden. And they teased him, saying that fear of his mother's scolding on losing the donkey had impressed him more than the Turkish rifle.

The white scar on his leg was still noticeable, but his wife Najla's war scars were invisible, and much deeper. His village was on the sub-tropical coastal plain where gardens produced food almost all year, but her family's mountain village and fields were inland in the Bekaa's cooler climate with only one harvest season. Besides the Allied coastal blockade stopping all imports, the Turks systematically tried to starve them by allowing no food by land, taking native crops for their troops and cutting fruit trees to fuel their trains. Disaster also descended from the skies during two successive summers in the horrifying black form of huge locust swarms. Banging pots and pans, little children joined their elders trying in vain to prevent the ugly and noisy insects from devouring the precious wheat plants. There in the famous "breadbasket" of the Middle East, starvation killed almost one-fourth of Lebanon's population by 1918.

Her memories were sad, but her stories of life in Lebanon were so entertaining that he listened as avidly as their American children, who begged for their retelling. She told them of hot summer nights when families took bedding up to the cool, flat roofs, where under the bright clear starlight, they looked down on the ancient caravan road used by conquering Egyptians, Assyrians, and Babylonians. Time lost all dimension as her uncle, oral historian of the village, described how it took the armies of Alexander the Great a full week to march by, so numerous were his troops. The children could almost see the spears glittering in the moonlight as the soldiers walked by night to avoid the burning sun. In their mind's eye, Roman Legions, Moslem horsemen and camel-riders, armored Crusader knights, and Napoleon's forces all passed below them on that eastern highway.

A history lesson actually seen from that hilltop vantage, the one that cut painfully in her memory, was the sight of hundreds of emaciated Armenians straggling along the road. She and her cousins sat watching, themselves too weak from hunger to play their usual games, when some of the refugees, who were forced out of their homes in Armenia by the Turks, stopped moving. They simply lay down at the roadside like small bundles of rags, and died.

Tragedy followed tragedy as their father left to build a life in America, only to die there in the influenza epidemic of 1919. Soon afterward, the beloved only son died in Lebanon, probably of typhoid and malnutrition. Najla, her sister, and widowed mother survived, aided by the American Near East Relief Agency and by American missionaries nearby. Is it any wonder that their love for an unseen country represented by such kind and generous people grew stronger?

Unaccompanied, the mother and young daughters came to their revered land, only to be detained on Ellis Island for months, and threatened with deportation because they had no means of support. Again, a church group rescued and subsidized them until vouchers from distant relatives arrived. Beyond all doubt, they were convinced that the gigantic "Saint of America" with the strange pointed halo, standing in the harbor, had answered their fervent prayers. Their faith in all things American and in its unfaltering goodness was embodied in that statue.

Through the Depression with its struggles and into the Second World War, their trust and optimism for the United States never flagged. A fierce patriotism erupted with enlistments and hopeful volunteers from the Lebanese-Americans. Celebrations, farewell parties, and original Arabic songs of praise sent young men off to war. The womenfolk who had perfected the technique in the Old Country, whimsically uttered the Arab war cry, a high-pitched, piercingly shrill vibrating sound produced by strong lungs and fluttering tongue. Supposed to incite warriors to deeds of bravery on the open desert, it probably gave most of the party-goers in the room headaches instead.

On the homefront, wives who had never before worked outside the home, gladly joined their husbands in Cortland's defense factories. With the war years went many traditional lifestyles as immigrants broke through speech barriers with co-workers on the job, and family closeness lessened from the disruptions of overtime work and from the increased social contacts of participating in war-related community activities. Even the youngest children gaily helped in the war effort by picking beans for the Halstead Canneries and by collecting scrap materials for re-use in manufacturing plants. The war's "melting pots" blended a heterogeneous people as surely as they recycled old parts into a new wholeness.

In 1943, before the end of the war, the French-mandated Lebanese Republic was declared an independent nation with an elective president and a parliamentary membership proportionately based on the uncounted "alleged" numerical strength of the different religious communities. And although the constitution had established no official state religion, these strictly sectarian divisions weakened the structure of the infant democracy from its birth. Perhaps with more years of political maturation the competing factions might have found accommodating solutions and stability. But the creation of Israel in 1948 displaced millions of Palestinians from their ancestral lands and created turmoil in the Middle East. The displaced Palestinians were at first sympathetically allowed into Lebanon until their increasing strength threatened the nation's sovereignty; the guests had overwhelmed their hosts.

Now they stood together, Sam Joseph and his oldest son, on the sidewalks of the Cortland they had left sixteen years ago in the depths of the Depression. At that time, Sam, a naturalized citizen, his American-born infant son, and his wife Rose had gone back to Lebanon to sell his properties and to have a "short" visit with relatives. The war broke out, keeping the family there, and it was 1948 before they could return, now with seven children, to the United States to stay.

The old ties of relatives, inheritances, and familiar mores could not hold back the parents who had already tasted the wonders of education, opportunities, and liberty in this country. Starting over again, working in the factories they had quit in 1932, everyone pitched in, including their son-in-law, Nahra Hage, a skilled tailor. Sheer hard work by the adults, and intense studying by the school-aged children brought quick successes to the persevering family. They eventually reaped the rewards of home ownership; scholarships toward advanced degrees in physics, engineering, anthropology; and success in other businesses and professions. Such was the pattern for most immigrants of that period, whether named Joseph, Sopp, Ferris, Isaf, Ossit, or Darweesh.

It was understood that the parents' main purpose in life and their constant priority was the advancement of the new generation. This single-minded idea was devoid of feelings of self-sacrifice or expectations of future repayment, or of any sense of personal unfulfillment. The immigrant parents simply and lovingly gave all their time and energy to their American children because they trusted and respected them in whatever they chose to do. With no regrets and only momentary nostalgia, they accepted their children's metamorphosis. And, naturally, their grandchildren would turn out even better! The Westernization which began with Phoenician traders sailing off the coast into the unknown to found Carthage and other colonies, was completed with Egyptian and Graeco-Roman acculturation; European Crusader influences; Italian, English, and American missionary schoolings; and the final impact of the French political legacy.

Cortland also made assimilation easy. The neighborly kindness of its friendly townspeople, the helpfulness of the clergy and of teachers in the schools and the college, the assistance from community services and organizations, combined for pleasant adaptations. The Cortland immigrant experience was better than the impersonality of large metropolitan areas and the ghetto atmosphere of tightly clustered ethnic colonies.

Recreation had its place in the daily routine of hard work in that pre-television era. The men often congregated at Fred Isaf's pub, as they had done in the coffee-houses of the Old Country. Rousing political and philosophical discussions vied simultaneously for their attention with the even more serious games of pinochle and back-gammon. Women and children walked to visit other housewives, weather permitting, since few had cars and fewer had driver's licenses. And those long, glorious summer evenings of Cortland! Empty lots and untrafficked streets were full of disorganized, un-uniformed, non-regulated, and ill-equipped ball games. Played by teams of mixed ages, genders and nationalities, everyone was too busy laughing to bother keeping score.

On summer weekends, families often drove to relatives in Bing-hamton, Syracuse, Utica, Elmira, and Oneonta, usually staying over-night with the little ones sleeping three or four in a bed. Checking the children's annual growth, exchanging news of the extended family here and abroad, and especially the cooking and eating of holiday foods, made them memorable occasions.

Even before "Victory gardens" were in vogue, Lebanese-Americans depended almost completely on their vegetable plots for summer meals. As a teenager, Ernie Sopp, weary of the repeti-tious garden fare, said, "Our daily summer dinners alternate from beans to squash to beans again, with the big Sunday 'treat' being squash and beans together." Unsurprisingly the wartime rationing of meat, butter and sugar was no hardship for most immigrant fam-ilies. Their diets were mainly vegetarian, with fruit for dessert. Meat, chiefly lamb, and sweet, rich pastries were served only on feast days and family celebrations. Candies and a single bottle of "arak" liquor were saved and hidden by parents, to mysteriously appear at the arrival of company.

Food-gathering to youngsters was adventure. Whether digging the tender, early spring dandelion greens along nearby railroad tracks, or riding off to state lands to pick wild strawberries, huckle-berries, blackberries and grape leaves, they felt the explorer's excite-ment of discovery.

Late summer climaxed with longer trips to the Finger Lakes orchards to pick peaches, pears, and the favored apricots. Bushels upon bushels filled the car. The gluttonous fruit-lovers stuffed them-selves, rationalizing that the slightly imperfect ones eaten, would not have passed the ultimate test to be purchased. Children forgot the hot, fatiguing work of their mothers canning and preserving food in steamy kitchens on old coal-burning stoves. They do remem-ber the colorful beauty of cellars with brimming bushels of apples and of shelves lined with glass jars of tomatoes, beans, and fruit for the long, gray winter. The simple splendor of abundant food in America made even the poorest immigrant feel rich, and his light-heartedness was contagious. Freedom from want replaced the fear of hunger and starvation.

Relating some of America's advantages to his family in Lebanon, Nahra Hage inspired his brother Farris, and later Nabih, to join him. Being the established older brother and now the patriarch of the American branch of the Hage family, he fostered them in his home until Farris married and bought his own home and tailoring business, and Nabih as well, but in real estate. The close-knit clan in 1986 continued to celebrate holidays and other occasions together, usually with all nine children attending. Their social life was often quite international with visiting relatives flying to and from Africa, Britain, Germany and of course Lebanon. Arabic hospitality at its best is personified by the Hages.

When teen-agers reached marriageable stages, most immigrant parents hesitantly encouraged sons and daughters of Lebanese extraction to become acquainted with one another. Annual summer festivals featuring both Arabic and American dance bands, entertainment, and Middle-Eastern dishes, were organized and attended by families from two hundred miles around. Though hopeful mothers noticed random glimmers of interest between suitable pairs, little if anything developed from the brief encounters.

Unlike the arranged marriages in the Arab lands where paternal first cousins often were pressured to wed for the economic benefits of keeping family properties intact, Lebanese here preferred the American way of free choice. Not only were eligible Lebanese mates very few in number and out of the local area, but the attraction was almost fraternal, so alike were they in appearance and manner. Much more interesting and mysterious were the American boys and girls seen daily. In fact, all first generation immigrant couples from Lebanon had Lebanese partners, but most of their children married non-Lebanese. So go the old matchmaking customs!

The American way of love in 1947 extended to a Lebanese mountain village, with some timely aid from Homer's Harry Calale. It seems that Nassir Ferris, son of Cortland native Ferris N. Ferris, was visiting Lebanon with his friend Harry, when he met and fell in love with the seventeen-year-old Esther Awad. The feeling was reciprocal, but she was very young and her family disapproved of the marriage. However, Harry, romantic bachelor that he was, had his own car there, and agreed with Nassir that true love must prevail. In the darkness of a moonless night, Esther escaped to her determined suitor in the car. Harry drove the eloping couple to the appointed priest for the ceremony, and the Beirut hotel where honeymoon reservations had been made. Always pleased with his role as "Cupid," Harry was doubly thrilled when the couple's daughter Jeanine Ferris Pirro in 1986 was chosen as running-mate to the Republican candidate for Governor of New York State. Although Jeanine eventually declined the offer to run for Lieutenant Governor, she continued as the Assistant District Attorney of Westchester County, at age thirty-two. But for Harry and his car. . .

Freedom in America does seem to bring out the innate talents and abilities that would have been suppressed or neglected in the insecure and often impoverished Middle East. How else could a people who came from those same tight, introverted sectarian enclaves, in the span of one generation, supply so many contributing individuals?

Some work quietly behind the scenes as volunteers (Eva Khoury and Rena Ferris), others as teachers (Vera Ferris, Jean Abdallah, Richard Calale, Laurice Darweesh, and Robert Isaf), and Michael Joseph serves as superintendent of Marathon schools.

The influence of Victor Bahou, former political science professor and for more than 20 years the Democratic Party Chairman for Cortland County has been nothing less than spectacular. By building the county's Democrats into a strong organization, he has proven time and again that a true two-party system serves the people in a democracy more equitably. His wife, Peg, also contributes a great deal to the community, in teaching and in many other county activities.

Many notables have left this region to go into other counties and states, mainly because a rural district cannot employ all the young people it has spawned. Those who have stayed here smile at the mention of their names and their successes, happily aware of the Arabic commonality. Recently, however, the repercussions of Middle Eastern events have saddened and upset the local Arab-Americans.

The newest immigrants come out of the Lebanese civil war like survivors of a holocaust. Hearts break at the recounting of compounded horrors of the bombings, atrocities and murders. They come thankfully, knowing that they are the few lucky ones, with immediate family members in Cortland or with valuable professions that permit entrance under tight immigration restrictions. The Chacras, the Chababis, and the Doctors El-Hassan and Salman have left the chaos and destruction of that fractured land.

As Arabs continue to migrate to Cortland and elsewhere, many Americans seem uncaring or unknowledgeable about the current suffering in Lebanon. Simplistic answers are given to complicated problems. Perhaps the finest contribution of Cortland's Arab-Americans will be to help build a bridge of understanding and compassion between the Arab world and America.

Puerto Ricans in Brentwood

By ELIZABETH GUANILL

M any cultures compose our nation, one of them, perhaps the major one is the Latin culture. The headlines of *"El Diario* and *La Prensa,"* Hispanic newspapers, in 1973 stated that immigration from the Latin American countries to the United States had risen by 72%. The greatest number of immigrants to the United States were the "Latinos." To this unique culture belongs the Puerto Rican, a citizen of an island known officially as the commonwealth of Puerto Rico, situated 1,000 miles southwest of Florida, 35 miles wide and 100 miles long, it is shorter but wider than Long Island. It is inhabited by 2.7 million people, all of whom are citizens of the United States, with full rights of citizenship, except for the right to vote in national elections, since islanders do not pay federal taxes. This also means that Puerto Ricans living in Puerto Rico cannot vote for the President of the United States.

The Jones Act of 1917 granted citizenship to the residents of Puerto Rico. The transition from political, economic, cultural, and linguistic ties with royalist Spain to an English speaking democracy was a drastic change. Without freedom of choice or opinion the citizens of the island of Puerto Rico were thrust from 400 years of Spanish rule to a completely different, culturally, linguistic and political English speaking regime. This drastic change has had effects that are still causing conflict in the political climate of the island today. Groups such as the Independentistas, Socialistas, Nacionalistas and Faln, are not only sources of dissent, but also of violence on the Island, as well as in the mainland itself. The bombings and terrorist tactics are of great concern not only to the Island's political leaders, but also to the Puerto Rican who is content with the commonwealth status shared with the United States and with those who advocate statehood for Puerto Rico. The present Governor of Puerto Rico, Carlos Romero Barcelo, has written a very inter-

Reprinted from Salvatore J. LaGumina, ed., *Ethnicity in Suburbia: The Long Island Experience* (1980), 37-41.

Elizabeth Guanill of the Suffolk Human Rights Commission lives in Bay Shore, New York.

esting book called, "Statehood Is For The Poor, " a worthwhile book to read, on the subject.

The relationship between the Island of Puerto Rico and the mainland United States had had two major effects:

1. The use of American technology has brought about a tremendous upheaval in the economy of the Island.
2. The migration of over a million Puerto Ricans to the United states mainland has had an impact on the social-standards of the Island.

The many cultural ties, and the easy facility for traveling (a round trip to Puerto Rico is $142.00, with no need for passports) has created a jet generation that reaches out from Isla Verde Airport to J.F. Kennedy Airport, making the Puerto Rican the largest airborne migrant to the United States. This consideration involves the philosophy of "Where a Puerto Rican settles a community is born," which certainly has been the case of the Puerto Rican community in Brentwood. We find, outside of the New York City limits, one hour car travel time, the largest concentration of Puerto Ricans in the State of New York, excluding the city itself. Dr. Seda Bonilla, a well known Puerto Rican anthropologist writes about Brentwood:

"Brentwood is a Puerto Rican community in Long Island, very much like the "matojos" type, in that, the Puerto Rican culture is preserved as a separate domain, never admixtured in the alloy that has begun to spread throughout Puerto Rico itself."

Here in Brentwood one finds first generation Puerto Ricans who adhere to the Puerto Rican culture, as faithfully as if they had been born in Puerto Rico. In 89% of these homes, Spanish is the language that is spoken. English then becomes the second language. A mixture of both languages has resulted in "spanglish," spoken by many of the first generation Puerto Ricans. This is a characteristic of the generation known as Neo-Ricans. The remaining 11 % are the Puerto Ricans who, because of a strong desire to assimilate, cannot communicate, even with their elders at home, in Spanish, they then become monolingual—English speaking only; in an ever increasing number of homes this is slowly becoming an accepted custom.

In 1939, names such as Sosa, Acevedo, Vasquez, Rivera first appeared on rural mail boxes along 5th Avenue, Brentwood, north of the Sunrise Highway. Newcomers were leaving their imprint on the sands of Long Island. By word of mouth and advertising in "El Diario," the word was out, you could own an acre of land, for $10.00 down and $10.00 monthly until the total sum of $150.00 was paid. For every customer that you brought to the real estate broker and if he purchased, $10.00 was applied to your purchase price, thus for 15 customers, an acre of land was yours. The sense of becoming land owners, of the rural "Finca" type as in Puerto Rico, suddenly became a reality, here given a 45 to a 60 minute ride from New York City, living in a typical Puerto Rican setting became possible.

The Brentwood area was formerly known as Victory farms, an underdeveloped tract of land in Islip Township, hamlet of Brentwood (transportation was afforded by the real-estate broker). The similarity to the land they had left behind in Puerto Rico was the greatest attraction with the similarity especially evident in the summer time. Brentwood was rural country. At that time in 1943 there was no electricity if you lived off the main road and unpaved roads. These environmental conditions presented a challenge; the challenge of pioneering. Besides presenting the homesite, the broker took you a little further down the road, to a place known as "Mason's General," but now known as Pilgrim State hospital. It was this institution which provided permanent employment, plus the benefits of becoming a State employee.

Puerto Ricans are very clannish, so one soon found complete families and members of a given community resettling in Brentwood. A good example and one which I shall refer to consistently throughout is the Sosa family, one of the pioneer, Puerto Rican families in Brentwood.

On June 2, 1979, Mrs. Josephine Sosa was honored as the "Pioneer Mother of the Year" by the Spanish Society of Suffolk County. Manuel Sosa and Josephine Sosa, his wife, first came to Brentwood in 1939, after a member of their Brooklyn community advised them of the Victory farm lands that were for sale. Mr. Sosa, a disabled individual, was at that time participating in a rehabilitation program sponsored by Republic Aviation through the Office of Unemployment. Farmingdale was certainly closer to Brentwood, than Brooklyn, and this was one of the factors in the Sosa's family's move to Brentwood; the other factor was their asthmatic youngest child Pedro for whom the family doctor had advised a change in environment which would be beneficial to his health. The pure air of "Brentwood in the Pines" was just what the doctor had ordered. The Sosas were parents of six children, all of whom, excepting the eldest son, resettled in Brentwood. Today from a resettled family of seven, there are now in Brentwood fifty-one, of which 29 are Long Island Ricans (L.I.R.). This is but one example of one family, and considering the 33,000 Hispanics in the Brentwood area, one can easily establish a family pattern.

The availability of employment at Pilgrim, not necessarily requiring any specific training or education, was essential in the development of the surrounding area. Puerto Ricans opened up businesses in the immediate vicinities, grocery stores (bodegas) barber shops, restaurants, gas stations,liquor stores, etc. Within ten years a typical Puerto Rican commercial area had developed on Fifth Avenue, Brentwood. This strip of choice industrial and commercial property was to become the visible and easily identifiable part of the Puerto Rican community.

Here can be found all of the delicacies enjoyed in Puerto Rico, and lately, not only the delicacies of Puerto Rico, but of Central and South America and the other Caribbean Islands. The first Puerto Rican business to open on Fifth Avenue was the "Tropical Market" owned and operated by the Sosa family and only recently sold outside of the Sosa family to a stranger. In thirty-five years this store has become a community entity. Here the news of the day is disseminated, politics, social and religious events are discussed and advertised. Browsing is a unique experience, for here are sold wares unknown to those that are not Hispanic consumers.

Then came the migrants, the men who come yearly to till the farms out further East. For them Brentwood was a beacon of light as it lured them to their community. No longer would they have the long ride into Spanish Harlem for a day of relaxation and indulgence in their typical foods and drinks; the migrants' trip was cut in half by making Brentwood become their "stop off" point and their "day off" trip. By the 1950's, Brentwood was definitely a Puerto Rican community.

It was the church that first focused in on the migrant problem out east. A program was instituted that weekly outreached to these men, the Puerto Rican migrants who came to work in the farms. Once the church addressed itself to the needs of this segment of the population, it came to the Catholic Puerto Rican community of Brentwood seeking volunteers to run the program, and the Puerto Rican Catholic community of St. Anne's responded. Weekly on Sundays two women from the church would travel to Camp Molloy, in Mattituck and cook a typical Puerto Rican meal for over 100 migrants. The church provided the food and transportation not only for the migrants, but also for the cooks. Brothers, sisters, priests and young college students provided back up services. They provided the spiritual needs of the migrants, i.e., mass and confessions, games, songs, music and swimming.

The Catholic church took notice of this "newcomer." Masses, confessions, and baptisms were conducted in Spanish. This was a growing community. Not only did the Catholic church expand into two parishes, but the Baptists, Seventh Day Adventists, Pentecostal and other Protestant sects made their presence visible. Churches that cost thousands of dollars along with botanicas also made their appearance in Brentwood. In its 22 square mile radius, Brentwood has seven churches that take care of the spiritual needs of the community all of different denominations, not counting the many aspirants to spiritualism and santerismo. Botanicas are stores that hold hope and faith for a better tomorrow. Here can be bought candles, prayers, colored beads, incense and incantations. Here the evils of life hold no fear, for somehow our failures can be dispelled, one must have someone or something to blame, and it makes life and defeat easier to accept. In Brentwood it is not uncommon to see men and women dressed completely in white professing their faith in "santerismo," a religion that had its origin in Africa and in which one finds relief from failure in the mystical.

In response to the presence of the ever increasing different religions and their impact on community life, "Pronto" came into existence. A group of concerned parishioners approached the priests of St. Anne's church, expressing a growing concern that the Puerto Rican Catholic was turning away from Catholicism and joining the Protestant sects that were rapidly opening up beautiful churches along 5th Avenue. Here because everyone spoke his language, understood his culture, was clearly visible and readily available, the Puerto Rican Catholic was easily convinced and converted. Leaders of the Puerto Rican Catholic community felt that the Catholic church had a spiritual and moral commitment to this newcomer. Accordingly, this Catholic church-sponsored store front operation (Pronto) was the answer to the needs of those Puerto Ricans who remained faithful to the religious upbringing of their ancestors. It was a minority that refused to be overlooked and thus planted the seed of Pronto. Today, Pronto has established itself to the degree that through community efforts it has purchased its own building and is a committed social, religious, and civic entity known throughout the Island.

To establish their presence in the community, civic groups and associations were formed: Pan American Civic, Bay Brent Civic, Good Neighbors, Adelante, The Spanish Society of Suffolk County, La Union Hispanica of Suffolk. These civic groups and associations served as a uniting force, with the result that leadership was established, political figures were encouraged, participation in community affairs became the order of the day and education became the name of the game.

These groups and others saw the need for equality in education, and in 1969 the first bilingual program was established in Brentwood. The local Puerto Rican realized that upward mobility was essential and that education was the key to this mobility.[1] A multi-lingual assessment program was established in the Brentwood community schools, and parents came together with one common purpose: equality in education. It functioned through interrelated efforts on the part of a community with a common cultural pattern.

"The Congress hereby finds that one of the most acute educational problems in the United States is that which involves millions of children of limited English speaking ability because they came from environments where the dominant language is other than English. Such priority shall take into consideration the number of children of limited English speaking ability between the ages of 3 and 18 each state."

This is the statement of the Title VII United States Elementary and Secondary Education Act.[2] In Brentwood 22% of the public school students have Hispanic surnames, or 3,842 students.[3] The bilingual program in Brentwood has faced and is still facing many problems. The Spanish Parent Teacher Association has charged that the school administrators are not implementing bilingual programs to the best interest of the student, and a class action suit has ensued. To this day there is much controversy regarding the success of Brentwood's bilingual program because it is too recent a development. The effects of bilingual education impact on a given community will be seen in about the next five years.

Following the traditional love for parades, the first Puerto Rican parade in Long Island was held in 1966, and every year thereafter the second Sunday in June has been designated Latin-American Day by executive proclamation. The parade is held along Fifth Ave., Brentwood, a colorful festive Latin event, including floats, dancers, bands, and shouts of "Viva Puerto Rico" as events of the day. The businesses along Fifth Avenue, the two mile parade route, are Puerto Rican merchants with great economic clout, a fact which has not been recognized by the non Puerto Rican community of Brentwood. The uniqueness of the Puerto Rican lies in the fact

---

[1] Dr. Seda Bonilla—Writing on the Acculturation of the "Nuyoricans' '—University of California, Multi-lingual Program, San Francisco, California [2] Title VII of the United States Elementary and Secondary Education Act—passed January 2, 1969—referred as the Bilingual Education Act. [3] Mr. John Finan, Director of Special Programs in the Brentwood school district.

that this community was founded, designed and built by Puerto Ricans from its inception. The Puerto Ricans did not take over what others left, and future generations knew that they were coming into an established Puerto Rican community.

Thus, another phenomenon was taking place, a first generation of Long Island Ricans (L.I.R.) came into existence, a first generation of Long Islanders of Puerto Rican parentage, which started in the early 50's. The Sosa family is a good contemporary example. Today, children, grandchildren and great grandchildren are residents of the Long Island community of Brentwood including professionals, business people, local leaders, students and laborers. Furthermore, a second generation of L.I.R. is on the rise. One finds Puerto Ricans in any of the 22 square miles that constitute the hamlet of Brentwood, although the largest concentration is still the area known as North Bay Shore. *Newsday*, writing on the occasion of the Bicentennial of America, recognized the change in the ethnic makeup of Long Island, and did a special section on the Puerto Rican community of Brentwood.

The rapidly growing outlying areas in the community still have reservations about their Hispanic neighbors; they do very little shopping or socializing, and they have learned to live within, yet apart. The areas of tension and stress are still the common ones relegated to minorities. The unknown is always feared and because the actions and cultural patterns of the Puerto Rican are still not acceptable nor understood in the Anglo community, the stereotyping, high welfare costs, property devaluation and high crime rate are considered the ills of the Brentwood Puerto Rican community; yet homes in Brentwood have the same trade and market value of those in any integrated community.

One of the greatest areas of concern in the Puerto Rican community is adequate representation in decision and policy making positions, a concern that is being addressed not only by the formation of political coalitions but also by a group of Puerto Rican leaders. We have developed in Suffolk a group called "La Union Hispanica" which has conducted studies that decry the fact that the Hispanic community is being snubbed by county, town and local authorities. "La Union Hispanica" is to the Long Island Rican what C.O.R.E. and N.A.A.C.P. are to the black communities. The Spanish Society of Suffolk County, another long established group has focused on and brought into the Anglo community the cultural and social aspect of Puerto Rican life. Puerto Rican leaders are tearing down areas of political and social apathy that exists among Puerto Ricans. The availability of higher education within walking distance in the Brentwood community is a help. The awareness of their roles as homeowners and taxpayers, the importance of having elected officials conscious of the potential voting power of the Puerto Ricans are beginning to have important consequences. The upward mobility that the Long Island Ricans represent is especially significant. With them rather than the older generation of migrants lies the full potential of raising a family and the ability to earn higher incomes. It must be noted that the median age for the Long Island Rican is 9.6 years compared to the average "other" American who is 28 years, and that therefore, the best years of the Long Island Rican are yet to be fully developed and their impact is yet to be felt. I feel a great future lies ahead for the Long Island Rican. It is with this knowledge that the Puerto Rican leadership has started the political wheels rolling.

The majority of Puerto Ricans are registered Democrats, yet a strong Hispanic Republican Club exists in Brentwood. Leaders include Irma Rivera and Robert Trice, who are respected by Republicans and Democrats alike. The Puerto Ricans of Brentwood have the distinct honor of postulating the first woman candidate to run for Islip Town Supervisor. For the first time in the 200 years of the establishment of Islip Town a major political party nominated a woman as its candidate for supervisor; the Democratic party nominated Elizabeth Guanill, a first generation Puerto Rican woman, and a resident of Brentwood for forty years. This was a feat that was a first not only in the community as a whole, but specifically in the Puerto Rican community. For the first time in the history of Islip Town was a Puerto Rican chosen to run for such a high political post. The showing was more than expected, 6000 more votes than for any previous Democratic candidate were cast. The Puerto Rican political clout and peer image were established and some definite barriers came tumbling down. Puerto Ricans from Brentwood have achieved other high ranking employment. The Assistant Director of the Suffolk County Human Rights Commission is a young Puerto Rican educated in the Brentwood school system and at one time two young lawyers became assistant district attorneys. Puerto Ricans serve as volunteers in many governmental agencies. The chairperson of the Suffolk County Human Rights Commission is a Puerto Rican woman. The Governor has appointed a Puerto Rican, resident of Brentwood, to the Mental Health Advisory Council and to the Board of Visitors of Pilgrim State Psychiatric Center. The County Executive of Suffolk has appointed a Puerto Rican woman to serve on the Criminal Justice Coordinating Council. Many lawyers, doctors and teachers of Puerto Rican descent now live and work in Brentwood. The Puerto Rican community has become a part of the progress, yet the older Long Islander, who is returning to Puerto Rico, is being filled by newer, younger migrants who bring with them not only socio-economic barriers, but cultural and language barriers that will take a number of years to surmount. Yet the picture is not as grim as the past; the new migrant is now met by fellow Puerto Ricans with acquired knowledge of the "American Way of Life"; Spanish newspapers, two all day major radio stations, social, civic and political clubs, and a tremendously growing Puerto Rican population, in Brentwood and elsewhere in the state, augurs well for the future.

If the Puerto Rican is to become an integral part of the given community in which he lives, there are special needs that have to be met. The earning power of the Puerto Rican must be raised above the tomato picker, the restaurant worker, and the custodial worker category. This can be achieved only through the educational process. Operation Upward Bound Program must be put into motion for these citizens with academic qualifications, either in English or Spanish. Such is the purpose of bilingual education, which proposes accessibility to educational programs, that will ensure active participation in the American way of life—to all its young citizens—including the Long Island Rican.   Since the 1970's we have experienced another trend, the return migration to Puerto Rico of the older retired Puerto Rican, something that has not happened with any other ethnic group. Yet the fact is that as American citizens (since the Jones Act of 1917) they enjoy ease of travelling at low fares between New York and San Juan, and have therefore kept up a continuous flow of transients between the two islands. Their American citizenship notwithstanding, Puerto Rican migrants continue to experience problems of adjustment and acceptance. Yet a nucleus of Puerto Rican leaders such as Congressman Robert Garcia, Deputy Mayor Herman Badillo and Resident Commissioner Baltassar Corrada Del Rio feel that the Puerto Rican community has nowhere to go but upward. The census of 1975 acknowledges that one of every twenty persons in the United States is Spanish-American and the Puerto Rican as part of that number will play an increasingly important role.

As long as politicians continue to woo the Latin vote with Spanish campaign literature, the future for Puerto Ricans is not completely rosy but neither is it grim or completely gray. As we mature, and become more knowledgeable and more experienced, we will in the next decade no longer be the silent majority. "It's Your Turn in the Sun." As long as people of all the nations are willing to join their efforts, talents and energy regardless of ethnic background, there is hope not only of a bright future for Long Island Ricans, but for all ethnic groups that may follow us into Long Island.

From One Island to Another: The Story of Long Island Cubans

By ELAINE ANNE PASQUALI

The migration of Cubans has added another facet to the population of Long Island. Since the fall of the Batista government at the end of 1958, hundreds of thousands of Cubans have gone into self-imposed exile and migrated to the United States in a series of stages or "waves." Within an Hispanic population of 101,975 (almost half of which is Puerto Rican), some 6,692 Cubans now reside in Nassau and Suffolk Counties, Long Island, the locus of my study.[1]

The migration of Cubans has contributed to the diversity of Long Island's Caribbean/Latin American population, comprised of different ethnic groups distinguishable by such characteristics as language, history, racial composition, reasons for migrating, and legal entry status. For example, the colonial history of the Caribbean or Latin American country of origin is reflected in the language spoken by immigrants. Thus, Cubans speak Spanish; Haitians may speak Creole or French; and Jamaicans speak English. While most Cubans migrated for political reasons, economic reasons may have been instrumental for the moves of other groups, such as Puerto Ricans and Dominicans. Moreover, the historical, political, and socioeconomic context surrounding immigration is often reflected in the residential status of Caribbean/Latin American people on Long Island. While most Cubans entered the United States as political refugees, Puerto Ricans hold citizen status, and Mexicans may be classified as immigrants or as illegal aliens.

This article is based on an ethnographic study that traces the migration of Cubans to Long Island. The first wave of migration

Reprinted from *Long Island Historical Journal* 2 (Spring 1990), 265-77.

Elaine Anne Pasquali is a professor of anthropology at Adelphi University.

1. *1980 Census of Population: General Population Characteristics. Part 34, New York* (Washington, D.C.: U.S. Government Printing Office, 1980), 653, 662. According to the Long Island Planning Commission, these are the latest available statistics for Cubans on Long Island, but do not reflect the addition of Marielitos to the population.

began in 1958; the most recent occurred in 1980. The experience
of immigration is examined within the context of Cuban studies
and United States-Cuban relations current at the time that migration occurred.

As an anthropologist, I used an ethnographic perspective which
is primarily descriptive. Migration experiences include the subjec-
tive accounts of refugees and the meanings they gave to them.
Ethnographic data was collected from three hundred Cuban refugees over a three-year period (1980-1983).[2] Ethnographic methods
of anthropological research were employed that combined the following fieldwork techniques: extensive participant-observation, life
history, genealogy, diary-keeping, guided interview, informal association, attendance at meetings and gatherings, and individual case
study. Key informants consisted of eleven Cuban refugees and their
families who were conversed with regularly and in-depth, and whose
behavior was observed throughout the entire three years of fieldwork. Casual informants were conversed with less frequently. I
associated with and observed the behavior of all informants at home
as well as at social gatherings, meetings, and places of employment.

BACKGROUND

The majority of Long Island Cuban informants came as political
refugees escaping from a repressive government, rather than as
immigrants looking to improve their standard of living. They stated
that the prior presence of relatives on Long Island was their primary reason for settling here. In addition, social networks of relatives and friends-of-friends channeled Cuban refugees into unskilled
jobs that required little knowledge of English. In this way, occupational niches were carved out that provided some degree of economic security for Long Island Cuban refugees.

In Cuba, most of the informants who became the refugees of the
1960s and 1970s had lived in Havana or other urban areas and had
belonged to Cuba's middle class. The majority had completed high
school, and some had graduated from or were enrolled in college
at the time of the Cuban revolution. Men customarily had been
employed in skilled, white-collar, or professional occupations. Almost
half of the women migrants had not been employed in Cuba, but
had remained at home supervising maids and nannies in the care

2. Ethnographic data were collected as part of my doctoral dissertation, "Assimilation and Acculturation of Cubans on Long Island," SUNY at Stony Brook, 1982,
and postdoctoral research in 1983. All informants were guaranteed anonymity and
clearance was obtained from the Human Subjects Committee, SUNY at Stony Brook.

of the house and the children. Those women who had worked in Cuba usually held positions as professionals (primarily teachers), government workers, or managers of family businesses, and they also had employed servants for housework and child care.

Immigration to the United States frequently necessitated the breakup of the immediate family unit of husband, wife, and children. In the 1960s and 1970s, for some refugee families the separation was temporary and short-lived, as when one spouse emigrated a few days or a few months before the other. For other families, the separation extended over a protracted period, as when children were sent out of Cuba to extended-family members in the Unites States, or to refugee-relocation centers that placed the children in foster homes. Frequently, these children were not reunited with their parents or siblings for many years.

Parenthetically, years later, the Mariel boatlift refugees of 1980, especially those who had been political prisoners in Cuba, also experienced the break-up of family. Many left Cuba without any opportunity to say goodbye to family members whom they left behind. Some boatlift refugees told of having a parent, spouse, or child removed from the boat just as it was ready to leave port. Some of these family members remained in Cuba. Others were sent to countries other than the United States.

MIGRATION

Most first-generation Long Island Cuban informants settled here in the 1960s and 1970s. Situated in the suburbs of Manhattan, the Nassau and Suffolk communities have Cuban populations residentially dispersed throughout the general population. Several of these communities—Freeport and Rockville Centre among them—have sizeable populations of Cubans, but in contrast to Miami, Florida, and West New York-Union City, New Jersey, no ethnic enclaves have formed.

The migration of Cubans from Cuba and to Long Island occurred in "waves," and can best be understood by viewing it in its social and historical context.

FIRST IMMIGRATION WAVE

The Batista government fell at the end of 1958. From January 1959 through June 1972, hundreds of thousands of Cubans chose self-imposed exile in the United States.[3] Similar to other Cubans fleeing at this time, Cuban informants who eventually settled on Long Island were mainly the Batista power elite (*Batistianos*) and other upper-class families whose lifestyles were undermined by the

Cuban Agrarian Reform Law of 1959 and the Nationalization and Confiscation of Businesses Act of 1960.

The group of Long Island Cuban informants who had been part of the professional army under Batista, or whose families had owned large businesses, was comparatively small. Most of them were able to obtain United States visas as immigrants or non-immigrants with relative ease. Those Cubans who fled in small boats did not have entry visas; they were unable to enter the United States as immigrants but were admitted as political refugees. In this period of American history, people emigrating from Communist countries received political refugee status.[4]

Many of the informants who emigrated from Cuba in this first wave considered themselves fortunate because they had been able to bring many of their assets with them. After the Bay of Pigs incident of 1961, Castro retaliated by restricting the assets that emigrating Cubans could take with them. The following account from an informant is representative of the experience of many Cubans who migrated during this period:

> You could only take $5 out of Cuba and your personal belongings in one suitcase and one bottle of rum per person which you could sell in the United States for American dollars. I was an adult and I came with my three brothers and two sisters. The youngest was thirteen. They confiscated two of the bottles of rum at customs because two of the children were under age. Some Cuban friends had heard we were coming and met us at the airport in Miami. They were very poor but they gave us $50, probably all they had.

This account illustrates the scarce economic resources with which many Cubans began their refugee lives. Informants explained that when families applied to leave Cuba, a government official inventoried the family's assets, including household possessions and financial savings, all of which had to be left in Cuba. Each family member was able to take one suitcase of personal belongings and a bottle of liquor (usually sold in the host country). This comprised the family's economic stake to a new life.

As many Cubans became disenchanted with the revolution, lower-and middle-class families, and frequently children unaccom-

---

3. Virginia R. Dominguez, *From Neighbor to Stranger: The Dilemma of Caribbean Peoples in the United States* (New Haven: Antilles Research Program, Yale University, 1975), 21-24.

4. Ibid., 21.

panied by parents, left Cuba via a holding country for the United States. Often, the decision to leave Cuba had to be hastily made and implemented, as one Long Island Cuban man explained:

> I had been a supporter of Castro during the Revolution but by 1960 I realized that Castro was a Communist and I joined the underground against Castro. One day, a friend who had married a captain in Castro's army came and told me that in two days Castro's men were coming to my town to arrest anti-revolutionaries and I was going to be arrested. I was eighteen years old at the time and I had forty-eight hours to get out of Cuba. I panicked. I had no relatives outside of Cuba. Then I thought, let me go back to my school [the Catholic high school from which he had recently graduated]. The priest told me I was not the first and would not be the last to leave Cuba. There was a classmate of mine whose mother had contacts in the Spanish Embassy in Cuba and she got me on a boat to Spain within two days.

Cuban youths, mainly pre-teen-agers or teen-agers, who emigrated without their parents were customarily met at their destinations by relatives, godparents, family friends, or friends-of-friends who acted as their guardians. The following accounts of two informants who left without their families represent the experiences of many youths who came to Long Island:

> I left Cuba by boat without any money. You weren't allowed to bring any money out of Cuba, but I had a letter of introduction to a priest in Spain.

> When the boat arrived in Spain, I had no one to meet me, only a letter of introduction. I had left my family, everything, behind me. I have a letter and I'm going to beg for help. While I was crying, a boatmate came and told me a priest was looking for me. The priest and one of my classmates (from Cuba) who was already in Spain had come to claim me.

> I lived at a *colegio*, the sister school to the one I had attended in Cuba, for one and a half months. The priests at the school told me that an invasion of Cuba was being planned in the United States...The invasion was the Bay of Pigs... After the unsuccessful invasion of Cuba, I decided to come to the United States. I came with no money but with three bottles of cognac for friends of my godmother. These were the only people I had in the United States...I lived with them.

and,

I came to the United States when I was twelve years old. I came with my fourteen-year-old brother. My brother and I stayed with an aunt for two years. My aunt had come to the United States in 1949. To me, it was like living with a strange person. I didn't know my aunt. When my brother was sixteen, he left school and got a job and me and my brother left my aunt's home and rented a room to live in. My brother supported me. I had a job too, selling newspapers on the street for sixty cents an hour. I worked for two hours each day after school. I made $6 a week. We ate a lot of hamburgers...In Cuba, we had been rich. We didn't know what it was to wear mended clothes. Once we came to the United States, we matured fast. It was like a survival struggle. We didn't have time to just be a kid.

These youths' migration experiences illustrate how social networks especially the secondary zone of friends-of-friends, were activated in order to leave Cuba, and the role of extended-family members in helping refugees to resettle on Long Island. Other studies of Cuban refugees of the 1970s have also noted the importance of social networks, especially secondary zones, in the resettlement process.[5]

Because the Castro government had placed a restriction on the emigration of boys within two years of military age, many families sent younger sons out of Cuba, but sons between the ages of fifteen and twenty-six had to remain in Cuba. As one Long Island Cuban man explained,

My mother had sent me and my brother out of Cuba to the United States to escape military service in Castro Cuba. But my other brothers were military age and they were not allowed to leave Cuba. My mother wanted to stay with my brothers. She didn't want to leave them alone in Cuba. It wasn't until the boatlift that my mother and my brothers were able to come to the United States.

When, in 1961, the United States ended diplomatic relations with Cuba, it became impossible for most Cubans to obtain visas to the United States without first going through a third country. Those Cubans who had obtained nonimmigrant visas prior to January 1,

---

5. Eleanor M. Rogg, *The Assimilation of Cuban Exiles: The Role of Community and Class* (New York: Aberdeen Press, 1974), 29-42; Alice James, "Economic Adaptations of a Cuban Community," *Annals of the New York Academy of Science* 293 (1977): 194-205.

1961 and who were able to book a flight on a commercial plane were still able to fly into Miami.[6]

Although informants recounted stories about other Cubans who obtained counterfeit nonimmigrant visas, they denied having done so themselves. Because Castro had set a lower age limit for the emigration of children from Cuba, one mother admitted that she had used an underground network to obtain a counterfeit birth certificate stating her daughter's age as one year more than it really was. Since so many Cubans were unable to qualify for nonimmigrant visas, the United States Immigration and Naturalization Service granted parolee status to Cubans who wanted to reside in this country but did not have visas.[7] Many Long Island Cubans had parolee status when they entered the United States.

SECOND IMMIGRATION WAVE

Following President John F. Kennedy's speech on the Cuban missile crisis, on 22 October 1962, Castro prohibited air flights between Cuba and the United States, and immigration dramatically declined. During this period, the main ways to emigrate from Cuba were to leave in small boats or to fly to third countries, usually Mexico or Spain.[8] A few Long Island Cuban informants emigrated at this time, living in Spain or Mexico for months before obtaining entry visas to the United States. Because of the cost of flying to the holding country and living there after arrival, immigration to the United States became very expensive.

THIRD IMMIGRATION WAVE

Not until December 1965, when Castro decided to permit Cubans with relatives in the United States to leave Cuba, did immigration to the United States resume. During this period, which lasted until the "Freedom Flights" were terminated in April 1973, more than one-third of the Long Island Cubans in the study arrived in the United States. Nationwide, approximately 285,000 Cubans took advantage of these Freedom Flights.[9] Early in this period, the United States government recognized that most Cubans who came as refugees would probably stay here permanently. On 2 November 1966, Public Law 89-732 was enacted to allow Cuban refugees to alter

---

6. Dominguez, *From Neighbor to Stranger*, 21-24.
7. Ibid., 22.
8. Ibid.
9. *Cuban Refugee Program Fact Sheet* (Washington, D.C.: Department of Health, Education and Welfare, United States Government Printing Office, 1972).

their legal status from parolee to permanent resident.[10] All but one of the Long Island Cubans in the study took advantage of the law and became permanent residents.

FOURTH IMMIGRATION WAVE

The termination of the Freedom Flights ushered in a seven-year hiatus in the immigration of Cubans to the United States. The next wave occurred with the Mariel boatlift of 1980. After approximately ten thousand Cubans took political asylum in the Peruvian Embassy in Havana, Castro decreed that those with relatives in the United States were free to leave. This wave of migrants primarily consisted of three groups: Cubans who had sought refuge in the Peruvian Embassy; Cubans who had relatives in the United States and had been unable to leave Cuba during the Freedom Flights; and Cubans who had been incarcerated in Cuban prisons, often for political offenses.[11]

The events leading up to this fourth wave of immigration date back to December 1978, when Castro decided to allow Cubans living in the United States to visit their families in Cuba. The visits were to be for a period of one week and took place between 1979 and early 1980. This period is often referred to as the "blue-jeans revolution" because, of all the gifts that visiting Cuban-Americans brought to their relatives, designer blue-jeans were the most prized.[12] Informants told of cramming suitcases with clothes and of returning to Long Island with only the clothes on their backs. Some of them suspect that opportunities and living conditions in the United States may have been exaggerated by returning emigres who were trying to impress their relatives. Still, relatives in Cuba began to realize that American emigres had a lifestyle superior to Cuba's.

Moreover, Cuba was in the midst of an economic recession. Its two main export crops, tobacco and sugar, were being ravaged by disease, and government austerity programs were on the increase. Disenchantment with Castro's government rose, as did political dissent. The boatlift benefited Castro by decreasing an acute housing shortage, by clearing the island of dissidents, and by providing scapegoats for the stagnating economy.[13] Some 20 percent of the

10. Dominguez, *From Neighbor to Stranger*, 22.

11. "Cuba: The Flotilla Grows," *Time* 115 (12 May 1980), 36-38; Anthony Ramirez, "After a Year Here, A Cuban Likes U.S., but Jobs Are Scarce," *Wall Street Journal*, 2 June 1984, 1, 18.

12. Thomas D. Boswell and James R. Curtis, *The Cuban-American Experience: Culture, Images and Perspectives* (Totowa, New Jersey: Rowman & Allanheld Publishers, 1983), 52.

13. Ibid., 52-53.

Mariel boat people were black.[14] However, because the vast majority of the Long Island Cubans of the '60s and '70s who participated in this study would be considered white, this was not true of *Marielitos* brought into their households.

During the boatlift, one-third of informant households brought relatives and long-time family friends out of Cuba. It cost Long Island Cuban informants an average of $5,000 for each person they brought out. Some Long Island Cubans took time off from their jobs to go to Miami (sometimes they sailed on boats to Cuba) in order to expedite emigration procedures. In addition to bringing out relatives and friends, many informants served as sponsors and helped Mariel refugees to resettle. Resettlement assistance included opening their homes to refugees or finding them apartments, enrolling refugees in English-language classes, and finding them jobs. Many Mariel refugees found employment and housing within days of arriving on Long Island. Social networks of relatives, friends, and friends-of-friends were activated to obtain jobs, housing, clothing, and food. As one long Island Cuban explained, "It's not imposing to ask. It was done for us when we came. Now we do it for others. It's paying back."

CROSS-CUTTING WAVES OF IMMIGRATION

The experience of Long Island Cuban families often spanned several waves of immigration, as illustrated by the account of Mrs. M. and her family. In 1956, Mrs. M. came to Long Island for a visit, liked the area, found a job, and decided to stay. She had left her husband and three-year-old son in Cuba. Mrs. M. divorced her husband and tried to get her son out of Cuba. In the interim, the Cuban Revolution occurred and she was unable to visit Cuba. Since her ex-husband refused to give the consent necessary under Cuban law for her son to come to the United States, the boy remained in Cuba. When her ex-husband died, she began proceedings for her son to emigrate from Cuba. He was granted permission to leave and went to Mexico, where he lived for one year with one of Mrs. M.'s sisters and eventually obtained a visa to the United States. Then, in 1967, by means of the Freedom Flights, Mrs. M.'s father, mother, another sister and her husband, and the first sister's daughter left Cuba and came to the United States. They all lived with Mrs. M., her second husband, and her son in a two-bedroom house

14. Ibid., 104.

on Long Island until Mrs. M.'s sister, brother-in-law, and niece were able to move into their own house in the same neighborhood. Lastly, in 1980, the brother of Mrs. M.'s second husband, who for twenty years had been a political prisoner in Cuba, came to Long Island in the Mariel boatlift.

RESETTLEMENT

For most informants, the presence of relatives was the primary reason for settling on Long Island. The importance of such "migration chains" in determining immigrant resettlement was first identified by Robert E. Park and Herbert A. Miller.[15] In their study of the same phenomenon, Thomas D. Boswell and James R. Curtis state that, "Social networks have proven to be very influential in determining where refugees finally settle in the United States."[16] Most informants immediately settled on Long Island and lived with already established relatives or close friends until they could afford to set up independent households. Before settling in Nassau or Suffolk, only a few lived in urban villages in Queens or Brooklyn, or in ethnic enclaves in Florida or New Jersey.

Settlement on Long Island followed a pattern of residential dispersement. Ethnic neighborhoods did not develop, and Long Island Cubans did not become residentially segregated from the non-Cuban population. This is different from other areas of the country where, "although there is considerable mixing among Cubans and other ethnic groups in the suburban areas there is still a tendency for clearly identifiable Cuban neighborhoods to develop."[17]

RESIDENTIAL MOBILITY

Residential mobility was common during the process of resettlement. Moves were usually made to be closer to a job, to have more living space, to reside in a more affluent neighborhood, or to change one's status from renter to home owner. A typical example is the L.'s, a newly married couple when they emigrated from Cuba and arrived in Florida. Although they had planned to settle in Florida, limited job opportunities led them to reconsider. When they heard that job opportunities were more plentiful in New York, they moved

15. Robert E. Park and Herbert A. Miller, *Old World Traits Transplanted* (New York: Harper, 1921), 43, 119-20, 145-224.

16. Boswell and Curtis, *Cuban-American Experience*, 50.

17. Ibid., 69.

north, staying with Mr. L.'s brother and his family in Freeport. Through friends of his brother, Mr. L. obtained a custodial job and his wife became a kitchen helper in a nearby community hospital. Once both were employed, they rented a furnished attic room. Two months later, they moved to a second furnished room in the community where they worked. In a few years they had saved enough money to buy a small house in a Long Island neighborhood zoned for residential housing and small businesses. Ten years later, they bought a larger house in an upper middle-class Long Island neighborhood.

SETTLEMENT PATTERNS

Long Island Cuban informants tend to reside in one of two types of neighborhoods. According to criteria adapted from W. Lloyd Warner and Leo Srole's classic study of American ethnic groups,[18] Type A neighborhoods are characterized by residential dwellings interspersed among retail establishments or adjacent to central business districts. Type B neighborhoods are zoned only for residential dwellings, which tend to be large, well-kept, and far removed from business establishments. Type A neighborhoods tend to have larger numbers of Cuban and Hispanic residents than do Type B neighborhoods. Because of the presence of Cubans and other Hispanics, bodegas and botanicas that sell Hispanic foods and religious ritual materials generally are found in Type A neighborhoods. When they first arrived on Long Island, most of the informant-refugees of the 1960s, 1970s, and 1980s settled in Type A neighborhoods.

As informants prospered and became upwardly mobile, they generally moved into Type B neighborhoods. Frequently, there was only one Cuban family in a Type B neighborhood. Rosemary B. Cooney and Maria A. Contreras's study of Cuban refugees of the 1960s and 1970s suggests that in communities in the United States where there are few Cuban elites, "ethclass" neighborhoods do not develop.[19] Cuban elites, therefore, move into non-Hispanic, upper-middle-class neighborhoods. Prosperous Long Island Cuban informants seem to follow a similar residential pattern.

18. W. Lloyd Warner and Leo Srole, *The Social Systems of American Ethnic Groups: Yankee City Series*, Vol. 3 (New Haven: Yale University Press, 1945), a classic study of American ethnic groups.
19. Rosemary S. Cooney and Maria A. Contreras, "Residence Patterns of Social Register Cubans: A Study of Miami, San Juan, and New York SMAS," *Cuban Studies* 8 (July 1978): 33-49.

Another reason for settling here was that Long Island suburban communities offered more job opportunities than did such Cuban enclaves as Miami, Florida, and West New York-Union City, New Jersey. Although most informant-refugees of the 1960s and 1970s were from Cuba's middle class, had high school educations, and possessed occupational skills or professional training, they had difficulty speaking English. These refugees took menial jobs which did not require fluency in English. People who, in Cuba, had been teachers, physicians, white-collar workers, or skilled workers initially worked as janitors, kitchen help, factory workers, or office cleaners. By parlaying jobs, Long Island Cuban refugees successfully used low-status, low-paying jobs to obtain higher status, better-paying positions.

In addition, the practice of holding two or more jobs helped to increase the incomes as well as the standard of living of Long Island Cuban informants. For example, when Mr. R., who had owned a tire recapping business in Cuba, came to Long Island his brother got him a job as a dishwasher. Through contacts he made in his dishwasher job, Mr. R. found work as a cook in a deli. Within eighteen months, he obtained a job as a cook in a local restaurant, which he held for eight years. Then he learned from a friend of two jobs, one with an office-cleaning service and the other in the kitchen of a local hospital. Mr. R. decided to work in the hospital kitchen during the day and for the office cleaning service in the evening. When the cleaning service went out of business, he persuaded the building owner to let him and his brother-in-law clean the offices, and, when the building owner agreed, Mr. R. went into business with his brother-in-law. Mr. R.'s wife and teenage daughter helped to clean offices. Eventually, five buildings engaged his service and he had to hire employees. Although his office-cleaning business prospered, Mr. R. kept his day job in the hospital kitchen.

When one Cuban refugee learned enough English to get a more highly skilled job, another Cuban refugee was channeled by a relative, friend, or friend-of-a-friend into the vacated job. In this way, occupational niches were carved out for Long Island Cuban refugees. Similar network functioning to facilitate employment was found among West New York and Tarrytown Cuban refugees.[20]

Occasionally, job-brokerage systems emerged. In contrast to other brokerage systems that exchange jobs for loyalty or political

20. Rogg, *Assimilation of Cuban Exiles*, 47-64; James, "Economic Adaptations of a Cuban Community," 194-205.

patronage,[21] this pattern was not part of the Long Island system. Although Long Island Cuban job-brokers were highly regarded and favors were exchanged for a job, most of the time reciprocity was not evident. Thus, networks comprised of extended-family members, friends, friends-of-friends, and/or job brokers have facilitated job hunting for Long Island Cuban informants. Rarely have they had to rely on private or government employment agencies to locate jobs. After becoming fluent in English and, when applicable, meeting educational requirements for licensing, many Long Island Cuban refugees have been able to transfer their occupational skills and reverse the trend of downward socio-economic mobility.

A third factor that attracted informants to Long Island was its geographical similarity to Cuba. Long Island is an island endowed with beaches and in close proximity to New York City, just as the suburbs of Havana have access both to beaches and the City. One Long Island Cuban succinctly expressed the attraction to Long Island that many informants have described: "I think that's why so many Cubans live on Long Island. . .It reminds people of Cuba."

CONCLUSION

Cubans are residentially dispersed throughout the communities of Nassau and Suffolk counties. Cuban neighborhoods have not formed, and physical barriers to intergroup relations, which often perpetuate social distance, have not developed. However, residential proximity does not assure integration into American social networks. Cultural differences and language may persist as barriers to assimilation.

In a culturally pluralistic society, degree of assimilation reflects a minority group's position in the society. Assimilation is a process in which, through social contacts, people and groups are incorporated, without prejudice or discrimination, into the cultural, social, economic, and political life of the dominant group. Assimilation usually occurs in two stages. In stage one, the minority group uses secondary-group associations to establish working relationships with the dominant group. In stage two, primary-group relationships

---

21. Stan Steiner, *La Raza: The Mexican Americans* (New York: Harper and Row, 1970), 40-50; Edward Wakin, *The Immigrant Experience. Faith, Hope and the Golden Door* (Huntington, Indiana: Our Sunday Visitor, 1977), 24-27, 67.

(recreational and friendship groups) are established with members of the dominant group.[22]

The assimilation of Long Island Cuban refugees of the '60s and '70s was influenced by two very different factors. On one hand, Americans responded to the flight of Cubans from an oppressive Communist government. Their plight "pulled at the very heart of American patriotism and sense of justice and compassion."[23] On the other hand, assimilation may have been slowed by the prejudice many Cuban informants encountered when they first migrated to Long Island. The most common prejudice was discrimination against Hispanics. In the 1960s and 1970s, the largest Hispanic group in New York metropolitan and suburban areas was Puerto Rican. Frequently, informant-refugees found that Americans did not differentiate between Puerto Ricans, who were predominately lower class and had come here for economic reasons,[24] and middle- and upper-class Cuban political refugees. It has been noted that "if Cubans are distinguished by their relative affluence among Hispanic groups, Puerto Ricans are known for their perseverance in the face of grueling poverty."[25] Most Long Island Cuban informants who emigrated in the '60s and '70s felt that they had to prove to their American neighbors that they were skilled, educated, hard-working people.

By 1980, most Long Island Cuban informants felt that they had achieved a good image in the eyes of American. Then, in May 1980, a new wave of Cubans arrived—the Mariel boatlift refugees. At that time, one informant succinctly stated the fears of many Long Island Cubans: "By sending undesirables, criminals, and homosexuals, Castro has undermined the good image we had established with Americans." Some Long Island Cuban informants referred to this practice as "Castro's revenge."

Many informants involved with the resettlement of Mariel refugees found more resistance among Americans to Cuban than to Vietnamese boat people. The Long Islanders involved with the

22. Milton M. Gordon, *Assimilation in American Life: The Role of Race, Religion and National Origins* (New York: Oxford University Press, 1964), a classic treatise on assimilation; Raymond H. C. Teske and Bardin H. Nelson, "Acculturation and Assimilation: A Clarification," *American Ethnologist* 1 (1974): 351-367; and A.J. Jaffe, Ruth M. Cullen, and Thomas D. Boswell, *The Changing Demography of Spanish Americans* (New York: Academic Press, 1980), 9-20; Joseph P. Fitzpatrick, *Puerto Rican Americans* (Englewood Cliffs, NJ, 1970), 34-43.

23. Boswell and Curtis, *Cuban-American Experience*, 4.

24. Dominguez, *From Neighbor to Stranger*, 24-27.

25. David M. Reimers, *The Immigrant Experience* (New York: Chelsea House Publishers, 1989), 120.

resettlement of Cuban boat people believed that Cubans suffered from a "bad press" that focused on the few criminals and trouble-makers in the group, and made no distinction between civil and political prisoners. This view has been shared by others. Boswell and Curtis conclude that the ". . .receptive posture (pre-boatlift) was tainted by the events surrounding the Mariel boatlift and its aftermath." These included the economic climate in this country at the time of the boatlift, marked by recession and high unemployment, and certain events that followed the boatlift, among them the disclosure that many boat people were prisoners, homosexuals, mentally ill, elderly, or infirm. This unfavorable perception was compounded by disturbances at resettlement camps, and crime sprees in New York and Miami perpetrated by a small number of *Marielitos*. American public opinion toward Cuban refugees had been tainted.[26]

Many informants who had lived on Long Island since the '60s and '70s began to feel the impact of a new wave of prejudice. As one informant explained,

> It used to be when I went some place, people (Americans and other Hispanics) would say, "Cuban people are nice," but now they are saying "Look what your *paesanos* are doing." Cubans began to hear Americans refer to "those lazy Cubans" and "those ungrateful troublemakers."

The most recent wave of migration's impact on the assimilation of Long Island Cubans awaits future evaluation. If negative public opinion has indeed affected assimilation, the nature of the effect needs to be determined. It is possible that the two stages of assimilation have been differently affected. Specifically, relationships may have continued to be established through secondary-group associations, while primary-group associations may have lagged.

In addition, we may speculate about the possible ramifications for Long Island Cubans of the wave of freedom and democratic reform that is washing over Eastern Europe. If Cuba ever responds in kind, will some Long Island Cubans decide to return in a "wave" of reverse migration? Although most refugees initially thought of their emigration as temporary and hoped to return to their homeland some day, to make such a decision today would be fraught with strains. After more than twenty years in the United States, Long Island Cubans have established themselves in jobs, friend-

26. Boswell and Curtis, *Cuban-American Experience*, 4-6.

ships, and families. Moreover, many of their children were born and raised in this country. These children, who have formed social networks with Americans and in many cases consider themselves more American than Cuban, might not respond well to uprooting and relocation. In addition, some Cubans who migrated as youths have married Americans; it is doubtful that these spouses would want to migrate to Cuba. Thus, there would be many encumbrances attached to deciding to go back to Cuba.

Hopefully, future research will continue to investigate the assimilation of Long Island Cubans, so that their place in life on Long Island will have on-going documentation.

The Chinese: New Immigrants in New York's Chinatown

By BERNARD WONG

N ew York City's Chinatown has changed significantly since 1965. The boundaries of Chinatown have been enlarged and demographic characteristics of the community—such as population size, occupational composition, social stratification, and attitudes toward the larger society have also changed.[1]

This community in the Lower East Side of Manhattan has always been socially diverse, but it has become even more so in recent years (Wong 1976, 1982, 1985). The population includes old settlers who came before 1965, second- and third-generation American-born Chinese, new immigrants, jumped-ship sailors, and refugees from Vietnam of Chinese descent. Among the new arrivals since 1965 are professionals and unskilled workers, millionaires and paupers. The community is now home to alienated youth gangs as well as rich corporations composed of experienced businessmen from Hong Kong.

One of the most important factors responsible for these population changes was the 1965 Immigration and Nationality Act. In the past 150 years, the United States has implemented several immigration policies affecting the Chinese (Kung 1962). At first, between 1850 and 1882 there was a period of free immigration when the Chinese were welcomed to this country as a source of cheap labor (Rose Hum Lee 1960). However, this period was followed by one of exclusion and restriction. In 1882 the Chinese Exclusion Law was passed by Congress, barring Chinese from admission to the United States, with the exception of certain special categories of people such as spouses and minor children of U.S. citizens, teachers, and

Reprinted from Nancy Foner, ed., *New Immigrants in New York* (New York, 1987), 243-72.

Bernard Wong is an associate professor of anthropology at San Francisco State University.

1. The data on which the present paper is based were obtained by field work in New York's Chinatown in 1972, 1974, 1980, and 1984. A total of twenty-four months was spent doing field research, principally in participant observation and interviewing informants. Written sources were also consulted.

ministers. Subsequent modifications of this law over the next sixty years were even more restrictive. It was not until 1965 that significant positive changes in immigration legislation were enacted. The 1965 law abolished the "national origins" quotas and established a system of preferences whereby immediate relatives, skilled and unskilled workers, refugees, scientists, and technical personnel were listed under different categories of preference. For the first time, Chinese immigrants were treated equally with other nationalities by U. S. immigration law, thus ending some eighty-five years of bias against the Chinese. Many Chinese once again flocked to the United States, and New York was a major area of settlement. According to the 1980 census, there were about 82,000 people born in China and Hong Kong living in the New York metropolitan area (Kraly, this volume). When we consider people of Chinese ancestry, not just Chinese birth, the numbers of course are even higher. The population of Chinese ancestry in the New York metropolitan area swelled to a high of 158,588 in 1980 (U. S. Bureau of the Census 1982). Of this number, 80,000 resided in the Chinatown area. Other areas of Chinese concentration are the southern part of Brooklyn and the Jackson Heights, Flushing, and Elmhurst sections of Queens.

The increase of the Chinese population in the Chinatown area has had a direct effect on the boundaries of Chinatown. Today's Chinese population on the Lower East Side has expanded beyond the Mott-Mulberry-Canal area north to Houston Street, south to the piers, east to Allen Street, and west to Broadway. The commercial areas of Chinatown have also branched out from the traditional core area (Mott, Pell, Bayard, Doyer Streets) to include Mulberry, Canal, the Bowery, East Broadway, Catherine, Hester, Elizabeth, and Grand Streets. Thus, both residential and commercial areas of Chinatown have expanded and other ethnic territories have been penetrated. There is an effort to establish another Chinatown in the Flushing area of Queens. All of these expansions are the direct result of population increases attributable to the 1965 immigration law.

The 1965 immigration law and the subsequent Chinese migration to New York City have not only changed the geographical boundaries and population size of Chinatown but also the social and economic characteristics of the people in the community. Chinatown is now mainly occupied by Chinese who intend to stay in the United States permanently, as opposed to the sojourners of the past (see Wong 1982). Before 1965 Chinatown was dominated by people from Kwangtung Province, mostly from the county of

Toysan. Not surprisingly, the lingua franca in those years was the Toysan dialect. Today, although people from Kwangtung still make up more than half of the population there are also many people from North China, Shanghai, Hong Kong, Fukien, and Taiwan. Standard Cantonese, as spoken in the cities of Hong Kong, Macao, and Canton, is now the lingua franca of Chinatown. Speakers of other dialects such as Mandarin, Fukienese, Shanghainese, and Hakka have to learn the Cantonese dialect of Chinatown in order to communicate with shopkeepers and coworkers. Mandarin speakers, however, are more likely to be understood in Chinatown today than before 1965 because many young Cantonese also learn the national language (Mandarin) and because Chinatown has many Mandarin-speaking immigrants from Taiwan and mainland China.

Before 1945, there were very few women and children in Chinatown, and the population mainly consisted of male sojourners. The female population in Chinatown has gradually grown since 1945—initially with the influx of Chinese war brides. Only after 1965, however, did the sex ratio narrow significantly. In 1960 the male/female ratio was 2:1. In 1980 it became nearly equal.

The recent migration stream includes some extremely wealthy individuals from Hong Kong who have fled with their capital, due to the uncertain situation in the colony. Hong Kong's lease will expire in 1997, when the People's Republic of China (PRC) will claim sovereignty over Hong Kong. Although an agreement between Great Britain and the PRC has been signed and an extension of the present system of capitalism has been pledged, there is still fear among the very rich in Hong Kong. Many have contemplated abandoning their businesses; some have transferred their major assets to New York City; and others have already migrated. As I will explore later, the availability of "flight capital" has been responsible for the speculative activities in real estate and for various modernization projects in Chinatown.

Most recent immigrants, of course, are not wealthy and most did not move to New York to protect their assets. In fact, most new immigrants came to New York to improve their economic well-being and for the future education of their children. The majority are of urban background; some came with considerable educational and professional attainments. As compared with old settlers, the new immigrants consider themselves to be more "genteel," more literate and more modern as most of them lived in Hong Kong at least for a period of time (having originally come from urban areas in the PRC) and some were born and raised in that international city. They feel that the old settlers are "country bumpkins" with unrefined manners who came from rural areas of the old land. Most old settlers do have peasant origins in China, and their lifestyles before emigration were very different from those of the new immigrants. That new immigrants and old settlers have such different social and economic backgrounds helps to explain why their experiences in New York have diverged in so many ways. This essay will show that other factors are also important, including the different resources and opportunities available to the two groups of immigrants in New York and the immigrants' intentions to stay, or eventually leave, the United States.

POLITICAL ADAPTATION OF NEW IMMIGRANTS

Moving to New York has led to numerous changes in the lives of new immigrants as they adapt to life in their new home. Many newcomers to Chinatown, as I already mentioned, have had to learn Cantonese to get by in the community. Many have also come to rely on American-style social service organizations and have become willing to use American political methods. Some have, on occasion, rallied together through new associations to further the interests of the Chinese community. Such political activities are a new feature of the Chinatown scene and represent a departure from the political behavior and beliefs of old settlers.

One major difference between new immigrants and old settlers is in the types of associations they form and use. The traditional power structure—the Consolidated Chinese Benevolent Association (CCBA) and affiliated associations—simply cannot adequately handle the problems of the new immigrants. These associations, established in the pre-1965 era, principally served the financial, social, and emotional needs of the old settlers who were single males, and they recruited members mainly on the basis of traditional kinship and friendship ties and locality of origin, family name, and dialect similarities. The leaders of the major traditional associations, who sat on the governing board of the CCBA, claimed to speak for the community as a whole. Even in the old days, the CCBA was not an effective organization in representing the community. The leaders were not familiar with U.S. society. Many could not even speak the English language. As sojourners, many old settlers were not interested in any kind of assistance from the American government. They wanted to socialize with people who spoke the same dialect, and they sought mutual financial and emotional support through various family name, hometown, and linguistic

associations. Some were primarily interested in having a burial service handled by their hometown or surname associations. In the
1940s, to be buried first in New York City and later exhumed and
reburied in China was a concern of many old settlers (Rose Hum
Lee 1960). New immigrants have no such wishes, since they intend
to make their permanent home in the United States, pursuing the
"American dream" (Hsu 1971). Such problems as housing, education, family disputes, teenage gangs, medical assistance, and social
security benefits are very much on new immigrants' minds. Realizing the inadequacies of traditional associations, new immigrants
have formed new associations and use modern social service organizations. In fact, the community is no longer controlled by the mono-
lithic power structure of the CCBA and its affiliates (James Lee 1972).

The community is coordinated today by three groups of associations: traditional, new, and modern social service organizations.
While some new immigrants belong to traditional associations, most
depend on new associations and social service organizations to
solve problems that they encounter in day-to-day living. In addition to the limitations of traditional associations, several other factors account for this preference. One is the new immigrants' educational background. Many have learned about the workings of
the U.S. government as well as the New York Chinatown community from books or newspapers published in Chinese. As I mentioned
earlier, the new immigrants tend to be urban and aggressive; they
are diligent in seeking information relevant to their new lives. Moreover, modern social service agencies get results. Newly arrived immigrants have learned from kinsmen or friends of the effectiveness of
the various social service organizations in Chinatown. Modern social
service agencies like the Chinatown Planning Council and Chinatown
Health Clinic have the financial resources and connections to help
the new immigrants. There is also the language factor. Most of the
modern social service organizations and new associations are run
by Cantonese-speaking people, many of whom are new immigrants
themselves. Similar background and linguistic convenience thus
facilitate communication. The new immigrants do not feel at ease
in their dealings with the old settlers who speak a different dialect
and who migrated form rural China with different sets of social
values and habits.

New associations, which recruit members on the basis of common interests, professions, or educational background, have multiplied in size and number in the past two decades, so that by 1980
there were over 200 in Chinatown. Most of these associations—
alumni groups, for example—are social and recreational in orien-

tation, although three, including the Organization of Chinese-Americans, are actively concerned with Chinese civil rights. As for modern social service organizations, they have assumed many of the functions that used to be performed by traditional associations. Such organizations include state- or federally funded agencies and nonprofit charitable groups that have appeared in the past two decades. The Chinatown Advisory Council, for example, established in 1970, is made up of representatives from the government and from schools, churches, and hospitals in the Chinatown area. It provides immigrants with help in finding housing and jobs and obtaining health care and also mediates between the immigrants and institutions of the larger society.

Many of the new associations and social service organizations have played an important role in introducing new immigrants to American customs. The leaders of these associations are often new immigrants who are familiar with the workings of U.S. society and who are capable social workers. Some work in Chinatown as career social workers, community developers, or volunteers. In any event, new immigrants who belong to new associations or utilize social service organizations are clearly interested in participating in the resource distribution of the larger society. Unlike their predecessors, who shunned the confrontational approach, a good number of new immigrants are willing to use such American methods as strikes, petitions and demonstrations to obtain their goals. They have learned these methods in this country through the mass media, especially television and newspapers. Further, instead of using Chinatown as a colony for the transmission of traditional culture as the old settlers did, new immigrants prefer to use Chinese ethnicity as a base for the formation of an interest group (see Wong 1977). Having lived in an era of intense racism against Chinese, old settlers came to feel that any intimate contacts with the larger society would invite trouble and they isolated, and still isolate, themselves from the mainstream of American life. Most of the new immigrants do not want to isolate themselves and the community from the larger society. On the contrary, they would like to see their community as an integral part of the city as well as of the wider U. S. society. Thus, Chinatown is not an "unmeltable" ethnic community (Novak 1972). Rather, it is an assimilable community with an interest in changing its ethnic boundaries (Fredrik Barth 1969).

The new immigrants, of course, are not a homogeneous group. Some are highly educated and sophisticated about the United States; others have little education and are unfamiliar with the politics of American society. As compared to old settlers, however, significantly more new immigrants have become knowledgeable about, and involved in, the American political process and this is in part due to the fact that new immigrants, as a group, are better educated than earlier settlers. Not only do new immigrants know they have to organize as a united front with all co-ethnics, they are also eager to cooperate with other ethnic groups to fight for equal rights and equal justice (Wong 1982). New immigrant leaders have on occasion sought alliances with other minority groups, especially with other Asians, who have similar cultural backgrounds and have encountered similar types of discrimination. Politically ambitious citizens have participated in city and state elections for various offices. Along with second-generation Chinese, some new immigrants have been instrumental in persuading the community to organize collective actions such as the 1983-84 fight against the decision to build a prison near Chinatown. Though this effort failed to change the New York City mayor's decision concerning the prison, the petitioning, picketing, and demonstrations have been important for the community: they indicate a determination to use American methods to obtain political goals. In recent years, moreover, various government institutions in the Chinatown area have been successfully pressured by the modern community organizations in Chinatown to employ more Chinese-Americans.

New immigrant activists have also learned that, to participate in the resource distribution of American society, they must organize their own interest groups to lobby the U.S. Congress for passage of favorable legislation and against enactment of unfavorable bills. Recently, the Organization of Chinese-Americans (OCA), one of the new associations with many new immigrant members, lobbied for passage of the Urban Jobs Enterprise Zone Act (1981) and the Voting Rights Act (1980). In 1983, the OCA also urged a Senate subcommittee to lift restrictive immigration quotas for colonies (Hong Kong was included). The limited quota for Hong Kong means that, apart from spouses, minor children, and parents of U.S. citizens, only 600 people born in Hong Kong may be legally admitted as immigrants each year. Many new immigrants from Hong Kong realize that brothers and sisters of U.S. citizens waiting in Hong Kong may face between six and eleven or more years to be reunited. Some new immigrant activists have formed coalitions with other ethnic groups who have similar incentives for wanting the colonial quota repealed. And on other occasions new Chinese immigrants have allied with Hispanic and West Indian immigrants on immigration-related issues. This kind of political involvement and interest in achieving results through political participation are notable only since the arrival of the new immigrants.

In the pre-1965 era, citizens in the community generally ignored American political life. After the influx of large numbers of educated immigrants, and a changed political climate that gave minority groups more political scope than before, many in the community began to learn the meaning of participatory democracy and to recognize that Chinatown cannot solve all its problems alone. The prison construction issue and the fight against gentrification that I discuss in a later section have made clear to many in the community how important it is for the Chinese population to be involved in city politics. In fact, editorials in various Chinese community newspapers have discussed the painful results of ignoring events of the larger society. The majority of these papers were founded by new immigrants and are alert to any anti-Chinese sentiments around the United States and elsewhere in the world.[2] The newspapers have frequently chastised "isolationists" in the community and stressed the need for developing public consciousness and the importance of political participation in the United States.

NEW IMMIGRANTS AND THE LAW

Recent immigrants also have a new orientation toward the law now that they have moved into the United States—one that differs from the attitudes of the old settlers. In the old country, the Chinese were passive toward law enforcement institutions. In traditional China, as well as in old Chinatown, a saying held that "one does not go to government offices while living, one does not go to hell when dead." Among new immigrants, this saying is no longer valid.

New immigrants are sensitive to social injustices against Chinese-Americans. Cases like the murder of Vincent Chin in Detroit (June 1982), the shooting of Asian-Americans in Davis, California (1984), discrimination against Chinese-American businesses in Washington, D.C., the assault on the Chinese in Grand Ledge, Michigan (January 1984), and the shooting death of a Chinese immigrant by police on Long Island (June 1982) not only aroused indignation in

2. In 1985, nine major Chinese dailies, all written in Chinese, were published in New York City's Chinatown: *The World Journal, Sing Tao Jih Pao* (New York edition), *The United Journal, Sino Daily Express, China Daily Express, China Daily News, The China Post, China Voice Daily, The China Tribune*, and *The Peimei News*.

the community, they also made immigrants aware of racism in America. Unlike their forebears, the new immigrants, as I already indicated, have learned that, to participate in American society, they have to fight individually and collectively for their rights, to use litigation, strikes, demonstrations, and other methods of confrontation.

Police harassment and brutality against citizens of Chinatown are reported in Chinese newspapers. Some citizens are not afraid to complain to the police or to civil rights organizations about official harassment. Most recently, in a case of alleged police brutality involving a Chinese immigrant motorist, the police accused the motorist of assault and resisting arrest. The immigrant claimed that he was beaten up by two police officers simply because he was asking questions about the parking ticket they were giving him, and he took his case to court. Disregarding the merits of the case and the outcome of litigation, the motorist's reaction is significant because it shows that some new immigrants are not afraid to go to court to redress grievances.

In the old days, there was a saying in Chinatown that "good son will not be a soldier." This premise is no longer relevant in Chinatown. Chinese-Americans now serve in various branches of the armed forces as well as in the police force. The Fifth Precinct in Chinatown employs Chinese police officers, translators, and civilians. The new immigrants are not hesitant to use the police to solve problems and to fight crime.

While old settlers shunned dealings with the U.S. courts, new immigrants have a desire to use the law enforcement system of the United States to keep the streets safe. Not only will new immigrants assist the police in apprehending criminals, but many also serve as witnesses when called, and some even become involved in cases against Chinese youth gang members. People outside the Chinatown community often believe that Chinese immigrants condone Chinese youth gangs. In fact, the majority in the community despise those *Tongs* (or secret societies) that engage in illicit activities such as extortion for protection, gambling, prostitution, and drugs—and the youth gangs that carry out orders from elders of the *Tongs*. In the old days, old immigrants were afraid to confront assailants, even in court. Several years ago, a leading businessman, who was a new immigrant in the community, gave a speech at a public meeting indicating that he would help put criminals in the youth gangs in prison, regardless of their ages. He was later stabbed. After convalescence, he identified the assailant in court. This kind of cooperation with the law is indeed a new phenomenon. New immigrants have learned the American way in handling criminals.

Although nearly all new immigrants want to rid Chinatown of gangs—and a few are even willing to help fight them—gang problems actually seem to be related to the new immigration. Betty Lee Sung (1979) found that almost all gang members in Chinatown were new immigrants from Hong Kong and all were under eighteen years of age. One reason for the predominance of Hong Kong emigrants among gang members is simply that most Chinatown residents come from Hong Kong (even if they only lived there for a while) and are Cantonese speakers. Children migrating directly from Taiwan or mainland China are fewer in number and many speak no Cantonese, so numerical and linguistic factors delimit gang membership (Sung 1979). While it is difficult to establish direct connections between New York gangs and secret societies in Hong Kong, gang activity is not uncommon in Hong Kong. It may well be that gang members in Chinatown were exposed to certain influences in Hong Kong at a young age that predisposed them to join gangs after they emigrated (Sung 1979). Perhaps some were already gang members in Hong Kong. Gangs are less of a problem in Taiwan and mainland China, where criminals, including young criminals, are severely punished (Sung 1979).

The gangs in Chinatown have a particular appeal to young people experiencing difficulties in adjusting to American life. The change from a Chinese-speaking school in Hong Kong to an English-speaking school in New York City creates many problems for newly arrived immigrant children. Instructional difficulty, alienation, loss of self-esteem because of poor school performance, ethnic conflicts, and confrontation in the public school system impose great pressures on young children, especially those who have no close family members in whom to confide. Socially, the "American dream" becomes an illusion. Many young people join gangs for protection and excitement, and some are under peer group pressure to affiliate with a gang.

Gang membership in New York's Chinatown, despite much publicity, is not large. Police think there are only several (two to three) hundred members. My informants suggested 500, including the inactive ones. Gang membership also fluctuates as gang members inevitably dissociate themselves after age 19 since American courts deal more severely with adults than with juveniles. In the past twenty years, gangs have disbanded and organized with names like Black Eagles, White Eagles, Quon Yings, Ernie's Boys, Fukien, etc. (Sung 1979). In 1984, the major gangs in Chinatown were the Ghost Shadows and the Flying Dragons. The major gangs in 1984 worked for two *Tongs*, the On Leong or Hip Sing Associations. The On Leong group controlled Mott Street, while the Hip Sing affiliates controlled Pell Street and the Bowery.

ECONOMIC ADAPTATION OF NEW IMMIGRANTS

The overall economic performance of the Chinese in the United States as compared to other nonwhite ethnic groups is impressive. In New York City, as in the rest of the country, many second-, third-, or fourth-generation Chinese have attended college or professional schools and, after graduation, they usually prefer to work for white American establishments. In fact, the professional Chinese in New York tend not to be Chinatown connected, living instead in middle-class neighborhoods. Although some go to Chinatown to practice their trades, most do not live in the community.

New immigrants who live in Chinatown are heavily concentrated in service and factory work. Indeed, whether they are new or old immigrants, most Chinatown residents depend on the ethnic niche — although, as I will demonstrate, new and old immigrant entrepreneurs differ in terms of the types of businesses they engage in and the management methods they use.

Occupational Patterns

Laundries, restaurants, and grocery stores were traditionally the stereotypical businesses of the Chinese in New York. These businesses are still important, but today the Chinese in the city have also moved into other lines of work.

Census data for 1970 on the occupational distribution of people of Chinese ancestry in New York City indicate that 36 percent of the Chinese men in the labor force were service workers connected with Chinese establishments, while 43 percent of the employed females were operatives, mostly seamstresses. The same census also shows that the second most important occupational group for males was professional and technical, accounting for 19 percent of the Chinese male labor force; for females, it was clerical work, with 25 percent of the Chinese female labor force. The relative importance of these four occupational groups was the same in 1985. The ethnic niche, which is composed of restaurants, garment factories, grocery stores, and other types of Chinese-run businesses, still employs the largest group of Chinese in New York City, including a very high proportion of new immigrants. According to my informants, in 1985, some 50,000 Chinese in the city worked in Chinese garment factories and restaurants. Chinese professionals and other white-collar workers are the second most numerous group. Although the majority of these workers are not connected with Chinatown, some new immigrants who live in Chinatown hold clerical and other white-collar jobs outside the community. Within Chinatown itself, people mainly work in ethnic businesses. Other occupations include a small group of professionals—physicians, accountants, lawyers, and journalists—who serve the Chinese-speaking residents in the community.

The unemployment rate is low in Chinatown. Census data for 1970 indicated a 2.8 percent unemployment rate among Chinese in New York City, and in Chinatown it was perhaps lower than 2 percent. The unemployment situation was similar in 1985. Yet behind these impressive statistics lies a distressing fact, namely, that many new immigrants are not working according to their potential, training, or education. Due to their lack of English proficiency and unfamiliarity with American society, many qualified technicians and professionals have to work at menial jobs and thus function under capacity.

Some of these workers, of course, will eventually improve their positions. In general, new immigrants who are not proficient in English mainly find avenues for mobility in ethnic businesses. Those who begin as workers may end up accumulating enough savings to start their own small restaurant, garment factory, or laundromat.

Business Activity and Family Firms

Business activity among new immigrants in Chinatown differs from that among pre-1965 arrivals in terms of the kinds of businesses entered and methods of management. In addition to traditional Chinese businesses like restaurants, gift shops, grocery stores, and laundries, some new immigrants operate travel agencies and bookkeeping offices. Garment factories now constitute the major ethnic niche in Chinatown and the vast majority of the 500 garment factories in the community in 1985 (actually "assembly plants" for American garment manufacturers) were controlled by new immigrants. Table 9.1 compares the kinds of Chinese businesses new and old immigrants run. New immigrants not only control garment factories but also laundromats, bookstores, and certain types of

Chinese restaurants in Chinatown, while old settlers monopolize most branches of the laundry trade and Cantonese restaurants. Many new immigrants organize and establish their businesses through the use of family members—something that is increasingly possible now that so many immigrant families have arrived in recent years. Family firms are much less common among old settlers, and most family firms in New York's Chinatown are run by new immigrant families.

In the pre-1965 era, few men in Chinatown had families with them, save those who sent for their children and wives before the 1924 Quota Act and those who sponsored their war brides shortly after 1945. Thus, for some time Chinatown was labeled a bachelor society (Wu 1958; Rose Hum Lee 1960; Beck 1898). Apart from traditional hand laundries and small-scale chop suey restaurants, there were few family member firms among old settlers. Old set-

Table 9.1. Relationship Between Types of Chinese Businesses in Chinatown and Types of Chinese (1984)

Type of Chinese Business	Subtypes	Controlled by
Laundries	Washer plants Presser plants Collection and delivery stores Complete service hand laundry	Old settlers
	Laundromats	New immigrants
Restaurants	Chop suey restaurants Snack and coffee shops Cantonese restaurants	Both old settlers and new immigrants
	Shanghai, Peking, Hunan, Szechuan restaurants	New immigrants
Garment factories	Skirts, blouses, and sportswear	New immigrants
Travel agencies, law, accounting and insurance firms		Mostly second-generation Chinese-Americans
Groceries		Both old settlers and new immigrants
Gift stores		Both old settlers and new immigrants
Bookstores		Mostly new immigrants

tlers who set up businesses often did so through partnerships with kinsmen and friends. Rich old settlers in the pre-1965 period tended to be partners in different businesses at the same time—multiple shareholders, as it were. As for second- and third-generation Chinese, born and raised in the United States, they are not particularly interested in returning to Chinatown to work. Some are college-educated and professionally trained and prefer to work in American establishments. Those second- or third-generation Chinese professionals who have returned to Chinatown tend to run travel agencies and law, accounting, and insurance firms which require fluency in English and Chinese. In fact, some educated new immigrants who have the capital also have become involved in these types of business. Chinatown is reputed to be a gold mine for bilingual lawyers and accountants. I met several American-born lawyers of Chinese descent who are studying Cantonese for the sole purpose of making money from the immigrants. The enterprises that appeal to bilingual members of the second and third generations, however, are not run along family lines. As in the past, family members of second- and third-generation Chinese are seldom involved in business activities in Chinatown; they feel it is more rewarding and more comfortable to work with U.S. firms. Indeed, new immigrants in Chinatown today hope that their children will not be dependent on traditional Chinese businesses and will enter such professions as medicine, engineering, and law.

New immigrants themselves, however, are still firm believers in family businesses. Not all new immigrant businesses, of course, are run by families. Some new immigrants are involved in partnerships and corporations that have been formed by shareholders and partners who are not related to each other. In a number of cases, new immigrants have learned about such business opportunities through notices in local Chinese newspapers inviting people to become shareholders or partners in well-known restaurants and garment factories. However, the majority of new immigrant entrepreneurs prefer to run family firms for the sake of flexibility, independence, and greater control over their workers. Use of family ties in the family firm environment can bring other advantages. Family members can be trained in business operations; they are trustworthy and able to keep trade secrets; they are willing to put in more hours; and they are an important source of financing, many firms having been established through pooling of family members' savings. Kinsmen of the family also constitute an inexpensive labor pool.

Many new immigrants are in the garment industry where flexibility is especially important. Garment factories are highly competitive and business is seasonal. Firms that cannot cope with fluctuating demands in the New York market can easily go bankrupt. However, those Chinese businesses run by the family have greater endurance and flexibility. When business is slow, family members do all the work themselves and thus cut down on outside help. In adverse situations, family members can simply stop their salaries or reduce the profit for every garment. Low profit margins and reduced production costs in the family firm environment have thus enabled many family-run garment factories to survive.

Family firms among new immigrants come into being due to the initial efforts of their founders who are usually heads of the families. Beyond this, however, there are several different ways that such firms are started. One way to set up a firm is for family members, who will work in the business, to pool resources to supply capital and equipment. A second method involves several years of hard work in New York on the part of the family head. After he has accumulated enough savings and has borrowed funds from friends, he sponsors family members so they can come to New York. All family members live under one roof, if possible, or try to live in the same neighborhood so they can eat together during the day, thus saving money, food, and time. A third way many family firms start is by a process of fusion and fission. Initially, a person will cooperate with friends of kinsmen to set up a firm. After some profits are made, one partner will buy the whole firm and the others will get a share of the profits and leave. The person who buys the firm then reorganizes it into one of the kinds of family businesses I discuss below.

Types of Family Firms

In general, there are three types of family firms run by new immigrants. Type 1 firms are owned, managed, and staffed only by family members and kinsmen; type 2 firms are run by a core group of family members with some outside employees; and type 3 firms are run by a core group composed of family members with a labor boss and his staff. In the family firm environment, the family head is often the major decision maker. He plays the role of father, patron, and friend in his relationships with family members, employees, and the labor boss. Thus, relationships among firm members are based on kinship, friendship, and patron-client ties.

Many small-size businesses in Chinatown are of the type 1 variety, run by an entire family group. Benefiting from the 1965 immigration law changes, some new immigrants arrived in this country with entire families—an important economic resource. In the type 1 family firm run by the entire family group, the family head is usually the father or the oldest effective male. The family is an economic unit both in production and consumption. Every family member who can help works in the firm and contributes to the common resources. Wives, parents (normally only one set of parents, either the husband's or the wife's), and children usually get only the money they need for daily living. Those who work in the firm take their meals together; food is provided from the common kitchen. Taking meals together saves manpower, since only one person cooks and shops. Communal eating also saves money in that costly equipment is purchased together and food can be bought in bulk. Although family members can bring expenditures up for discussion, the decisions are generally made by the family head. The family firm is also a business training center for family members. Children learn various aspects of business operation from working in the family firm.

Family firms of the type 1 sort are extremely durable, enduring through sagging economic conditions and slow business seasons. They also facilitate the generation of family wealth among new immigrants, since everyone contributes to the family resources through savings. The wealth accumulated in this way is generally spent on family necessities such as houses, cars, and education of the children. The dream of many new immigrants is to send their children to college to train them to be professionals.

The second type of family firm is run by a core group of family members with some assistance from outsiders, who are hired only because the family cannot supply all the needed workers. Usually, this kind of family firm has a sizable group of employees. Many garment factories in Chinatown have thirty to eighty employees, so outsiders must be hired. Likewise, medium-sized Chinese restaurants need outside help. Members of the core group are insiders who are familiar with business operations, and they also make routine day-to-day decisions. Family members usually contribute both capital and expertise to the firm, since, as new immigrants, no one person commands enough capital for a medium-sized business. Thus, many new immigrants in this kind of family firm are both shareholders/business partners and workers at the same time.

The third kind of family firm, run by the family with assistance from a labor boss and his staff, is commonly found in medium- and large-sized Chinese establishments. What differentiates this type of family firm from the type 2 sort is that here there are two separate groups of personnel in the firm, and an outsider labor boss heads one of these groups, composed of his hired employees. The other group, made up of family members, is supervised by the family head, who is also responsible for the management and operation of the entire firm. In terms of authority structure, the family head is thus the supreme authority, a superpatron for everyone in the firm. The outsider labor boss is a patron for his staff (compare Bennett and Ishino 1963 on the Japanese labor boss system). He may work alongside his subordinates, and a close esprit de corps may develop among them. The labor boss trains his employees and, at times, even assumes the position of foster-father-cum-teacher of his younger staff members. He can hire his own workers, recruiting his relatives, friends, and people with whom he has ties of locality of origin and dialect.

To sum up, then, many firms in the post-1965 era have been established with the help of family members because these people are available. In fact, the use of family members in the new immigrant businesses represents a successful economic adaptation in a competitive urban environment. Family firms allow flexibility and can withstand market fluctuations. Moreover, family members are important for capital formation and they also provide labor resources and generate high productivity.

Methods for Obtaining Employment

The discussion of family firms clearly indicates how important family and kinship ties are for new immigrants looking for employment. There are also other ways to obtain employment: through friendship networks; various family and alumni associations; and employment and social service agencies. Although many immigrants have had to accept lower-status jobs than they held before emigration, the fact is that obtaining employment in Chinatown is easy if one is willing to work at a menial job. Indeed, the Chinatown Study Group (1969) found that a major reason why Chinese immigrants moved to Chinatown in the first place was that they had friends and relatives—and knew there were job opportunities—in the area.

Family members, kinsmen, and friends in the New York Chinese community, as in overseas Chinese communities elsewhere (Wong 1984:230), are given priority in employment. The unique aspect of employment in the New York Chinese community today is the special preference given family members and relatives who may not even be in the United States. That is, the cohesiveness of the kinship network is not necessarily diminished by geographical distance.

Since 1965, U.S. immigration policy has favored the migration of immediate relatives, and Chinese businessmen, especially after they have their own firms, want to sponsor relatives from Hong Kong or Taiwan who will work for them when they move to New York. Major reasons for this preference are: (1) the belief that family members and kinsmen are more trustworthy than outsiders; (2) the expectation that kinsmen will work harder; (3) the fact that it is cheaper for a businessman to sponsor kinsmen employees from Hong Kong or Taiwan than to hire a Chinese or an American from this country; and (4) the desire to live up to the cultural expectation that successful immigrants will sponsor family members so they can migrate to the United States. Chinese employers prefer to hire friends as well as kinsmen, and they also give priority to people from their locality back home and those who speak their dialect. No high degree of specialization exists along kinship lines in today's Chinatown so that, for example, Chans or Lees do not dominate any sector of Chinatown's economy. Yet there is some specialization along regional and linguistic lines. All Cantonese hand laundries are run by people form Kwangtung, and most owners are from the county of Toysan in Kwangtung Province. Shanghainese, Szechuan, and Peking restaurants are run by Mandarin-speaking people, which means northerners. Real estate companies, and garment factories tend to be controlled by, and give preference in hiring to, Cantonese-speaking immigrants from Hong Kong.

In addition to using traditional kinship, friendship, and family relationships, new immigrants sometimes secure employment through social networks in various Chinatown associations (Wong 1977), especially the Consolidated Chinese Benevolent Association (CCBA). New immigrants also use alumni groups and regional and dialect associations to obtain jobs. Increasingly, new immigrants turn to employment agencies in the community, which have played a more important role in the past twenty years with the expansion of Chinatown and the growing number of Chinese businesses. These agencies principally place job seekers with Chinatown establishments. Since the agency owner and staff are bilingual immigrants, they can also negotiate with American employment brokers in mid-Manhattan. They refer suitable Chinese applicants to the mid-Manhattan brokers and, in return, receive a commission fee for the referrals. Social workers in Chinatown social agencies such as the Chinese Development Council and Chinatown Planning Council are also instrumental in helping new immigrants obtain jobs outside of Chinatown. Thus, these social workers are not simply employment brokers, but culture brokers linking the

Chinese community with the outside world. Traditionally, this function was performed mainly by the CCBA. Today, due to funding available from the federal and state government, many bilingual social workers have established social agencies that not only serve the Chinese community but make the community more open to the larger society.

A major change, then, from the pre-1965 era is that there are new avenues for gaining employment—social agencies, for example, new associations, and commercial employment organizations. Moreover, in the pre-1965 era most Chinese worked within the community. Today, more jobs are available to Chinese outside the Chinatown area because of reduced discrimination. Given their educational backgrounds, many new immigrants have been able to obtain such positions.

NEW IMMIGRANTS AND THEIR IMPACT ON NEW YORK CITY

The new immigrants have not simply adapted to life in New York City. They have influenced the city as well: in housing, banking, labor unions, travel businesses, and the real estate market. Indeed, they have changed Chinatown itself in many crucial ways.

Gentrification of Chinatown

The recent influx of new immigrants as well as capital from Hong Kong have led to dramatic transformations in the Chinatown community. Not only have the borders of Chinatown expanded but there are growing pressures for gentrification.

Since 1965, Chinatown has experienced a marked housing shortage. Most recently, Chinatown has spread into nearby neighborhoods of Manhattan's Lower East Side. Some real estate developers have called this expansion the "modernization" of the community. This term is used because expansion also involves the upgrading of buildings, the construction of new high-rises, and the replacement of small business firms by high-rent office facilities. Meanwhile, long-time Chinatown residents face rising rents, and many traditionally family-run restaurants and garment factories have had to move to sections of Brooklyn or Queens.

This process of upgrading, or gentrification, has split the community. Some residents are determined to fight gentrification for practical, economic, or philosophical reasons. Practically, older residents are used to the convenience of shopping and to the warmth of the old culture which the community engenders. One can stroll through Chinatown's streets, speaking a familiar dialect and addressing others with traditional kinship terms, something that is especially important for older Chinese who cannot speak English. Economically, some believe that building new offices at the expense of traditional Chinese businesses will ruin the livelihood of many people. It is said that new offices will provide few jobs for community residents, since not many have training in English. Many small garment factories and restaurants, which have been important economic bases for the community, also face increased rent. Their absence would deprive many people of jobs and change the nature of the community. Philosophically, the argument is that expansion is a case of the "haves" expelling the "have-nots"—big businesses driving out small businesses. In fact, modernization appears to be favored by wealthy Chinese rather than by economically disadvantaged newcomers. Community groups such as Asian Americans for Equality and the Asian-American Legal Defense Fund have launched great efforts to fight gentrification, and among their concerns is the fate of new immigrants who are still to come. Manhattan's Chinatown is not just an economic center, but also an ethnic and enculturation center for new immigrants, who use Chinatown as an entrepôt—a transitional place, a stepping-stone to American society.

The plans for the modernization of Chinatown typify two common phenomena in the United states: the disappearance of traditional ethnic neighborhoods that preserved many Old World features, and emerging conflicts between old and new immigrants (Wong 1976). Early arrivals who have established themselves see no problems with the modernization or gentrification of Chinatown. They believe Chinatown should have more office spaces for professionals, for instance, and better housing for middle-class Chinese. Real estate brokers, condominium developers, landlords, speculators, and bankers are also in favor of modernization projects for they cannot afford the exorbitant rents for their residential or business facilities that modernization will bring.

What factors are responsible for the trend toward modernization or gentrification in the community? As I have emphasized, Chinatown needs more living space given the tremendous influx of new immigrants since 1965, and there is a pressing demand for better housing from the general Chinese population. Other Asians, and some non-Asians, also want to live in the community for convenience and local color. People who work in the Wall Street area find that Chinatown is not only close to their offices but peaceful and full of excellent and inexpensive restaurants. In addition to the demand for housing, two other forces have contributed to gentrification: the city government's encouragement of high-rise housing construction in the area and the influx of capital from Hong Kong.[3] Part of the capital influx is a result of the deliberate movement of cash by some wealthy Hong Kong Chinese who are worried about the future of Hong Kong, and part appears to be attributable to a "natural inflow" since the United States is the British colony's primary trading partner. Among the rich in Hong Kong there is a saying that Hong Kong Chinese already own Vancouver, half of San Francisco, half of Toronto, and what is left is part of New York City. The availability of Hong Kong capital has driven up Chinatown's real estate values, and the demand for real estate now far exceeds supply. As a result, the value of land per square foot is on a par with that in the fashionable areas of Manhattan's Fifth Avenue. So far, real estate purchases by Chinese and Chinese-American investors have been estimated at $150 million in 1983 and most of the transactions have been in Manhattan (*New York Times*, September 21, 1984).

Manhattan's Chinatown may be the main area for real estate investment by Chinese and Chinese-Americans, but parts of Brooklyn and the Flushing section of Queens are also prime areas. Real estate developers and the New York Chinese press have been spreading rumors about the establishment of a "second Chinatown" in Flushing, and newcomers from Hong Kong have purchased property there with "flight capital."[4] Indeed, people and businesses have moved to Flushing, although these movements have not been as great as expected. The craze for real estate in Manhattan's Chinatown and in Flushing may well be an artificial phenomenon, directly related to, and therefore subject to, changing political and economic arrangements between China and Great Britain.

Other Changes

In addition to influencing the real estate market, the new Chi-

3. This observation was voiced by many realtors in Chinatown. Several newspapers made similar statements (e.g., *The Christian Science Monitor*, January 3, 1985; *New York Times*, September 21, 1984).
4. Since the agreement was signed between Great Britain and the PRC in December 1984, there is a slight indication of the return of "flight capital" to Hong Kong. However, the amount of this return flow cannot be determined at this time.

nese immigration has had other effects—both within and outside of the Chinatown community.

The presence of so many new immigrants has stimulated the growth of the banking industry in Chinatown. Immigrants, as many economists note, tend to work hard and are eager to accumulate savings, and the Chinese are no exception. They are frugal and save money for such major expenditures as houses, appliances, and automobiles. As a result, many major banks in New York have opened branch offices in Chinatown. Realizing the lucrative nature of banking in Chinatown, some affluent Chinese businessmen from Hong Kong and Taiwan have also organized banks to cater to new immigrants. By 1985, in an area of less than two square miles, there were already fifteen banks and, according to one informant's estimate, they employed more than 400 people, mainly non-Chinese New Yorkers. This is in marked contrast to the pre-1965 era when there were only a handful of banks in the community, employing not more than 100 people.

Various labor unions will soon have to deal with the increasing number of Chinese union members in their ranks. In 1985, there were more than 20,000 Chinese factory workers, most union members, in the 500 Chinese garment factories. So far, the higher echelons of the International Ladies Garment Workers' Union (ILGWU) have been white Americans. To serve members better, the ILGWU needs more Chinese professionals (such as lawyers, accountants, and managers) who can speak both English and Chinese. In the restaurant trade, Chinese workers fear that the existing labor union will discriminate against Chinese because of traditional prejudice and racism and because no union officials speak Chinese. As a result, Chinese restaurant workers have talked about organizing their own labor union without affiliation to any unions of the larger society. Whether this possibility will lead the existing restaurant workers union to organize its locals to cater to the needs of Chinese restaurant workers is unclear.

In the entertainment field, especially in restaurant and travel businesses, new immigrants have been important culture brokers for New Yorkers. New Yorkers' interest in regional Chinese foods other than Cantonese has been stimulated by the culinary talents of new immigrant chefs from different parts of China and also by improved U.S.-China relations since President Nixon's 1972 China visit.

In the field of travel, a number of new immigrants have used their expertise in Chinese culture and their ability to speak Chinese to organize special tours for Americans to visit China. Many Chinese travel agents have considerable contact with Chinese consulates and the Chinese government's travel organizations, and help customers obtain visas and arrange trips for handsome fees. While these travel agents serve as "culture brokers" for American tourists, they also, in the process, learn more about the workings of American society.

The recent U.S.-China normalization has also opened up entrepreneurial opportunities in the import-export sector for new immigrants. In turn, this new business activity has had an impact on the city at large, not only making Chinese goods widely available but also making the Chinese a more visible presence outside the Chinatown community.

New immigrants are particularly suited for import-export trades since these businesses require knowledge of Chinese as well as American and Chinese cultures. In fact, these new immigrant entrepreneurs must improve their facility in English to be able to deal with American businessmen. Such business interaction leads to social interaction, and many new immigrant entrepreneurs—in the import-export trade as well as in other businesses—have considerable contact with people outside of Chinatown. A number of Chinese businessmen have moved out of Chinatown to live among white business associates. Some of these associates have identified pleasant residential areas or have recommended their realtors to help Chinese immigrants find better housing in Queens, Brooklyn, or even on Long Island.

CONCLUSION

The examination of new immigrants' adaptation to New York City in this essay shows that new Chinese immigrants differ significantly from the old settlers. The urban origins of new immigrants, coupled with the assistance of family members, have turned out to be important assets in their creation of a new life in the New World. Many new immigrants come from highly literate backgrounds and a good number have had higher education or specialized training. Unlike the old sojourners who arrived in this country years ago, the new immigrants are more committed to participate in the realization of the "American dream." They came here with business plans and, often, even with savings.

The social and economic backgrounds of the new immigrants, however, cannot alone explain why their adaptation patterns differ from those of old settlers. New immigrants have also benefited from the 1965 immigration law which permitted migration of family members and talented individuals, a change that helped immigrants in the financing, establishment, management, and stability of many new business firms. Moreover, changed attitudes in the larger society toward ethnic groups, the equal opportunity and affirmative action programs, and the general interest in "things Chinese" since normalization of U.S.-China relations in 1972 have also given new immigrants more scope in pursuing their goals. Although racist and discriminatory attitudes toward the Chinese still exist, they have diminished.

New immigrants have more contacts outside Chinatown than old settlers did, and the community has expanded geographically, penetrating surrounding areas in lower Manhattan. There is even indication that a second Chinatown will soon be established in Flushing, Queens. Socially, more successful new immigrants have begun interactions with the white middle class, and some live among and work with white Americans as colleagues. Politically, new immigrants are more interested than old settlers in their rights. They are committed to making the United States their permanent home, and, though still novices, they have gradually become involved in American political life. New immigrant activists in particular see the need to participate in the resource distribution of the larger society. Furthermore, political candidates from the neighborhood have been testing the waters in their recent efforts to participate in the 1984 elections for various offices in city and state government.

Although the Chinese are increasingly accepted in New York City, certain barriers still limit economic opportunities. Most new immigrants still have to depend on the ethnic niche. Restaurants, garment factories, and grocery stores remain the lifeblood of new immigrants. However, the size, scale, management, and organization of present businesses differ substantially from those of the past. The old sojourners intended to stay briefly in America, make some quick money, and then return to China. New immigrants, intending to make America their permanent home, are more determined than old settlers to achieve economic success through business achievement and are more entrepreneurial in style. New immigrant businessmen are also more willing to venture into non-Chinatown areas, and they have been pioneers in developing the new Chinatown in Queens.

While carving out their ethnic niche in New York City, new Chinese immigrants also play an important role in the vitality of the host culture. They generate profits for New York garment manufacturers and, by creating a demand for housing, have supported construction as well as real estate businesses in Chinatown. New immigrant businesses have multiplier effects on non-Chinese enterprises in such fields as transportation, fashion, textiles, construction, and the grocery trade. With the influx of new immigrants, Chinatown has also become a more important neighborhood for non-Chinese Americans, and new immigrants' grocery stores, travel agencies, and laundries provide important services for cosmopolitan New Yorkers. Indeed, new immigrants help introduce New Yorkers to aspects of the otherwise "mysterious" Chinese culture: traditional Chinese festivals, Chinese regional cuisine, the Chinese way of entertaining, and the language of China. These activities and customs enhance the cultural life of New Yorkers and facilitate intercultural communication.

The Chinese community of New York's Lower East Side is no longer the "quiet" community it used to be. It has changed greatly. New immigrants in today's active community have to deal with problems of family disorganization, union disputes, aging, housing shortages, and gangs—some of these problems, perhaps, the social costs of rapid Americanization. On the positive side, new immigrants have established flourishing businesses and enriched the cultural, social, and economic life of Chinatown and New York City itself. New immigrants, moreover, are gradually changing the conservative, apolitical community into a dynamic urban enclave with political and economic power. New York's Chinatown is, in fact, changing from a "voluntary segregated community" (Yuan 1963) into a voluntary "ethnic interest group."

REFERENCES

Barth, Fredrik. 1969. *Ethnic Groups and Boundaries*. Oslo: Universitetesforlaget.
Barth, Gunther Paul. 1964. *Bitter Strength: A History of the Chinese in the United States, 1850-1870*. Cambridge: Harvard University Press.
Beck, L. 1898. *New York's Chinatown*. New York: Bohemia.
Benedict, Burton. 1968. "Family Firms and Economic Development." *Southwestern Journal of Anthropology* 24:1-19.
Bennett, John W. and Iwao Ishino. 1963 *Paternalism in the Japanese Economy*. Minneapolis: University of Minnesota Press.
Chinatown Study Group. 1969. *Chinatown Study Group Report*. Manuscript. New York.
Hsu, Francis L. K. 1971. *The Challenge of the American Dream*. Belmont, Calif.: Wadsworth.
Kung, S. W. 1962. *Chinese in American Life: Some Aspects of Their History, Status, Problems and Contributions*. Seattle: University of Washington Press.
Lee, James. 1972. "The Story of the New York Chinese Consolidated Benevolent Association." *Bridge Magazine* 1:15-18.
Lee, Rose Hum. 1960. *The Chinese in the United States of America*. Hong Kong: Hong Kong University Press.
Novak, Michael. 1972. *The Rise of the Unmeltable Ethnics*. New York: Macmillan.

Sung, Betty Lee. 1976. *A Survey of Chinese-American Manpower and Employment.* New York: Praeger.

――― 1979. *Transplanted Chinese Children.* New York: Department of Asian Studies, City College of New York.

U.S. Bureau of the Census. 1982. *1980 Census of Population and Housing. General Population Characteristics, New York.* Washington, D.C.: U.S. Government Printing Office.

Wong, Bernard. 1976. "Social Stratification, Adaptive Strategies and the Chinese Community of New York." *Urban Life* 5:33-52.

――― 1977."Elites and Ethnic Boundary Maintenance: A Study of the Roles of Elites in Chinatown, New York City." *Urban Anthropology* 5:1-25.

――― 1982. *Chinatown: Economic Adaptation and Ethnic Identity of the Chinese.* New York: Hold, Rinehart and Winston.

――― 1984. *Patronage, Brokerage, Entrepreneurship and the Chinese community of New York City.* New York: AMS Press.

――― 1985. "The Chinese Family in New York with Comparative Remarks on the Chinese Family in Manila and Lima, Peru" *Journal of Comparative Family Studies* 16:231-255.

Wun, Cang-tsu. 1958. "Chinese People and Chinatown in New York City." Ph.D. dissertation. Ann Arbor: University Microfilms.

――― 1972. *"Chink!" A Documentary History of Anti-Chinese Prejudice in America.* New York: World Publications.

Yuan, D.Y. 1963. "Voluntary Segregation: A Study of New York's Chinatown." *Phylon* 24:255-268.